Barriers to
Conflict
Resolution

Barriers to Conflict Resolution

P O N B o o k s

Cambridge, Massachusetts

EDITED BY

Kenneth J. Arrow
Stanford University

Robert H. Mnookin
Harvard University

Lee Ross
Stanford University

Amos Tversky
Stanford University

Robert B. Wilson
Stanford University

PON Books
published by
Program on Negotiation
at Harvard Law School
500 Pound Hall
Harvard Law School
Cambridge, MA 02138

Library of Congress Catalogue Data
Barriers to Conflict Resolution
editors, Kenneth Arrow, Robert H. Mnookin, Lee Ross, Amos Tversky, Robert
Wilson
p.   cm.
Includes bibliographical references and index
1. Conflict Management—Congresses.   2. Negotiation—Congresses.
I.   Arrow, Kenneth Joseph, 1921–.

ISBN 1-880711-15-x.

CONTRIBUTORS

Kenneth J. Arrow
Departments of Economics and Operations Research, Stanford University

Max H. Bazerman
Kellogg Graduate School of Management, Northwestern University

Robyn M. Dawes
Department of Social and Decision Sciences, Carnegie Mellon University

John T. Dunlop
Lamont University Professor, Emeritus, Harvard University

Jon Elster
Department of Political Science, University of Chicago

Ronald J. Gilson
School of Law, Stanford University; School of Law, Columbia University

Daniel Kahneman
Woodrow Wilson School for Public and International Affairs, Princeton University

Robert H. Mnookin
School of Law, Harvard University

Margaret A. Neale
Kellogg Graduate School of Management, Northwestern University

John M. Orbell
Department of Political Science, University of Oregon

Wolfgang Panofsky
Stanford Linear Accelerator Center, Stanford University

Edward A. Parson
John F. Kennedy School of Government, Harvard University

Howard Raiffa
Schools of Business and Government, Harvard University

Lee Ross
Department of Psychology, Stanford University

Ariel Rubinstein
Department of Economics, Tel-Aviv University

James K. Sebenius
Harvard Graduate School of Business Administration, Harvard University

Lawrence Susskind
Department of Urban Studies and Planning, Massachusetts Institute of Technology

Amos Tversky
Department of Psychology, Stanford University

Robert B. Wilson
Graduate School of Business, Stanford University

Richard Zeckhauser
John F. Kennedy School of Government, Harvard University

Preface to the Paperback Edition

Like the best of wines, some scholarly works seem to get better with age. This volume, *Barriers to Conflict Resolution*, falls into that welcome class. The book was conceived in 1993, when the Stanford Center on Conflict and Negotiation proposed to convene a conference on a theme that seemed to provide a useful frame for the current period of broadly interdisciplinary research into conflict resolution: barriers to negotiated settlement. The theme had resonance, and attracted the attention and precious time of many a diverse group of distinguished scholars drawn from many fields, including psychology, economics, management, organizational behavior, and law.

Their papers were first published in this award-winnning collection, and many have since provided the grist for more extended theoretical developments within their respective disciplines. Equally important, by focusing specifically on the issue of barriers to conflict resolution as an interdisciplinary enterprise, they also opened a new way of thinking about the old problem of conflict resolution, and, in so doing, helped build an early bridge between the theory and practice of the field.

These foundational works continue to represent a remarkable and vibrant collection of seminal thinking. In collaboration with the Stanford Center on Negotiation and Conflict, Harvard Law School's Program on Negotiation is pleased to make it more widely available as a paperback work. This would not have been possible, however, without the time, patience, and good will of many people, most notably Drake McFarley and Sarah Stewart of W.W. Norton & Co., which published the hard-bound edition of the book, and Sara Cobb, Teresa Hill and Richard Reuben of the Harvard Program on Negotiation, who took stewardship of the work as it moved toward the broader accessibility that a paperback edition can provide. With appreciation and hope, we look forward to our fields' progress in recognizing, and overcoming, barriers to conflict resolution.

Robert H. Mnookin
Cambridge MA, October 1999

Contents

Preface

*T*his book is a project of the Stanford Center on Conflict and Negotiation (SCCN) and the end product of a conference held at Stanford
University in February 1991. During that conference, contributors presented
"working drafts" and engaged in a broad-ranging interdisciplinary dialogue
on the theory and practice of dispute resolution. These working drafts were
then revised in response to the conference dialogue and subsequent editorial
input. Also, an introductory chapter was added identifying the major themes
of the conference and SCCN's continuing concerns.

The Stanford Center was founded in 1988 with a grant from the William
and Flora Hewlett Foundation, which has continued to contribute gener-
ously to its maintenance. The major undertaking of the Center has been one
of conceptual analysis and theory building, with a particular focus on the
barriers—at all levels of analysis from the cognitive processes of individuals
to the structures and constraints of social institutions—that impede negotiation and dispute resolution. Its cofounders and principal investigators (Kenneth Arrow, Robert Mnookin, Lee Ross, Amos Tversky, and Robert Wilson)
are the editors of this volume. Mnookin was the director of the Center from
1988 to 1993, and with his departure to the Harvard School of Law, Arrow
has assumed the directorship.

The Center provides a home for seminars, workshops, and topical dialogues involving SCCN graduate fellows, affiliated faculty, and distinguished practitioners form many arenas of dispute resolution. It also sponsors
graduate student research, graduate and faculty seminars, and dialogues
between groups and societies in conflict. Throughout, its approach is deeply
interdisciplinary, reflecting our conviction that no one discipline or level of
analysis is sovereign, or sufficient, when it comes to the daunting task of
understanding conflict and eliminating obstacles to successful negotiation
and dispute resolution. These commitments to interdisciplinary scholarship
and the integration of theory and practice were evident throughout our conference and, we trust, will be faithfully reflected in this volume.

The editors wish to thank the National Institute for Dispute Resolution

(NIDR) for its generous underwriting of our conference and of the book. NIDR's support allowed us to bring an exceptional group of scholar/practitioners to Stanford, and to subsidize their efforts in preparing chapters. Our publisher, W. W. Norton, has similarly been more than generous in its support.

We also owe a large debt to Richard Birke and Melanie Greenberg, who, respectively, served as SCCN's associate directors from 1991 to 1993 and from 1993 to the present, and to Judy Slater, SCCN's administrative assistant from 1990 to 1993. Without their skill and tireless efforts, neither the conference nor the book would have materialized. Finally, we want to thank Stanford Law School for providing us with an administrative home and a continuing base of support for our efforts.

PART ONE

Introduction

CHAPTER ONE

Introduction

Robert H. Mnookin
and Lee Ross

C onflict is inevitable, but conflict resolution that best serves the interests and aspirations of the disputants is not. Conflicts can persist—as
the long history of ethnic and religious strife in the Middle East, Ireland,
and many other parts of the world so vividly reminds us—even though there
may be a number of possible resolutions that would better serve the interests
of the parties. In our everyday personal and professional lives we similarly
witness disputes where the absence of a resolution imposes substantial and
avoidable costs on all parties. Moreover, many resolutions that are
achieved—whether through negotiation or imposition—conspicuously fail to
satisfy the economist's criterion of efficiency. Let us cite a few here in
which, at least with the benefit of hindsight, alternative resolutions easily
can be identified that surely would have left both parties better off.

- Mary and Paul Templeton spend three years fighting over the custody of
  their seven-year-old daughter Tracy after Mary filed for divorce in 1985.[1]
  Mary wants sole custody; Paul wants joint physical custody. This middle-
  income family spends over $37,000 on lawyers and experts. In the process
  they traumatize Tracy, who feels caught in the middle, and inflict great
  emotional pain on each other. Worst of all, they damage each other's rela-

---

This chapter's organization and content borrow heavily from two previous works: Mnookin
1993 and Ross and Stillinger 1991. It also reflects the general interdisciplinary orientation
of the Stanford Center on Conflict and Negotiation and the diverse contributions of its
principal investigators, who are the co-editors of this volume.

[1] This example involves a divorcing family in California included in the Stanford Child
Custody Study. The results of the study, which involved some eleven hundred families,
are described in Maccoby and Mnookin *Dividing the Child: Social and Legal Dilemmas of
Custody* (1992).

tionship with their daughter in a way that renders them less able to sustain Tracy when she needs them most. The ultimate resolution is unexceptional: the divorce decree provides that Mary will have primary physical custody of Tracy and that Paul will be entitled to reasonable weekend visitation. But the costs borne by mother, father, and daughter alike—emotional as well as financial—are far greater than they needed to be.

- In March 1989, after three years of skirmishes at Eastern Airlines, during which Frank Lorenzo, the new owner, had pressed the airline's unions for various concessions and had laid off workers to reduce costs, Eastern's machinists went out on strike. They were later joined by the company's pilots and flight attendants. To exert further pressure on the unions, and to avoid creditor claims, Eastern's management filed for bankruptcy, hired permanent replacements for the strikers, and began to sell off assets. The pilots and flight attendants returned to work, but the machinists union persisted in its strike, determined to get rid of Lorenzo at whatever cost. In one sense, they succeeded, for in 1990 the bankruptcy court forced Lorenzo to relinquish control of Eastern. This "victory" for the union, however, turned out to be a pyrrhic one (see Bernstein 1990). For on January 18, 1991, Eastern Airlines permanently shut down operations. Can there be any doubt that management and workers alike would have been better served by an agreement that responded to the needs and aspirations of both (for example, through a contract tying future employee compensation to company profitability)?

- The titanic struggle between Texaco and Pennzoil over Getty Oil had a clear winner and loser: in 1988 Texaco paid Pennzoil $3 billion in cash to end the dispute. The case nonetheless suggests a bargaining failure, although of a somewhat subtler sort. The parties reached the settlement in question only after Texaco endured a yearlong bankruptcy proceeding and after protracted legal wrangling in various courts. While the dispute dragged on, the combined equity value of the two companies was reduced by some $3.4 billion (Cutler and Summers 1988). A settlement *before* Texaco filed for bankruptcy would have saved resources and offered more to the shareholders of both companies (if not to Texaco's management) than the resolution created by the bankruptcy court.

- Our last example involves Art Buchwald's dispute with Paramount Pictures. In 1989, Buchwald and his partner Alain Bernheim sued Paramount for breach of contract, claiming that the studio had based Eddie Murphy's film *Coming to America* on Buchwald's story treatment without offering appropriate acknowledgement or compensation. Buchwald later wrote:

> When I got involved, I expected to be in a business dispute that I assumed would be resolved early in the game for a minimal sum of money and, hopefully, an apology. . . . One of the discoveries of a suit such as this is that it makes you hurt deeply, and you don't forgive easily. [Another thing

I discovered:] Do not count on any money in a lawsuit—this is as true if you win as if you lose. (O'Donnell and McDougal 1992, xvii–xviii)

Buchwald's observations capture the nature of the process and the settlement. After three years of bitter litigation, a trial judge awarded Buchwald $150,000 and Bernheim $850,000. But this hardly made them winners, for the award was only a small fraction of the $6.2 million they had requested in their final arguments. Moreover, it was far less than their legal expenses. Despite the contingency arrangement limiting the legal expenses actually paid to his attorney, Buchwald ended up losing money (to say nothing of time, energy, and frustration) in the resolution of his dispute.

Nevertheless, Buchwald was accurate in ridiculing Paramount's claim of victory. How, he asked, could it be a victory for the defendant to pay out nearly $1 million in damages, and face additional legal fees in excess of $3 million?[2] No Solomon is required to imagine a more satisfactory resolution—for example, the apology plus modest settlement proposed by Buchwald, perhaps accompanied by a soothing statement on his part acknowledging the absence of any fraudulent or malicious intent on the part of the studio.

These cases, as well as the ever-expanding list of religious, ethnic, and political conflicts that impose staggering costs on the peoples of our world, raise a central question for those of us concerned with dispute resolution: Why do negotiations so often fail even where there are possible resolutions that obviously would serve disputants better than protracted struggle? And why, when resolutions are achieved, are they so often suboptimal for the parties, or achieved only after heavy and avoidable costs? In other words, what barriers stand in the way of successful negotiation and effective resolution of conflict?

The Stanford Center on Conflict and Negotiation was established to explore this question through a program of interdisciplinary scholarship and research. This book, and the interdisciplinary conference from which it arose, represents a part of the Center's work. We will not attempt in this introductory chapter to summarize the chapters that follow. Suffice it to say that the reader will find discussions of several different strands in the Gordian knot of conflict resolution, including approaches illustrated by game-theoretic models (Rubinstein; Wilson), psychological research (Ross; Kahneman and Tversky; Dawes; Bazerman and Neale) and analysis of competing

---

[2] Paramount executives, and theorists seeking a normative account for Paramount's decisions, might seek to justify such expenditures on "reputations" grounds—i.e., as an investment to discourage other potential litigants. Such explanations, however, may often reflect after-the-fact rationalizations rather than authentic accounts of calculated decision making or risk-taking.

institutional incentives (Gilson and Mnookin; Parson and Zeckhauser; Arrow). These discussions are set in a variety of contexts, ranging from international diplomacy (Panofsky; Raiffa) to constitution making (Elster), from labor disputes (Dunlop) to environmental negotiations (Sebenius; Susskind; Arrow). Our purpose is to explicate the concept of negotiation barriers and to show how an analysis of such barriers provides a useful departure point both for considering specific instances of conflict perpetuation and for developing a more coherent approach to the problem of dispute resolution. To this end we begin by introducing and distinguishing among three broad categories of barriers.

The first category concerns *tactical and strategic barriers,* barriers which arise from the efforts of bargainers to maximize their short-term and / or long-term outcomes, and which have long been the concern of game theory and the economic analysis of bargaining. In describing the operation of these barriers, we shall be calling attention to the ways that "rational" bargaining strategems—notably, concealment or misrepresentation of one's true interests and priorities and other hardball tactics—preclude the achievement of the greatest possible "gains in trade" at the lowest cost. As such, these tactics make it impossible for the bargainers to reach efficient agreements. Strategic barriers can cause rational, self-interested disputants to act in a manner that proves to be both individually and collectively disadvantageous.

The second set of barriers are *psychological* and, as the label suggests, they are the special concern of a number of subdisciplines of psychology. These barriers do not arise from any calculated pursuit of self-interest. Instead, they reflect cognitive and motivational processes, or more precisely, biases in the way that human beings interpret information, evaluate risks, set priorities, and experience feelings of gain or loss. These barriers also reflect the fact that bargaining is an interactive social process, one in which parties make attributions and inferences not only about each other's proposals, but also about each other's motives and character.

The third category is something of a grab bag. What the barriers in this category have in common, however, is that they relate not to self-interested calculation or individual psychological processes, but rather to broader *organizational, institutional,* and other *structural* factors that compromise the interests and aspirations of disputing parties. These factors range from bureaucratic structures that restrict the free flow of information to political considerations that restrain the freedom of leaders to make necessary compromises, abandon past promises and rhetoric, or risk alienating powerful factions in their constituency. Understanding these barriers takes one into the domains of political science, organizational theory, and transaction-cost economics. We shall note some of these factors a bit later in this chapter, and describe one, the familiar *principal / agent* problem, more thoroughly. Several chapters in this volume dealing with specific environmental, economic, or political conflicts also discuss the operation of institutional and structural barriers in considerable detail.

We would be first to concede that the tripartite classification scheme to be presented in this chapter is somewhat arbitrary, and that the list of barriers within each category is far from exhaustive. But the particular classifications and lists are less important than the general approach we are championing. The defining feature of this approach is its assumption that the problem of efficient dispute resolution profitably can be examined at very different levels of analysis—from the cognitive and motivational processes of the individual to the dynamics of institutions or even whole "bodies politic" (Saunders 1991). As such, the pursuit of efficient agreements in the face of conflict is inherently an interdisciplinary enterprise. We further maintain that beyond understanding the nature of particular barriers or types of barriers, it is important to recognize the ways in which these barriers may *interact* to multiply each other's effect in thwarting the negotiation process. Finally, our approach emphasizes the importance of recognizing that frustrated disputants are apt to misdiagnose or misattribute the sources of a given stalemate—in particular, to make inferences about each other's negotiation motives and behavior that are not only uncharitable but often erroneous and bound to exacerbate existing feeling of ill will and mistrust.

The succeeding chapters in this volume make it clear that different arenas of conflict, even different specific disputes, may bring into play very different resolution barriers. Indeed, dialogue with dispute resolution practitioners invariably makes one appreciate how important it is to understand the specific history and content of a given dispute, and to appreciate the social, political, or institutional context surrounding a given negotiation. Nevertheless, we think the analysis of barriers offered in this chapter does have some general implications for third parties who seek to facilitate the negotiation process. Accordingly, after outlining the various strategic, psychological, and institutional barriers of concern, we offer some suggestions for those who seek to overcome such barriers.

TACTICAL AND STRATEGIC BARRIERS

Self-interested actors may fail to achieve efficient outcomes because their rational calculations induce them to adopt strategies and tactics that preclude such efficiency. Negotiators characteristically face a dilemma arising from the inherent tension between two different goals. The first goal consists of maximizing the joint value of the settlement—that is, the pool of benefits or size of the "pie" to be divided. The second goal consists of maximizing their own share of the benefit pool—that is, the size and attractiveness of their particular "slice" of the pie. Disputants, as we shall make clear, can affect the size of the pie and of their own slice in several ways; but often the strategies and tactics that maximize the size of the pie compromise their ability to achieve the largest possible slice. Conversely, negotiation ploys designed to increase the size of their own slice tend to stand in the way of maximizing, and may even shrink, the size of the pie.

The Practice of Secrecy or Deception

The "negotiators' dilemma" (Lax and Sebenius 1986) that we have described is particularly clear with respect to the question of revealing versus concealing interests. Clearly, the parties have a strong incentive to ascertain each other's true interests. Accurate information about goals, priorities, preferences, resources, and opportunities is essential for the principals (or those negotiating on their behalf) to frame agreements that offer optimal "gain of trade"—that is, agreement tailored to take fullest advantage of asymmetries of interests. Such information may even allow the parties to create additional value, that is, to contribute complementary skills or resources that combine synergistically to offer the parties "win-win" opportunities that might not heretofore have been apparent (See Fisher, Ury, and Patton 1991).

At the same time, parties have a clear incentive to conceal their true interests and priorities—or even to mislead the other side about them. By feigning attachment to whatever resources they are ready to give up in trade, and feigning relative indifference to whatever resources they seek to gain (while concealing opportunities and plans for utilization of those resources), each party seeks to win the best possible terms of trade for itself. In other words, total frankness and "full disclosure"—or simply greater frankness and fuller disclosure than that practiced by the other side in a negotiation—leave one vulnerable in the distributive aspects of bargaining. Accordingly, the sharp bargainer is tempted, and may rationally deem it advantageous—to practice secrecy and deception.

Such tactics, however, can lead to unnecessary deadlocks and costly delays or, more fundamentally, to failures to discover the most efficient trades or outcomes. A simple example illustrates the dilemma facing negotiators, and the barrier imposed by the strategic concealment or misrepresentation of information. Suppose Bob has ten apples and no oranges, while Lee has ten oranges and no apples. Suppose further that, unbeknownst to Lee, Bob loves oranges and hates apples, while Lee, unbeknownst to Bob, likes them both equally well. Bob, in service of his current resources and preferences, suggests to Lee that they might both be made better off through a trade.

Now, if Bob discloses to Lee that he loves oranges and doesn't eat apples, Lee might "strategically" but deceptively insist that he shares Bob's preferences and, accordingly, propose that Bob give him nine apples (which he says have relatively little value to him) in exchange for one of his "very valuable" oranges. Bob might even agree, and thus sell his apples more cheaply than he could have sold them if he had concealed his taste for oranges and suggested a trade of five oranges for five apples (on the grounds that they "both might enjoy a little variety in their diet").

Note, however, that such an "even trade," while more equitable, would not really be efficient, because it fails to take full advantage of the differing tastes of the two parties. That is, a more efficient trade would be accomplished by an exchange of Bob's ten apples for Lee's ten oranges, perhaps with some "side payment" to sweeten the deal for Lee, or better still, with linkage to some other efficient trade—one in which it was Bob who, at little or no cost to himself, accommodated Lee's particular needs or tastes.

Intransigence and Other "Hardball" Tactics

Even when both parties in a negotiation know all the relevant information and are fully aware of the potential gains available from a negotiated deal, strategic bargaining over how to divide the pie can still lead to deadlock (with no deal at all), or to protracted and expensive bargaining that essentially shrinks the pie. Suppose, for example, that Selma has a house for sale for which she has a reservation price of $245,000, and suppose further that Barbara is willing to pay up to $295,000 for the house. Any deal within a bargaining range from $245,000 to $295,000 would make both parties better off than they would be if no sale occurred at all.

As in our previous example, secrecy or deception on the part of the principals could put the transaction in jeopardy. For example, if Selma disclaimed any eagerness to sell, and Barbara claimed interest only in picking up a "bargain" (because Selma's house "wasn't exactly what she had in mind"), buyer and / or seller both could lose heart and consummate a deal with some other party that was less advantageous to both of them. But even if Selma and Barbara know, or guess, each other's reservation price, there still may be no deal—if they disagree about how the $50,000 "surplus" should be divided.

If Selma and Barbara engage in hardball negotiation tactics, in which each tries to persuade the other that she is committed to walking away from a beneficial deal rather than accept less than $40,000 of the surplus, the negotiation may end up in deadlock. Selma might claim that she won't take a nickel less than $285,000, or even $294,999 for that matter. Indeed, she might go so far as to give a power of attorney to an agent to sell only at that price (or at least tell Barbara that she has done so) and then leave town in order to make her claim credible. Of course, Barbara could play the same type of strategy, with the result that no deal is made, and both parties suffer for their strategic display of intransigence.

Tough, intransigent bargaining tactics, which may be rational for self-interested parties concerned with maximizing the size of their own slice of the pie, can often lead to inefficient outcomes. Those subjected to such tactics often respond in kind, and the net result typically is at best additional cost of the dispute resolution process (frustration, fees to agents, and loss of opportunity arising from delay) and at worst the failure to consummate a mutually beneficial agreement. This unfortunate scenario, it should be noted, is particularly likely to unfold when one or both parties believes that "time is on their side"—that they have greater patience or greater resources, or that delay will exact greater costs from the other side than their own side or, more generally, that the passage of time will weaken the other side's bargaining position relative to their own.

Indeed, in the search for strategic advantage the parties in a conflict or negotiation may threaten to escalate the costs of deadlock, and may carry out their threats (thereby shrinking the size of the pie and the prospect for an outcome satisfactory to both sides). Those experienced in the civil litigation process see this all the time. One or both threaten extensive and costly pre-trial discovery as leverage to force the other side into agreeing to a more favorable settlement. They even make their threat credible, by producing a great deal of "paper" for the other side to deal with, to which the other side responds in kind. And the net result, too often, is simply that both sides unnecessarily spend a great deal of money in the process. *Buchwald v. Paramount Pictures* was such a case, one in which the economic costs of hardball litigation obviously and substantially shrunk the pie, leaving all of the litigants poorer, and angrier, than was necessary.

PSYCHOLOGICAL BARRIERS

Psychological barriers, in contrast to strategic ones, do not arise from calculated attempts by the disputing parties to maximize immediate or long-term outcomes. Rather, they arise because the parties are subject to psychological processes that render them unable to recognize as advantageous (or unwilling to accept despite their advantages) settlement terms that seemingly meet the requirements of rational self-interest. Again, our list of such barriers is no doubt incomplete, and our classification scheme is far from neat. However, two basic insights, neither of which depends on the specifics of our list, are important.

First, it is critical to recognize that basic cognitive and motivational processes do in fact create barriers to dispute resolution that augment and interact with barriers arising from strategic calculation. Second, it is important to appreciate that disputants who are frustrated by the other side's apparent intransigence are apt to misdiagnose or misattribute the source of the deadlock, both by failing to recognize the impact of various psychological processes and biases on their *own* evaluations and responses and by erroneously inferring subtle, devious, strategic motives on the part of their adversary. As a result, disputants are likely to make unwarranted inferences about their adversaries' good faith, character, or intent, and to proceed to negotiate—or even *refuse* to negotiate—accordingly.

Equity or Justice Seeking

A proposed change in the status quo, one calling for an exchange of concessions or an allocation of gains and losses, may be rejected even when it offers indisputable advantages over maintenance of that status quo, and even when the future offers no realistic hope of more favorable terms, simply because the proposal violates one party's or both parties' sense of fairness or equity (see Adams 1965; Homans 1961; also Berkowitz and Walster 1976; Walster, Berscheid, and Walster 1973).

In cases where the parties have an identical basis for claiming gains (for example, where two partners hold a winning lottery ticket they purchased jointly, bearing both their names) the equitable division may be apparent to all (i.e., a "fifty-fifty" split). Moreover, neither party, is likely to propose, much less agree to, any other division. Indeed, it is interesting in this connection to take note of research on the "ultimatum game," in which (at least in the simplest form of the game) one party is given the opportunity to propose some division of a given purse, and the other party is obliged either to accept that "ultimatum" or to reject it (in which case neither party gains any portion of that purse). Two results from such research are important in terms of our present discussion. First, ultimatums offering the recipient less than 50 percent of the purse, especially ones offering *much* less than 50 percent, are frequently rejected even though the rejecting party thereby forfeits its only opportunity for gain. Second, the most common offer is a fifty-fifty split, and extremely unequal offers are relatively uncommon, which suggests that the party offering the ultimatum accepts the equity principle, or at least anticipates correctly that the other party would rather see the entire purse forfeited than accept a grossly inequitable division of its purse (Guth, Schmittberger, and Schwarze 1982; Ochs and Roth 1989).

Unfortunately, in allocation dilemmas and other bargaining situations outside the laboratory, the requirements of equity often are less obvious and less easily satisfied. In many cases what parties seek is not an *equal* advance over the status quo (for example, equal shares of material resources, or equal gains in security) but rather an advance that is *proportionate* to the weight and legitimacy of their respective claims (see Bazerman, Loewenstein, and White 1992). Such a requirement becomes particularly difficult to satisfy when the bases for the contending claims are different. If Jones wrote two-thirds of the chapters in a coauthored text and Smith one-third, or if Jones put up two-thirds of the money for a speculative stock purchase and Smith one-third, they are likely to agree without difficulty or ill will on a similar two-thirds / one-third allocation of any returns on their investment. But if Jones wrote more first drafts and did more of the library research, while Smith provided the outlines from which Jones worked and did more of the subsequent revisions and prose polishing, or if Jones provided more of the capital for the joint enterprise, while Smith provided more time, effort, and expertise, the search for an equitable allocation of returns is apt to be more difficult and contentious.

The pursuit of equity is apt to be especially difficult when the contending parties are longstanding adversaries and the claims in question are not only varied in nature but subject to dispute about facts and relevance—i.e., who started the conflict, who has endured greater wrongs, who made more concessions or exerted more energetic and sincere attempts at conflict resolution in the past, whose present needs and privations are most pressing, who has the most attractive alternatives to negotiated settlement, and so forth. Furthermore, adversaries are more apt to insist on proportionality or equity rather than mere improvement over the status quo when at least one of the parties feels that it has received inequitable treatment in the past, or when it believes that the momentum of history is on its side—i.e., that in future, perhaps through imposition of terms rather than negotiation, it will be more able to achieve what it "deserves."

By contrast, the search for agreement may be facilitated, and issues of equity may be pointedly avoided, when the parties in question already enjoy and wish to maintain a positive relationship. For example, longstanding collaborators negotiating future publication royalties, like friends negotiating the payment of a restaurant meal, may readily agree upon simple "equality"—that is, equal rather than proportional shares of the royalties—precisely because such an allocation avoids any consideration of equity or proportionality, thereby sparing the parties any potentially disagreeable discussion of respective claims or relative contributions.

Indeed, the "script" in such situations seem quite clear. The party with the stronger claims for a personally advantageous division of cost or benefits (i.e., the colleague who contributed somewhat more to the writing of the book, like the friend who ordered the less expensive restaurant entrée) is obliged to propose simple equality. At the same time, the other party, who stands to gain from equal division of current costs or rewards, is obliged to acknowledge that an unequal division (in favor of the first party) would be more equitable, but to yield graciously when the first party, perhaps citing the quality and / or continuing nature of their joint activities, insists on simple equality.

Our discussion of equity seeking suggests a paradox—one that some theorists and practitioners will no doubt find distasteful. As many thoughtful analysts (e.g., Fisher and Ury 1984) have noted, the art and science of successful dispute resolution demands the discovery (or if necessary the creative construction) of terms that the relevant parties feel are fair and responsive to their underlying needs and concerns, not mere "half-a-loaf" compromises. Our observation here is simply that the explicit pursuit of fairness or proportionality may itself pose a barrier to dispute resolution. To some extent, the resolution of this paradox involves a simple distinction between short-term and long-term perspectives. Agreements that satisfy equity concerns may be more difficult to design, and in many cases may not be achievable; but if they *can* be achieved they are apt to prove relatively stable. Conversely, terms agreed upon that do not satisfy such concerns are apt to come undone in the future, and to create the prospect of renewed hostility (especially if one party or the other increases its power, and feels able to redress the "injustice" of existing arrangements). To some extent, however, satisfaction of the partisans' subjective senses of equity—at least as an explicit negotiation goal—may simply be an unrealistic and undesirable burden to place on the negotiation process. That is, negotiation may proceed more productively when all that is explicitly sought is the generally obtainable goal of mutual advantage, with no requirement or implication that the disputants thereby concede explicitly or implicitly that the settlement reached reflects the relative merits of their respective cases.

Biases in Assimilation or Construal

As we have noted, disputants are bound to have differing recollections and interpretations of the past—of causes and effects, promises and betrayals, conciliatory initiatives and rebuffs. They are also bound to have differing interpretations or construals not only of the *context* of their dispute, but also of the *content* of any proposals designed to end that dispute.

Such differences may reflect the operation of both cognitive and motivational biases—that is, the tendency for people to "see," and remember, what their theories, beliefs, and expectations on the one hand, and their needs, wishes and self-interest on the other hand, dispose them to see (Abelson 1981; Bartlett 1932; Bruner 1957a, 1957b; Fiske and Taylor 1991). At the same time, they fail to recognize the influence of such biases on their own views, believing that they see things as they are in objective reality, and that it is only those who fail to share their views who are subject to such biases (Griffin and Ross 1991; Ross and Ward, in press).

Cognitive and motivational biases alike thus lead disputants to feel that they have acted more honorably in the past, have been more sinned against than sinning, and are seeking no more than that to which they are entitled. Each side in the dispute, moreover, is apt to feel that *its* interests are the ones that most require protection in any future agreement—for example by avoiding ambiguities in language that could be used as a loophole by its adversary, while at the same time avoiding rigidities in formulation that could compromise its own legitimate need to guard itself against unforeseen future developments. And, when its adversaries make parallel claims, or when third parties offer relatively evenhanded summaries of the past or commentaries about the legitimacy of respective claims, each side is apt to perceive bias in such effort and to infer unreasonableness, hostility, or devious strategic intent on the part of that third party.

The disputants, as we have noted, may show similarly divergent biases in the way they interpret prospective settlements of their conflict. Specifically, each side may interpret its potential concessions in a manner that maximizes their apparent significance and value but interpret the other side's potential concessions in a manner that minimizes their apparent significance and value. Thus the "impartial review board" proposed by the mayor's task force to deal with alleged incidents of police brutality is apt to be interpreted very differently by the members of the outraged community ("a bunch of political hacks who don't understand our experiences and would take the word of the police over that of people like us") and by the police ("outsiders who would worry too much about political implications and wouldn't understand our problems and frustrations"). Acceptance of such an "impartial" board, accordingly, would be seen as a far greater concession to the community by the police officers who would be subject to its review than by the community members who would gain the opportunity to air their grievances before it.

Often, a difference in construal may reflect a difference in perception of motives and intent. For example, one adversary in an arms negotiation may feel that a package deal that would increase its ability to launch a successful first strike but decrease its ability to retaliate to such a strike would represent a major concession on its part (because it has no intention to launch a first strike, while the other side has yet to prove its trustworthiness). By contrast, the other adversary will feel the proposal to be equitable or even generous (because, from *its* viewpoint, it is the other side's trustworthiness rather than its own that remains to be proven).

When such differences in construal and / or evaluation are great enough, a conflict that appears to be quite tractable (i.e., amenable to agreements offering mutual advancement of interests) from the viewpoint of outsiders proves highly intractable in light of the views of the adversaries. But even when the differences in perceptions and evaluations are not great enough to render the conflict totally intractable, these differences may be great enough to make the two sides disagree about which side would be making the larger concessions and, therefore, which would be entitled to receive more generous concessions in the future. And again, the net result of these biases will be a tendency for the adversaries to assess the overall valence or balance of a given proposal (especially when the matter of equity is taken into account) in terms that would strike an outside observer as biased and self-serving. Moreover, when the adversaries hear *each other's* characterization of the proposals' content and equitability, the result is likely to be heightened enmity and distrust.

"Reactive" Devaluation of Compromises and Concessions

Beyond the barriers posed by biased assessment of content and context there is a further problem resulting from the dynamics of the negotiation process. The evaluation of specific package deals and compromises may *change* as a consequence of knowing that they actually have been offered, especially if they have been proposed by an adversary.

Evidence for such "reactive" devaluation, obtained in both laboratory and field settings, is reviewed in Chapter 3 of this volume. It appears that a given compromise proposal is rated less positively when proposed by someone on the "other side" than when proposed by an apparently neutral third party (or, of course, when proposed by a representative on one's own side). Furthermore, it appears that proposed concessions are rated more positively than withheld concessions, and that a given compromise is rated less positively after it has actually been put on the table or unilaterally enacted—less positively, that is, than it had been rated beforehand, when it was merely a hypothetical possibility (see Ross and Stillinger 1991; Ross and Ward 1994, Stillinger, Epelbaum, Keltner, and Ross 1990). A range of cognitive and motivational processes, discussed in more detail in Chapter 3, has been proposed to account for such phenomena. These range from the perfectly rational tendency for negotiators to view an adversary's willingness to offer rather than withhold a given concession as informative of that concession's *value*, to the motivational bias that frequently makes people devalue whatever is at hand or readily available relative to whatever is unavailable or withheld.

It seems likely that different reactive devaluation mechanisms may operate to different degrees in different negotiation contexts (depending on the *ambiguity* of the terms of the proposal, the nature of the *relationship* between the source of the proposal and the potential recipient, and other contextual factors). It also seems likely that reactive devaluation will be most pronounced and most destructive in its effects when concessions are offered *unilaterally*, with the explicit or implicit suggestion that they should be reciprocated. In such cases the recipient of the unilateral concession is apt to believe that its adversary has given up nothing of real value and, therefore, to resist the suggestion that it should offer something of real value in return.

As a result, strategies that would attempt to build goodwill, break deadlocks, and stimulate reciprocal concessions through initial unilateral concessions (see Osgood 1962, 1980; also Lindskold 1978) face a formidable obstacle. When such concessions are *large*, they may increase the recipients' level of aspiration and their conviction that further large gains can be won by hard bargaining (see Siegel and Fouraker 1960). Nontrivial unilateral concessions may even invite exploitation (and reinforce the position of the "hardliners" within the adversary camp who have urged intransigence). When such concessions are *small*, they are apt to be perceived as trivial, token, and manipulative in intent. Against a background where each side feels that it historically has been more flexible and reasonable than its adversary—i.e., where each side feels that it is now the other side's turn to make concessions—the prospects for disappointment, distrust, and misattribution seem great, and alternative strategies seem called for.

Loss Aversion

In an important series of studies, Daniel Kahneman and Amos Tversky (1979, 1984) showed that decision makers tend to attach greater weight to prospective losses than to prospective gains of equivalent magnitude. This work is reviewed in Chapter 3 of this volume. The most obvious implication of such "loss aversion" for the art and science of negotiation is worth emphasizing here, namely, that parties in a dispute will prove reluctant to trade concessions—even when a dispassionate analysis of the parties' interests and expressed values suggests that the relevant trade would be mutually advantageous.

Consider, for example, a conflict between a management determined to cut costs and a union determined to advance the interests of its workers. In principle, a third-party mediator should be able to serve both sides in the conflict by identifying benefits currently held by workers that have been highly costly to management but only moderately valuable to the workers (for example, a health insurance policy that calls for no copayment) and prerogatives currently held by management that have been highly aversive to the workers but only moderately valuable to management (for example, the ability to dictate working hours rather than allowing flexible work schedules). The phenomenon of loss aversion, however, suggests that the obvious proposal by a mediator—i.e., that the union trade its "no copayment" insurance benefit for management's willingness to give up its scheduling prerogative—may meet a cooler-than-expected reception from both sides, unless the mediator finds a way to discourage them from framing what they are ceding as "loses" and what they are receiving as "gains" (see Neale and Bazerman 1991).

In other negotiation contexts a proposed trade of "land for peace," or more flexible custody arrangements for more generous child support terms, may meet a similarly cool reception for a similar reason—even without the equity concerns and without the problems of biased construal and reactive devaluation that we have outlined earlier. And again, the prospects for misunderstanding and misattribution are obvious. Each side is apt to see the other side's reluctance to trade concessions, or its apparent unwillingness to offer "fair value," as unreasonable, or as strategic in intent, or as evidence of its lack of "seriousness" in the negotiation.

The phenomenon of loss aversion also manifests itself in the tendency for decision makers to risk large but uncertain losses rather than accept smaller but certain ones. This tendency, in turn, holds an obvious implication for civil litigation. Defendants may unwisely decide to litigate rather than settle out of court—i.e., risk a large loss or award to the plaintiff rather than accept the certainty of a small one. By contrast, plaintiffs may unwisely decide to settle when their expected gain would actually be increased by undertaking the risks of litigation. In other words, the plaintiffs would show the familiar bias of "risk aversion" in the domain of gains by accepting a modest but certain gain rather than gambling on the prospect of a potentially large but uncertain one (Rachlinski 1994).

Judgmental Overconfidence

Litigants deciding whether to go to trial, political leaders deciding whether to undertake a military adventure, and labor negotiators deciding whether to risk a strike may all be led to decide affirmatively rather than reach negotiated settlements because of a phenomenon that Kahneman and Tversky (in Chapter 3 of this volume) term "optimistic overconfidence." Such overconfidence (which is but one aspect of the more general and much documented tendency for people to place unwarranted confidence in their predictions about future events) would be reflected in the tendency for the disputants to overestimate the likelihood and probable extent of their success in achieving their objectives. The primary source of this overestimation is an obvious asymmetry in the availability of information. That is, each side tends to have greater access to the factors that strengthen its position or would promote its success than to the factors that would weaken its position or promote its adversary's success. In particular, disputants know their own goals, assumptions, and plans better than they know their adversary's; and they fail to make adequate inferential allowance for such gaps in their knowledge by lowering their subjective certainty of success. Essentially, they adopt an "insider's" rather than an "outsider's" perspective, one that focuses too much on what they know or assume about the particular case at hand, and too little on the type of base-rate information or historical precedent that ought to alert them to the possibility of miscalculation and protracted, costly struggle.

One might imagine that the decision makers would be protected from the consequences of their overconfidence by the opportunity to compare their own assessments with those of peers and advisers. But a number of organizational or institutional factors (of the sort to be described in the final section of this chapter) limit the value of such consultation. As Irving Janis noted in his well-known discussion of "groupthink" (Janis 1972), counselors may hold their position precisely because they share the views of their leader; moreover, they may be reluctant to express doubts or disagreement lest their courage and loyalty be doubted. Indeed, even in the absence of shared norms and conformity pressures, group deliberation may generally serve to heighten rather than temper judgmental overconfidence. Recent research conducted by Dunning and Ross (1992) and by Heath and Gonzalez (in press) suggests that group deliberation in the context of estimation or prediction—even the simple exchange of predictions and numerical confidence assessments in the absence of real discussion—increases judgmental overconfidence. In other words, exposure to the views of one's peers seems to increase subjective certainty more than it increases objective accuracy.

Optimistic overconfidence can also be expected to occur where the outcomes in question involve predictions about judgments of others. In particular, disputants are apt to overestimate the degree to which their assessments will be shared by peers (Ross, Greene, and House 1977). The unwarranted assumption made is that other individuals—at least if they are objective and fair-minded—will come to one's own views, once they are exposed to the "truth." This assumption is apt to prove particularly costly in litigation contexts, where attorneys and their clients must decide whether to reach negotiated settlements or risk the inevitable costs and uncertainties of trial before judge or jury.

Dissonance Reduction and Avoidance

People involved in protracted conflict or unsuccessful negotiation are likely to try to minimize the amount of psychic regret or "cognitive dissonance" (see Festinger 1957; also Aronson 1969) to which they are subject. Such attempts at reducing and / or avoiding dissonance create obstacles to dispute resolution in two respects. First, disputants are continually motivated to rationalize or justify both their past failures to settle and whatever costs they are bearing in continuing the struggle. This objective is accomplished by convincing themselves (and telling others) that the rejected proposals were even more one-sided, or that those offering them are even more untrustworthy, or that the causes for which they are struggling are even more noble, or that the prospects for better terms in the future are even more favorable, than they had seemed prior to the disputant's decision not to settle. These additional justifications, which successfully reduce the parties' dissonance, in turn constitute additional psychic barriers to settlement.

Second, the prospect of settling a longstanding conflict threatens new dissonance—especially when additional costs and suffering have been borne since the rejection of similar terms in the past, and especially when such refusals have been buttressed with public pronouncements and actions. Rather than embracing today what could have been achieved yesterday without any additional financial, economic, human, or political costs, it is enormously tempting to "stay the course" and to convince oneself, and anyone else who can be persuaded, that more advantageous terms (terms that could truly justify one's past expenditures and sacrifices) can be won in future.

The implications of dissonance theory, however, are not entirely bleak for the process of dispute resolution. The human tendency to avoid and reduce psychic pain can also ease the process of acceptance and reconciliation. Once the agreement in question is a fait accompli, and resumption of conflict has become an unattractive option, the same dissonance-reduction or rationalization processes will lead all concerned to find new justifications for and new advantages in the agreed-upon terms of settlement.

INSTITUTIONAL, ORGANIZATIONAL, OR STRUCTURAL BARRIERS

The third set of barriers to be considered does not involve motives or biases in the judgments and behavior of the principal parties involved in conflict. These barriers reflect the fact that conflicts typically involve individuals and interest groups other than the principals. They also reflect the contexts within which conflict and negotiation occur and the institutions through which disputes are likely to be managed. Again, the list we offer is meant to be illustrative rather than complete or definitive.

Restricted Channels of Information and Communication

Sometimes channels of communication are nonexistent, or so restricted that the parties have no opportunity to air their grievances or to provide each other with the information about priorities and interests necessary for them to frame efficient settlement proposals. Such barriers to information transfer can be bureaucratic and institutional, reflecting divided or even conflicting responsibilities and areas of expertise (for example, the responsibilities of technical experts, financial officers, advisory boards, elected officials, and decision makers). They can also be political, or even legal. When countries break off diplomatic relations, undertaking discussions with the "enemy" can open politicians and citizens alike to political charges of disloyalty, lack of resolve, or broken promises. Lawyers, officeholders, entrepreneurs, and union officials all face restrictions on whom they can meet with and what they can discuss privately. (See Chapter 12 for Elster's account of the costs and benefits of public versus private diplomacy, and Chapter 13 for Arrow's discussion of some problems in the social organization of information acquisition.)

Multiple Interest Groups

As the chapters later in this volume on environmental disputes and negotiations attest, a number of structural problems or barriers arise when negotiations involve multiple interest groups. Often, people affected by a decision or settlement plan will not or cannot be represented at the bargaining table (and while their absence may actually increase the odds of an agreement's being reached, it may decrease the likelihood that the agreement will address all relevant interests). The problem of multiple interest groups becomes particularly intractable when very different interests, and stakes, are involved for different parties—for example, in negotiations about the placement of waste disposal sites, parks, hospitals, or halfway houses. In such cases a small well-defined set of individuals stand certain to gain or lose a great deal of money, while larger and less easily defined groups of individuals face prospective gains and losses that are less certain and involve less concrete matters of "quality of life." The institutions available for handling such disputes may be poorly equipped to weigh and resolve such competing claims. They may even be prevented by legal, ethical, or political constraints from entertaining settlement plans and procedures of the sort that might offer the greatest efficiency (e.g., use of "side payments," and creation of "markets" for distribution of costs and benefits).[3]

The Principal / Agent Problem

A final barrier to be discussed is suggested by recent work relating to transaction-cost economics, and is often called "the principal / agent problem" (Pratt and Zeckhauser 1985). The basic idea is familiar. The personal interests of an agent (whether it be a lawyer, employee, or officer) serving as a negotiator may be quite different from the interests of the principal party that agent represents. Indeed, aligning such interests—whether by formal

---

[3] In this regard, it is also worth noting the formal arguments demonstrating the "impossibility" of satisfying simultaneously a set of desirable conditions or requirements for the aggregation of individual preference orderings (Arrow 1963).

contract or norms—proves very difficult; and this difficulty may constitute a barrier to efficient resolution of conflict.

Litigation is fraught with such principal / agent problems. In civil litigation, for example—particularly where the lawyers on both sides are being paid by the hour—there is very little incentive for the opposing lawyers to cooperate. Indeed, the incentive structure of the situation may induce them to favor costly, noncooperative litigation. This may be particularly true if the clients have the capacity to pay for trench warfare and if they are angry enough to derive satisfaction from the costs they impose on the other side. Clients who crave a decisive, formal judicial decision that would offer them "vindication"—something that negotiated settlements can rarely offer—are especially likely to line the pockets of their agents in this fashion. Commentators have suggested that such asymmetries of interest help us understand why so many cases settle on the courthouse steps, and not before. Such a late settlement allows the attorneys to avoid the possible embarrassment of an extreme and unfavorable outcome, while at the same time providing substantial fees. (P'ng 1983). All the agents remain obliged to do is to explain their sudden eagerness to settle to clients who crave outright victory in court, who are now overly optimistic about the prospect of such victory, and eager for the trial to begin.

The Texaco / Pennzoil dispute may have involved a principal / agent problem of a different and subtler sort. Mnookin and Wilson (1989) have argued that the interests of the Texaco officers and directors diverged from those of the Texaco shareholders. Although the shareholders would have benefited from an earlier settlement, the litigation was controlled by Texaco directors, officers, and lawyers who were themselves defendants in fourteen lawsuits (eleven of them derivative shareholder actions, brought after the original multibillion-dollar Pennzoil verdict in the Texas trial court.)[4]

Facing the risk of personal liability, the directors and officers of Texaco had an incentive to pursue protracted litigation (paid for by the shareholders) in the remote hope of a total victory and exoneration, rather than accept a negotiated resolution. In any case, they rejected initial settlement offers, even though in so doing they subjected the corporation to the risk of a $10 billion judgment, along with ever mounting litigation costs. The case ultimately did settle, but only after a bankruptcy proceeding in which the bankruptcy court eliminated the risk of personal liability for Texaco's officers and directors.

---

[4] In 1985, a Texas jury awarded $7.53 billion in compensatory damages and $3 billion in punitive damages to Pennzoil. See *Texaco, Inc. v. Pennzoil Company*, 626 F. Supp. 250 (S.D.N.Y. 1986).

The principal / agent problem, we should emphasize, does not relate exclusively to the distribution of *financial* costs and benefits. Agents may bargain and respond to settlement possibilities in a manner that gives heavy weight to their "reputations" either for "toughness" or "cooperativeness." They may have ideological axes to grind, or may feel that their clients do not know their own best interests. Alternatively, they may feel that their clients give their own interests too much weight and the "public's" interest too little weight. In a real sense, agents and other third parties bring their own mix of strategic concerns and psychological biases to the negotiation process—all of which can constitute barriers to efficient dispute resolution.

OVERCOMING BARRIERS: THE ROLE OF MEDIATORS

The study of barriers can do more than help us understand why negotiations sometimes fail when they should succeed. It can also contribute to the appreciation, development, and evaluation of techniques for overcoming these barriers. In this regard, let us briefly consider the role of third-party mediators, and discuss some of the ways that "neutrals" can facilitate the efficient resolution of disputes.

First, let us consider strategic barriers. To the extent that a neutral third party is trusted by both sides, it may be able to induce the parties to reveal information about their underlying interests, needs, priorities, and aspirations that they would not disclose to their adversary. This information can permit a trusted mediator to help the parties formulate the most efficient "trades" possible, or even to "enlarge the pie" by helping the parties to combine their resources and opportunities in ways that had not previously been considered by either party.[5] Moreover, a skilled mediator can lessen the adversaries' incentive, and hence their temptation, to engage in the various hardball tactics that waste resources and breed ill will.

Mediators can also do much to overcome or attenuate psychological barriers. Perhaps most importantly, they can foster a problem-solving atmosphere, one that encourages the parties to move beyond political posturing and recriminations about past wrongs to recognize fully the gains from an efficient and fair resolution of the dispute and to work to achieve them. In a sense, the mediator can turn the parties' attention away from the direct pursuit of equity to the pursuit of enlightened self-interest. While divergent

---

[5] This perspective poses interesting theoretical and empirical questions for further research: From a game-theoretical perspective, when would a "rational" strategic party reveal information to a mediator that would not be disclosed to the other party? To what extent do mediators succeed in securing accurate revelations?

views of the past are inevitable, the mediator can employ techniques designed to at least help each side understand the case from the other side's perspective. The mediator can also endeavor to reframe the status quo, the impact of particular resolutions, and the costs of continued struggle in a manner that minimizes (or even takes advantage of) the participants' aversion to accepting losses, especially losses that are certain. The mediator similarly can dampen the principals' overconfidence about the prospects of pursuing a non-negotiated settlement—perhaps by offering the disputants' relative "base rate data" regarding outcomes and costs, or by exposing them to the reactions of disinterested parties apprised of the essential facts of the case.

The phenomenon of reactive devaluation sometimes can be avoided (and almost always can be reduced) if the settlement proposal in question can be made to come, or seem to come, from the third party or some collaborative effort rather than one of the principals acting unilaterally. Indeed, this blurring of authorship is one of the objectives accomplished when, after talking separately to each side about what might or might not be acceptable, the mediator takes responsibility for generating a proposal that he or she presents as a response to the principals' own stated priorities. The mediator can also help the parties to understand *why* a particular concession is being offered, and why it is being offered *now*—lest attribution be made which would encourage devaluation rather than reciprocation of those concessions. Such explanations could also reduce some of the dissonance associated with making concessions and accepting the various costs associated with ending protracted struggle.

The skilled mediator similarly can help overcome organizational barriers, such as those posed by principal / agent problems. A mediator may bring clients themselves to the table, and help them understand their shared interest in minimizing legal fees and costs, in circumstances, where the lawyers themselves might not be doing so. Similarly, in circumstances where a middle manager is acting to prevent a settlement that might benefit the company but might be harmful to the manager's own career, an astute mediator can bring another company representative to the table who does not have a personal stake in the outcome.

Finally, the mediator can serve as educator and relationship builder. Parties can be made aware of the barriers to dispute resolution discussed in this chapter and can be encouraged to seek ways of overcoming them, or at least to recognize that they often spring from the nature of conflict and negotiation rather than the character flaws of their adversary. Through such education and the many confidence-building measures and personal opportunities for more informal and humanizing contact that skilled mediators encourage, personal relationships can be built and improved. In this way the enmity that heightens the impact of virtually all of the barriers we have described can be attenuated.

CONCLUSION

In closing, we would like to underscore three basic ideas. The first concerns the important task around which this chapter has been organized, that is, recognizing the existence and exploring the nature of the many barriers to be overcome in the pursuit of efficient and fair dispute resolution. We trust that this chapter, and the chapters that follow, will help the reader to appreciate the importance of this task, not only for researchers, but for practitioners as well.

The second idea concerns the inherently interdisciplinary nature of the field of dispute resolution. This book is an example of how barriers can be explored from a variety of different perspectives. It draws principally on work relating to game theory and the economics of bargaining, principal / agent economics, cognitive psychology, and social psychology. Other disciplines, however, also have much to offer. Our understanding of conflict resolution would surely be enriched by careful exploration of barriers from the perspectives of other social sciences, including anthropology, sociology, and political science. History, literature, philosophy, theology, and other humanities similarly offer potentially useful contributions.

The third idea is a corollary of the second. No theoretical perspective, and no single discipline, has a monopoly on useful insights concerning the barriers to the fair and efficient resolution of conflict. Indeed, progress with respect to our understanding of conflict is going to turn very fundamentally on the ability of people from different disciplines to learn from one another and to work together to improve both theory and practice. One goal of this research should be to go beyond a better understanding of why negotiations fail when they ought to succeed—to help us, both as disputants and third parties, to overcome the barriers and achieve greater and more consistent success in the negotiated resolution of conflict.

PART TWO

Social and Psychological Perspectives

CHAPTER TWO

Reactive Devaluation in Negotiation and Conflict Resolution

Lee Ross

*A*dversaries seeking to settle conflict through negotiation face the familiar problem of achieving "gains in trade." The parties stand ready to make concessions, such as forfeiting valued resources or opportunities, provided that they can receive concessions that they value even more. Thus, by exploiting differences in needs, values, or preferences it generally should be possible for the adversaries themselves (or third parties interceding on their behalf) to propose a trade of concessions offering both sides an improvement over the status quo. (See Homans 1961; Pruitt 1981; Raiffa 1982). Only when the contending parties have *already* achieved all potential gains of trade, and one party can improve its position only at the expense of the other—i.e., only when the status quo already represents a *Pareto-efficient* state—should a conflict logically become "intractable." Otherwise, the failure of the parties to negotiate mutually acceptable terms reflects a kind of market inefficiency—in much the same sense as there is an inefficiency when a motivated buyer and a motivated seller are unable to consummate a deal under conditions where the buyer privately is willing to pay a greater amount for the relevant goods or services than the seller privately is willing to accept.

Sometimes, of course, the interests of parties involved in conflict are so dramatically opposed—or at least appear to be in the eyes of the disputants—that the difficulty of achieving success in negotiation seems not only explicable but inevitable. Israel and Syria both may have long recognized the perils of their continuing deadlock; and Syria fervently wished to regain the Golan Heights from Israel, while Israel was equally fervent in its desire for a Syrian pledge of nonaggression. But no conflict-reducing trade of concessions was likely to be negotiated as long as Israel valued the Heights more than the pledge and Syria deemed the pledge too high a price for the Heights. Enmity and distrust may even reach the point where the specifics of the concessions sought or proposed cease to matter. The disputants may view their struggle as a "zero-sum" game, one in which any gain achieved by the other side is perceived to be a loss, of equal magnitude, to their own side—so that the very idea of a mutually advantageous trade of concessions becomes a psychological, if not a logical, impossibility (see Pruitt and Rubin 1986). But many if not most disputes are at least somewhat tractable; and gains of trade through mutual concession making seem readily achievable provided that the parties are willing to bargain in good faith and patiently explore possibilities for mutual advantage.

One need only pick up the morning newspaper, however, to see that negotiations frequently fail and deadlocks persist even in conflicts where preservation of the status quo clearly seems to be against the best interest of the relevant parties. To some extent, the problem can be traced to barriers—strategic, psychological, or situational—that make it difficult to formulate, and / or get on the table, a proposal that both parties, given their different interests and views and their conflicting strategic goals, deem preferable, at least temporarily, to perpetuation of the status quo. (See Chapter 1.) But even when such a "mutually-acceptable-in-principle" proposal *can* be formulated, there may be an additional barrier to be overcome, one that arises, at least in large part, from the dynamics of the negotiation process. This barrier has been termed *reactive devaluation* (Ross and Stillinger 1991; Ross and Ward 1995; Stillinger, Epelbaum, Keltner, and Ross 1990). It refers to the fact that the very offer of a particular proposal or concession—especially if the offer comes from an *adversary*—may diminish its apparent value or attractiveness in the eyes of the recipient.

The same newspaper articles that describe failed negotiations and prolonged deadlocks generally provide anecdotal evidence of the parties' negative characterizations of each others proposals. It is easy to dismiss such uncharitable responses as tactical posturing rather than authentic reflections of the parties' private perceptions and evaluations. Labor has obvious incentives to denigrate the wage concessions that management proposes at the outset of contract negotiations. Parties in legal or political disputes similarly have ample reason to characterize the other side's current offer as ungenerous and inadequate. In so doing the negotiators simultaneously demonstrate their toughness to their constituencies, make a bid for the sympathy of interested third parties, and perhaps even convince the other side to up the ante. However, in such cases the question remains whether devaluation occurs in the proposal recipients' *private* evaluations—or at least in the evaluations they express when they have no strategic motives for misrepresenting their actual sentiments.

Ideally, one would like to answer such a question by gaining access to the candid evaluations, or rather to the *changes* in evaluation, that occur in the context of a broad sample of face-to-face negotiations. But the researcher rarely enjoys such access—certainly not under circumstances where suitable experimental control and measurement are possible and where sample sizes are adequate for purposes of statistical inference. However, a variety of survey and experimental techniques have been employed to furnish evidence of genuine, as opposed to strategically feigned, devaluation. That is, in the research to be described, recipients seem inclined to devalue concessionary proposals even when they know that their ratings will never come to the attention of the party offering the proposal, or for that matter to the attention of anyone they might have reasons to deceive about their actual feelings and assessments.

SUMMARY OF EMPIRICAL RESEARCH

Initial evidence for the reactive devaluation barrier was provided in a 1986 sidewalk survey of opinions regarding possible arms reductions by the U.S. and the U.S.S.R. (Stillinger et al. 1991). Respondents were asked to evaluate the terms of a simple but sweeping nuclear disarmament proposal—one calling for an immediate 50 percent reduction of long-range strategic weapons, to be followed over the next decade and a half by further reduction in both strategic and short-range tactical weapons until, very early in the next century, all such weapons would have disappeared from the two nations' arsenals. As a matter of history, this proposal had actually been made slightly earlier, with little fanfare or impact, by the Soviet leader Gorbachev. In the Stillinger et al. survey, however, the proposal's putative source was *manipulated*—that is, depending on experimental condition, it was ascribed by the survey instrument either to the Soviet leader, to President Reagan, or to a group of unknown strategy analysts—and only the responses of subjects who claimed to be hearing of the proposal for the first time were included in subsequent analyses.

The results of this survey showed, as predicted, that the proposal's putative authorship determined its attractiveness. When the proposal was attributed to the U.S. leader, 90 percent of respondents thought it either favorable to the U.S. or evenhanded; and when it was attributed to the (presumably neutral) third party, 80 percent thought it either favorable to the U.S. or evenhanded; but when the same proposal was attributed to the Soviet leader, only 44 percent of respondents expressed a similarly positive reaction.

While such results, and related ones reported a generation ago by Stuart Oskamp (1965), are unlikely to violate the reader's intuitions and experience, there is a point about research methodology or strategy that is worth emphasizing. It would be relatively easy for any competent experimenter to illustrate that the perceived valence of a proposal can be influenced by the perceived valence of its source. All the experimenter would have to do is frame a fictional proposal and contrive a negotiation context that featured lots of ambiguity or uncertainty—for example, ambiguity about what the parties would do and receive, or about the conditions under which they could exercise an "escape clause," or about the consequences they would face for not living up to the proposal's terms. But it should be noted that in the case of the proposal offered by Gorbachev, the framer's interest presumably lay not in *producing* such reactive devaluation but in *preventing* it (to which end, presumably, he was obliged to formulate terms that either would be clear and forthcoming or else ambiguous in ways specifically designed to win a positive rather than a negative reaction from the intended audience). Accordingly, the Stillinger et al. demonstration cannot be dismissed as a hothouse product of the psychological laboratory, one irrelevant to the real world. Nor could the cool reception that Stillinger et al.'s subjects afforded the Gorbachev proposal relative to the Reagan or third-party proposal be attributed to some strategic goal. For, unlike players on the real-world diplomatic stage, these subjects obviously were not trying to coax further concessions from the other side or to win the hearts and minds of partisan constituents or third parties.

Although this initial reactive devaluation study provided positive results, the findings are unlikely to seem particularly surprising or provocative to negotiation theorists or practitioners. The reason for this is clear. While the tendency to devalue the adversary's concessions and proposals undeniably is a barrier to dispute resolution, such a tendency can readily be defended on normative grounds. Certainly there is nothing counternormative about treating a proposal's authorship as informative with respect to the balance of advantages and disadvantages that would accrue to its author. ("They wouldn't have offered those terms if those terms didn't advance their interests.") And, where the author in question is presumed to be a foe who seeks to dominate the proposal's recipients, there may be nothing counternormative about also treating such authorship as potentially informative about the proposal's prospects for the recipient. ("They wouldn't have offered those terms if those terms strengthened our position relative to theirs.")

It was such normative considerations, at least in part, that dictated the design and procedural details of the next set of reactive devaluation studies conducted by Stillinger et al. In these studies the responses contrasted were not ones made to proposals from hostile versus nonhostile sources. In fact, the responses examined were made in reaction to compromise measures offered by a source who was perceived by most recipients as not opposed to their own interests, but merely acting in that source's interests. The context of this research was a campus-wide controversy at Stanford about the university's investment policy. Students generally favored a policy calling for total and immediate divestment by the university of all stock holdings in companies doing business in South Africa. The university, claiming to share the students' opposition to apartheid, but to be constrained by its responsibilities to maximize the value of its portfolio and earnings, set up a committee to study the problem and devise a divestment policy that would be both financially prudent and socially responsible. Once again using a real-world issue, and once again relying upon the use of an experimental manipulation within the context of a survey, Stillinger et al. seized this opportunity to study further the phenomenon of reactive devaluation.

In the first such study, students simply were asked to read a booklet describing the divestment controversy, then to evaluate two potential compromise proposals. One of these proposals, which was termed the "Specific Divestment" plan, entailed immediate divestment from corporations doing business with the South African military or police. The other alternative, termed the "Deadline" plan, proposed to create a committee of students and trustees to monitor "investment responsibility," with the promise of total divestment two years down the road if the committee was not satisfied with the rate of progress shown in dismantling the apartheid system in South Africa. Subjects were randomly assigned to three experimental conditions, identical in all respects except for the particular program that the university was purported to be on the verge of enacting. One group read that the university planned to undertake Specific Divestment; another group read that the university planned to undertake the Deadline plan; and the remainder were given no reason to believe that the university was considering the immediate adoption of either alternative. The experimental hypothesis, of course, was simply that the "offered" concession plan would be devalued relative to the "non-offered" one.

The results obtained in this study seemed once again to offer straightforward evidence for the predicted reactive devaluation phenomenon. That is, students tended to rate whichever of the two proposals the trustees had ostensively offered as a smaller and less significant compromise than the alternative, non-offered, proposal. Thus, when Stanford purportedly was ready to implement the Deadline plan, 85 percent of the respondents ranked Specific Divestment as a bigger concession than the Deadline. By contrast, when the university purportedly was ready to pursue Specific Divestment, only 40 percent rated Specific Divestment as the more consequential of the two compromise plans. Not surprisingly, when neither concession plan was purported to be imminent, the percentage of students rating Specific Divestment as a bigger and more significant concession than the Deadline plan was between the extremes in the two experimental conditions—i.e., 69 percent. Clearly, the "offered" versus "non-offered" status of the relevant divestment plans influenced the student respondents' evaluation of their apparent significance and attractiveness.

The same basic result was replicated in a follow-up laboratory experiment, in which students selected specifically on the basis of their strong and active support for immediate and total divestment negotiated with a middle-aged man (actually a confederate of the experimenter) who expressed a willingness to defend the university's interests and current policies. To prepare the students for their forthcoming negotiation session, a packet of information materials calling for their careful examination was mailed to them beforehand, detailing the university's holdings in firms doing business in South Africa and indicating the record of those firms with respect to fair employment and affirmative action policies. The packet also included a list of the most common arguments offered by opponents and supporters of divestment.

During the negotiation itself, which often proved to be quite heated (despite the participants' awareness that any "agreements" they reached would have no impact on actual university policy), the confederate for a time stubbornly but articulately defended the university's current "nonpolitical" investment policy. In two experimental conditions, however, he ultimately made a proposal that offered his student adversary a concession—either the Specific Divestment plan (the same one used in our survey study) or a rather surprising and peculiar "Reward for Disinvestment" plan (whereby the university would not divest itself of anything but would channel $20 million in additional investments into companies, such as General Motors, which had already withdrawn from all business activities in South Africa). The experimental design also included a control condition in which the confederate offered no concession at all.

Subsequently, the subjects rated the attractiveness and significance of a number of different proposals, including, of course, the ones that had been offered in their negotiation session. And, as predicted, these ratings again reflected the "offered" versus "non-offered" status of the relevant proposals. Specifically, the familiar Specific Divestment plan received a more positive rating than the peculiar Reward for Disinvestment plan, both when no concession was offered and (even more so) when the confederate offered the Reward for Disinvestment plan. Only when Specific Divestment was the compromise plan explicitly offered did its ratings dip below those of the Reward for Disinvestment plan.

The magnitude of the differences obtained in this laboratory experiment, however, was not particularly impressive, and the investigators set out to design a follow-up experiment that they thought would yield more conclusive results. But this plan was thwarted by a new development in the unfolding divestment drama at Stanford. As the academic year was drawing to a close, the university at last reached a decision and prepared to announce the enactment of its divestment plan—one, not coincidentally, that closely resembled the Specific Divestment plan that had been employed in the two earlier Stillinger et al. studies. This turn of events precluded further laboratory or field experiments. At the same time, however, it presented the investigators with a golden opportunity to do one final study—this time looking at evaluations of an actual compromise measure before and after it had been publicly proposed in the context of an ongoing political struggle.

Having learned of the details of the university's still unannounced plan (by which it would divest itself of shares in ten companies, for a total of about $3 million), Stillinger et al. quickly prepared a new survey asking students to evaluate a number of possible compromise plans, including, of course, the university's soon-to-be-announced Specific Divestment plan. This survey was administered to a sample of Stanford students on two occasions—once *before* the university made its new divestment plan public (with all proposed compromise plans, including the university's actual plan, described as merely "hypothetical") and once shortly *after* the university's well-publicized announcements (this time accurately characterizing the university's plan as "about to be enacted," while again characterizing the alternative plans merely as other hypothetical alternatives).

Participants' responses in these two surveys provided the basis for a simple before / after comparison to test for reactive devaluation. And the results of this comparison were clear-cut, albeit no doubt disappointing to the university. On the key measure involving apparent magnitude and significance of concessions, the students' mean ratings of Specific Divestment declined after its planned enactment had been announced by the university. By contrast, none of the other merely "hypothetical" plans showed any such decline in ratings. Indeed, slight increases in ratings were more typical for these "non-offered" plans. In other words, it was only the *offered* compromise plan, not compromise plans in general, that came to be seen as less significant by the students over the critical three-week period following the university's announcement. Thus, consistent with the results of Stillinger et al.'s previous study, the change in the students' assessment of the relevant compromise plan appeared to be a direct consequence of, and a reaction to, the fact that the plan actually had been initiated.

To the extent that adversaries devalue the compromises and concessions put on the table by the other side, they exacerbate an already difficult dilemma: that of forging an agreement that the relevant parties, with their differing views of history and their differing perceptions of entitlement, will perceive to be better than the status quo and not offensive to their sense of equity. Beyond alerting us to this dilemma, the Stillinger et al. studies raise two important, ultimately related, questions. First, what processes or mechanisms might cause the offer of a concession or compromise proposal to decrease its attractiveness in the eyes of the recipient? Second, what steps might be taken, either by the adversaries themselves or by third-party mediators, to overcome this barrier?

Research on reactive devaluation initially was undertaken to show that biased construal of an adversary's concession or compromise proposal could lead to devaluation—and hence could launch a downward spiral of misunderstanding and mistrust, whereby dismissal and lack of reciprocation by the recipient of a proposal discouraged further initiatives. As that research program evolved, however, it became increasingly clear that a number of different psychological processes might underlie reactive devaluation—processes that differ considerably both in their normative status and in their implications for negotiation theory and practice. Two specific processes, or rather *types* of processes, merit consideration in more depth.

One set of underlying processes involves changes in *perception, interpretation, or inference,* either about individual elements in a proposal or about the overall valence of that proposal. To the extent that the other side's initiative seems inconsistent with our understanding of their interests and / or past negotiation behavior, we are apt, perhaps even logically obliged, to scrutinize their offer rather carefully. That is, we are inclined to look for ambiguities, omissions, or "fine print" that might render the terms of that proposal more advantageous to the other side, and perhaps less advantageous to our side, than we had assumed them to be (or would have assumed them to be, had the question been asked) prior to their being offered. The results of such skeptical scrutiny—especially if the terms in question are unclear, complex, or imperfectly specified, and especially if trust vis-à-vis implementation of these terms is called for—are apt to be a revised assessment of what we stand to gain, both in absolute terms and relative to what we believe the other side stands to gain, from acceptance of the relevant proposal.

This process of inference and deduction, as psychologists would be quick to note, could be even simpler and less cognitively demanding. Several theories of psychological consistency (e.g., Osgood and Tannenbaum 1955; also Abelson and Rosenberg 1958; Festinger 1957; and Heider 1958) hold that any relevant object of judgment (including, presumably, a concession offer or a negotiation proposal) will be evaluated more negatively as a consequence of its linkage to a negative source (including, presumably, an enemy or adversary). In other words, no reinterpretation, in fact no consideration of content at all, need take place for devaluation to occur. One might simply reason that if "they" are offering a proposal it must be good for them; and if it is good for them (especially if "they" are adversaries who wish us harm) it must be bad for "us." Once again, although it is difficult to criticize such inferential leaps on purely normative grounds, the danger should be obvious. One can be led to conclude that any proposal offered by the "other side"— especially if that other side has long been perceived as an enemy—*must* be to our side's disadvantage, or else it would not have been offered. Such an inferential process, however, assumes a perfect opposition of interests, or in other words, a true "zero-sum" game, when such is rarely the case in real-world negotiations between parties whose needs, goals, and opportunities are inevitably complex and varied.

The second type of underlying process or mechanism, suggested by demonstrations of the devaluation phenomenon in the Stanford divestment studies in which the source of the devalued proposal was not really an enemy of the recipient, is very different. This mechanism involves neither mindful nor mindless changes in interpretation, but rather changes in underlying *preferences*. Human beings, at least in some circumstances, may be inclined to reject or devalue whatever is freely available to them, and to covet and strive for whatever is denied them. Moreover, they may be inclined to do so even when no hostility is perceived on the part of the individual or institution determining what will or will not be made available. (See Brehm 1966; Brehm and Brehm 1981; also Wicklund 1974, for theoretical accounts of such "psychological reactance"). The familiar aphorism that "the grass is always greener on the other side of the fence" captures this source of human unhappiness and frustration very well, and it is easy to think of anecdotal examples in which children or adults, rather than "counting their blessings," seem to place inordinately high value on whatever commodity or opportunity is denied them.

A simple role-play study by Lepper, Ross, Tsai, and Ward (1994) documents this "change of preference" process quite clearly. At the same time, this study provides further evidence that the reactive devaluation phenomenon depends neither on an adversarial relationship nor on ambiguity in proposed terms. The subjects in the study, all social science majors, were asked to imagine that they had undertaken a summer job with a distinguished professor, one which entailed low pay and unrewarding and difficult library research. They further were asked to imagine that they later discovered that the professor was on the verge of publishing, and receiving a hefty royalty for, a chapter based heavily on their work. The fictional professor, however, offered them neither additional money nor a coauthorship in recognition of their efforts (two rewards that had been vaguely alluded to as "further possibilities" if the student's efforts led to a publishable article). Next, they were asked to imagine that, after writing a polite but firm note to the professor complaining about the lack of fair recognition or compensation and reminding the professor of the vague assurances offered them at the outset of the project, they had received one of two possible concessions—either a "third authorship" (with their name following that of a second author who to their knowledge had contributed little to the project) or a sum of $750. Finally the students were asked to assess, among other things, the attractiveness and value of the two relevant concessions—the one that they had been granted by the professor and the alternative concession that had not been granted.

Reactive devaluation was found, just as predicted. That is, it was the students who had been granted the money who found the third authorship to be the most attractive and of greater interest to them, and the students who had been offered the third authorship who found the money most attractive and valuable. These students, it is worth noting, gave no evidence of having reinterpreted the meaning or reassessed the objective worth of the two relatively unambiguous compromises in question. They simply expressed preferences and values that seemed to be tilted in the direction of whichever one of the two compromises had proven "unavailable" or been "withheld."

A second study reported in the same paper by Lepper et al. extended these findings and clarified two parameters that may influence the magnitude of reactive devaluation. In this follow-up study, students again evaluated a "cash settlement" (this time $900 instead of $750) versus a "third authorship" compromise granted by the professor. This time, however, two factors were explicitly manipulated. These factors were the *reputational status* of the professor and the exact nature of the promises that heightened the students' sense of *entitlement* to the concessions in question (both of which deliberately had been left somewhat vague in the initial study). Thus, half the students in the following study were told that the professor had been cold and harsh in dealings with them, and exploitative in past dealings with other prior research assistants, while half were given no such negative information about the professor's reputation or past dealings. At the same time, half of the students within each "reputation" condition were told that the professor had explicitly promised that publication would lead to additional rewards in the form of money and / or authorship, while half were given no information suggesting any prior assurances or other basis for heightened feelings of entitlement.

The results of this follow-up study by Lepper et al. again were clear-cut. Both the presence of a negative relationship and reputation based on past dealings and the presence of prior assurances promoting a sense of entitlement seemed to enhance the magnitude of the reactive devaluation phenomenon. But neither factor proved *necessary* to produce the phenomenon. That is, the fictional professor's action in granting one particular concession rather than another seemed to shift the recipient's assessments and underlying preferences even when there was neither an existing negative relationship or reputation with respect to the source nor a strong basis for feelings of denied expectation or prior entitlement on the part of the recipient.

A number of other psychological processes and mechanisms which may also contribute to reactive devaluation merit at least brief mention even though they have not yet been pursued explicitly in the context of reactive devaluation research. For instance, a seemingly equitable proposal for a trade of concessions can become unattractive and inequitable in the eyes of the recipient because of a judgment bias that Daniel Kahneman and Amos Tversky (1984) have termed *loss aversion* (see also Chapter 3 in this volume). What these investigators have documented is the fact that the aversiveness of a given loss tends to be greater than the attractiveness of a gain of the same objective magnitude. Thus, the very act of framing a proposal in a manner that invites the other side to give up some things it values in order to receive some other things it also values may leave the recipients of the proposal convinced that the loss in question will not be commensurate with the gain—even when a prior elicitation of the recipients' values might have led one to anticipate that the proposed trade of concessions would be welcomed quite eagerly.

The receipt of a specific concession or conciliatory proposal also can alter the recipients' *aspiration* or *comparison level*. The mere fact that one's adversary is willing to offer a concession can change one's assessment of that adversary's flexibility and eagerness to deal. Accordingly, there is apt to be an altered perception of the gains that might be achievable through further toughness in bargaining, and also a new standard for comparison and a higher level of aspiration. Such changes may thus broaden the gap between what is sought and what is on the table—leading the recipient to rate the concession less positively than it would have been rated beforehand, when it was merely hypothetical. Indeed, it is this consequence that the practice of "strategic intransigence," discussed as a barrier to conflict resolution in Chapter 1 of this volume, is designed to avoid; for early displays of intransigence can serve to lower the adversary's expectations and aspirations and perhaps encourage that adversary to show more flexibility.

Still another possible mechanism may involve the "polarizing" effect of *mere attention* or *heightened scrutiny*. Abraham Tesser (1978) has provided evidence that instructions or procedures that "lead" experimental subjects to consider various objects of judgment more deeply, or even simply for a longer period of time, increase the positive or negative valence of those objects. That is, favorable evaluations become even more favorable and, more to the point, negative evaluations (including, presumably, negative evaluations of concessionary proposals or compromises that inevitably offer less than the recipient seeks and feels entitled to receive) become more negative.

Furthermore, *interpersonal* processes can play a role in encouraging critical scrutiny and resulting devaluation. When a compromise is proposed in the context of a social or political struggle, it inevitably becomes the object of pointed debate and propagandizing. As the aftermath of the Stanford divestment conflict showed, "hard-liners" search for and find shortcomings, or at least ambiguities, in the proposed terms; and they are apt to put their objections forward forcefully, both in informal discussion and in their comments to the media. This process subjects the less militant members of the group to persuasion and social pressure alike—both of which exert a force in the direction of public devaluation of the other side's proposal, and perhaps private devaluation as well.

The preceding list of potential underlying mechanisms is by no means intended to be exhaustive. Nor is it likely that all of these mechanisms were operating in the reactive devaluation studies reviewed in this chapter. (Indeed, the designs and measures employed by the investigators precluded the operation of at least some of these mechanisms, showing that they are not necessary to produce the phenomenon). But the list should be sufficient to illustrate that the reactive devaluation phenomenon is likely to reflect the operation of different types of processes in different contexts. Some of these processes may seem more defensible on normative grounds than others, and some may more commonly play an important role in producing the phenomenon. But all of them potentially may contribute to the difficulty of achieving conflict reduction through compromise and negotiation in the social, political, economic, and ideological deadlocks that seem so pervasive a feature of contemporary life.

IMPLICATIONS: OVERCOMING REACTIVE DEVALUATION

The preceding discussion of the reactive devaluation phenomenon, and of the various processes that might underlie it, has some implications for those who seek to resolve disputes. Foremost, of course, is the likelihood that compromise proposals or concessions designed to demonstrate goodwill and prompt reciprocation will fail in their objectives. All too often, they will be dismissed as trivial and token, or received with coolness and expressions of distrust that serve to thwart the goal of negotiated agreement and to weaken rather than strengthen the hand of those who urge conciliation. Furthermore, such public dismissals or cool receptions are themselves apt to be misattributed—to be seen as the product of calculated strategy rather than genuine sentiment, or to be taken as evidence of a lack of good faith and seriousness in the pursuit of agreement. Anticipating disappointing pitfalls in the negotiation process, and correctly attributing them when they occur, is important. But the research and analysis reviewed in this chapter also point to some specific strategies that could prove helpful in overcoming reactive devaluation and facilitating dispute resolution; and it is to these applied concerns that the last section of this chapter will be directed (see also Ross and Stillinger 1991)

The Use of Prior Elicitation and Concession Menus

Two strategies for reducing reactive devaluation follow rather directly. Both are designed to discourage the recipients of a concession or compromise proposal from reinterpreting its terms or reordering their own preferences in ways that make the proposal seem less advantageous to them. The first strategy involves explicitly eliciting the potential recipients' values and preferences before making any concessionary proposal, and then explicitly linking the content of the subsequent proposal to those expressed values and preferences. An invitation could be offered to exchange lists of concessions, each side not only indicating what it seeks and what it might be willing to offer in "trade," but also stipulating the relative importance it attaches to those concessions. Each side could then use the other side's responses to help formulate and justify the specifics of the concessions offered and / or sought in subsequent proposals. Again, the goal of such a strategy is twofold—first to formulate mutually beneficial terms, and second to discourage reactive devaluation by prompting the recipients of such proposals to attribute the specifics of the proposed terms to their own expressed preferences and priorities (rather than to hidden motives or private knowledge on the part of the proposal's initiator). The advantages of candid pre-negotiation exchanges of goals and preferences are rather obvious. But such a strategy is probably realistic only in negotiations characterized by a lack of enmity or distrust, negotiations in which the parties have already embraced the objective of maximizing mutual benefit.

A related strategy (one that offers less temptation for strategic misrepresentation of goals, intentions, opportunities, or priorities) would be for one side simply to offer the other a "menu" of unilateral concessions that it is willing to make as a gesture to initiate a cycle of future *reciprocal* concessions; and then to invite that other side to select the "pump-priming" concession of its choice. It is worth contrasting the "menu of concessions" technique described here with the well-known tension-reduction and agreement-seeking strategy suggested by Osgood (1962). Osgood's proposal called for the initial unilateral concession to be chosen by the *offerer*. Such a choice, however, is apt to be seen as informative about its cost to the offerer and perhaps even its value to the recipient. Furthermore, the recipient's preferences and priorities may change as well, making the offer seem less significant and attractive. In the proposed "menu" strategy, the initial unilateral concession is to be chosen by recipients in accord with *their* preferences, thereby minimizing such perceptions of informativeness or changes in preferences. What we are suggesting here is a dispute resolution principle even simpler than the suggestion to seek gains in trade: Tell your adversaries that you are willing to take the first small step; stipulate or at least outline some possibilities that clarify the magnitude of that step; and ask your adversaries what *they* want (i.e., which initial, necessarily modest, pump-priming measure *they* would value and deem worthy of reciprocation). Then, insofar as the nature and magnitude of their request is consistent with the "menu" offered, *give them what they ask for.*

Process Debriefing and Forewarning

It is worth exploring the possibility that insight or awareness about reactive devaluation and the mechanisms or processes that underlie it could serve to forestall or weaken such devaluation. In practical terms, the suggestion is that the negotiation agenda include a pointed preliminary discussion of barriers and underlying processes—including not only reactive devaluation but other psychological and strategic barriers as well. It is apparent from previous investigations in the field of judgment and decision making that forewarning or inoculation concerning particular biases and the mechanisms that underlie them sometimes "works" and sometimes does not work (see Fischhoff 1981; Lord, Lepper, and Preston 1984; Ross, Lepper, and Hubbard 1975). Clearly, the usefulness of such educational techniques vis-à-vis reactive devaluation and dispute resolution is an empirical question worthy of investigation. In fact, there are really two questions to be addressed. The first and most obvious question concerns the value of pre-negotiation discussions or briefings about reactive devaluation and the mechanisms that may underlie it. The second, more general, and ultimately more provocative question involves the value of educating fledgling negotiators about the psychological processes that create barriers to dispute resolution and that foster misunderstanding and distrust between parties involved in negotiation.

Addressing Attributional Concerns

As the discussion of mechanisms and potential remedies offered thus far suggests, the psychological barrier of reactive devaluation hinges in part on the assumption that disputants are bound to make attributions about each other's offers of compromise and concessions. Why is *this* particular compromise being offered? Why is this particular exchange of concessions being proposed? And why is the offer or proposal coming *now?*

When the stakes are high, these questions inevitably are considered. And the answers likely to be deemed most plausible (for example, "they must not value what they are proposing to concede" or "they must know something about the current situation that we don't" or even "they don't intend to honor their side of the proposed agreement") are ones that may serve to encourage devaluation, to discourage reciprocation, and to preclude the desired creation of goodwill. Such attributions and consequences seem particularly likely when the relationship between parties is adversarial or hostile, and trust is in short supply. The solution to this attributional dilemma is simple, at least in theory. The side offering the proposal or concession must help the other side to arrive at more *benign* attributions—in particular, by clarifying the forces, constraints, or motives that are prompting it to compromise or offer such attractive terms. At times such candor may have a strategic cost—one may be obliged to acknowledge weaknesses in one's bargaining position, or to reveal goals and plans that one would prefer to keep hidden. But the benefit of such candor—that is, the increased prospects of having one's proposal taken at face value—may outweigh the strategic cost more often than standard bargaining and negotiation lore would suggest.

Beyond pointing to the value of greater candor in the conduct of negotiation, an awareness of attributional issues leads to the suggestion that negotiating parties might benefit from the *creation* of additional external forces compelling compromise and agreement. Setting deadlines (after which some cost or loss of opportunity will be incurred), making plans or commitments contingent on negotiation success, or even staking reputations on the promise of success are all strategies that not only prompt disputants to offer each other concessions but also permit or even encourage them to take such offers at face value.

Role of Third Parties

The "Reagan versus Gorbachev" disarmament proposal study discussed earlier provided some evidence that attributing a given proposal to a neutral third-party source instead of an adversary can reduce or eliminate reactive devaluation. While the possibilities for such deceptive manipulations are very limited in the conduct of real-world bargaining and negotiation, the skilled third-party mediator can assume some responsibility for the framing of proposals, especially proposals that the mediator explicitly links to the parties' expressed goals and priorities. The mediator can also encourage a "problem-solving" orientation (Fisher and Ury 1981) in which the parties seek to create additional value or to capitalize upon differences in the two sides' needs, preferences, and opportunities, rather than merely to accept compromises that apportion dissatisfaction. More generally, third parties can play a useful role in neutralizing the mechanisms that underlie reaction devaluation and its potentially negative consequences. They can alert the parties to the existence of the phenomenon and to its psychological rather than strategic basis, thereby forestalling attributions and responses that might heighten rather than attenuate conflict and mistrust. They can create deadlines, incentives, and other pressures that not only encourage concessions or compromise but also prompt benign attributions when they occur. They can help create trust and goodwill. Most important, they can help the parties to recognize that they are not in a zero-sum struggle; to see that mutual as well as opposing interests exist, and that the other side's author-ship of a proposal is not *necessarily* evidence that their own side's interests would be better served by rejecting that proposal than by accepting it.

Negotiation Ideology and Expectation

The analysis of reactive devaluation and the barriers that underlie it, as well as the more general discussion of negotiation barriers featured in this volume, can leave the reader with unwarranted pessimism about the pros-pect of successful dispute resolution. It is important, therefore, to remind ourselves that difficult, even seemingly intractable disputes often do reach resolution. In fact, in many potentially difficult negotiations (including the passing of the federal budget, the election of a pope, and many labor-man-agement confrontations) it is success rather than failure that history suggests to be inevitable. In such cases, ideology and expectation seem critical. When pessimism is widespread and rooted in a history of past negotiation failures, the parties will find it difficult to offer meaningful compromises and equally difficult to accept as meaningful any concessions offered in the proposals of their adversaries. But when all parties enter the dispute resolution process with the absolute conviction that their negotiations must and will succeed, especially when such convictions are rooted in a history of consistent past success, the parties are more likely not only to offer concessions but to inter-pret "charitably" the concession offers they receive—i.e., as genuine com-promises dictated by the imperative of reaching an agreement, and not deceptive ploys that conceal private knowledge and hidden motives. Only when failure is somehow "unprecedented" and "unthinkable" can one be relatively certain that reactive devaluation, and the other barriers to dispute resolution discussed throughout this volume, will be overcome. As a result, parties are more likely to reciprocate the compromises they receive, thereby moving the negotiation process closer to resolution.

CHAPTER THREE

Conflict Resolution: A Cognitive Perspective

Daniel Kahneman and Amos Tversky

*M*any different disciplines deal with the resolution of conflict. Even within the single discipline of psychology, conflict can be approached from different perspectives. For example, there is an emotional aspect to interpersonal conflict, and a comprehensive psychological treatment of conflict should address the role of resentment, anger, and revenge. In addition, conflict resolution and negotiation are processes that generally extend over time, and no treatment that ignores their dynamics can be complete. In this chapter we do not attempt to develop, or even sketch, a comprehensive psychological analysis of conflict resolution. Instead, we explore some implications for conflict resolution of a particular cognitive analysis of individual decision making. We focus on three relevant phenomena: optimistic overconfidence, the certainty effect, and loss aversion. Optimistic overconfidence refers to the common tendency of people to overestimate their ability to predict and control future outcomes; the certainty effect refers to the common tendency to overweight outcomes that are certain relative to outcomes that are merely probable; and loss aversion refers to the asymmetry in the evaluation of positive and negative outcomes, in which losses loom larger than the corresponding gains. We shall illustrate these phenomena, which were observed in studies of individual judgment and choice, and discuss how these biases could hinder successful negotiation. The present discussion complements the treatment offered by Neale and Bazerman (1991).

Some preliminary remarks are in order. First, the three phenomena described above represent departures from the rational theory of judgment and decision making. The barriers to conflict resolution discussed in this chapter, therefore, would be reduced or eliminated if people were to behave in accord with the standard rational model. It would be inappropriate to conclude, however, that departures from rationality always inhibit the resolution of conflict. There are many situations in which less-than-rational agents may reach agreement while perfectly rational agents do not. The prisoner's dilemma is a classic example in which rationality may not be conducive for achieving the most desirable social solution. The present chapter focuses on the obstacles imposed by the presence of optimistic overconfidence, the certainty effect, and loss aversion. We do not wish to imply, however, that these phenomena are necessarily detrimental to conflict resolution.

I. OPTIMISTIC OVERCONFIDENCE

In this section we discuss two phenomena of judgment that have both attracted a considerable amount of research attention in recent years: over-confidence and optimism. Overconfidence in human judgment is indicated by a cluster of related findings: uncalibrated assignments of probability that are more extreme than the judge's knowledge can justify (Lichtenstein, Fischhoff, and Phillips 1982), confidence intervals that are too narrow (Alpert and Raiffa 1982), and nonregressive predictions (Kahneman and Tversky 1973). Overconfidence is prevalent but not universal, and there are different views of the main psychological processes that produce it. One source of overconfidence is the common tendency to undervalue those aspects of the situation of which the judge is relatively ignorant. A recent study by Brenner, Koehler, and Tversky (1992) illustrates this effect, which is likely to be common in situations of conflict.

Participants were presented with factual information about several court cases. In each case, the information was divided into three parts: background data, the plaintiff's argument, and the defendant's argument. Four groups of subjects participated in this study. One group received only the background data. Two other groups received the background data and the arguments for one of the two sides, selected at random. The arguments for the plaintiff or the defendant contained no new evidence; they merely elaborated the facts included in the background data. A fourth group was given all the information presented to the jury. The subjects were all asked to predict the percentage of people in the jury who would vote for the plaintiff. The responses of the people who received one-sided evidence were strongly biased in the direction of the information they had received. Although the participants knew that their evidence was one-sided, they were not able to make the proper adjustment. In most cases, those who received all the evidence were more accurate in predicting the jury vote than those who received only one side. However, the subjects in the one-sided condition were generally more confident in their prediction than those who received both sides. Thus, subjects predicted the jury's decision with greater confidence when they had only one-half, rather than all, of the evidence presented to it.

Conflicts and disputes are characterized by the presence of asymmetric information. In general, each side knows a great deal about the evidence and the arguments that support its position and much less about those that support the position of the other side. The difficulty of making proper allowance for missing information, demonstrated in the preceding experiment, entails a bias that is likely to hinder successful negotiation. Each side will tend to overestimate its chances of success, as well as its ability to impose a solution on the other side and to prevent such an attempt by an opponent. Many years ago, we suggested that participants in a conflict are susceptible to a fallacy of initiative—a tendency to attribute less initiative and less imagination to the opponent than to oneself (Tversky and Kahneman 1973). The difficulty of adopting the opponent's view of the chessboard or of the battlefield may help explain why people often discover many new moves when they switch sides in a game. A related phenomenon has been observed in the response to mock trials that are sometimes conducted when a party to a dispute considers the possibility of litigation. Observers of mock trials have noted (Hans Zeisel, personal communication) that the would-be litigators are often surprised and dismayed by the strength of the position put forth by their mock opponent. In the absence of such a vivid demonstration of their bias, disputants are likely to hold an overly optimistic assessment of their chances in court. More generally, a tendency to underestimate the strength of the opponent's position could make negotiators less likely to make concessions and thereby reduce the chances of a negotiated settlement. Neale and Bazerman (1983) illustrated this effect in the context of a final arbitration procedure, in which the parties submit final offers, one of which is selected by the arbitrator. Negotiators overestimated (by more than 15 percent, on the average) the chance that their offer would be chosen. In this situation, a more realistic appraisal would probably result in more conciliatory final offers.

Another cognitive mechanism that may contribute to overconfident optimism is the tendency to base forecasts and estimates mostly on the particular features of the case at hand, including extrapolations of current achievements and assessments of the strength of relevant causal factors. This preferred "inside approach" to prediction is contrasted with an "outside approach," which draws the prediction of an outcome from the statistics of similar cases in the past, with no attempt to divine the history of the events that will yield that outcome (Kahneman and Lovallo 1993; Kahneman and Tversky 1979a). The neglect of relevant statistical information in the inside approach to forecasting is one of many manifestations of a general tendency to represent any situation in terms of a concrete (and preferably causal) model, rather than in more abstract, statistical terms. This tendency can produce an inconsistency between people's general beliefs and their beliefs about particular cases. One example of such an inconsistency applies to the overconfidence effect: respondents who are on the average much too confident in their opinions about a series of questions are likely to be less optimistic, or even slightly pessimistic, in their guess about the total number of questions that they have answered correctly (Gigerenzer, Hoffrage, and Kleinbolting 1991; Griffin and Tversky 1992). The effect is not restricted to laboratory studies. Cooper, Woo, and Dunkelberg (1988) interviewed entrepreneurs about their chances of success, and about the base rate of success for enterprises of the same kind. Over 80 percent of the respondents perceived their chances of success as 70 percent or better, and fully 33 percent of them described their success as certain. The average chance of success that these entrepreneurs attributed to a business like theirs was only 59 percent, an estimate that is also too optimistic: the five-year survival rate for new firms is around 33 percent (Dun and Bradstreet 1967). In general, of course, the individuals who freely choose to engage in an economic activity tend to be among those who have the most favorable expectations for that activity, and for their own prospects in particular. This is a version of a statistical selection effect that is known in other contexts as the "winner's curse." It is possible in principle for an agent to anticipate this bias and to correct for it, but the data suggest that the entrepreneurs studied by Cooper et al. did not do so.

The inside approach to forecasts is not by itself sufficient to yield an optimistic bias. However, in the special case of a decision maker considering a course of action, the preference for the inside view makes it likely that the forecast will be anchored on plans and intentions and that relevant statistical considerations will be underweighted or ignored. If we plan to complete a project in a couple of months, it is natural to take this date as a starting point for the assessment of completion time, maybe adding an additional month for unforeseen factors. This mode of thinking leads us to neglect the many ways in which a plan might fail. Because plans tend to be best-case estimates, such anchoring leads to optimism. Indeed, the optimism of forecasts made in the planning context is a well-documented effect (Arnold 1986; Merrow, Phillips and Myers 1981; Davis 1985). In the context of conflict, unwarranted optimism can be a serious obstacle, especially when it is bolstered by professional authority. Optimistic overconfidence is not a desirable trait for generals recommending a war or for attorneys urging a lawsuit, even if their expressions of confidence and optimism are pleasantly reassuring to their followers or clients at the time.

There are other sources and other manifestations of optimism than those mentioned so far (Taylor and Brown 1988). For example, there is evidence that most normal people expect others to rate them more favorably than they actually do, whereas mildly depressed people tend to be more realistic (Lewinsohn, Mischel, Chaplin, and Barton 1980). Similarly, people rate themselves above the mean on most desirable qualities, from effectiveness to sense of humor (Taylor and Brown 1988). People also exaggerate their ability to control their environment (Langer 1975; Crocker 1981) and accordingly prefer to bet on their skills rather than on a matched chance event (Howell 1971; Heath and Tversky 1991).

The claim that optimistic delusions are often adaptive has recently attracted much attention (Taylor and Brown 1988; Seligman 1991). To put this claim in perspective, it is useful to consider separately the effects of optimistic overconfidence on the two main phases of any undertaking: the setting of goals and plans, and the execution of a plan. When goals are chosen and plans are set, unrealistic optimism favors excessive risk-taking. Indeed, there are indications of large biases of optimistic planning in the domain of business decisions (Davis 1985), and the daily newspaper offers many examples in the political domain. However, decision makers are also very risk averse in most situations. The conjunction of overconfident optimism and risk aversion brings about a situation in which decision makers often accept risks because they deny them (Kahneman and Lovallo 1993; March and Shapira 1987). Thus, the benefit of unrealistic optimism in the decision phase may be to prevent paralysis by countering excessive aversion to risk, but this is hardly an unequivocal blessing—especially in situations of conflict.

The main advantages of optimism may be found in increasing persistence and commitment during the phase of action toward a chosen goal, and in improving the ability to tolerate uncontrollable suffering. Taylor (1989) has reviewed the role of irrational hope in promoting the adjustment of some cancer patients, and Seligman (1991) has claimed that an optimistic explanatory style, in which one takes credit for successes but views failures as aberrations, promotes persistence in the face of difficulties in diverse activities, ranging from the sale of insurance to competitive sports. The role of optimism in sports is of particular interest for a treatment of conflict. On the one hand, optimistic overconfidence will sometimes encourage athletes to take on competitors that are too strong for them. On the other hand, confidence, short of complacency, is surely an asset once the contest begins. The hope of victory increases effort, commitment, and persistence in the face of difficulty or threat of failure, and thereby raises the chances of success. A characteristic of competitive sports is that the option of abandoning the contest is not normally available to a competitor, even if defeat is certain. Under those circumstances, stubborn perseverance against the odds can only be beneficial. The situation is more complex when leaving the field is a viable option, and continuing the struggle is costly. Under these conditions, it is rarely easy to distinguish justified perseverance from irrational escalation of commitment.

In other situations of conflict, as in sports, optimism and confidence are likely to increase effort, commitment, and persistence in the conduct of the struggle. This is particularly true in conflicts that involve severe attrition. When maximal effort is exerted by both contestants, then it would appear that optimism offers a competitive advantage. In some competitive situations, the advantages of optimism and overconfidence may stem not from the deception of self, but from the deception of the opponent. This is how intimidation works—and successful intimidation accomplishes all that could be obtained by an actual victory, usually at a much lower cost. An animal that is capable of intimidating competitors away from a desirable mate, prey, or territory would have little need for techniques of conflict resolution. It is also recognized in analyses of conflict, from the game of chicken to treatments of pariah [or "outlaw"] states, that the appearance of complete confidence often pays off. Because complete confidence may be hard to fake, a tendency to sincere overconfidence could have adaptive advantages (see Frank 1989).

II. CERTAINTY AND PSEUDOCERTAINTY

A significant aspect of conflict resolution is the presence of uncertainty not only about the nature of an agreement but also about its actual outcomes. The outcomes of agreement can be classified into three types: (1) assured or certain outcomes—exchanges that are executed immediately, or promises for future actions that are unambiguous, unconditional, and enforceable; (2) contingently certain outcomes—enforceable undertakings that are conditional on objectively observed external events; and (3) uncertain outcomes— consequences (e.g., goodwill) that are more likely in the presence of agreement than in its absence. Uncertain outcomes are often stated as intentions of the parties in the "cheap talk" that precedes or accompanies the agreement.

Sure things and definite contingencies are the stuff of explicit agreements, contracts, and treaties; but the uncertain consequences of agreements are sometimes no less important. For example, a mutually satisfactory agreement between a supplier and a customer on a particular transaction can increase the probability of long-term association between them. A peace treaty between Israel and Syria might reduce the probability that Syria would seek to build or acquire nuclear weapons, but this significant consequence is not guaranteed. As these examples illustrate, an increase in the other side's goodwill is sometimes an important outcome of agreement, albeit an uncertain one. Future goodwill differs from many other consequences in that it is not necessarily in limited supply; negotiations in which goodwill is (implicitly or explicitly) a significant factor present a sharp contrast to zero-sum games. However, the characteristics of the way people think about uncertain outcomes favor a systematic underweighting of such consequences of agreement, compared to certain and to contingently certain benefits that are assured in the formal contract. This tendency reduces, in effect, the perceived value of an agreement for both parties in a dispute.

Research on individual decision making has identified a major bias in the weights that are assigned to probabilistic advantages and to sure things, which we have called the *certainty effect* (Kahneman and Tversky, 1979b, 1984). The classic demonstration of this effect is the Allais paradox, named after the French Nobel laureate in economics who in 1952 demonstrated to an audience of famous economists (several of them future Nobel laureates) that their preferences were inconsistent with expected utility theory. More specifically, these preferences imply that the difference between probabilities of 0.99 and 1.00 looms larger than the difference between 0.10 and 0.11. The intuition that the two differences are not equally significant is compelling. Indeed, it comes as a surprise to the uninitiated that the standard analysis of rational choice (expected utility theory) requires that a probability difference of, say 1 percent, be given equal weight, regardless of whether the difference lies in the middle of the range (0.30 to 0.31) or whether it involves the transition from impossibility to possibility (zero to 0.01) or from near-certainty to certainty (0.99 to 1). Intuitively, however, the qualitative distinctions between impossibility and possibility and between probability and certainty have special significance. As a consequence, many people consider it prudent to pay more to increase the probability of a desirable outcome from .99 to 1 than from .80 to .85. Similarly, people may well pay more to reduce the probability of harm from .0005 to zero than to reduce the same risk from .0015 to .0005 (Viscusi, Magat, and Huber 1987). The certainty effect has been confirmed when the probabilities are associated with well-defined chance processes and are expressed numerically. Most decisions under uncertainty, however, involve vague contingencies and ambiguous probabilities. The evidence suggests that the certainty effect is further enhanced by vagueness and ambiguity (Hogarth and Einhorn 1990; Tversky and Fox 1994). Thus, there is good reason to believe that uncertain outcomes, such as goodwill, are underweighted when people evaluate alternative agreements.

The principle that uncertain benefits are underweighted does not apply to *contingently certain outcomes*. The payment of insurance in the event of a specified property loss or in the event of a medical need is a prime example of a contingently certain outcome. The evidence indicates that people are willing to pay disproportionately more for insurance that will certainly be provided if the relevant contingencies arise than for insurance that is merely probabilistic. There is also strong evidence for a closely related phenomenon, which has been labeled the *pseudocertainty effect* (Kahneman and Tversky 1984; Tversky and Kahneman 1986), and is illustrated using the following pair of decision problems.

Problem 1. Consider the following two-stage game. In the first stage there is a 75 percent chance to end the game without winning anything and a 25 percent chance to move into the second stage. If you reach the second stage you have a choice between

A. a sure win of $30
B. an 80 percent chance to win $45

Your choice must be made before the game starts, i.e., before the outcome of the first stage is known. Please indicate the option you prefer.

Problem 2. Which of the following options do you prefer?

C. 25 percent chance to win $30
D. 20 percent chance to win $45

Because there is one chance in four to move into the second stage of problem 1, prospect A offers a .25 probability to win $30 and prospect B offers a .25 × .80 = .20 probability to win $45. Problems 1 and 2 are therefore identical in terms of probabilities and outcomes. However, the two problems elicit different preferences, which we have observed with both real and hypothetical payoffs. A clear majority of respondents preferred A over B in problem 1, whereas the majority preferred D over C in problem 2 (Tversky and Kahneman 1986). We have attributed this phenomenon to the combination of the certainty effect and the tendency to focus on the outcomes that are directly relevant to the decision at hand. Because the failure to reach the second stage of the game yields the same outcome (i.e., no gain) regardless of whether the decision maker chooses A or B, people compare these prospects as if they had reached the second stage. In this case, they face a choice between a sure gain of $30 and a .80 chance to win $45. The tendency to overweight sure things relative to uncertain outcomes (the certainty effect) favors the former option in the sequential version. Because an uncertain event (reaching the second stage of the game) is weighted as if it were certain, we called the phenomenon the pseudocertainty effect.

A study by Viscusi, Magat, and Huber (1987) provides compelling examples of both the certainty and the pseudocertainty effects. Participants in that study were exposed to a container of insecticide that was allegedly available for a stated price. After reading the warning label, they were asked to state their willingness to pay more for a product that would be safer in various ways. Two risks were mentioned (inhalation and child poisoning), each with a .0015 probability. The average willingness to pay to reduce both risks from .0015 to .0005 was $2.38 (in families with children), but the respondents were willing to pay an additional $5.71 to eliminate the last .0005 chance of harm. This large difference illustrates the certainty effect. The same respondents were also willing to pay $2.69 or $4.29, respectively, to eliminate the risk of inhalation or of child poisoning, without reducing the other risk. However, they were only willing to pay $1.84 to reduce both risks to .0005. This is an instance of a pseudocertainty effect. The respondents were willing to pay for the comfort of completely eliminating an identified risk, but the certainty they wished to purchase was illusory: the pesticide they would buy would still be associated with some danger, and in any event the amount paid to eliminate the risk of toxic inhalation or child poisoning would only reduce the overall risk of such harms, which can also occur in many other ways.

Contingently certain outcomes are important in many negotiations, in at least two ways. First, there are penalties and insurance provisions that are intended to protect one party against a failure of the other to comply with the agreement. The present analysis suggests that these provisions will loom large in the parties' view—but of course only to the extent that they are fully enforceable, and therefore contingently certain. Second, contingent certainty is involved in a less obvious way in negotiations about assets that will be significant if conflict breaks out between the parties. The negotiations between Israel and its neighbors provide many examples. Strategic assets, such as the Mitla Pass in the Sinai, or the Golan Heights near the Syrian border, provide contingently certain benefits to Israel in case of war. However, the retention of such assets raises tensions and surely increases the probability of armed conflict. An Israeli leader intent on minimizing the probability of catastrophic defeat should consider the probability that war will occur, multiplied by the probability of defeat given a war—separately for the case of withdrawal and nonwithdrawal. We do not presume to assess these probabilities; we merely suggest that the side that argues for retaining the strategic asset is likely to have the upper hand in a political debate—because of the superiority of contingent certainty over mere probability. Thus, the definite advantage of a strategic asset in case of war is likely to offset the uncertain reduction in the probability of war that might be brought about by a strategic or territorial concession.

The tendency to undervalue uncertain benefits sometimes leads to the *pseudodominance effect*. If it is advantageous to hold strategic assets both in war and in peace, territorial concession appears to be dominated by the strategy of holding on to key strategic positions. The fallacy in this argument is that it does not take into account the possibility that an agreement based on territorial concessions can decrease the chances of war. Even if holding to the strategic positions in question is in a country's best interest both in war and in peace, it could still make sense to give them up if this act could greatly reduce the probability of war. Since this outcome is uncertain, and its probability is in some sense unknowable, both politicians and citizens are likely to undervalue or neglect its contribution. The present discussion, of course, does not imply that strategic concessions should always be made. It only points out that the perception of dominance in such cases is often illusory.

III. LOSS AVERSION

Loss aversion refers to the observation that losses generally loom larger than the corresponding gains. This notion may be captured by a value function that is steeper in the negative than in the positive domain. In decisions under risk, loss aversion entails a reluctance to accept even-chance gambles, unless the payoffs are very favorable. For example, many people will accept such a gamble only if the gain is at least twice as large as the loss. In decisions under certainty, loss aversion entails a systematic discrepancy in the assessments of advantages and disadvantages (Tversky and Kahneman 1991; Kahneman, Knetsch, and Thaler 1991). The general principle is quite simple: When an option is compared to the reference point, the comparison is coded in terms of the advantages and disadvantages of that option. A particularly important case of loss aversion arises when the reference point is the status quo, and when the retention of the status quo is an option. Because the disadvantages of any alternative to the status quo are weighted more heavily than its advantages, a strong bias in favor of the status quo is observed (Samuelson and Zeckhauser 1988). The argument has been extended to the context of international conflict and negotiation. Jervis (1992) notes: "If loss aversion is widespread, states defending the status quo should have a big bargaining advantage. That is, a state will be willing to pay a higher price and run higher risks if it is facing losses than if it is seeking to make gains" (p. 162).

The location of the reference point also affects the evaluation of *differences* between other pairs of options. Differences between disadvantages will generally have greater weight than corresponding differences between advantages because disadvantages are evaluated on a steeper limb of the value function. For example, the difference between salary offers of $40,000 and $45,000 will be viewed as a difference between two gains by someone whose current income is now $35,000, and as a difference between two losses if current income is $50,000. The psychological differences between the alternatives is likely to be greater in the latter case, reflecting the steeper slope of the value function in the domain of losses. Acceptance of the lower salary

---

Section III is borrowed from Kahneman 1992.

will be experienced as an increased loss if the reference point is high and as a foregone gain if it is low. It will be more painful in the former case.

The following classroom demonstration illustrates the principle of loss aversion (Kahneman, Knetsch, and Thaler 1990; see also Knetsch and Sinden 1984). An attractive object (e.g., a decorated mug) is distributed to one-third of the students. The students who have been given mugs are *sellers*— perhaps better described as owners. They are informed that there will be an opportunity to exchange the mug for a predetermined amount of money. The subjects state what their choice will be for different amounts, and thereby indicate the minimal amount for which they are willing to give up their mug. Another one-third of the students are *choosers*. They are told that they will have a choice between a mug like the one in the hands of their neighbor and an amount of cash; they indicate their choices for different amounts. The remaining students are *buyers:* they indicate whether they would pay each of the different amounts to acquire a mug. In a representative experiment, the median price set by sellers was $7.12, the median cash equivalent set by the choosers was $3.12, and the median buyer was willing to pay $2.88 for the mug.

The difference between the valuations of owners and choosers occurs in spite of the fact that both groups face the same choice: go home with a mug or with a prespecified sum of money. Subjectively, however, the choosers and owners are in different states: the former evaluate the mug as a gain, the latter as something to be given up. Because of loss aversion, more cash is required to persuade the owners to give up the mug than to match the attractiveness of the mug to the choosers. In the same vein, Thaler (1980) tells of a wine lover who will neither sell a bottle that has gained value in his cellar nor buy another bottle at the current price. The experimental studies of the discrepant valuation of owners, choosers, and buyers demonstrate that loss aversion can be induced instantaneously; it does not depend on a progressive attachment to objects in one's possession. Unlike the differences between buyers and sellers observed in some bargaining experiments (Neale, Huber, and Northcraft 1987), the above effect does not depend on the labels attached to the roles.

The market experiments conducted by Kahneman, Knetsch, and Thaler (1990) demonstrated a significant consequence of the discrepancy between the valuations of owners and buyers: far fewer transactions take place than economic theory would predict. Consider an experiment in which half the subjects are given mugs, and a market is set up where these subjects can sell their mugs to potential buyers. Economic theory predicts that when all market changes are completed, the mugs will be in the hands of the subjects who value them most. Because the initial allocation was random, half the mugs initially allocated should change hands. In an extended series of experiments, however, the observed volume of trade was about one-fourth, that is, only half the number predicted. The same result was obtained when owners and potential buyers had an opportunity to bargain directly over a possible price.

Concession Aversion

Loss aversion, we argue, could have a significant impact on conflict resolution. Imagine two countries negotiating the number of missiles that they will keep and aim at each other. Each country derives security from its own missiles and is threatened by those of the other side. Thus, missiles eliminated by the other side are evaluated as gains, and missiles one must give up are evaluated as losses, relative to the status quo. If losses have twice the impact of gains, then each side will require its opponent to eliminate twice as many missiles as it eliminates—not a promising start for the achievement of an agreement. The symmetry of the positions might help negotiators reframe the problem to trade missiles at par, but in most negotiations the sacrifices made by the two sides are not easily compared. In labor negotiations, for example, a union may be asked to give up a third pilot in the cockpit, and might be offered improved benefits or a more generous retirement plan in return. These are the circumstances under which we expect to find *concession aversion*, a systematically different evaluation of concessions made and of concessions received.

Concession aversion appears similar to the phenomenon of *reactive devaluation*, a negotiator's tendency to value a possible concession less if it is made by the opponent than by one's own side, as discussed in the previous chapter. However, the processes are quite different: reactive devaluation reflects a change in the evaluation of a proposal in response to an offer by an opponent, while concession aversion reflects the asymmetric valuation of gains and losses. Both processes could operate together to make agreement difficult.

Loss aversion does not affect all transactions: it applies to goods held for use, not goods held for exchange. Three categories of exchange goods are money held for spending, goods held specifically for sale, and "bargaining chips," goods that are valued only because they can be traded. The significance of missiles, for example, is substantially reduced when they are treated not as strategic assets but as bargaining chips. Concession aversion, we suggest, will only inhibit agreement in the latter case. Loss aversion plays little role in routine economic transactions, in which a seller and a buyer exchange a good and money, both of which were held for that purpose. In contrast, many of the objects of bargaining in labor negotiations (e.g., job security, benefits, grievance procedures) are "use goods" rather than exchange goods. Labor negotiations in which both sides seek to modify an existing contract to their advantage therefore provide the paradigm case of concession aversion.

The analysis of concession aversion has an immediate prescriptive implication. It suggests that the most effective concessions you can make are those that reduce or eliminate your opponent's losses; the least effective concessions are those that improve an attribute in which the other side is already "in the gains." Reductions of losses are evaluated on the steep lower limb of the value function—and the eliminations of losses are evaluated at its steepest region. In contrast, increments to already large gains are expected to add relatively little value.

The suggestion that it is more efficient to reduce the opponent's losses than to offset them by gains is compatible with a negotiating strategy discussed by Pruitt (1983). The *cost-cutting strategy* requires a side that seeks a concession to find ways to reduce the costs of that concession to the other side—in other words, to avoid imposing losses. The cost-cutting strategy is implicitly preferred to a strategy of offering concessions that the other side will evaluate as gains. In the terms of the present analysis, the losses that the cost-cutting strategy eliminates are evaluated in the steep region of the value function, whereas the marginal value of offsetting gains is relatively slight.

Gains, Losses, and Fairness

"I only want what is fair" is a common cry in negotiations, although adversaries who make this claim are not necessarily close to agreement. In addition to their effect on the valuation of outcomes, reference points also affect negotiations by influencing judgments of what is fair or unfair. Such judgments have impact on the outcome of bargaining—perhaps because offers that are perceived as unfair as well as disadvantageous are especially likely to evoke anger and resistance. It is generally accepted, of course, that fairness does not always govern behavior, that the rules of fairness are often ambiguous, and that disputants' interpretation of these ambiguities are likely to be self-serving (Messick and Sentis 1983; Thompson and Loewenstein 1992).

The role of reference points in judgments of fairness has been studied in the context of business practices. Judgments of fairness were obtained in a series of telephone surveys, in which the respondents assessed vignettes describing actions of price or wage setting by merchants, landlords, and employers (Kahneman, Knetsch, and Thaler 1986). The judgments appeared to be governed by a small number of rules of fairness, which treated gains and losses asymmetrically. The most prominent rule of fairness is that a firm should not impose a loss on its transactors (customers, employees, or tenants) merely in order to increase its own gain. For example, people consider it extremely unfair for a hardware store to raise the price of snow shovels after a blizzard, and they also think it unacceptable for a firm to cut the wages of employees merely because they could be replaced by cheaper labor. On the other hand, the standards of fairness allow a firm to protect itself from losses by raising the price it charges its customers or by reducing the pay of its employees. Thus, a firm can fairly use its market power to protect its reference profit, but not to increase it. In a further indication of the asymmetric treatment of gains and losses, the rules of fairness do not obligate a firm to share increases in its profits with its customers or employees. We summarized these rules by a *principle of dual entitlement:* the firm is entitled to its reference profit; customers, employees, and tenants are entitled to a reference price, wage, or rent; and in case of conflict between these entitlements the firm is allowed to protect itself from a threatened loss by transferring it to its transactors. Note that the principle defends the *rights* of both parties to a reference state, without imposing a more general egalitarian norm of sharing both pain and gain.

What determines the reference transaction? The precedent of previous transactions between the firm and the same individual transactor can be important. Thus, it is unfair to reduce the wage of an employee during a period of high unemployment, although an employee who quits can be replaced at a lower wage. The previous history of transactions between the firm and its employee defines an entitlement, which does not extend to the replacement. Note also that the wage that the new employee was paid elsewhere is entirely irrelevant. Thus, it is not the task of the firm to protect new employees from a loss relative to their previous earnings, because these are not part of the relevant reference transaction. The prevailing wage is the standard reference transaction for a new contract, especially if the new employee's job is not directly comparable to that of anyone currently in the organization.

Similar principles find expression in legal practice. Cohen and Knetsch (1992) have compiled an illuminating review of the judicial impact of the distinction between losses and foregone gains. They cite a legal expert to the effect that "To deprive somebody of something which he merely expected to receive is a less serious wrong, deserving of less protection, than to deprive somebody of the expectation of continuing to hold something which he already possesses." The familiar expression that possession is nine points of the law is another manifestation of the importance of the reference point.

The asymmetric treatment of losses and gains has generally conservative implications for judgments of economic fairness as well as for individual choice. We saw earlier that loss aversion induces a bias toward the retention of the status quo; the rules of fairness exhibit a similar bias favoring the retention of the reference transaction. There are other similarities between the two domains. For example, losses are given greater weight than fore-gone gains in individual choice, in judicial decisions (Cohen and Knetsch 1992), and also in lay rules of fairness. A firm is (barely) allowed to deny its transactors any share of its gains, but is definitely prohibited from impos-ing losses on them. No one would seriously suggest that these principles extend to all human interactions. There are domains in which fairness demands that gains be shared, and competitive contexts in which the impo-sition of losses on others is sanctioned. It appears, however, that one com-mon principle may apply across contexts: Actions that impose losses relative to an acceptable reference standard are viewed much more severely than actions (or omissions) that merely fail to provide a gain.

The notion of rights or entitlements is associated with a more extreme form of loss aversion called *enhanced loss aversion*. Losses that are com-pounded by outrage are much less acceptable than losses that are caused by misfortune or by legitimate actions of others. An example is the differ-ence between two customers who face a steep increase in price, which one of the customers regards as unfair and the other as legitimate. According to the present analysis, both customers face the same loss, but whether they perceive that a right has been violated depends on their coding of the sup-plier's choice. Suppose, for example, that the supplier follows others in raising the price. If the prevailing price is accepted as a legitimate refer-ence, the option of maintaining the old price would be coded as a loss to the supplier, which the rules of fairness do not require. If the price charged by other merchants is considered irrelevant, maintaining the old price merely foregoes an illegitimate gain.

As this example illustrates, the rules of fairness are often ambiguous, and the ambiguity typically involves the selection of the specific reference standard, rather than a more general principle. Customer and supplier could agree on the general principles that prices should be fair and that arbitrary increases beyond a proper reference price are unfair, but disagree on the proper reference price for the case at hand. Another important possi-bility is that the reference point by which an action is evaluated may not be unique. "Seeing the other person's point of view" might make a differ-ence even when one does not fully accept it. There is at least a possibility that a discussion of fairness may have some persuasive effect even when it does not achieve a complete conversion.

CONCLUDING REMARKS

In this chapter we have discussed three major phenomena (optimistic overconfidence, the certainty effect, and loss aversion) which have emerged from the cognitive analysis of individual judgment and decision making.

These phenomena represent systematic departures from the standard rational theory in which individuals are assumed to have realistic expectations, to weight outcomes by their probabilities, and to evaluate consequences as asset positions, not as gains and losses. We have argued that these biases in the assessment of evidence and the evaluation of consequences can hinder the successful resolution of conflict. In particular, optimistic overconfidence is likely to make opponents believe that they can prevail and hence they do not have to make concessions. The certainty effect leads disputants to undervalue some outcomes, such as goodwill, because they are not certain. Finally, loss aversion is likely to reduce the range of acceptable agreements because one's own concessions are evaluated as losses and the opponent's concessions are evaluated as gains. Although these phenomena do not exhaust the psychological barriers to the successful resolution of interpersonal conflict, they represent serious obstacles that often stand in the way of successful negotiation.

An understanding of the cognitive obstacles to conflict resolution could provide insight on two levels. On the first level, a negotiator may recognize that her opponent may not behave according to the standard rules of rational behavior, that he is likely to be overconfident, to undervalue uncertain concessions, and to be loss averse. In the spirit of Raiffa's prescriptive analysis (see Bell, Raiffa, and Tversky 1988), a rational negotiator may wish to take into account the fact that her opponent may not be entirely rational. On a higher level of insight, a negotiator may realize that she, too, does not always behave in accord with the maxims of rationality, and that she also exhibits overconfidence, the certainty effect, and loss aversion. The literature on judgment and choice (see Bazerman 1994; Dawes 1988; Kahneman, Slovic, and Tversky 1982) indicates that biases and cognitive illusions are not readily eliminated by knowledge or warning. Nevertheless, knowing the opponent's biases, as well as our own, may help us understand the barriers to conflict resolution and could even suggest methods to overcome them.

CHAPTER FOUR

The Benefit of Optional Play in Anonymous One-Shot Prisoner's Dilemma Games

Robyn M. Dawes and
John M. Orbell

T it for tat is the strategy in playing repeated prisoner's dilemma games of cooperating on the first move and subsequently making the same choice the other player made on the previous move—thereby rewarding cooperation with cooperation and punishing defection with defection. In both empirical investigations with human subjects and computer simulations of repeated-play prisoner dilemmas, tit for tat is superior to other strategies. It is not just a satisfactory, "satisficing" strategy; playing against a multiplicity of other strategies, it is the best (Axelrod 1984). Moreover, the general principle of cooperating with another agent prior to knowing how that agent will respond, and then reciprocating either cooperation or defection, appears from casual observation to be one many people adopt to their advantage outside the experimental laboratory as well as within it. Be friendly, cooperative, and nice when initiating an interaction or negotiation, but don't hesitate to counterpunch if the other party punches first; moreover, having a reputation for adopting this policy may obviate the need to counterpunch (and hence the pain of initially being punched). Tit for tat works.

We would like to begin this paper with an analysis of tit for tat that is somewhat different from that most usually made, by such people as Anatol Rapoport (1965) and Robert Axelrod (1984). This analysis will lead to hypotheses about how cooperation can yield desirable—even optimal—results in situations that do not have the characteristics commonly associated with the success of tit for tat, such as situations in which there is no further

The research reported in this paper was supported by the National Science Foundation, grant SES-9008157. Pam Ferrara played an important role in administering all stages of the experiments reported here, and was a valuable source of insight about behavior in these experiments.

interaction between the parties involved, and hence no possibility that behavior can yield reciprocation or have an effect on personal reputation. We will limit the analysis to bilateral interactions in prisoner's dilemma situations, but will exclude those in which agreements and promises may be made on a verbal level. Hence, we're studying anonymous "negotiations without words." If, however, we can understand when it is that cooperation can be personally beneficial when iterations and agreements are absent, we might gain insight into basic processes favoring cooperation that also operate when they are present. Our emphasis is on *when*. We are not claiming that in all situations involving one-shot and anonymous interactions, cooperation is beneficial; there are certainly situations in which "nice guys finish last"— particularly in zero-sum games such as baseball, and in some mixed-motive games as well. What we will attempt to do, however, is to suggest through our unorthodox analysis of tit for tat that there is at least one nonrepeated and anonymous situation in which cooperation in prisoner's dilemmas is beneficial, sometimes optimal, and we will then present data from an experiment (Orbell and Dawes 1993) that supports the suggestion.

The traditional analysis of tit for tat is based on the effects of reciprocity of reward and punishment over an extended interaction, specifically between two parties confronted with an iterated prisoner's dilemma. As Axelrod puts it (1984, p. 182): "The foundation of cooperation [achieved through tit for tat–type approaches, however they came about] is not really trust, but the durability of the relationship." Moreover, Axelrod stated when an experimental subject himself (Hofstadter 1983) that "of course" he defects if a prisoner's dilemma is played only once. This emphasis on reciprocity—and hence the *necessity* of repetition—for the development, the success, and the invulnerability to "invading" strategies of tit for tat has been present ever since its inception by Anatol Rapoport, and this emphasis was reinforced by Amnon Rapoport's (1967) demonstration that in repeated plays (without a known end point) tit for tat could be an optimal strategy, provided there is the *possibility* of reciprocity.

Both (unrelated) Rapoports studied cooperation and defection in multiple-play situations, and most subsequent experimenters have followed their lead. While the importance of repetition and consequent reciprocity should logically be studied by comparing situations with and without repetition, the standard research paradigm has been to compare tit for tat with other strategies in situations involving repetition. (Those few studies involving single plays have, counter to the standard rationale for tit for tat's success, demonstrated rather high levels of cooperation; these levels are often dismissed in terms of "habitual responding" due to the similarity of the one-shot experiment to situations in which repetition and reputation are involved outside the laboratory, often with an aside that the one-shot laboratory situation lacks "ecological validity." Of course, such an analysis cannot explain the rather extreme variations in cooperation rate found under different social conditions in one-shot experiments; see Dawes [1991], or Orbell, van de Kragt, and Dawes [1988].)

There are two characteristics of tit for tat that, although mentioned by Axelrod (1984), have often escaped attention. First, tit for tat can be expressed in a manner that is impervious to reward, punishment, or attempts to secure reciprocity for cooperation. The usual expression of tit for tat is captured in two simple mandates (or program instructions):

1. Cooperate on trial 1.
2. On trial $n + 1$, make the choice the other player did on trial n.

Here, we propose substituting for these two mandates a single one:

1'. Defect only if behind.

Unlike rules 1 and 2, rule 1' has the appearance of being ethical and social, rather than strategic. When payoffs are identical for both players, however (as is almost always true in the experiments and simulations investigated), the results of following instruction 1' are identical with those of following 1 and 2. (The initial choice is cooperation, which continues so long as the other cooperates; defection is followed with reciprocal defection only until a cooperative response occurs, at which point the players are "even," and rule 1' "resets" to cooperation.) In contrast to focusing on the consequences of behavior, however, mandate 1' embodies a simple social heuristic: "Neither an exploiter nor a sucker be." This rule finds descriptive support in the preferences people (claim to) have for distributing the payoffs for joint effort (Loewenstein, Thompson, and Bazerman 1989), in which a desire for equity is complemented by an aversion to being "one-down" that is much stronger than a desire to be "one-up." The rule is also supported in the emphasis people place on the *fairness* of joint distributions—to the point of preferring an egoistically satisfying distribution of rewards only when some dimension or meaning of "fairness" can justify it (Messick and Sentis 1983). The rule finds normative support in that, as noted, it leads to behavior identical to that of the successful tit-for-tat strategy. We note here that a strategy, instruction, or rule of thumb need not be based on motivation or strategic concerns in order to thrive and evolve; all that is necessary is that its consequences be benign—for whatever reason (just as the circumstances by which it came about are not important). If a concern for social / ethical equity yields desirable consequences in many circumstances (as it does when playing tit for tat), so be it. Such a concern does not have to be motivated by a desire for these consequences.

The second characteristic of tit for tat is that it does not gain more points than are gained by any single strategy against which it plays; yet it is optimal when it plays against many strategies. This "smell" of Simpson's paradox (equaling each strategy singly but surpassing all others in aggregate) will be extended directly and explicitly in the model we will later propose. What is important to note here, however, is that a behavioral decision-making strategy can be one that is optimal over many occasions while simultaneously being optimal on none. Later we will demonstrate that *in some circumstances* the type of "optimism" embodied in tit for tat (i.e., "anticipating" cooperation—by cooperating on trial 1—until the evidence contradicts this anticipation) can lead to an interactive strategy that in fact is superior over multiple occasions while simultaneously being inferior on each.

There is a corollary implication to this characteristic. Consider a single extended dyadic iterated prisoner's dilemma game as constituting a "negotiation." Whatever strategy the other player adopts, it will do at least as well as tit for tat. Were we then to compare strategies by examining their relative efficiency opposed to a single other strategy (as is commonly done in experimental work on negotiations), or even a series of strategies without summing overall, we would conclude that tit for tat was not a very good strategy. A simple vote count, for example, would give it a number of minuses, some zeros, and no pluses.

Finally, we point out that tit for tat is a cognitively simple strategy to pursue. Except for the optimistic anticipation evidenced in the first trial, there is no need to anticipate anything at all about the consequences of a choice (in fact, no need to make a prediction even on trial 1). There is no necessity to recall anything but the previous trial. The strategy can be expressed as a single instruction. Thus, the person adopting it is the antithesis of the optimal decision maker, who carefully weighs the plethora of potential consequences of each single act chosen from a multitude of possibilities, and who judges both probabilities and consequences in terms of what is known theoretically or "learned from experience." (It is a Ulysses S. Grant strategy rather than a Robert E. Lee one.)

The part of our model we present here concerns single interaction in social dilemma (Dawes 1980) situations, specifically those involving two-person prisoner's dilemmas. It is based on two observations. The first is that people often have a choice as to whether to become involved in such situations. There are some in which they do not. For example, people can "free ride" on public broadcasting, or fear that their individual contributions will be wasted and therefore conclude that a dominating strategy is not to contribute their "fair share." Or people asked to ride bicycles during a pollution alert can easily conclude that such a time is the worst possible one for being on a bicycle, and that they therefore have a dominating strategy to drive. Public broadcasting and pollution exist independent of the individual's choice. In contrast, people can choose to enter or refrain from entering a joint business, research, romantic, or friendship situation that has payoffs expressible in prisoner's dilemma terms. We are often not required to put ourselves in situations where—despite a "cooperative surplus" (Gauthier 1986)—we can exploit others or be exploited or end up with the mutual-defection payoff.

The second major observation on which we base our model is that people have a bias to expect others to choose what they choose in dilemma situations. Throughout fifteen years of experimentation, we have repeatedly observed positive correlations between one's own choice and estimates of the proportion of others in one's group who will cooperate, and such "projective" reasoning appears to us to occur with great frequency outside the laboratory as well. It is not necessarily a *false* consensus effect: by definition, most of us make majority choices most of the time. Thus, for example, in our experimental situations where a majority of subjects cooperate, the tendency to believe that a majority of other subjects will "do as I do" is correct for the cooperators, who constitute a majority of our subjects. The same conclusion follows for those situations where a minority cooperate, in which case the projection tendency is correct for the majority of subjects who defect. This tendency is irrational and "egoistic" only under certain conditions. First, it should not lead to estimates that are insufficiently regressive (for, after all, oneself is a sample of size only $n = 1$). Second, it is false if in those situations where judges have knowledge of another single person's response, they give their own response greater weight in making their estimates (for a discussion, see Sherman and Presson 1984). Third, it is false if the projection—in the absence of any differentiating knowledge—leads to differential predictions about those with whom judges have a "special" relationship (Messe and Sivacek 1979), in which case it devolves into "magical thinking." For a fuller discussion of the rationale for the normative use of such projective reasoning, see Dawes (1988b, 1990).

Others have claimed that the correlation observed is due purely to subjects' making a strategic choice based on what they think others will choose. One problem with that reasoning is that in a dilemma situation a "rational" strategic choice dictates defection no matter what others do, because defection is a dominating strategy. This rational expectations argument can then be "rescued" by postulating a utility for "doing the right thing" that has greater relative weight if the subjects expect generally high external payoffs, due to others' cooperation, than if they expect relatively low ones, due to others' defection (as Dawes [1980] once suggested). The problem with this hypothesis is that it doesn't explain the lack of a "downturn" in step-level public goods dilemmas as more and more people are expected to contribute (Dawes, Orbell, Simmons, and van de Kragt 1986). In these public goods step-level experiments, defectors (noncontributors) do indeed expect too few others to contribute to allow their own contribution to make a difference in obtaining that good. Cooperators, in contrast, expect their own contributions to be redundant (the median and modal expectation being that everyone will contribute in sets of experiments where expectations about exact number of contributors were assessed). This differential relationship between expectation and behavior for cooperators and defectors supports the view that expectations are more dependent on choice than vice versa. Finally, in one experiment (Dawes, McTavish, and Shaklee 1977, study 2), the variance of the expectations (about the proportion of others who would contribute) of subjects who actually made choices was greater than the variance of expectations of those who observed them making choices, with decision makers who cooperated skewing the distribution toward 1 and those who defected skewing it toward zero. This difference as well contradicts the simple "form expectations and then act" model, because the decision makers and the observers had equal information from which to form their expectations—except for the decision maker's own choice.

An important qualification of this projection hypothesis is that both cooperators and defectors make specific predictions about specific other people, even though these predictions are influenced by projection. That is, people do not apply their "base rate" beliefs about the proportion of cooperation, which they obtain in part from their own tendencies, to all others in a blanket manner—independent of what they believe to be individuating information about others' propensities and independent of the situation, such as the parameters in the payoff matrix (Orbell and Dawes 1991b). For example, throughout fifteen years of experimentation, we have found that people believe women to be more cooperatively inclined than men—but neither cooperators nor defectors make identical predictions for all men and for all women.

Despite claims to the contrary based on our own data (e.g., on study 1 in Dawes, McTavish, and Shaklee 1977), we have found that these differential predictions are invalid—except for a higher rate of cooperation, consistent with the correlation outlined above. For example, study 2 of Dawes, McTavish, and Shaklee (1977) examined the residual accuracy of individual predictions corrected for the overall rate of cooperation (that is, percent accurate minus $PQ+(1-P)(1-Q)$ where P is the predicted rate of cooperation across others and Q the actual rate). They found its average to be $-.02$, in contrast to $+.03$ in their study 1. Moreover, except for one particular subset of studies involving group discussion, women are no more cooperative than men; also see Javine (1988), who investigated gender differences in cooperation directly rather than on a post hoc basis, and who found none.

Our model (Orbell and Dawes 1991a) is simple. In a situation where subjects have an option to play or not play a prisoner's dilemma with negative payoffs for mutual defection, no one will wish to play with a defector (the payoff for being exploited being even more negative than the payoff for dual defection). People who have a tendency to cooperate when considering a particular set of payoffs will be more optimistic that others will also cooperate than those who have a tendency to defect. Hence, they will offer to play—or avoid opting out—more often than will potential defectors, and they will accept such an offer—again opt out less—more often than potential defectors. If there are p proportion of potential cooperators in a population, each will then end up playing with a fellow cooperator with probability qpq, where q is the probability that a cooperator judges a specific other person to be a cooperator; each will end up playing with a defector with probability $q(1-p)r$, where r is the probability that a defector plays; each will opt out with a probability $1-q$; and each will offer but be refused play with probability $q[p(1-q)+(1-p)(1-r)]$. The comparable weightings for potential defectors are: rpq, $r(1-p)r$, $1-r$, and $r[swp(1-q)+(1-p)(1-r)]$. As demonstrated by Orbell and Dawes (1991a), while the payoffs in a prisoner's dilemma matrix are always higher for defectors than for cooperators on any single game, the *expected* payoffs weighted by these probabilities (including a zero payoff if either party opts out) can be higher for cooperators than for defectors provided $q>r$. That inequality follows, of course, from the projection heuristic.

Thus the model embodies the simple rule that "I should expect in general others to do as I would in this situation," "and when given the option to play or not play to act in accord with that expectation." This heuristic assumes no knowledge of the other person, whether through past interactions or through "translucency" (Gauthier 1986; Frank 1988). It is a rule which, like tit for tat, will always provide a payoff inferior to that of a defecting rule whenever it encounters one, but which may nevertheless come out ahead overall. For potential cooperators, it is a rule which never exploits, but which never expects (through their optimism) to be exploited. Here, again, it mirrors tit for tat in that it can be exploited on the first play, which for the situations to which this rule is applied is the only play. For the defectors, it is a rule that severely limits the amount they play—thereby benefiting everyone involved (including other defectors). Finally, this rule is consistent with our observations that outside the laboratory those who are themselves untrustworthy do not trust others and consequently avoid interactions (particularly those involving financial or emotional "dependency").

There are two side conditions. First, payoffs must always be negative for playing with a defector; otherwise, there would be no reason not to offer to play or to opt out. Second, the rule cannot be extended to seek a Nash equilibrium solution (where each "rational" player assumes all others will play according to the same principles of rationality—in this case, make the same choices concerning cooperating, defecting, or opting out); for—as will be elaborated later—it is self-defeating if it is. (Such an extension would lead the players to become "rational fools" [Sen 1977] who forgo a cooperative surplus.) It turns out that our subjects—who are of above-average sophistication compared to the general public—do not attempt to seek a

Nash equilibrium by extending the rule. (Otherwise, a potential defector would reason that someone willing to play must be a cooperator and thereby change their own unwillingness to play, which would in turn negate that judgment, etc.) In the experiments we will present, potential defectors opt out with much greater frequency than potential cooperators, resulting in the defectors' doing worse with such optional play than they do when play is mandated, while cooperators do better—to the point that with one set of prisoner's dilemma parameters, cooperators make a higher net payoff than do defectors. Moreover, the average payoff of the group increases with the addition of a mechanism for not offering to play or refusing an offer. These results occur in the absence of any accurate knowledge or estimates of how particular others will play, just as predicted by our model.

OVERVIEW OF EXPERIMENTS

Six subjects seated around a large room were required to play one prisoner's dilemma game with each of the remaining five. All these games involved negative dollar payoffs for mutual defection, and hence even greater negative payoffs for unilateral cooperation (i.e., "being suckered"). Because our model applies only to situations where people experience such losses when they play against defectors, and because we could not ethically take money away from our subjects, they were first paid a flat rate of $20 for spending a half hour evaluating and rating their responses to political campaign rhetoric, in what was presented as a separate study. Following completion of that task, they took part in the experiment itself—which was presented as a decision-making study in which it was possible to gain as much as an additional $20 (for a total of $40), or to lose all their $20 starting money. Our hope was that our subjects would take the possibility of loss from their "earned" base more seriously than if we had simply given them an endowment of $20, which could easily be framed as "house money." (See Thaler 1980, 1985.)

A test of our prediction that defectors would opt out more than cooperators in playing these games requires us to estimate which choices would have been made were the subjects not allowed to opt out. Simply asking subjects what they would have done had they not been able to opt out, or equivalently asking them to choose both between cooperating and defecting and between playing and not playing, would have had the obvious disadvantage that subjects who had decided to opt out could attempt to create a good impression (on the experimenters or themselves) by claiming that they would have cooperated had they played. Alternatively, making the choices sequentially would have worked only if the cooperate versus defect choice were made first, but pretesting demonstrated that this method led to very

FIGURE 1

The structure from binary to trinary choice experiments

Binary:

Proportion cooperating	Proportion defecting
p	$1-p$

Trinary:

Proportion cooperating	Proportion opting out		Proportion defecting
	opting out cooperators	opting out defectors	
q	$p-q$	$(1-p)-r$	r

little opting out, either through a commitment to the choice already made or through inertia.

Our solution was to run two parallel experiments: a *binary choice* experiment in which subjects had only the choice of cooperating versus defecting, and a *trinary choice* experiment in which subjects had a simultaneous choice of cooperating, defecting, or opting out. With everything else in the structure of the choices constant, we could then extrapolate from the numbers cooperating or defecting in the binary choice experiment to the number of potential cooperators and of potential defectors who opted out in the trinary choice experiment.

This extrapolation is illustrated graphically in Figure 1. In it, p is the proportion cooperating in the binary experiment when playing a given game, and thus $1-p$ is the proportion defecting; q is the proportion cooperating in the trinary experiment and r the proportion defecting; hence $1-(q+r)$ is the proportion opting out. Given random assignment (so far as possible) to the binary and trinary experiments, our estimate of the proportion of cooperators who opted out is $p-q$, and of the proportion of defectors opting out is $(1-p)-r$.

EXPERIMENTAL METHOD

Subjects

We recruited our subjects through an advertisement in the University of Oregon's student newspaper. This advertisement promised between $5 and $40 for participating in two studies that would last about an hour or a little more—with the particular amount depending on "decisions you make and the simultaneous decisions of others in the experiment." People who responded to the advertisements were assigned to various time slots according to their convenience, and the time slots were then assigned arbitrarily to experiments, conditions, and replications. Every effort was made to prevent friends or relatives from signing up for the same time slots (e.g., by assigning people who called as a group to different ones). About 80 percent of the subjects were students. Because in over ten years of experiments involving similar dilemma choices we have never found consistent gender differences or consistent differences between students and townspeople, no effort was made to balance these factors in scheduling subjects.

Procedure

Subjects first read a series of politicians' statements from Oregon Voters' pamphlets and completed questionnaires about their responses to these candidates. They were then handed $20 "payment for this work," which they carried with them to a large experimental room a few doors away. On arrival, they put their $20 in a plastic bag labeled with an identification letter between A and F, and then placed that bag on a table in the center of the room. Subjects then sat in one of the corresponding six chairs clearly labeled A through F. The experimenter in charge, at the head of the room, also sat down and read the instructions.

These instructions emphasized that the money they would take home would depend on decisions that they made and decisions simultaneously made by others in the room. The instructions also emphasized that no one else in the room—other than the experimenters—would know what decisions they personally had made, and that as a further protection of their anonymity, each person would be paid individually and asked to leave the experimental area before the next was paid.

In half the conditions, this introduction was followed by a period of "irrelevant discussion"—prior to the time the experiment proper was explained. This discussion concerned a "Schelling coordination problem," in which the subjects discussed where they would go in Eugene, Oregon, during a week's duration in which a millionaire had promised them and another unknown person $100,000 each if they would be at the "same place" ("within a few yards of each other") at the same time at least once during that week. After ten minutes of discussion, they proceeded to the prisoner's dilemma games. In the other half of the conditions (crossed with the binary versus trinary conditions of major importance), subjects were immediately introduced to the prisoner's dilemma games they would be playing.

No further discussion was permitted. The prisoner's dilemma was first explained with a simple matrix that was not one to be played later. The two choices were labeled X (the cooperative one) and Y (the defecting one). The terms "cooperation" and "defection" were avoided. Subjects were then told that they would be making one decision about choosing X or Y paired with each other person in the experiment. The payoff matrices would be different for each choice. Each member of each pair would be responding to the same payoff structure as the other, but (because it was logistically impossible) members of each pair would not be making choices at the exact same time.

The experimenter emphasized that subjects should pay attention to the differences in the five payoff matrices, because "those differences will have consequences for how much money you leave here with." There were many opportunities for questions, which were encouraged and answered as fully as possible. Subjects then completed a four-item quiz, which was checked for accuracy, and further explanations were provided if there were any errors. The experimenters initiated the choice part of the experiment only after they were satisfied that all the subjects understood the structure of the payoff matrices, the sequencing and privacy of the choices made, and the laboratory logistics after the experiment was over. (The understanding of only one subject was questionable.) The instructions for the binary experiment and for the trinary one were identical, except that the latter involved an additional opting-out choice of zero. The experimenter emphasized that if *either* member of a pair chose this option, then *neither* would receive or lose any money—i.e., the person who didn't choose the zero would gain or lose nothing as well.

Subjects were then given a booklet containing a set of five decision sheets, each with the identification letter specifying one of the five other subjects, a different prisoner's dilemma matrix, a place for recording a choice between an X and a Y—or between an X and a Y and a zero—and a place for recording expectations about what the other subject would choose. These sheets were completed one by one, with all subjects having completed each before any were permitted to proceed to the next.

Once all were completed, these decision forms were collected and taken to an adjoining "payroom," where each subject's aggregate pay was computed. During that time, subjects completed a final questionnaire concerning feelings and thoughts about the experiment. They were then escorted one by one to the payroom, paid appropriately, and dismissed.

A total of 216 subjects were in the experiment, consisting of 36 groups of 6; 9 groups were first engaged in the irrelevant communication task and then made choices in the binary experiment, 9 groups were first engaged in the irrelevant communication task and then made their choices in the trinary experiment, 9 groups directly made choices in the binary experiment, and 9 in the trinary experiment.

FIGURE 2

a.

2,2	-7,5
5,-7	-5,-5

(High greed incentive; high sucker loss; low mutual defect loss.)

b.

2,2	-7,5
5,-7	-2,-2

(High greed incentive; high sucker loss; low mutual defect loss.)

c.

2,2	-2,3
3,-2	-1,-1

(Low temptation; low sucker loss; low mutual defection)

d.

2,2	-2,4
4,-2	-1,-1

(Modest greed incentive; low sucker loss; low mutual defect loss.)

e.

2,2	-2,3
3,-2	-1,-1

(Low temptation; low sucker loss; low mutual defection.)

The Matrices

The five monetary prisoner's dilemma matrices in both the binary and the trinary experiments all had the structure $t > c > 0 > d > s$, where t is the "temptation" payoff (for unilateral defection), c the "cooperative" payoff (for joint cooperation), d the (negative) "defect" payoff (for joint defection), and s the (more negative) "sucker" payoff (for unilateral cooperation).

Consistent with the requirement that subjects should be able to lose all their starting money or double it, the five temptation payoffs summed to $20 while the five sucker payoffs summed to $-$20. It was also, of course, possible for subjects to take home any amount in between $0 and $40—including, in the trinary experiment, their $20 starting money, which they could ensure for themselves by simply opting out of all five games. The five matrices actually played are presented in Figure 2, together with a verbal description of the relative magnitudes of their incentive structure.

An examination of the incentives reveals that the five matrices can be ordered in terms of "difficulty" as $a > b > d > c$ and e.

Matrices *a* and *b* are "hard" in that both provide substantial incentives to defect, while the other three are relatively "easy." We made matrices *c* and *e* identical in order to provide a reliability check, but they were nevertheless presented separately, and subjects played them with different others. The exact sequence of plays followed a balanced design, with subjects randomly assigned to positions A through F.[1]

RESULTS

We found virtually no differences in choice depending on whether the subjects initially had discussed our Schelling coordination problem. Consequently, we have collapsed across irrelevant communication versus no communication prior to prisoner's dilemma choices in the data analyses that follow. Table 1 presents the numbers of *paired* choices for each matrix in the binary and trinary conditions.

The total amount gained by all 108 subjects in the binary choice experiment was −$150, for an average loss of 6.9 percent of the $20 stake. The total amount gained by all 108 subjects in the trinary choice experiment was +$332, for an average profit of 15.4 percent. The difference is nontrivial in terms of its economic implications.

Consistent with our expectation that subjects would respond to the incentive structure of the matrices, there is a perfect correspondence between the frequency of opting-out choices in the trinary experiment and the order of matrix difficulty specified in our methods section. In matrix *a*, 55 percent of our subjects chose not to play; in matrix *b*, 42 percent opted out; in matrix *d*, 30 percent; and in (identical) matrices *c* and *e*, an (identical) 21 percent. Contrary to our expectations, however, there is only a weak and erratic correspondence in the binary experiment between defection rates and matrix difficulty: 49 percent for matrix *a*, 65 percent for matrix *b*, 59 percent for matrix *d*, and 47 percent and 46 percent respectively for (identical) matrices *c* and *e*. The perfect rank order between matrix difficulty and opting out in the trinary experiment is consistent with subjects' expecting more defection when playing the harder matrices and hence

---

[1] In several initial runs of the binary experiment, subjects—without prior warning—were allowed to return to their choices after all had been completed and to opt out if they desired to do so. Few chose this option. It was this result that led us to construct the design of parallel binary versus trinary choice conditions. Because subjects in their initial runs of the binary condition did not know at the time they made their choice that they might be able to opt out of making it later, we see no problem in pooling these runs with the later ones. We are comfortable in assuming that future choice cannot affect a past choice when the availability of the future choice is unknown at the time the past choice is made.

TABLE 1*

MATRIX	a	b	c	d	e
Binary choice					
CC	30	8	32	18	32
CD	25	30	25	26	26
DC	25	30	25	26	26
DD	28	40	26	38	24
Trinary choice					
CC	16	6	26	20	26
CO	26	28	14	16	22
CD	4	18	32	32	28
DO	28	30	14	20	18
DD	2	10	12	10	10
OO	32	16	10	10	4

*C refers to cooperation, D to defection, O to opting out; hence, CC refers to mutual cooperation, and so on.

tending to avoid play. The *lack* of association between matrix difficulty and defection in the binary experiment suggests that there is no empirical justification for this expectation.

Because the same players made choices across the five different matrices, these choices are not independent. We cannot analyze our data (Table 1) using the individual as the unit of analysis, however, because our model does not postulate a *general* disposition to cooperate or to defect independent of the payoffs in the matrices. Instead, it is based on the principle that when faced with a *particular* choice, subjects will use their own disposition to cooperate or to defect as a cue to what to expect the other player to do, and will hence play or opt out if given the opportunity depending on their own disposition to cooperate or to defect *in that particular choice*. Accordingly, we must analyze the results matrix by matrix. To control for the probability of an experimentwide type 1 error (erroneous rejection of at least one null hypothesis that is "true") that results, we required that the analysis of each separate matrix yield a result significant at the .01 level to consider it "significant," thereby assuring by the Bonferroni inequality that the results across all five matrices will have a maximal error rate of .05. (Because the probability of a union of events is less than or equal to the sum of the probabilities of its constituent events, the probability of committing a type 1 error on *any* of *n* tests is less than or equal to the sum of the probabilities of committing a type 1 error on each.)

Our model requires an absence of translucency in these conditions of no or minimal communication. This absence implies that the rate with which cooperators play with other cooperators is no higher than would be expected to result from the base rate of cooperation and independence of choice. In the binary experiment, the chi-squares testing the actual number of mutually cooperative choices against this chance expectation are .19, 2.45, .17, .00, and .03 for matrices *a* through *e* respectively. Even considered singly, none of these values would have achieved significance at the .05 level, and the one that comes closest (for matrix *b*) assesses a contingency opposite that implied by translucency (i.e., fewer mutually cooperative choices than predicted by our chance null hypothesis).

In the trinary experiment, the chi-squares evaluating the actual number of mutually cooperative choices against our chance null hypothesis are 6.17, .44, .81, .29, and .20 for matrices *a* through *e* respectively. Our Bonferroni procedure does not permit us to conclude that there is dependent pairing for matrix *a*, but it must be kept in mind that the contingency (which is in the direction predicted by translucency) would have been significant had it been considered singly. Thus, if subsequent tests of our model led to positive results only for matrix *a*, we should be dubious of its support (but they don't).

Estimating the number of potential cooperators and defectors in the trinary experiment from the number observed in the binary experiment will not be free of error, but this error is biased neither systematically for nor against our hypothesis that potential defectors will be more likely to opt out than potential cooperators. Table 2 presents the results for opting out, using our estimate. In all cases, the results are in the predicted direction, with phi values ranging from .21 to .49. The chi-square values assessing contingency between potential cooperation versus defection and opting our or not are 5.46, 7.80, 4.68, 25.99, and 7.47 for matrices *a* through *e* respectively. All but those for matrices *a* and *c* would have been considered significant at the .01 confidence level considered singly, and can therefore be considered significant at the .05 confidence level by the Bonferroni inequality.

The result is that while in all conditions in the binary experiment defectors receive higher payoffs than cooperators, potential cooperators do relatively better in the trinary experiment. (Again, we split those opting out into potential cooperators versus potential defectors according to the proportions in the binary experiment.) Moreover, the change in average payoff is always

TABLE 2

Potential cooperators' and defectors' opt-out choices by matrix.

MATRIX a	Experiment 2		Experiment 1
	Stay	Opt out	
Potential cooperators:	31	24	55
Potential defectors:	18	35	53
Experiment 2:	49	59	108

Chi-square = 5.46;   Phi = .22;   p < .025

MATRIX b	Experiment 2		Experiment 1
	Stay	Opt out	
Potential cooperators:	29	9	38
Potential defectors:	34	36	70
Experiment 2:	63	45	108

Chi-square = 7.80;   Phi = .27;   p < .005

MATRIX c	Experiment 2		Experiment 1
	Stay	Opt out	
Potential cooperators:	49	8	57
Potential defectors:	35	16	51
Experiment 2:	84	24	108

Chi-square = 4.68;   Phi = .21;   p < .05

MATRIX d	Experiment 2		Experiment 1
	Stay	Opt out	
Potential cooperators:	44	0	44
Potential defectors:	36	28	64
Experiment 2:	80	28	108

Chi-square = 25.99;   Phi = .49;   p < .000

MATRIX e	Experiment 2		Experiment 1
	Stay	Opt out	
Potential cooperators:	51	7	58
Potential defectors:	33	17	50
Experiment 2:	84	24	108

Chi-square = 7.47;   Phi = .26;   p < .005

TABLE 3

*Mean dollar payout for cooperators and defectors in Experiment
1 compared with mean dollar payout in Experiment 2 for
potential cooperators and defectors, by matrix.*

Choice	Binary Experiment		Trinary Experiment		Change with opting out	
	C	D	C	D	C	D
M A T R I X a	-2.08	-.28	.33	.00	2.41	.28
M A T R I X b	-5.50	1.00	-1.16	.36	3.89	-.64
M A T R I X c	.25	.96	.35	.69	.10	-.27
M A T R I X d	-.36	1.03	.18	.84	.54	-.19
M A T R I X e	.21	1.08	.43	.60	.22	-.48

higher for potential cooperators than for potential defectors—to the point
that despite the payoffs, potential cooperators actually have a higher average
payoff than potential defectors in matrix *a*. The results by matrix are presented in Table 3. Note that the magnitude of the difference in payoff
changes from binary to trinary experiments is greatest for the two "hard"
matrices *a* and *b*.

If we were to use actual payoffs for the statistical analysis of these changes
from binary to trinary, the large number of zero payoffs in the trinary condition would create a huge difference in the variance within conditions—of a
factor of about 10 (the binary condition) to 1 (the trinary condition). Also, a
standard statistical analysis of the payoffs *per se* would violate virtually all
parametric assumptions a priori in that the payoffs to cooperators are always
different from those to defectors, with the exception of the zero payoff in
the trinary condition. We therefore decided to employ a nonparametric analysis. We computed the Spearman rank order correlation (rho) within each
condition between cooperate versus defect (with cooperation ranked higher)
and ordinal level of payoff. (This correlation may be regarded as an ordinal
analogue of a point-biserial correlation.) Because rho is equivalent to a Pear-
son correlation between ranks, we then converted to Fisher Z scores to test
whether there were any significant differences between the ranks in the
binary versus trinary experiments. The results are presented in Table 4.
(The reader who finds this procedure dubious may be content with noting
the significant results in Table 2, which in fact imply the effect we are evaluating.)

TABLE 4

Rank order correlations and the z-values testing their difference

Matrices	Bindary Condition	Trinary Condition	z Testing Difference
a	−.16	+.55	5.64*
b	−.31	−.25	4.10*
c	−.16	+.16	1.60
d	−.20	+.07	1.98+
e	−.19	+.12	2.27+

*$p<.01$ considered singly, hence $p<.05$ by our Bonferroni procedure
†$p<.05$ considered singly but not $<.05$ by our Bonferroni procedure

DISCUSSION

The experimental work demonstrated the potential for a "cooperators' advantage," at least a relative one in that cooperators did much better in the optional play situation relative to defectors than they did in the forced play one. This surplus translated into actual superiority in one matrix. Whether or not the relative advantage will result in an absolute one is, of course, dependent on the actual payoffs in the games involved—and on a number of other factors to be discussed here.

First, the advantage is to cooperators, plural. There must be enough so that the differential willingness of cooperators versus defectors to interact can lead to a weighting of consummated games toward mutual cooperation. We—consistent with the work of Axelrod and simulations of "genetic programming" with randomly altered strategies (e.g., Miller 1987)—make no claims about the initiation of cooperation, but only of its potential success. Again, evolutionary theorizing is concerned with consequences, not initiation or motives. Whether some other factors may yield an "initial kick" (Maruyama 1963) toward cooperation which the projection heuristic will then exacerbate, or whether this heuristic will itself provide the kick to be exacerbated by other factors, or both, is not at issue. The point is that in optional play situations the belief that "others will do as I do" clearly favors the evolution of mutual cooperation.

Second, payoffs for mutual defection must be negative, or there is no reason to avoid play. We believe that such negative results from mutual defection are quite frequent outside our experimental situation. In fact, the use of all-positive payoffs in previous work has obscured a strategy that is often superior to tit for tat in such situations: Reciprocate defection by quitting. This strategy has been investigated by Vanberg and Congleton (1992), who found it superior to tit for tat when one player's defection led to negative payoffs for the other.

Thus, the special status of zero in our model must be stressed. Our binary choice condition is one in which $t>c>0>d>s$ (where t, c, d, and s have the usual interpretations of "temptation," "cooperation," "defect" and "sucker" payoffs respectively). We could extend the structure to one in which $t>c>a>d>s$, where a stands for "abstain," and all five payoffs can be monotonically transformed without changing the original implications of the payoff matrix. Specifically, these implications are that cooperation is dominated by defection, and if by standard game theory logic we thereby eliminate cooperation as a viable choice, abstention weakly dominates defection. Games with such a structure might be termed (somewhat awkwardly) *quasi half-dilemmas*. We have previously (Dawes, Orbell, Simmons, and van de Kragt 1986) used the term "half-dilemmas" to refer to those game structures in which weakly dominating strategies converge on deficient equilibria (e.g., in binary choice prisoner's dilemmas that eliminate "greed" by setting $t=c$, or eliminate "fear" by setting $d=s$, but not both). Here, we introduce the term "quasi" to specify structures that become dilemmas only after domi-nat*ed* structures are eliminated from consideration. There may be many such quasi-dilemma games.

We believe, however, that the zero point is psychologically important, both in our experiment (especially given that subjects do *not* choose it in overwhelming numbers) and in choice outside the laboratory. We concur with that aspect of prospect theory (Kahneman and Tversky 1979) which maintains that people frame choices in terms of gains or losses from a status quo, or zero point (which can occasionally be manipulated). Consequently, we believe (although without empirical evidence) that choice would *not* remain invariant under ordinal transformations of the payoffs—that the prospect of loss if a game is consummated with a defector is critical in explaining choice.

Third, the model assumes no "translucency." In fact, we found none, with one possible exception. While the model is applicable to situations where it doesn't exist, there are clearly many in which it does. There may well be cues in other situations that signal intentions (Frank 1988), and people in many situations clearly bring with them reputations for being cooperative or exploitive. Even in these, however, projection of one's own intentions may be important. For example, Hoch (1987) has found that such projection has normative use in predicting others' responses, and in fact is used less often than it could be to enhance accuracy. (He argued that weighting one's own response was a normatively correct strategy when done by a single individual across different stimulus items, but maintained that such projection would still constitute a "false consensus" when different people's estimates concerning frequency about the same item is related to their own responses. As pointed out by Dawes [1990], the problem with such a position can be easily illustrated by considering two people and two items. If person A answers yes to item 1 and no to item 2, then—according to Hoch—it is legitimate for that person to give a higher estimate for item 1 than for item 2; if person B's response pattern is no / yes, then it is legitimate for that person to give a higher estimate for item 2 than for item 1; but if $x > y$ and $y' > x'$, then either $x > x'$ or $y' > y$, or both.)

Fourth, there may well be reciprocation in many circumstances. As pointed out earlier, however, the model we have developed is applicable to the first play in an iterated situation, and the first play is an essential feature of the success of tit-for-tat, or an attempt at tit-for-tat followed by withdrawal if it doesn't work in a context of negative payoffs for mutual defection.

Fifth, people cannot be good game theorists in the sense of searching for Nash equilibria on the assumption that others will act as they do. As pointed out earlier, that would mean that a potential defector would assign a propensity to withdraw to other potential defectors, and hence should wish to play on the assumption that anyone else wishing to play would be prone to be a cooperator, which would then negate the original belief concerning defectors' lack of propensity. A cooperator who reasons similarly would also be caught in a "circle." The result would, of course, be a mixed strategy, with a consequent negation of the cooperators' advantage. Our response to this problem is twofold. First, people have to be taught to understand game theory equilibria, and particularly those that result from a mixed strategy. Second, our experimental results indicate that our subjects simply don't reason that way, and they are relatively sophisticated mathematically in comparison to the general human population of people deciding whether to interact with others in a dilemma situation.

Sixth, and relatedly, people cannot "choose" to have a cooperative disposition or an exploitive one in order to maximize payoffs, or even to get satisfactory ones. Here, we point out that in any consummated interaction, defection yields better payoffs (again, in our one-shot situation), and there is therefore no reason to choose to have a cooperative disposition in order to maximize payoffs.

Seventh, as pointed out by our critic McLean (see our response, Orbell and Dawes 1991b), people must be selective about with whom they play; moreover, a critical aspect of our model is that such selectivity does not mirror the actual play of those with whom they interact. Otherwise, cooperators or defectors would always play or always refrain from playing—with the result that either no one would play, everyone would play, or all cooperators would play and all defectors would refrain (given that defectors' expectations are less optimistic than cooperators'). We simply don't observe that, either in all our past experiments in which we have collected expectations data or in the present one. While there is a strong correlation between what people do and what they expect others to do, our subjects nevertheless make differential predictions about others' choices. People use cues—often bad ones, such as gender in our experiments, or "you can't trust people with mustaches" (an academic job candidate years ago addressing an audience in which over half the males—including the department head—sported mustaches). Just as your mother often told you to try to be a nice guy (i.e., play tit for tat) and not to play with the nasties (i.e., opt out), she also probably gave you some often dubious advice about "who to look out for" whom you hadn't met. Following this last piece of advice can, of course, result in prejudice, irrationality, and discrimination. But since mother's advice turned out to be right a lot of the time, how are we to know? Moreover, by failing to interact with the people we incorrectly assume would exploit us, we can never find out that they wouldn't.

Eighth, our model can obviously be extended to situations where there is some degree of translucency (although of course there is no problem when it is total; given negative payoffs for mutual defection, no one would play with a defector, and the world would be benign—except for the defectors). We are not currently doing so ourselves, because we are interested in another type of extension.

That extension yields our ninth qualification. People do receive feedback in the world, not just about particular others, but about their own payoffs and in particular how these payoffs relate to the payoffs of others, as a reference group. We are currently investigating what effects which types of feedback would have on the basic finding. Consider, for example, feedback only about the results of one's own interactions (again, excluding knowledge about particular others' choices). Cooperators could be reinforced in believing that the world consists of primarily cooperative people, while defectors could be reinforced in their belief that they can "spot suckers"— even if the world itself consists primarily of defectors like them.

In contrast to such selective availability (usually a source of irrational and self-defeating judgments), knowledge of how propensities are distributed in the general population could negate the cooperators' advantage in optional play situations. Recently I spent seven hours at an airline lounge at Kennedy Airport prior to a European trip. There were no sports events on the television, so it reiterated the news that day, seven times. One item in the news concerned results of a poll in which people were asked whether they would murder a stranger for a million dollars if they were sure that they wouldn't be caught. The figures (quoted from memory) were that almost 20 percent of the men sampled had answered that they would, and close to 10 percent of the women. Each time that report came on, there were gasps and negative comments from the viewers, all from comparatively affluent backgrounds. While some of these viewers had no doubt engaged in dubious business or tax dealings, it is unlikely that they or the people with whom they interact would be particularly tempted to commit murder for money—or at least not the murder of a stranger. Could this poll have had some effect on their subsequent views of *each other?* Consider now our model. If the proportion of cooperators in the population is .5 and cooperators play with probability .8 while defectors do so with probability .2, then 80 percent of a cooperator's consummated plays will be with other cooperators, which is exactly what cooperators should expect—except for belief in the validity of their selective judgment. But now suppose a cooperator discovers that in fact 50 percent of the population consists of people who will defect were they to play. That could well affect the initial propensity, perhaps even to the point of reducing it to .5; similarly, defectors would discover that "there are a lot more suckers out there than I ever believed," and the result would be a total destruction of selectivity plays leading to a cooperators' advantage.

Finally, our whole model is based on the premise that people who are untrustworthy themselves tend to not trust others, and vice versa. We believe that is true, generally. Others have investigated that contingency on an individual difference basis across varying situations; here, we have restricted ourselves to propensities to cooperate or defect given a particular payoff structure.

We wish to end by stressing one important implication of our model and our results. To the degree to which our model is applicable, society would benefit by providing people maximal choice about whether to interact with each other. Societies without choice are dismal anyway, but they may have the added problem that—when mutual defection results in negative payoffs to the society itself—forcing people to interact will exacerbate the total magnitude of that negative payoff. Prisons and prep schools come to mind. Also, negotiations that are required, e.g., by an experimenter or at the end of a contract, should result in less benign outcomes than those that are optional. Freedom to choose may have positive effects not only on incentives and individual psychological functioning, but on the net payoff to society as a whole. When, for example, our subjects were forced to play in our binary game, 47 percent of the choices were cooperative ones. When given the option of playing in the trinary game, 57 percent of the choices actually made were cooperative ones. Given the overall lack of contingency, that translates into a 50 percent increase in the incidence of mutual cooperation and a 38 percent decrease in the incidence of mutual defection. We have recently observed the relative success of a free market economy.[2] Others have emphasized "market" as an essential component of this success. We suggest that "free" may be an equally important, if not more important, component.

---

[2]One of us (RMD) witnessed a speech in which President Ronald Reagan said he welcomed an arms race with the USSR because "it will bankrupt them before it bankrupts us." He proved himself to be a superb political economist because he was right—on both counts.

CHAPTER FIVE

The Role of Fairness Considerations and Relationships in a Judgmental Perspective of Negotiation

**Max H. Bazerman and
Margaret A. Neale**

*P*eople claim a right to fairness and they give weight to fairness in evaluating outcomes, but assessments of what is fair are often biased by self-interest. For example, it is quite common for all negotiators in a conflict to suggest viable solutions that are self-serving but to justify them based on abstract fairness criteria. Thompson and Loewenstein (1992) found that self-serving, biased attention to available information in a conflict affected negotiator perception of the fair settlement, and the magnitude of this bias affected the length of a strike in a simulated labor dispute. Similarly, White and Neale (1994) argue that the relative salience of differing alternative focal points that exist in the negotiation context can alter dramatically one's perceptions of what is fair.

Negotiators can focus on the market price, their expectation of the midpoint of the bargaining zone, or the midpoint of their aspiration zone as indicative of what a fair outcome would be. White and Neale (1994) manipulated negotiators' aspiration zone while holding constant their (true) bargaining zone. That is, negotiators were either given an optimistic aspiration level (a target that greatly exceeded their walk-away position in the negotiation) or a pessimistic aspiration level (a target that was only slightly in excess of their walk-away point). When negotiating dyads were composed of individuals with optimistic and pessimistic aspiration levels, they found that the parties' estimations of what was fair were inconsistent. As a result, the impasse rate was significantly higher than when negotiators' estimations of their own and others' midpoints were relatively consistent (optimistic versus optimistic; pessimistic versus pessimistic). In the inconsistent case, each side pushed for the midpoint that favored its side. The resulting conflict in perceptions of what constituted a fair agreement frequently caused a breakdown in the negotiation, resulting in impasse.

While fairness concerns can have dramatic effects on the outcomes of negotiations, little empirical work has been done that specifically investigates fairness in a negotiation context. A central theme of this chapter is that concerns about fairness result in systematically different behavior than that which we would expect from a purely rational model. We argue that fairness is an important component of negotiation outcomes and should be incorporated into the emerging judgmental perspective of the field.

Following the descriptive work of Tversky and Kahneman (1974, 1981; Kahneman and Tversky 1979, 1982), and the prescriptive framework of Raiffa (1982), our past work has focused on identifying the ways in which individual judgment systematically deviates from rational models of behavior in the context of negotiation. This research has suggested that negotiators tend to be inappropriately affected by the positive or negative frame in which risks are viewed (Neale and Bazerman 1985; Bazerman, Magliozzi, and Neale 1985), to anchor their number estimates in negotiations on irrelevant information (Neale and Northcraft 1986; Northcraft and Neale 1987), to rely too heavily on readily available information (Neale 1984), and to be overconfident about the likelihood of attaining outcomes that favor themselves (Bazerman and Neale 1982). Negotiators also tend to assume that negotiation tasks are necessarily fixed-sum and thereby miss opportunities for mutually beneficial trade-offs between the parties (Bazerman, Magliozzi, and Neale 1985), to escalate commitment to a previously selected course of action when it is no longer the most reasonable alternative (Neale and Bazerman 1991), and to overlook the valuable information that could be gained by considering the opponent's cognitive perspective (Bazerman and Carroll 1987).

While we believe that the judgmental perspective offered by this research has extended our understanding of negotiation in a new direction, this work, like much of the work that it criticizes, has ignored the important role played by fairness concerns. The present chapter integrates much of what we know about how concerns for fairness can affect the judgmental processes of negotiators. In the first half of this chapter, we will show how such concerns can promote irrationality in the way that negotiators make decisions and respond to allocations. In the second half of the chapter, we will examine how social relationships influence perceptions of fairness and the role that such perceptions play in the negotiation process.

IRRATIONALITY IN JUDGMENTS OF FAIRNESS

Research on fairness has focused primarily on decisions concerning the distribution of scarce resources and the fairness of procedures for distributing scarce resources (Thibaut and Walker 1975; Adams 1963; Lind and Tyler 1988). Most of this literature examines objective outcomes or procedures.

What is missing from these literatures is adequate consideration of the subjective perceptions of allocators and recipients in the distribution process.

Clearly, people care about fairness; it affects their decisions and lives. A number of authors have argued that fairness considerations account for the lack of explanatory power of economic models. For example, Kahneman, Knetsch, and Thaler (1986), Okun (1981), and Solow (1980) argue that fairness considerations explain why many employers do not cut wages during periods of high unemployment, despite the potential offered by the supply / demand levels. This unwillingness to exploit market conditions is consistent with the perceptions of third parties who view such cuts as unfair.

Concerns for fairness can lead to three effects that deviate from traditional conceptions of rational economic behavior. First, people often question the legitimacy or fairness of decisions dictated by traditional supply / demand considerations. Second, fairness considerations can lead negotiators to opt for joint outcomes that leave both parties worse off than they could have been had fairness considerations been ignored. Finally, and perhaps most significantly in terms of the challenge presented to standard conceptions of economic rationality, fairness considerations can lead to inconsistencies and intransitivities in expressed preferences.

Fairness and the Violation of Supply / Demand Considerations

The impact of fairness concerns on responses to exploitation of the laws of supply and demand is persuasively documented in the work of Kahneman et al. (1987). For example, subjects were asked to evaluate the fairness of the action in the following example:

A hardware store has been selling snow shovels for $15. The morning after a large snowstorm, the store raises the price to $20. Please rate this action as:

Completely Fair   Acceptable   Unfair   Very Unfair

The two favorable and the two unfavorable categories were combined to indicate the proportion of respondents who judged the action acceptable or unfair. Despite the economic rationality of raising the snow shovels' prices, 82 percent of respondents ($N = 107$) considered this action unfair. In addition, informal research showed that many of the respondents who viewed the price increase as fair reversed their decisions when the commodity was generators after a hurricane—yet the problem is conceptually quite closely related. Kahneman et al. (1987) illustrate quite clearly that individual judgments about fairness are not consistent with basic economic theory concerning supply and demand.

Interestingly, someone who acts according to the laws of supply and demand (e.g., increases the price of the shovels after a snowstorm) may fare less well economically than someone who considers norms of fairness, since others (e.g., the shovel customers) may punish the unfairness of an economically rational action in their future behavior or purchases. Thus, following the "rational" economic model in circumstances where it is deemed unfair may not be rational (Raiffa 1982). Rather, optimal decision making requires consideration of the expectations and standards of the other parties with whom one is transacting business (Bazerman and Carroll 1987; Bazerman and Neale 1992).

The work of Kahneman et al. (1987) shows persuasively that fairness concerns moderate the predictive power of market predictions. Yet, this research is only a starting point for clarifying the role of fairness considerations in negotiation. While some individuals do view raising the price of snow shovels as fair, these same individuals do not believe that it is fair to raise the price of generators after a hurricane, and certainly not to "sell" organs for transplantation to the highest bidder. Yet, as noted, these three situations have some parallelism. Future research is needed to clarify the variables that determine when fairness considerations lead to predictions that are distinct from traditional models of economic behavior.

Fairness and Pareto Optimality

The results discussed in the previous section can be incorporated into an economic model if one recognizes that fairness is an attribute that individuals value. However, concerns for fairness can also lead to inefficiency, where all parties are worse off as a result of fairness considerations. This is demonstrated in a set of experiments employing "ultimatum games" (Güth, Schmittberger, and Schwarze 1982; Roth 1991). In Güth et al.'s (1982) study, player 1 divided a known, fixed sum of money any way s / he chose, by filling out a form stating "I demand DM   " (the study was conducted in West Germany using Deutsche Marks). Player 2 could accept the offer and receive his / her portion of the money as divided by player 1, or reject the offer, leaving both parties with nothing. Game-theoretic models predict that player 1 would offer player 2 only slightly more than zero, and that player 2 would accept any offer greater than zero. The results, however, showed that subjects incorporated fairness considerations in their offers and their choices. The average demand by player 1 was for less than 70 percent of the funds, both for first-time players and for players repeating the game one week later. This behavior is inconsistent with the game-theoretic prediction.

In addition, individuals in the role of player 2 rejected profitable offers and took zero 20 percent of the time. In doing so, it should be emphasized that they were choosing a Pareto-inefficient result. An agreement is defined as Pareto inefficient when there is another agreement that would make at least one party better off, without reducing the outcomes to the other party. Güth et al. (1982) concluded that ". . . subjects often rely on what they consider a fair or justifiable result . . . subjects do not hesitate to punish if their opponent asks for 'too much.' "

Ochs and Roth (1989) studied a situation in which player 2 could reject player 1's offer, and counterpropose, but in doing so face a reduction of x percent (40 percent and 60 percent were used in various conditions of the study) of the available funds. They found that 81 percent of rejected offers were followed by counteroffers that provided less money to the party who rejected the initial offer. They referred to these behaviors as "disadvantageous counteroffers." These counteroffers were Pareto inefficient. Ochs and Roth (1989) argued that the players' utilities for fairness explained the results. However, they also argued that a simple notion of equality does not explain the data, since in most cases player 1 asked for more than 50 percent of the resources. Rather, parties realized that the other side may very well refuse offers perceived as unfair, economic arguments aside. Thus, intuition tells us that the other party will not always follow the logic of Pareto efficiency. Bolton (1991) incorporates these findings within a formal model that argues that individuals behave as if they are negotiating over both absolute and relative money. This is consistent with the model of social utility developed in the next section.

In a related study, Forsythe et al. (1988) employed either an ultimatum game as described above, or a "dictator" game in which player 1 could simply decide how the resources would be split without player 2's acceptance. While player 1 typically chose a 50-50 split in the ultimatum game, none proposed a 100-0 split. However, under the dictator format, player 1 took the entire amount 36 percent of the time. It should be emphasized, however, that even in the dictator game, 64 percent of the subjects still chose to give the other party some portion of the resources. This evidence supports the argument that people give weight to fairness norms even when there is no economic reason to do so. In addition, people realize that others will sacrifice gains rather than accept "unfair" allocations. Again, we see that acting in accordance with purely economic models may not be rational in a world where your opponent is following other systematic patterns of behavior.

The violations of Pareto efficiency, like the violations of supply / demand considerations, can be incorporated into a social utility function (Messick and Sentis 1985) that includes some nontraditional attributes. Loewenstein, Thompson, and Bazerman (1989) examined the preferences for outcomes to self and outcomes for others in various role-play situations. They asked subjects to assess their satisfaction with different monetary outcomes for themselves and another person in a dispute. A social utility function for each subject was then computed by regressing the subject's satisfaction with each outcome on its value to the subject and on the difference between that value and the other person's outcome. The precise form of the estimated function, selected by goodness of fit tests over a variety of forms, was:

$$U = \beta_1 \text{self} + \beta_2 \text{posdif} + \beta_3 \text{posdif}^2 + \beta_4 \text{negdif} + \beta_5 \text{negdif}^2$$

(a specification adapted from a model suggested by Messick and Sentis [1985] where posdif indicates positive differences between one's own and the other's payoff [advantageous inequality] and negdif indicates the absolute value of negative differences [disadvantageous inequality]). In general, disputants preferred equal outcomes over inequalities, so that the signs of both β_2 and β_4 were negative. At the same time, as one might expect, advantageous inequalities were preferred over disadvantageous inequalities—the absolute magnitude of the β_4 coefficient was greater than that of β_2.

This function is quite consistent with many of the violations created by fairness considerations discussed above. If people were preoccupied with the difference between themselves and other parties, acting against supply / demand considerations and violating Pareto efficiency are easily explained. However, this model still allows for consistency. That is, if an individual's utility were defined in a stable way within the model's parameters, consistency would exist.

Fairness and Inconsistency

The previous two sections document the role of fairness in creating predictions that are inconsistent with traditional economic models. However, many individuals would argue that fairness has utility to decision makers (Messick 1991), and thus it is reasonable for fairness concerns to be included in a rational model of decision making. This reasoning would suggest that decision makers should be allowed to value any attribute, including nontraditional variables such as the difference between their outcome and the outcome of another party. We now discuss additional research suggesting that fairness judgments cannot be reconciled even with a more flexible definition of rationality. Specifically, we will argue that social utility preferences, which encompass concerns for the outcomes to other parties, can be rendered inconsistent by normatively irrelevant information.

Bazerman, Loewenstein, and White (1992) have shown that while individuals care far more about social comparisons when rating a specific outcome, absolute individual outcomes are more important in actual choice behavior. For example, while 70 percent rated the outcome of $400 for self, $400 for the other party as *more* acceptable than $500 for self, $700 for the other party when they evaluated these outcomes separately, only 22 percent chose the outcome $400 for self and $400 for the other party over $500 for self and $700 for the other party when asked to choose between the two. This basic pattern is consistent across many other comparisons and a wide variety of contexts.

Bazerman et al. (1992) argue that when joint outcomes are evaluated separately, others' outcomes become the referent point. When choosing between two outcomes for oneself—even when others' outcomes are involved—no referent is needed, as outcomes to self can be easily compared. Others' outcomes are no longer needed as referents and appear to be unimportant in most people's choices. The salient attribute in a choice task is outcome to self.

Loewenstein et al. (1992) have extended this result to a real situation involving real payoffs. In addition, they showed that the critical determinant of the instability on the Bazerman et al. (1992) study was not the ratings / choice distinction, but whether the parties evaluated one or two options at a time. They agreed to recruit subjects for a colleague's experiment. One group of potential subjects was offered $7 to participate in a forty-minute experiment, knowing that all subjects would be receiving $7. A second group was offered $8 to participate in a forty-minute experiment, knowing that some subjects were arbitrarily (based on the last digit of their social security number) being offered $10. A third group was given an opportunity to (1) participate in a forty-minute experiment in which everyone was being paid $7, (2) participate in a forty-minute experiment in which some subjects, including themselves, would receive $8 and others would receive $10, or (3) not participate. While significantly more subjects in the first group chose to participate (72 percent) than in the second group (55 percent), the majority of subjects (56 percent) in the third group chose to participate in the experiment that gave them $8 while some others were given $10 (16 percent chose the experiment in which everyone received $7; 28 percent chose not to participate in either). Thus, in evaluating whether to participate in one specific experiment, the outcomes of other potential subjects were critical. However, when multiple opportunities were available, the outcomes of others became less important. Subjects were able to simply compare what they would receive across the multiple experiments.

The Loewenstein et al. study (1992) has also been generalized to a more realistic decision context. Bazerman, Schroth, Pradhan, Diekmann, and Tenbrunsel (in press) recruited second-year MBA students at Kellogg (in October 1991) to respond to a question which asked them whether they would accept or reject a job offer from a consulting firm under a deadline. In all cases, they were told to imagine that it was January 15, 1992, and that they had one (or two) job offers, and that the job offer(s) expired today. They were then asked whether they would accept (one of) the offer(s). Two of the jobs that were assessed were described as follows:

Job A: The offer is from Company 4 for $75,000 a year. It is widely known that this firm pays all starting MBAs from top schools $75,000 . . . [additional descriptive information about the firm]

Job B: The offer is from Company 9 for $85,000 a year. It is widely known that this firm is paying some other graduating Kellogg students $95,000 a year . . . [additional descriptive information about the firm].

One group of subjects was asked to assess twelve single job offers (single condition), each time being told that this was their job offer, and asked whether they would accept each of the individual job offers. Another group of subjects was exposed to six situations in which they had pairs of job offers (jobs A and B are one such pair) (dual condition), and asked if they would accept either job offer, and if so, which one. The six pairs covered the same twelve jobs as the earlier group, and in each case set up a comparison between equality and the maximization of outcomes to self. The confirmed expectation was that individuals examining one job offer at a time were more likely to accept job A than job B, but that individuals examining job A and job B simultaneously would prefer job B over job A. Bazerman et al. (in press) were not concerned with single-condition subjects who accepted neither or both of the job offers in a pair, or with dual-condition subjects who rejected both offers. Of the 32 subjects who accepted one of the two jobs listed above in the single condition, 22 accepted job A and 10 accepted job B. In contrast, of the 30 subjects who accepted one of the two jobs in the dual condition, 5 accepted job A and 25 accepted job B. This is consistent with the earlier Loewenstein et al. (1992) study, and generalizes the findings to a realistic context with subjects who could easily identify with the decision context.

Finally, Bazerman et al. (in press) explored the question of whether social comparisons are simply one of many possible sources of social information that are used inconsistently. They argue that when individuals are assessing any single outcome to self, and lack a metric to assess the worth of that outcome, they will search for some social information to make sense of that outcome. However, when evaluating more than one option, outcomes to self across the multiple options provide evaluative information about the worth of each of the specific outcomes to self. Bazerman et al. (in press) substituted procedural justice information for social comparison information, and asked MBA students to assess either six single job offers or three pairs in the same format as described in the previous experiment. In past studies, procedural justice research always had subjects assess one situation at a time, never allowing subjects a choice between options (Lind and Tyler 1988). Thus, one interesting question is whether procedural justice information is only used in contexts where decision makers are deprived of the information necessary to assess the worth of their outcomes.

Bazerman et al. (in press) described jobs to set up a conflict between obtaining procedural justice and maximizing salary. For example, the following pair of job offers were in the set:

Job A (low salary, high procedural justice): The first offer is from company 1 for $60,000 a year. . . . New associates are given the opportunity to participate in decisions typically made by upper management . . . new associates are allowed to voice their preferences regarding client and project assignments. . . . The firm encourages all consultants, both junior and senior, to voice their opinions for changes and improvements to the company's policies. . . .

Job B (high salary, low procedural justice): The second offer is from company 2 for $75,000 a year. . . . New associates are assigned by senior partners to specific clients, projects, and engagement teams in which a senior partner is in charge and are not allowed to request changes. Decisions involving company policies, including MBA training, job objectives, career advancement and salary increases, are made by senior management. The new MBAs are not encouraged to voice their opinions or objectives. . . .

It was expected that when individuals assessed jobs individually, procedural justice information would be more important than when individuals assessed pairs of jobs. In the single condition, of the 40 subjects who accepted one of the two jobs listed above, 29 accepted job A and 11 accepted job B. In contrast, in the dual condition, of the 37 subjects who accepted one of the two jobs, 14 accepted job A and 23 accepted job B. Thus, it does appear that social comparison information is simply one type of social information that individuals use to make sense of outcomes when they lack a way to assess the worth of the outcome itself.

Inconsistencies in fairness considerations can also be seen in Kahneman et al.'s demonstration (1986) that fairness judgments were affected by the framing of the problem. Consider these questions:

Question A: A company is making a small profit. It is located in a community experiencing a recession with substantial unemployment but no inflation. There are many workers anxious to work at the company. The company decides to decrease wages and salaries 7 percent this year.

(N = 125) Acceptable 38 percent   Unfair 62 percent

Question B: A company is making a small profit. It is located in a community experiencing a recession with substantial unemployment and inflation of 12 percent. There are many workers anxious to work at the company. The company decides to increase wages and salaries 5 percent this year.

(N = 129) Acceptable 78 percent   Unfair 22 percent

Despite very similar changes in real income, judgments of fairness were starkly different. A wage cut was typically coded as an unfair loss; a nominal gain that does not cover inflation was more often acceptable.

Research also suggests that individuals are affected by normatively irrelevant information. Kramer, Pradhan-Shah, and Woerner (in press), for instance, found that the effectiveness of the examples used to explain ultimatum games influences the subjects' aggressiveness. A vivid example (Tversky and Kahneman 1974) overwhelms a rational assessment of the ultimatum game: subjects exposed to President Kennedy's successful ultimatum in the Cuban Missile Crisis were far more aggressive than subjects exposed to the air controllers' unsuccessful ultimatum in the PATCO strike. Loewenstein, White, and Bazerman (1991) and Boles and Messick (1990) also show inconsistency in how subjects respond to the ultimatum game. They find that when individuals are asked for the lowest amount they will accept in an ultimatum game, they specify a higher amount than the minimum they will actually accept when asked to make a choice between accepting and rejecting an ultimatum.

The results of research highlighted above suggests that fairness concerns increase the likelihood that decision makers will violate the tenets of supply and demand, prefer Pareto-inefficient outcomes over Pareto-efficient ones, and make inconsistent choices among essentially equivalent options. Thus, concerns for fairness should be included in any analysis of a negotiating opponent's likely behavior. However, it is the case that what is perceived as fair in one situation may be perceived as unfair in another. So, not only do fairness norms not necessarily generalize across situations, they also do not seem to generalize across actors within the same situation. One particularly important aspect of the situation concerns the relationship that exists between parties, and this is the focus of the second half of this chapter.

SOCIAL RELATIONSHIPS AND FAIRNESS

Most studies on barriers to conflict resolution can be faulted because they ignore the context of negotiation (Barley 1991). One set of contextual variables most often mentioned as missing from experimental paradigms involves the social aspects of relationships, a particularly unfortunate omission given that the relationship patterns created by social interaction are the primary basis for conflict, coalitions, and the allocation of resources in society (Granovetter 1973; Simmel 1955; Tilly 1978). The first half of this paper examined ways in which fairness considerations could affect parties' attempts to achieve rational and mutually beneficial agreements. The second half of this paper focuses on the systematic effects that social relationships have on the negotiation process. Specifically, we are interested in the role that social factors play in heightening or attenuating concerns for fairness and the subsequent rationality of negotiated agreements.

Previous research exploring the impact of relationships on allocation decisions has typically found that individuals expecting future interactions with the recipient of the allocation tend to invoke an equality norm. For example, Austin (1980) examined the effect the tie between the two parties had on the distribution norm used. Subjects in one condition worked on a task with their roommate, while those in the other condition worked with a stranger. The apparent contributions of the two parties to a task were also manipulated. After both parties completed the work task and received feedback about their relative performances, one party, the "decision maker," was given the assignment of allocating the resource ($5) between herself and her partner (subjects were all female). She was instructed to allocate the money based on each individual's performance on the work task, along with any other factors she deemed appropriate. The results confirmed Austin's predictions. Subjects who participated in the experiment with their roommates overlooked performance on the work task and allocated the money equally. By contrast, subjects who participated in the experiment with a stranger allocated the money on an equal basis when they performed less well than their partner, but divided the money based on an equity norm when they outperformed their partner. In other words, in the stranger condition, the decision maker used whichever norm was in her best interest.

Others similarly have attempted to examine varying degrees of social interaction and resource allocation. Researchers have compared the decisions made by romantic couples and strangers (Fry, Firestone, and Williams 1983), and by people in "exchange" (operationalized as no potential for future interactions) versus "communal" (having potential for future interactions) relationships (Clark and Mills 1979). The results of these studies are consistent. People either in close personal relationships or with the potential for communal relationships (i.e., relationships in which members give benefits in response to a need for that benefit) typically chose equality allocation norms; those in nonpersonal or potential exchange relationships (i.e., relationships in which benefits are given in response to the receipt of a benefit) typically chose allocation norms based on principles of equity or proportionality of rewards to contributions.

All of these previously cited studies examining relationships required the subjects to specify an allocation. They did not examine the impact of relationships on the negotiation process itself. In an attempt to examine this question, Sondak, Pinkley and Neale (1994) manipulated three independent variables—relationship, task performance, and need—within the context of a distributive negotiation. Subjects were assigned either a stranger or their roommate as a negotiating partner and first asked to allocate 100 points between themselves and their partner. They were told that they could allocate the points in any way they chose, based on any factor they considered important. After each member of the negotiating dyad completed the initial allocation, they were told they had twenty minutes in which they could negotiate, face-to-face, the final allocation of points. While all dyads reached agreement, stranger dyads were more likely to allocate their points based on task performance (i.e., an equity norm) while roommate dyads were more likely to split the points (i.e., an equality norm).

Relationships, Social Comparisons, and Fairness

The earlier reviewed work of Loewenstein et al. (1989; Loewenstein et al. 1992; Bazerman et al. 1992; Bazerman et al., in press) suggested that fairness and social comparison concerns resulted in social utility preferences that were Pareto inefficient and inconsistent. In this subsection, we examine how social or interpersonal comparisons affect these social utility preferences. Loewenstein et al. (1989) found that the positivity or negativity of the relationship between parties played a role in dictating social utility preferences. Modal subjects in positive and neutral relationship conditions tended to dislike advantageous inequality ($\beta_2 < 0$), while those in the negative relationship condition derived positive utility from advantageous inequality ($\beta_2 > 0$).

Loewenstein et al. (1989) also examined how choice behavior in interpersonal decisions by parties in positive or negative relationships differed from intrapersonal decisions. All subjects participated in two phases of this experiment. In one phase, they made simple binary choices, each a selection between a sure thing and a risky alternative. In the other phase, subjects made binary choices that had implications not only for themselves but for the other party as well. The only difference between the two phases (the order was reversed for half the subjects) was the individual versus interpersonal nature of their choices. Thus, in the individual choice condition, the risky choice involved gains / losses only to the self, while in the interpersonal choice condition, the risky choice involved gains / losses to the self and another party. Subjects were randomly assigned to positive and negative relationship conditions.

The interpersonal choices began with the instructions: "Below you are given a description of an incident involving you and a neighbor. Please read the description and then answer each question." The description specified that either a positive or negative relationship existed between the disputants. The questionnaire then described situations in which the subject and neighbor either jointly owed, or were jointly to be paid, $10,000. Subjects were then given a choice between accepting a settlement proposed by the neighbor and taking a risky option of arbitrating. The interpersonal choices involved payoffs to the subject that were identical to the three choices in the individual choice set. The first choice in both conditions was between a sure $5,000 and a risky alternative offering a .7 chance of $6,000 and a .3 chance of $4,000 (expected value = $5,400).

The results of this experiment were dramatic. In the individual decision (intrapersonal) condition, 19 percent chose the sure thing and 81 percent chose the risky alternative. In the positive relationship (interpersonal) condition, 85 percent opted for the sure $5,000 / $5,000 (self / other) split rather than a .7 chance of $6,000 / $4,000 and a .3 chance of $4,000 / $6,000. However, in the negative relationship (interpersonal), only 27 percent opted for the sure, equal split. The choices in the interpersonal / positive condition were significantly different from those in the individual and interpersonal / negative relationship conditions.

These data are consistent with the predictions of the social utility functions described earlier. Subjects in the individual condition were willing to take risks to increase their expected values. However, in the interpersonal / positive condition, the equal-split alternative predominated; both unequal outcomes, even the one offering a greater payoff to the subject, offered lower utility than the equal split. Subjects in the interpersonal / negative condition were willing to risk the disadvantageous inequality in order to maximize their own expected outcome and to increase the likelihood of obtaining (positively valued) advantageous inequality.

The social utility functions from the earlier study by Loewenstein et al. (1989) also explain the reversal of preference in the negative relationship condition. A negative relationship has two effects on the utility function: it causes a "selfish shift" which increases the desirability of the high-valued risky alternative, and it increases the slope of utility as a function of positive differences between the disputants' payoffs. Now, getting more than the other person is valuable; without the negative relationship, differences provided negative utility. Negative affect within the context of potential relationships can remove fairness barriers.

Another item in Loewenstein et al.'s third study involved losses rather than gains. In the individual decision condition, as prospect theory (Kahneman and Tversky 1979) predicts, 75 percent of subjects preferred a fifty-fifty chance of losing $10,000 or losing nothing over a sure loss of $5,000. However, in an interpersonal context, 85 percent of subjects in the positive relationship condition and 82 percent of the subjects in the negative relationship condition preferred equal losses of $5,000 over a lottery giving a 50 percent chance of either side paying the full amount. The positive and negative interpersonal relationship conditions differed significantly from the individual (intrapersonal) condition, but not from each other. In this situation, we see a pattern of concern for equality of payoffs dwarfing the general preference for risk in the domain of losses.

In the Bazerman et al. (1992) study, subjects similarly were assigned to either a positive or a negative relationship condition. The basic finding in this study was that subjects rated $400 for self, $400 for other preferable to a split of $500 for self, $700 for other, but opted for the latter in actual choice situations. This finding proved to be consistent across positive and negative relationships. Bazerman et al. (1992) also had subjects assess outcomes in which payoffs to self were held constant, but the outcomes to the other party varied. For example, subjects assessed the outcome $500 for self, $500 for other versus the outcome $500 for self, $700 for other. This time, the choice / rating manipulation was found to interact with the relationship manipulation. When a negative relationship existed, $500 for self, $500 for other was preferred over $500 for self, $700 for other, regardless of the elicitation mechanism (86 percent had this preference under rating and 90 percent had this preference under choice). However, when a positive relationship existed, 79 percent preferred $500 for self, $500 for other over $500 for self, $700 for other under rating, but subjects were fairly evenly divided under choice—only 52 percent preferred $500 for self, $500 for other over $500 for self, $700 for other. Thus, subjects were even less likely to accept disadvantageous inequality when they did not receive something for doing so. It was only when a positive relationship existed and the subjects were directly confronted with the question of whether they wanted their nice neighbors to receive the extra $200 were subjects even open to the consideration of allowing the Pareto superiority of $500 for self, $700 for other over $500 for self, $500 for other.

Relationships and the Facilitation of Agreements

We have discussed a number of inefficiencies and inconsistencies in resource allocations that concern the weight that people give to fairness considerations. In this section, we explore how positive relationships can facilitate rationality in negotiation outcomes. In particular, we explore how positive relationships can help create agreements in the ultimatum game, can solve the winner's curse in negotiation, and can improve the integrativeness of agreements.

Relationships, fairness, and behavior in the ultimatum game. As noted earlier, researchers have been particularly perplexed by the seeming irrationality of subjects in ultimatum games. Most explanations have focused on notions of fairness, suggesting that such concerns cause individuals making the allocation to forgo relatively small sums of additional money for greater certainty that the individuals making the decision will accept the proposed allocation. While people can be expected to be even more concerned with the fairness of agreements in long-term relationships, preliminary evidence suggests that relationships may facilitate transactions in the ultimatum game—where parties may otherwise develop egocentric notions of fairness (White and Neale 1994; Thompson and Loewenstein 1992).

Consider the usual ultimatum game: The interaction is typically between strangers and is a one-time experience. While most previous ultimatum games have used strangers, it may not be the case that those in relationships will make similar allocation decisions and respond similarly to ultimatums. Polzer, Neale and Glenn (1993) had player 1 divide $7, with allocations being divisible by 50 cents. Simultaneously, player 2 in the dyad noted, for each possible allocation, whether s / he would accept or reject the proposal. Subjects in the experiment were required to come with a friend. A minimum of two sets of friends were scheduled to come together. Thus, a minimum of four subjects were required for each data collection. Subjects were paired with a friend or stranger in the first round and with the other (stranger or friend) in the second round, controlling for the order of bargaining opponents.

Player 1 allocated significantly more to player 2 when they were friends than when they were strangers ($4.90 versus $4.74). Player 1 was more likely to use a norm of equality as the basis for his / her allocation to a friend. When allocating to a stranger, player 1 was more likely to use an equity norm. Interestingly, player 2 required, on average, significantly less in the friend condition than in the stranger condition ($2.58 versus $3.67). That is, when offering a portion of a resource to a friend, an individual is more likely to use an equality norm of allocation. However, in determining the minimum acceptability of that resource, a friend (i.e., player 2) is likely to demand significantly less. The obvious implication of player 1's offering more and player 2's requiring less is that the rejection rate should fall. Unfortunately, Polzer et al. (1993) obtained too few rejections to test this prediction. It should be noted, however, that these differences—while significant—are not large. This probably reflects the reliance on a combination of the equity and equality allocation norms in both conditions. The differences may simply be a function of the increased weight one places on the equity norm with strangers and the equality norm with friends.

Positive relationships thus provide a partial solution to reducing dysfunctional impasses in contexts that parallel the ultimatum game. Before one decides to apply this finding too generally, however, it should be noted that while friends may be willing to accept a small gain or even a loss if it provides the other with a large gain, the critical component of such a willingness is a belief in the duration of the relationship. Thus, one must be relatively certain that the other will not break off the relationship when he or she is "in the gains." It is likely that the duration of the relationship allows for flexibility in the relative outcomes and interaction of the parties; however, one might expect that even for relationships that have considerable temporal continuity, a consistent pattern of inequality or inequity would eventually damage the relationship.

The winner's curse. Research in bilateral bargaining has found that, under asymmetric information, negotiators act irrationally by failing to incorporate valuable information about the decisions of their opponents. This results in negative profits—the "winner's curse": you complete the transaction, but probably lose money as a result (Samuelson and Bazerman 1985; Carroll, Bazerman, and Maury 1988). The most common documentation of the winner's curse involves the "acquiring a company" problem, in which one firm (the acquirer) may offer to buy another (the target). However, the acquirer is uncertain about the ultimate value of the target firm. It only knows (a) that the target firm's value under current management is between $0 and $100, with all values equally likely, (b) that the target firm knows its exact worth, and (c) that the target firm is expected to be worth 50 percent more under the acquirer's management than under the current ownership. Under such circumstances, it appears to make sense for a transaction to take place. The problem is, what price should the acquirer offer for the target?

While analytically quite simple, the problem defies most people's intuition. Many studies have documented that the common response is between $50 and $75. How is this $50 to $75 decision reached? One common (wrong) explanation is: "On average, the firm is worth $50 to the target and $75 to the acquirer. Consequently, a transaction in this range will, on average, be profitable to both parties."

Now consider the solution. If the acquirer offers any positive value, $X, and the target accepts, the current value of the company is worth anywhere between $0 and $X. As the problem is formulated, any value in that range is equally likely. Therefore, the expected value of the offer is equal to $X / 2. Since the company is worth 50 percent more to the acquirer, the acquirer's expected value is 1.5($X / 2), which equals only 75 percent of the offer price. Thus, on the average, the acquirer obtains a company worth 25 percent less than the price it pays when an offer is accepted. In other words, for any value of $X, the potential acquirer's best strategy would be not to make any offer ($0 per share).

The paradox of the situation, of course, is that even though the firm is worth more to the acquirer than to the target, any offer above $0 leads to a negative expected return to the acquirer. *The source of this paradox lies in the high likelihood that the target will accept the acquirer's offer when the firm is least valuable to the acquirer—i.e., when it is a "lemon"* (Akerlof 1970). As a result, the "winning" bidder, on average, loses money: it suffers the "winner's curse."

The correct answer to this problem is so counterintuitive that it has proved to be amazingly robust across a wide variety of subject populations, including many that have unique analytical and experiential characteristics that could have helped them (Samuelson and Bazerman 1985; Bazerman and Carroll 1987). In addition, this finding has been extended to contexts in which subjects were paid according to their performance and allowed multiple trials to learn the correct response (Ball, Bazerman, and Carroll 1991). Overall, a set of findings emerged that documented the winner's curse in the acquiring-a-company problem in virtually every experimental context suggested to the experimenters.

In light of these robust findings, it is noteworthy to examine the impact of relationships and face-to-face discussion. Valley, Moag, and Bazerman (1992) specifically examined whether the existence of a relationship between the parties in a face-to-face negotiation would protect the less informed party from the dysfunctional consequences of the winner's curse. They rewrote the acquiring-a-company problem into buyer and seller roles. The buyers were told the basic information in the earlier version, including the fact that the target company would be worth 50 percent more to them than to the sellers. The sellers were told the structure of the problem and the true value of the firm to them (randomly determined between $0 and $100), but they were not told the degree to which the value of the firm to the buyer would exceed its value to them. The parties were then allowed to negotiate an acquisition price of the firm. All parties were told that their objective was to make as much money as they could.

Dyads were assigned to one of two relationship conditions. In study 1, one condition included Kellogg MBA dyads who knew each other very well (strong relationship condition)—using converging network methodologies to assess relationships (Valley 1992). The other condition included Kellogg MBA dyads who did not know each other (weak relationship condition). It was predicted that the strong relationship condition would help eliminate the dysfunctional aspects of the winner's curse to the less informed party. The results of the study did not confirm this prediction: the vast majority of dyads in both conditions reached agreements that were mutually beneficial for both parties. This mutually beneficial outcome occurred because the sellers did not take advantage of their information advantage. Generally, information was openly and honestly shared, and this information sharing eliminated the winner's curse. Again, it is important to emphasize that this occurred in both the weak and strong relationship condition. Valley et al. (1992) offered the tentative conclusion that most members of a common subculture will not directly lie to their counterparts—the implications for future interactions in that subculture, beyond the experiment, are too high.

Valley et al. (1992) next manipulated relationship by assigning MBA dyads to either a within-school dyad (two University of Chicago MBA students or two Kellogg MBA students negotiating with each other) or a between-school dyad (a University of Chicago MBA student negotiating with a Kellogg MBA student). All discussions were conducted by phone, with both members calling in their results separately to a telephone answering machine. The expectation was that the relationship formed by group membership would solve the winner's curse in the within-school dyads, but that the curse would exist, and barriers to trade would exist, in the between-school dyads. But this expectation once again proved to be wrong. Again, the vast majority of dyads in both conditions reached agreements that were mutually beneficial for both parties. The evidence pointed to the argument that even highly competitive MBA students could solve the dyadic winner's curse by simply talking to each other.

In a third study, Valley et al. (1992) manipulated whether the communication between Kellogg MBA dyads was face-to-face or in writing. In both conditions, the communication time was ample and the volume of communication unlimited. The face-to-face dyads continued to solve the winner's curse. However, in the written form, the winner's curse re-emerged with many buyers losing money, and many more impasses occurring. It appears that face-to-face dialogue was required to create the personal relationship necessary to eliminate the winner's curse and reach mutually beneficial agreements.

Integrativeness of agreements. Research in negotiation has revealed many ways by which negotiators can increase their chances of maximizing individual and dyadic utility (Northcraft and Neale 1990). Many of these studies, however, have considered negotiators who have had no previous relationships and anticipate no future ones (Thompson 1990). In contrast, many negotiations take place between parties with a history of exchange and expectations of future interactions.

The few studies that consider the ways in which the relationship between the parties affects the process and outcome of negotiation use friendship or romantic involvement as their relationship variable (Fry, Firestone, and Williams 1983; Schoeninger and Wood 1969; Thompson and DeHarpport 1990). Even within this limited scope and these few studies, there have been inconsistencies. Schoeninger and Wood (1969) compared the negotiating process and outcomes of married couples to a control group of uninvolved mixed-sex couples. They found that married couples made lower offers and took less time to reach agreement. Husband and wives, more willing to incur losses or accept minimum agreements, attained lower joint outcomes. Similarly, Fry et al. (1983) found that romantically involved couples had lower aspirations, generated fewer integrative offers, were less inclined to use pressure tactics, and settled on outcomes with lower joint utility than did stranger couples.

However, romantic ties are not the norm with organizational relationships. Thompson and DeHarpport (1990) examined the effects of long-term relationships in a negotiation using friendship as the relationship focus. They found that individuals bargaining with friends tended to reach more mutually beneficial agreements. In other aspects of the negotiation, they found few other differences that could be attributed to relationships.

Pruitt (1983) suggested that an ongoing or potential relationship was a major requirement for parties to reach integrative agreements. However, if parties did not have high aspirations as well, the likely outcome would be highly cooperative but Pareto-inefficient outcomes. These two requirements for integrative agreements may well explain why negotiators who are romantically involved do poorly while friends do well. If individuals have as their primary goal the maintenance of the relationship, it is likely that they will not view reaching the best possible agreement as consistent with their relationship goals. This is especially likely as most novice negotiators view bargaining as an adversarial process (Bazerman and Neale 1983). Conveying what may be interpreted as a lack of trust in the other party by attempting to negotiate may send a message with which neither party is comfortable. However, in the context of a more collegial relationship, the parties may believe the relationship to be important *and* at the same time have high achievement aspirations in the negotiation.

Valley and Neale (1992) set out to test these differences by extending the work of Thompson and DeHarpport (1990). They used a network methodology to measure the strength of the relationship between the subjects. With this methodology, they were able to assess the strength of the relationship between parties and assign negotiating opponents based on that measurement. Subjects in this study were first-year master's of management students who participated in this negotiation as part of ongoing classroom activities.

Prior to the negotiation, individuals completed a sociogram and a questionnaire about their relationships within the class. Based on this assessment, half of the negotiating dyads were composed of close friends while the other half were mere acquaintances. Once assignments were made, dyads were given the role information to conduct a multi-issue negotiation with integrative potential. Upon reaching agreement, the dyads completed a postnegotiation questionnaire, exploring the participants' perceptions of the way in which each party had negotiated. Thus, data were collected on the outcomes the dyads achieved as well as self-reports of the subjects. Analysis of the data indicated, as predicted, that friends negotiated outcomes that were more integrative than did acquaintances. Unlike the studies that used married or romantically involved couples, these results suggest that collegial types of relationships may enhance the parties' ability to reach high-quality agreements.

The results of this study, combined with the results of previous research, suggest that relationships between the parties can have a significant impact on negotiator performance. These results suggest that when there is no relationship between the parties or an extremely close relationship between the parties, negotiator performance suffers. When parties have more of a collegial relationship they seem more able to combine the benefits of the relationship in terms of trust and information exchange with the high achievement expectations necessary to reach integrative agreements. Those with no relationships have no basis for trust and thus are likely to behave more competitively. Those with too close a relationship are likely to value the relationship significantly more highly than the outcomes that could be achieved within the context of the negotiation.

SUMMARY AND CONCLUSIONS

Behavioral decision theory has provided a number of breakthrough discoveries, and has fueled new research approaches across a wide variety of applications (Tversky and Kahneman 1974, 1981; Kahneman and Tversky 1979, 1982; Dawes 1988; Gilovich 1991). In our own work, the research approach and values of this literature have enabled us to identify a large set of systematic mistakes that are made by negotiators. This chapter has provided an opportunity to extend this list by focusing on the unique role of fairness concerns and relationships in a judgmental perspective to negotiation.

Specifically, this chapter has examined the impact of fairness in creating barriers to agreements. We have illustrated that fairness concerns are often the cause of impasses, even when the parties would be better off by reaching an agreement. However, fairness is not a unitary concept and, as such, it may be difficult for parties to ascertain the fairness norm used by their opponents. Even more problematic is the notion that the norms of fairness may change based on the type of opponent or the relative position of the parties.

We have also provided evidence to suggest that an important component in the evaluation of the fairness of a negotiation is the relationship between the parties. In fact, the relationship between the parties can serve as either an additional barrier to agreement or a means of enhancing both the likelihood and quality of agreements. The primary conclusion that we draw from the work presented here is that a cognitive perspective of negotiators must add issues of fairness and relationship to the equation in predicting negotiator behaviors and negotiation outcomes. Such concerns provide the lens through which information is evaluated and preferences determined. As a result, these interpersonal factors may lead to enhancing agreements or exacerbating the barriers to high-quality negotiated outcomes.

PART THREE

Strategic and Analytical Perspectives

CHAPTER SIX

Strategic and Informational Barriers to Negotiation

Robert B. Wilson

M any of the difficulties encountered in negotiating settlements of disputes stem from practical considerations. Often these difficulties can be eased by altering the context or procedures or by helping participants to appreciate the advantages of a cooperative resolution of conflict. In recent years, however, the literature of economics and game theory has identified a fundamental barrier to negotiation that stems from differences in information between participants. The purpose of this chapter is to review the theoretical basis for this prediction and to assess some implications for practical affairs. We also outline how theory suggests the design of procedural innovations to minimize the inefficiencies caused by informational disparities. The exposition relies on hypothetical examples in a legal context of negotiations between litigants prior to a trial, and in an arbitration context of wage negotiations between an employer and an employee. We begin with an explanation of the basic problem described by George Akerlof (1970).

1. AKERLOF'S EXAMPLE

Akerlof studied what he called the market for "lemons," namely, used cars. He made the plausible assumption that a seller's information about her car's quality (durability, reliability, etc.) is superior to the buyer's information in ways that the buyer cannot overcome by inspection or testing. Further, a seller cannot warranty quality due to "moral hazard"; that is, the subsequent performance of the car will depend on both its intrinsic quality and its use and care by the buyer, which is too expensive to monitor. In this circumstance, the buyer encounters the dilemma that any price he might propose or accept would be unacceptable to owners of high-quality cars but might be proposed or accepted by those owners with low-quality cars. Indeed, there may be no price low enough so that the average quality of the cars offered by owners justifies payment of that price.

This scenario is a paradigm of how negotiations can fail even when both parties know beforehand that the gain from trade is positive. For instance, suppose each car's quality is represented by an index q such that $0 < q < 1$ and q is uniformly distributed in the population of cars. If, say, the value to the buyer is $3q$, and to the seller it is $2q$, then the gain from trade is $3q - 2q = q$, which is surely positive, although only the seller knows its magnitude. At any price p the average quality among those owners willing to sell (those for whom $p > 2q$) is $q(p) = p/4$ and so the buyer would be willing to pay at most $3q(p) = \frac{3}{4}p$, which is less than p. Thus, no price attracts a sufficiently high quality on average to justify its payment by the buyer, and the gain from trade goes unrealized. The possibility of an agreement is thwarted by the buyer's apprehension that the division of the gain from trade will be to his disadvantage; in particular, he is likely to pay a price that exceeds his valuation of the quality obtained.

This pessimistic conclusion is not always necessary. For instance, it might be that the seller can provide credible assurance that her car's quality is better than average, say $q > \frac{1}{2}$. In this case the average quality is $\frac{3}{4}$ and both parties profit from any price in the range $2 < p < 2.25$, so a deal is feasible. A variety of other devices might be possible to ease the buyer's apprehension, such as a process of "discovery" to reveal the seller's records of maintenance and repair, or a partial warranty to share the risk of inferior quality; or it might be that as a continuing business the seller benefits from a reputation for truthful revelation of the qualities of the cars offered for sale. Another possibility is regulation that imposes on the seller either strict liability or a minimal quality standard (like $q > \frac{1}{2}$ above). However, we adhere below to the original scenario, which presents starkly the impediment posed by informational asymmetries between the parties.

The generality of Akerlof's analysis can be seen using methods devised by Roger Myerson and Mark Satterthwaite (1983). They represent the outcome of negotiations by a probability $s(q)$ that the parties settle on a trade and an expected payment $r(q)$, both conditional on the true quality q. Thus, if the seller's valuation is $u(q)$ and the buyer's is $v(q)$ then their expected net gains are $U(q) = r(q) - s(q)u(q)$ and $V(q) = s(q)v(q) - r(q)$ respectively. But one must recognize also that the seller could dissimulate by imitating a seller with the quality $\hat{q}$. One can account for this possibility of strategic behavior by providing incentives sufficient to ensure that the maximum $U(q) = \max_{\hat{q}} r(\hat{q}) - s(\hat{q})u(q)$ is achieved at $\hat{q} = q$. This condition implies the properties:

$$U'(q) = -s(q)u'(q)$$

by the envelope theorem,

$$\int_0^1 U(q)dq = U(1) + \int_0^1 s(q)u'(q)q\,dg$$

via integration by parts,

$$\int_0^1 V(q)dq = -U(1) + \int_0^1 s(q)\{v(q) - [u(q) + qu'(q)]\}dq.$$

The last line indicates that if the seller's expected net gain is to be nonnegative (at least $U(1) \geq 0$), then the most the buyer can get is obtained by trading (i.e., *s(q) > 0) only when* $v(q) \geq u(q) + qu'(q)$. In Akerlof's example, however, $v(q) = 3q$ and $u(q) + qu'(q) = 4q$, so this condition for profitable trading cannot be satisfied. Consequently, the only strategy that enables the buyer to obtain a nonnegative net gain is to refuse trade entirely: $s(q) = 0$. This strategy is optimal for the buyer even if he knows that the actual gain from trade $v(q) - u(q)$ is positive. The difficulty is that the seller's incentive to state an inflated report of the car's quality creates a risk that the buyer will pay more than the car is worth to him. Or, one can say that the cost of providing sufficient incentives to induce the seller to report truthfully exceeds the gain from trade: in Akerlof's example this cost is $qu'(q) = 2q$, whereas the gain from trade is only q.

One wonders whether the dilemma posed above is relevant in practice. After all, a mediator could suggest to the seller that the possibility of deception destroys the prospect of trading with the buyer, whereas a commitment to truthfulness would be more profitable since then they could agree on a price that splits the gains from trade. A central issue, therefore, is whether commitment to truthfulness and cooperative behavior is credible when there are no exogenous sanctions. The primary example of endogenous sanctions occurs in repeated negotiations where reputational effects enable a strategy of truthful reporting to be credible. Suppose the parties engage repeatedly in similar negotiations and after each one the buyer observes the actual quality of the item purchased. There is an equilibrium of this game in which the buyer accepts the seller's report of the quality and makes a purchase only if the previous quality received was as high as the seller reported. In response to this strategy of the buyer, an optimal strategy for the seller is to report truthfully—though she must accept a lower price after every inflated report. Nevertheless, to keep the focus on fundamental impediments to negotiation, I will consider only an isolated negotiation that precludes reputational effects. In this context, the buyer cannot rely on the seller to provide truthful reports.

The analysis of Akerlof's example depends on a special economic and informational structure. To extend its implications to negotiations in other contexts, in the next sections we examine simple models of pretrial negotiations and wage negotiations.

Robert Mnookin and Lewis Kornhauser (1979) emphasize that in legal contexts negotiations between litigants are conducted "in the shadow of the law." The plaintiff and defendant know that if they fail to agree on a settlement, and the plaintiff pursues the suit, then the dispute will be resolved by a trial. Moreover, in most cases they or their attorneys have similar expectations about the outcome of the trial. This being the case, their shared gain from settling privately is simply the saving in subsequent costs of litigation, about which also they have similar expectations. The matter therefore reduces to agreeing on a settlement that splits this known gain between them. Because there are no substantial informational disparities, obstacles of the sort in Akerlof's example are absent and one expects that most suits will settle without a trial. This prediction seems to be verified by the evidence that most civil cases in the U.S. are settled without trials. This conclusion is reinforced by the strong legal tradition ensuring that statutes, precedents, evidentiary rules, and trial procedures provide litigants with relatively clear indications about what they can expect if they resort to a trial. Moreover, it explains in part the key role of pretrial discovery to reduce informational differences between the parties and thereby promote settlements.

On the other hand, this same line of reasoning suggests that informational differences between the parties could partly explain why a minority of cases proceed to trial. In particular, one anticipates that the fraction who settle should diminish as the disparity of their predictions about trial outcomes increases. To illustrate this proposition, consider the following simple model. Suppose that the trial outcome will be a judgment that awards an amount v to the plaintiff from the defendant; in addition, each party must pay an expected cost c for the trial. Thus, the plaintiff gets the amount p of the settlement or (assuming she brings the suit to trial) the amount $v - c$ of the judgment net of her trial cost; and the defendant pays either p or $v + c$. One can think of v as the value of a zero-sum game between the parties; thus it can be the net result of elaborate strategies pursued before and during the trial. If the parties' payoffs are measured relative to the trial outcome, then this structure corresponds to the plaintiff's being the seller of a suit worth $v - c$ and the defendant's being a buyer for whom a pretrial settlement is worth $v + c$. To allow for informational differences, suppose that neither party knows the judgment beforehand, but their attorneys privately provide estimates x and y to their respective clients. All other data are known to both parties; in particular, both know the precision of the attorneys' estimates, and they know that their joint gain from settling is the trial cost $2c$.

Our aim is to show that the proportion of settlements declines as the precision of the attorneys' estimates declines. To make this relationship precise, suppose that (v,x,y) has a joint normal distribution such that each estimate is an unbiased estimator of the judgment with the conditional variance $\frac{1}{2}\sigma^2$, and the marginal variance of the judgment is so large as to make prior information insignificant compared to the attorneys' estimates. The procedural rules of the negotiations may also matter, but to capture the main effects it suffices to study the procedure that achieves the maximum expectation of the realized gains from trade were the parties' information independent, as in the case of a seller and a buyer with independent valuations; cf. Kennan and Wilson 1993. This procedure has them settle whenever $x \leq y - \sigma\delta$, where δ is a parameter, possibly negative, that varies directly with the standardized cost ratio $2c / \sigma$.[1] Highly precise estimation corresponds to a small σ, a large standardized cost, a small δ, and a large fraction settling.

This procedure can be implemented in various ways. A mediator might use the scheme in which the parties report their estimates and then settle for $p = \frac{1}{2}[x+y]$ if $x \leq y - \sigma\delta$. Alternatively, the parties could directly propose settlements X and Y and then settle for $p = \frac{1}{2}[X + Y]$ if $X \leq Y$. For the mediation scheme the construction of the parameter δ is designed to ensure that truthful reporting is optimal for each party given the hypothesis that the other will be truthful. But this works also for the direct proposal scheme since in that case their optimal strategies are to propose $X = x + \frac{1}{2}\sigma\delta$ and $Y = y - \frac{1}{2}\sigma\delta$, from which it follows that they settle under the same circumstances as in the mediation scheme. In either scheme, the settlement p is the conditional expectation of the judgment given *both* parties' estimates. Observe, however, that in the latter scheme each party's proposal differs from his / her estimate: this difference represents an optimal exploitation of his / her informational advantage. These differences also appear in the mediation scheme as the imputed cost of providing sufficient incentives to induce truthful reporting. In either interpretation, litigants do not settle if the plaintiff's estimate of the trial judgment is sufficiently larger than the defendant's estimate.

The features of this model are indicative of conclusions derived from other formulations. Unlike the extreme represented by Akerlof's example, in which no settlements are possible, in this model settlements are possible, and if the estimating precision is high then most suits settle without trials. In most models the optimal procedure resembles an auction, like the one above. In practice, however, one expects negotiations to proceed over time via a series of offers and counteroffers. This reflects again an inability to commit: while the gain from settlement remains unrealized, the parties have incentives to continue negotiations. However, if delay is not costly then there is no motive to settle early, so offers need not be serious and progress

---

[1]The parameter δ solves the equation $[1 - F(\delta)] / f(\delta) = 2c / \sigma$ using the standard normal distribution function F and its density f. The fraction of cases that settle is $1 - F(\delta)$.

may be deferred until the trial is imminent. If delay is costly then continual negotiation can increase the fraction of cases that eventually settle because the implicit exchange of information signaled by serious offers reduces the informational differences between the parties. But this increase in the gains realized is partially or entirely offset by costs of delay incurred along the way.

Discovery procedures pose a peculiar dilemma. They contribute to an equalized evidentiary basis for the trial, and before the trial they can narrow the informational gap and promote settlements; even the prospect of costly discovery can encourage early settlement. On the other hand, to the extent they impose costs on the other party they can enable a war of attrition; and they pose an agency problem if an attorney sees that his provision of an accurate estimate of the judgment can be made contingent on payment of the fees required to conduct discovery. That is, attorneys need not have incentives to balance the cost of discovery against the client's benefit from improved prospects of settling without incurring the costs of a trial. This is the familiar problem of the physician who prescribes and also provides treatment to a patient: the patient lacks the expert knowledge required to assess whether the benefits and costs of the treatment mode have been optimized.

Some observations can also be made at the level of the design of the judiciary system. Models of this kind make specific predictions about "bargaining in the shadow of the law." To the extent that trial outcomes are so predictable that attorneys' estimates are unlikely to differ greatly, most suits can be settled privately for the expectation of the judgment and little reliance on the courts will be required. But this prediction reflects a subtle equilibrium of supply and demand reflected in the standardized cost ratio $2c/\sigma$ introduced above. If standardized trial costs decline then fewer cases settle, more cases require adjudication, the demand for attorneys' services in trials increases, and then (to the extent legal services are supplied inelastically) attorneys' fees increase, and the cost of trials increases. To the extent this scenario is accurate, therefore, the settlement rate is also dependent on an equilibrium in the market for attorneys' services. The demand function for trials is derived from the fraction of cases that do not settle (as a function of the "price" $2c$ of trials) and the equilibrium price is determined by the intersection of this demand curve with an exogenous supply function for attorneys' services. Greater precision in estimating trial outcomes can shift downward the demand for trials, but all or part of the predicted reduction in the number of trials might be offset by the effects of the resulting decline in attorneys' fees and trial costs. In the extreme case that attorneys' services are supplied inelastically in the short term, the immediate effect is entirely a reduction in fees with no reduction in the number of trials. Similarly, an exogenous increase in the supply of attorneys reduces their fees in the market equilibrium and thereby stimulates demand for trials that use their services. Even in advising an individual client, an attorney might have an incentive to understate the precision of his estimate if that would increase the chance that his services would be needed for discovery and / or a trial. These features indicate that implicit in the sort of model described above is a host of problems about the principal / agent relationship between the client and the attorney, and about the nature of the market for legal services.

3. FINAL-OFFER ARBITRATION

The model above implies that the settlement rate varies directly with the ratio of the trial cost to the standard deviation of estimates of the judgment. This conclusion applies equally to quasi-judicial contexts such as private judging and arbitration where an impasse is ultimately resolved by the decision of a third party. The standardized cost ratio may differ from the norm represented by legal adjudication but the logic that predicts the settlement rate is not altered materially. For instance, it may be that compared to a legal trial, arbitration costs less and the judgment is less predictable so that fewer cases settle: the social cost could still be less because the product of the cost and frequency of "trials" is smaller.

An exception is final-offer arbitration, in which the judge or arbitrator is constrained to choose between proposals submitted by the two parties. As the default outcome when negotiations reach an impasse, final-offer arbitration differs materially from judicial determination of the judgment. It seems fundamental to legally sanctioned judicial procedures that the judgment is independent of the prior history of negotiations: the defendant's liability is measured according to exogenous standards (e.g., established by statute) that take no account of the parties' efforts and offers to settle the dispute. This is less true of ordinary arbitration, and indeed it is rare that an arbitrator's decision lies outside the range of the parties' offers, but the principle remains that the arbitrator is essentially unconstrained by prior negotiations and relies on the history of prior offers only for informational purposes. The novel feature of final-offer arbitration is that the set of possible outcomes is chosen endogenously by the participants via their submissions of "final offers." One expects, moreover, that these offers influence the arbitrator's choice between them. Thus the above model of litigation does not describe final-offer arbitration. We describe in this section how the previous results extend to this procedure. (Our results differ significantly from those derived by Samuelson [1991], who assumes that each party's private information is statistically independent of the other's.)

Final-offer arbitration is mostly confined to wage negotiations, so we cast the data within that interpretation. The plaintiff or seller is a worker whose wage p is negotiated with the buyer or employer. As before, let x and y be the seller's and the buyer's private estimates of the value v of the worker's future profit contribution, which is not observed directly. In addition, to take account of possible overlap in the data on which their estimates are based, we allow that conditional on v the correlation between any two estimates is ρ, which could be positive or negative.

To stay close to the previous model, suppose again that based on their respective estimates the parties negotiate by proposing X and Y, and they settle for the wage $p = \frac{1}{2}[X + Y]$ if $X < Y$. The novel feature is that if they fail to settle then an arbitrator chooses either X or Y. Several models of the arbitrator's decision process are possible. Here we simply suppose that the evidence elicited in the arbitration hearing provides the arbitrator with the parties' estimates x and y and also a further estimate z from which he can construct the conditional expectation of the worker's contribution given the three estimates. The arbitrator then selects whichever proposal is closer to this conditional expectation.

One possibility is that the arbitrator's estimate z has the same precision as the parties' estimates. In this case the parties' optimal proposals are $X = x + \frac{1}{2}\delta r\sigma$ and $Y = y - \frac{1}{2}\delta r\sigma$, where $r^2 = 1 - \rho$ and again δ is a parameter that depends on the standardized cost ratio.[2] Another is the extreme possibility that the arbitrator's estimate is perfect: the same result holds in this case except that the parameter is constructed slightly differently.[3] In either version, among those cases arbitrated, each party wins half and the expected wage is the conditional expectation of the worker's contribution.

Comparing these results with the previous model of legal adjudication reveals slight differences. The basic conclusion remains that the fraction of cases that settle is large only if the gain from settlement is large relative to the standard error of the parties' estimates of the consequences of a trial or hearing. In this sense, the obstacle to settlement caused by informational disparities appears unaffected by procedural innovations such as final-offer arbitration. This conclusion is premature, however, and next we show how the settlement rate can be improved by altering the arbitration procedure.

Penalties and Rewards to Improve the Settlement Rate

The seller's (and symmetrically the buyer's) calculation of an optimal proposal represents a balance between two considerations. Increasing the seller's proposal by \$1 produces a gain of 50 cents if they settle and \$1 if they don't settle and she wins the judgment. Against this benefit she counts the increased probability that they won't settle and the other party will win

---

[2] If $R^2 = 6r^2/[1 + r^2]$ then $2R\delta f(0) + [2c/r\sigma]f(\delta) + F(\delta) = 2$. The fraction of cases that settle without a hearing is $1 - F(\delta)$.

[3] The difference is that one uses $R^2 = r^2/[2 - r^2]$.

the judgment. This calculation can be manipulated in the following way to increase the likelihood of settlement. Suppose that instead of choosing between the parties' final offers X and Y the arbitrator chooses between $X+d$ and $Y-d$, where d is a specified parameter. Faced with this arbitration rule, the seller's calculation is exactly the same, except that now she sees that in the event that the $1 increase switches the outcome from settlement to the other's winning the judgment the switch loses $\frac{1}{2}[X+Y]$ from settling and gains $(Y-d)-c$ from arbitration: because $X \approx Y$ in this event, the net cost of the switch is approximately $c+d$.[4] Thus, if the parameter d is positive then this procedural change simulates the effect of inflating the cost of the arbitration hearing from c to $c+d$, and the result is that a greater fraction of cases settle without arbitration.

This procedural change has no distributional consequences: it is still true that they settle for the conditional expectation of the judgment; failing settlement they each have a fifty-fifty chance of winning the judgment; and the expectation of the settlement is the conditional expectation of the worker's contribution. The difference is that the enforced magnification of the disparity between the options from which the arbitrator chooses encourages the parties to settle for the expectation of the judgment rather than risk the prospect of an unfavorable outcome.

Fundamentally this is always the goal of measures designed to increase settlements and discourage reliance on judicial resolution of disputes. Final-offer arbitration is peculiar in that it provides a ready means of accomplishing this objective because it allows the arbitration process to be linked to the negotiation process. In the trading context studied in section 1, failure to settle yields "no trade" as the default outcome; and in the legal context studied in section 2, failure to settle yields the decision of a judge or jury. Arbitration differs from these only in that one can alter the implicit property rights of the parties by penalizing the loser and rewarding the winner by the amount d. This is consonant with the practice of final-offer arbitration because it is usually invoked in compliance with a clause of an employment contract previously negotiated between the parties. The insertion of penalty and reward provisions into such a contract could be justified on the grounds that it reduces the expected frequency and costs of arbitration.

Penalty provisions cannot be added arbitrarily to judicial procedures in legal contexts without infringing on the parties' constitutional rights to a judge's or jury's verdict on the merits of the suit. There are notable excep-

---

[4]The parameter d also affects the other part of her calculation, which is the switch from winning to losing the judgment, conditional on not settling. Consequently, having d positive is not exactly the same overall as using the cost $c+d$. The settlement rate is $1-F(\delta)$ where $2R[\delta+2d/r\sigma]f(0)+[2(c+d)/r\sigma]f(\delta)+F(\delta)=2$.

tions allowed by statutes, such as triple damages in civil antitrust actions and punitive awards in some other types of cases; also, the legal requirement that the defendant must be found "guilty" or liable before damages can be assessed works partially as a penalty against the plaintiff. However, in legal contexts I see no systematic design of penalties and rewards to encourage pretrial settlements. Penalties and rewards may encourage settlements but they are justified by other considerations; in particular they are not linked to the history of negotiations.

One should note that the analysis relies on the supposition that the arbitrator chooses between true final offers; that is, each party has the prior option to accept the other's submission to the arbitrator. The inducement to settle does not rely on a presumption that either party is risk averse, although aversion to risk could enhance the motive to accept the sure amount of the settlement. In practice there are practical limits to the magnitude of the parameter d, and therefore also the settlement rate, because the liability of the defendant is bounded below by the prospect of bankruptcy, and large rewards for successful plaintiffs attract nuisance suits.

A possible application of these ideas is to the interpretation of the data on final-offer arbitration of the salaries of baseball players. About half the negotiations result in filings of "final offers" for arbitration hearings, but the majority of these disputes settle in the weeks between the filing deadline and the hearings. Thus, it appears that the parties' last "final offers" are closer and enable more settlements than the earlier "final offers" filed for the hearings. This scenario fits the formulation above except that it is the distinction between the offers filed relatively early in the negotiations (in January), which tend to be further apart, and the last offers made at the conclusion of negotiations (in February, "on the courthouse steps" or the hallway of the hearing room), that one interprets as accounting for the high settlement rate. From this perspective it seems evident that after the "final offers" are filed each party perceives that settling now for the expected outcome of the hearing is as good (actually better because hearings are costly) as proceeding with the hearing, since there is no further opportunity to affect the data and options considered by the arbitrator.

4. SUMMARY REMARKS

The three sections of this chapter examine simple models of negotiation in the three contexts of economic exchange, litigation, and final-offer arbitration. In the first of these, Akerlof's example suggests that informational disparities can thwart negotiations entirely. This result depends on a particular economic structure and asymmetric information, but less restrictive models support the conclusion that differences in information can prevent settlements. Or, such differences can require costly delays as each party tries to exploit his or her private information or to communicate it credibly via the offers he or she makes. A strike between a union and a firm is a typical example of costly delay caused by, say, the union's uncertainty about the firm's valuation of labor's contribution; cf. Kennan and Wilson 1989. In these situations, one party's uncertainty about the gain from trade is sufficient to prevent or impede a quick and efficient settlement.

The model used to represent litigation is substantially simpler in that the gain from pretrial settlement is assumed known to both parties and consists only of the avoided cost of a trial. Informational disparities are represented in this context by differing estimates about the judgment resulting from a trial. The fraction of cases that settle without a trial is explained mainly by the magnitude of the trial cost compared to the precision of the estimates. Thus the results are not so bleak as those obtained from Akerlof's example, and indeed the model predicts that if litigants "bargain in the shadow of the law" with relatively precise estimates of trial judgments then most cases will settle without recourse to trials.

The model of arbitration shows that this conclusion is not altered by the procedural innovation of constraining the judge or arbitrator to choose between the parties' final offers. On the other hand, it is changed substantially if the procedure can be amended to allow penalties and rewards for losers and winners. In principle, it seems, amendments of this sort can induce all cases to settle for the expectation of the arbitrated outcome. Punitive provisions alter fundamentally the participants' implicit property rights, but there is some evidence of their use in statutory provisions of the law. And, in the context of wage determination where final-offer arbitration is commonly used, the punitive provisions themselves could be negotiated as clauses of long-term employment contracts.

In sum, the analyses of these three examples indicate that (1) the economic and informational structure can impede negotiations, (2) the incidence and magnitude of these effects depend sensitively on the structural features, and (3) measures that invoke supplementary penalties and rewards linked to the negotiation process can overcome these impediments and encourage negotiators to settle for the expectation of the default outcome. In a larger sense, if promoting settlement is socially efficient then its implementation is designed mainly to induce disputants to accept a sure thing now rather than pursue the costly and risky consequences of an impasse. Because the two parties have differing private information, each can expect to gain from a trial or arbitration, even if it is costly to pursue and they both know a priori that ultimately the outcome is zero-sum—so one party must be mistaken. Constructive use of supplementary penalties and rewards can deflate these divergent expectations and thereby encourage settlement.

CHAPTER SEVEN

On the Interpretation of Two Theoretical Models of Bargaining

Ariel Rubinstein

INTRODUCTION

*T*his chapter is devoted to a discussion of the interpretation of two game-theoretic models of bargaining: Nash's bargaining model and the alternating offers model. The standard image of the ideal game-theoretic model of bargaining is one which gives a clear prediction of the outcome in a wide range of bargaining situations (i.e., situations in which there exists a common interest to reach an agreement and a conflict of interest as to its content). Personally, I have never understood how a game-theoretic model of bargaining, even when it attains a "clear-cut result," can be viewed as a functional prediction of a bargaining outcome in a specific scenario; neither have I ever understood how such a model can provide a bargainer with tips on how to bargain. Therefore, I believe that theoretical models of bargaining need better justification and interpretation.

The need to interpret bargaining models is no different from the need to interpret other models in game theory, where questions and doubts are raised. One expects the theory to provide useful tools for achieving concrete goals, testable predictions of the outcomes of game situations, and even tips on how to play games. But the predictions offered by game theory are not comparable to those offered by the natural sciences; nor do they provide advice on how to play games. The usefulness of game theory is therefore questioned.

Bargaining theory is a convenient test case for this inquiry since in contrast

Numerous discussions with friends inspired me to the ideas included in this paper. I would especially like to thank Asher Wolinsky, who forced me to provide response to his perpetual questioning of my approach, and Hugo Sonnenschein, whose criticism of the alternating offers model in his presidential address to the Econometric Society presented me with a challenge I cheerfully accepted. I am also grateful to Peter Barsoon, Zvika Safra and Bob Wilson for their very helpful comments.

to most other areas of game theory, it provides several models that produce clear predictions. This allows us to focus on the content of the prediction rather than on the interpretation of its indeterminacy.

The approach taken in this paper takes the criterion for a bargaining resolution to be its being protected against certain types of objections which have simple and intuitive verbal meanings. In this respect, the approach here is close to that of cooperative game theory. The paper aims at provoking a shift of interest from the functional forms of the solution concepts to the verbal forms of the objections.

First, let us review Nash's model, the most fundamental and important model in bargaining theory.

NASH'S BARGAINING SOLUTION: A REVIEW

Nash's bargaining solution is a theory which looks for a sharp prediction of the bargaining outcome based on the bargainers' preferences defined over the set of possible agreements and their attitudes toward risk. The theory is organized around two concepts: the *bargaining problem* and the *bargaining solution*. The description of a Nash bargaining problem includes the elements which are conceived by Nash's theory to be relevant: a set of feasible agreements, an event called "disagreement," the preferences held by the bargainers, and their attitudes toward risk.

According to Nash, "risk" appears in bargaining theory through the possibility of a breakdown in negotiations. Therefore, preferences are taken to be those over the set of lotteries whose "certain prizes" are the agreements and the disagreement event.

Formally, a *Nash bargaining problem* is defined as a four-tuple $<X,D,\succsim_1,\succsim_2>$, where X is a set of feasible alternatives, D is the disagreement event, and $\succsim_1$ and $\succsim_2$ are preferences defined in the space of lotteries in which the prizes are the elements in $X \cup D$.

The above definition of the Nash bargaining problem (see Rubinstein, Safra and Thomson 1992) is different from the conventional presentation of his bargaining theory (see Nash 1950), which defines a bargaining problem in its "reduced form," $<S,d>$ where S is a set of pairs of numbers and d is a specified element in S. Any element in S is thought of as a pair of *von Neumann-Morgenstern utilities* derived from some feasible agreement. Formally, the condensed model is derived from the more detailed model through the representation of the preferences by their VNM utility functions, u_1 and u_2, and by taking $S = \{(u_1(x),u_2(x)) \mid x \in X\}$, the set of all pairs of utilities which can be derived from the elements in X, taking $d = (u_1(D), u_2(D))$. Implicit in this identification is the assumption that nothing in the physical description of the set of agreements is relevant to the bargaining outcome. A certain pair $<S,d>$ can be derived from *many* different quadruples $<X,D,\gtrsim_1,\gtrsim_2>$. In particular, Nash's space of problems $<S,d>$ is spanned either by varying preferences over a fixed set of alternatives or by keeping preferences on a universe of possible alternatives fixed, but varying the set of alternatives. Nash's hidden assumption is that all problems that produce the same pair $<S,d>$ have the same payoff vector outcome.

Nash's theory imposes some restrictions on what is a "bargaining problem." To avoid degeneracy, it is required that there is at least one agreement which Pareto-dominates the disagreement event. Since the agreements differ only through preferences, any two agreements for which the two players are indifferent are indistinguishable; it is thus convenient to assume that there are no such pairs of agreements. The set X is assumed to be compact and the preferences are continuous. Most importantly, it is assumed that a bargaining problem is convex in the sense that for all $x,y \epsilon X$ and for all $\alpha \epsilon [0,1]$ there is $z \epsilon X$ such that both players are indifferent between z and $\alpha \cdot x + (1-\alpha) \cdot y$, the lottery which gives x with probability α and y with probability $1-\alpha$. Denote by $\alpha \cdot x$ the lottery which gives x with probability α and gives the disagreement event D with probability $1-\alpha$, i.e., $\alpha \cdot x = \alpha \cdot x + (1-\alpha) \cdot D$.

The second central concept in Nash's theory is that of a "bargaining solution." A *bargaining solution* is a *function* which assigns a *unique* agreement to every bargaining problem. Thus, a bargaining solution tries to give a prediction of the bargaining outcome to each of the problems in its domain.

The standard definition of the Nash bargaining solution is the agreement which maximizes the product $[u_1(x) - u_1(D)][u_2(x) - u_2(D)]$ over all agreements which Pareto-dominate the disagreement event. For the bargaining problems under consideration, the above formula defines a unique prediction. Nash (1950) not only proposed this solution concept, but also showed that this solution is unique in satisfying the following three postulates: *symmetry* (SYM), *Pareto optimality* (PAR) and *independence of irrelevant alternatives* (IIA). Nash's fourth axiom, the *invariance to positive affine transformations* (INV), is redundant in the current setting, since we start from the players' attitudes toward risk and not from utility representations.

The first axiom is easy to accept. It captures the idea that the prediction rests only on the information included in the bargaining situation. A bargaining problem is called symmetric if players 1 and 2 are "indistinguishable" (presented in its reduced form $<S,d>$, a bargaining problem is symmetric if the set S is symmetric with respect to the main diagonal and d is a point on the main diagonal; for a definition in terms of preferences, see Rubinstein, Safra, and Thomson 1992). SYM requires that for symmetric problems, the predicted agreement does not discriminate between the two players (in utility terms, the solution concept should assign equal utilities to both players).

PAR requires that, for any bargaining problem, there is no agreement in X which Pareto-dominates the solution outcome. The axiom excludes the possibility that bargaining will result in disagreement.

The most problematic axiom is the IIA: its standard definition is that "if $X \subseteq X'$ and the solution to the problem $<X',D,\succsim_1,\succsim_2>$ is in X, then it is also the solution to the problem $<X',D,\succsim_1,\succsim_2>$". An alternative formulation of the IIA is suggested in Rubinstein, Safra, and Thomson 1992. Assume that y^* is the solution to the problem $<X,D,\succsim_1,\succsim_2>$ and let $\succsim_i'$ be a preference which agrees with $\succsim_i$ on the set of deterministic agreements X such that:

1. for all x such that $x \succsim_i y^*$, if $p \cdot x \sim_i y^*$ then $p \cdot x \precsim_i' y^*$, and
2. for all x such that $x \precsim_i y^*$, if $x \sim_i q \cdot y^*$ then $x \sim_i' q \cdot y^*$.

Then, y^* is also the solution to the problem $<X',D,\succsim_i',\succsim_j>$. The switch of agent i's preference from $\succsim_i$ to $\succsim_i'$ reflects his increased aversion to the risk of demanding alternatives which are better than the outcome y^*. Though player i still prefers x to y^*, he is less willing to risk demanding x. The axiom captures an intuition that the bargaining solution outcome y^* should be defensible against possible objections. The change in player i's preference described in the axiom makes player i "less eager" to object. The axiom states that this change does not affect the bargaining outcome.

THE INTERPRETATION OF THE NASH BARGAINING SOLUTION

One of the main reasons for the popularity of the Nash bargaining solution among economists is that it is defined by a very simple formula which is easily embedded in any larger model that includes a bargaining component. The analytical convenience is an important reason to use it in economic models. If the task of bargaining theory is to provide a "clear-cut" prediction for a wide range of bargaining problems, then Nash bargaining theory carries out the task perfectly well. The Nash bargaining solution is well defined and the axioms lend the solution a sense of non-arbitrariness for a wide range of problems. However, I cannot see the formula being tested as similar simple formulae in sciences are. In the absence of testability, we search for a meaning for the formula. What is the product of two von Neumann-Morgenstern utility numbers and what is the meaning of the maximization of that product? Can we consider the maximization of a product of utilities as an intelligent principle for resolving conflicts? The negative answer to these questions prompts us to look for alternative definitions of the Nash bargaining solution. Such a definition is required to have an attractive verbal (as opposed to analytical) meaning in ordinary language. It has to be defined by a simple sentence which includes only the terms "alternative," "disagreement," and "preference."

One may argue that the conjunction of the Nash axioms is an attractive alternative definition for the Nash bargaining solution. The axioms are defined in quite nontechnical terms and the Nash theorem can be interpreted as a proof that the conjunction of the axioms provides an implicit definition of the Nash bargaining solution. However, this is an implicit definition and we are looking for an explicit definition, one which will specify the outcome of a particular problem directly in terms of the problem's primitives without the need to search for consistency with the outcomes assigned by the solution for other problems.

I would now like to propose such an alternative definition (see Rubinstein, Safra, and Thomson 1992; the idea is close in spirit to Zeuthen's [1930] though it is quite different).

Definition: The agreement y^* is the ordinal Nash solution for the problem if and only if for any player i, any agreement $x \epsilon X$ and any probability $p \epsilon [0,1]$, if $p \cdot y^* <_j x$ then $p \cdot x <_i y^*$.

Thus, a Nash bargaining solution is an agreement y^* such that for any objection by player i, who proposes x rather than y^* and who takes steps which may cause disagreement with probability $1-p$, either

(1) it is credible for player j to reject the objection and to insist on the agreement y^*, even when he takes into consideration the possibility of breakdown, or,
(2) it is not credible for j to reject the objection ($p \cdot y^* <_j x$) but player i prefers not to take the risk ($y^* >_i p \cdot x$).

In other words, the Nash bargaining solution is the agreement such that any argument of the type "You should agree to my request, x, since x is better for you than insisting on the convention y^* given the probability $1-p$ of breakdown" is not profitable to the objector when he takes into account the same probability of breakdown.

The Gulf war provides a concrete example of this definition. The bargainers were Iraq and the U.S. The set of agreements contained the various possible partitions of the land in that region. The disagreement event was a war. When Saddam Hussein moved his troops he deliberately took a chance that the situation would deteriorate into an unpleasant war before the U.S. gave up. He preferred the lottery in which he would find himself in a war with a probability $1-p$ and that he would annex Kuwait with the probability p to the alternative of maintaining the status quo. However, his mistake was that the U.S. preferred the risk of war in demanding a return to the status quo rather than giving in to Iraq's demands. If the U.S. had given in to Iraq it would have meant that the pre-invasion borders were not part of a Nash bargaining outcome.

The first thing we notice about the ordinal definition is that in the expected utility case it leads to the same outcome as does the conventional definition of the Nash solution. Without loss of generality, we can choose the utility representation so that for both players $u_i(D) = 0$. Then, the alternative y^* satisfies $u_1(y^*)u_2(y^*) \geq u_1(x)u_2(x)$ for all x for both i *if and only if* for all i, for all $x >_i y^*$ for all $p \lesssim 1$, if $u_i(x)/u_i(y^*) > p$ then $u_i(y^*)/u_i(x) > p$ *if and only if* for all i and x, $py^* <_j x$ implies $px <_i y^*$.

In recent years there has been a growing interest in nonexpected utility theories of decision making under uncertainty since they explain a wide range of behavior patterns and experimental results which are inconsistent with expected utility theory. The ordinal definition above uses the language of agreements and preferences without a reference to utilities, thus it has the advantage that it can be extended to bargaining situations in which the preferences do not satisfy expected utility theory conditions.

The above explanation of the Nash bargaining solution also has a normative version. One can say that the Nash bargaining solution is an agreement in which no player i can make the following claim against player j: "You should agree to x since I prefer x to y^* so much that I am ready to take the $(1-p)$ probability risk of breakdown while you are not."

Notice also that in the (ordinal) definition of the Nash bargaining solution, there is a symmetry in the two bargainers' beliefs concerning the possibility of a breakdown. One can imagine other scenarios in which there is a systematic asymmetry in the beliefs about the possibility of breakdown. If we refine the definition of the Nash bargaining solution so that the probability p appears in player 1's considerations and is not the same as the probability p that appears in player 2's considerations, then we can arrive at a solution called an "asymmetric Nash bargaining solution."

THE ALTERNATING OFFERS MODEL: A REVIEW

This section is a brief review of the infinite-horizon alternating offers model (see Rubinstein 1982). Actually, I will present a variation of the model (see Binmore, Rubinstein, and Wolinsky 1986) in which the primitives of the model are the four-tuple $<X, D, \gtrsim_1, \gtrsim_2>$ as in the Nash model. The model is built upon a specific procedure used to reach agreement in which the players alternate turns in having the right to make offers. In each period, one of the players must make a proposal and the other must either accept or reject it. Acceptance ends the game. In the case of rejection, the responder has the right to make a proposal. However, before he does so, "nature" may interfere and cease the game, causing the outcome D. The probability of breakdown is fixed, $1-p > 0$. One interpretation of fixing $(1-p)$ is that the risk of breakdown is a function of the length of the time interval between a rejection and a counteroffer; the equal probability of breakdown reflects the assumption of the equal length of time between responses and counteroffers.

The above procedure, together with the preferences, forms an extensive game. Under the assumptions made on the bargaining problem in section 2, there is a unique subgame perfect equilibrium which is characterized by the unique pair of Pareto-optimal agreements x^* and y^*, so that player 1 is indifferent between y^* and the lottery $p \cdot x^*$ and player 2 is indifferent between x^* and the lottery $p \cdot y^*$. The following are subgame perfect equilibrium strategies: player 1 always makes the offer x^* and accepts any offer as good as y^*. Player 2 always makes the offer y^* and accepts any offer as good as x^*.

The current version of the alternating offers model has an interesting connection with the Nash bargaining solution which was discovered by Binmore (1987) and clarified by Binmore, Rubinstein, and Wolinsky (1986). Let $x^*(p)$ and $y^*(p)$ satisfy $p \cdot x^*(p) \sim_1 y^*(p)$ and $p \cdot y^*(p) \sim_2 x^*(p)$. Where $p \rightarrow 1$, both $x^*(p)$ and $y^*(p)$ converge to the Nash bargaining solution of the problem $<X, D, \gtrsim_1, \gtrsim_2>$. In other words, where the probability of breakdown is very small, the agreement reached is very close to the Nash bargaining solution, independent of which player makes the first proposal.

As in the case of the Nash bargaining solution, the above analysis achieves the standard objectives of game theory. Here we have quite a natural model which has a unique subgame perfect equilibrium and whose outcome is a clear-cut prediction of the outcome of bargaining.

By using the noncooperative approach, we have added a procedure to the description of the bargaining problem. The set of subgame perfect-equilibrium outcomes is sensitive to the procedure of bargaining. The sensitivity of the model to the procedure is an advantage of the noncooperative approach and one reason for its popularity in economic theory, as it allows for the modeling of trading institutions.

An agreement in a bargaining problem is taken in this paper to be stable if no bargainer can raise a *valid* argument which is *worthy* of raising. The contents of the term "valid" and "worthy of raising" differentiate the two models discussed in this paper. In the interpretation of the Nash bargaining solution, raising an objection z to y* is accompanied with creating conditions so that disagreement may happen. A valid argument is a statement of the type: "you better agree to z; for you, insisting on y* does not merit taking the risk of breakdown". The reference point in this type of argument is the current agreement y*. As to the objector, he assesses the value of raising an objection by taking into account that the risk of breakdown applies to him as well.

In the alternating offers model, on the other hand, the risk of breakdown is endogenous to the situation. As long as he believes that the partner will accept his objection, an objector does not take into account any risk when he raises an objection. The structure of a valid argument is "you better agree to z since anything I would accept is worse for you given the risk you face if you reject the offer". Thus, the reference point of the responder is the acceptance set of his opponent.

Other modifications of the alternating offers procedure lead to less attractive conclusions. If player 2 is allowed to make offers only once in three periods, the only subgame perfect equilibrium outcome is close to the partition (2/3,1/3) (when $1-p$ is small). When the probability of breakdown is small, it seems strange that such a relatively small change in the procedure should make such a significant impact on the bargaining outcome. This observation, together with the fact that real-life bargaining only rarely has a rigid procedure, was the main source of criticism against the alternating offers model (see for example Kreps 1990b and Sonnenschein 1991).

AN ALTERNATIVE INTERPRETATION OF THE ALTERNATING OFFERS MODEL

The above criticism is derived from the classical interpretation of the game form as a full description of the physical events in the modeled situation. In contrast I wish to follow Nash's approach: "Of course one cannot represent all possible bargaining devices as moves in the non-cooperative game. The negotiation process must be formalized and restricted, but in such a way that each participant is still able to utilize all the essential strengths of his position" (Nash 1953, 129). I view a game as a description of the *relevant* factors involved in a specific situation as perceived by the players rather than as a presentation of the physical rules of the game. According to this understanding, the alternating offers model is a model which captures the interaction between two bargainers whose reasoning is using choices between an offer on the table and a possibility to achieve a better agreement if they take a certain risk of a breakdown of negotiations. Thus, if the alternating offers model is interesting, it is not because it describes a real-life bargaining process but because it embeds an interesting type of consideration which players use in bargaining. Thus, a variant of the model in which the probabilities of breakdown after rejection by player 1 and 2 are distinct captures an asymmetry in player evaluations of breakdown. On the other hand, the version of the model, suggested by the critics, in which player 1 makes offers only once during three periods, fails to capture any sensible consideration. In the rest of this section, I will suggest a somewhat different model, one that allows us to analyze the strategic considerations which appear in the alternating offers model without using noncooperative games.

The new model is based on a view of a social order as an automaton. The automaton consists of the following elements: a set, S, interpreted as the set of "states of the system" and an initial state, s_0. Each state is accompanied by two sets of agreements $A_1(s)$ and $A_2(s)$, with the interpretation that at state s offers in the set $A_i(s)$ made by player i are expected to gain acceptance. (In the automatae jargon, this is the output function of the automaton). The automaton responds to events in the bargaining session. In the present context, the events are offers and responses; in alternative models we could also include other types of actions as events (walking away from the table, making commitments, etc.). The transition function describes the moves from one state to another as a function of the possible events in the game.

For a social order to be stable, we require that:

1. For each s and for every $b \notin A_i(s)$, the system moves to state s' after player i makes an offer b and there is an agreement $x \in A_j(s')$, so that $p \cdot x \gtrsim_j b$. (Note that p is here a constant). In other words, if b is not acceptable, there must be an acceptable counteroffer made by player j, so that it is optimal for player j to reject b and to insist on x even when he takes the risk of breakdown into account.

2. If $a \in A_i(s)$, then if i offers a and j rejects a, the system moves to state s' so that there is no $b \in A_j(s')$ that satisfies $pb >_i a$.

It can be shown that the only automaton that satisfies the above conditions has the property that for any s, $A_1(s) = \{x \mid x \lesssim_1 x^*\}$ and $A_2(s) = \{x \mid x \lesssim_2 y^*\}$.

In light of this result, which characterizes the acceptance sets, a convention must be included in the set $\{x \mid x \gtrsim_1 y^*$ and $x \gtrsim_2 x^*\}$ in order to be stable in face of acceptable objections. Consider, for example, an agreement x, so that $x <_1 y^*$. It is profitable for player 1 to raise the acceptable objection x^*, because he prefers the lottery px^* over the agreement x. Notice that here, the response to an unjustified demand is not to insist on the status quo (such as in the interpretation of Nash's bargaining solution) but to raise a counterdemand which has to be acceptable. A bargainer may be deterred from starting negotiations (rather than maintaining the status quo) by his anticipation of a counterdemand which is worse for him than the status quo.

The equivalence between the above model and the alternating offers model results from the fact that the notion of subgame perfect equilibrium in the alternating offers model has the following "one deviation property": a pair of strategies is a subgame perfect equilibrium if and only if there is no history after which a player can gain by a one-time deviation.

The advantage of the new concept lies in the fact that it models strategic considerations directly and avoids the need to use the problematic notion of an "extensive game strategy," which requires a player to make plans for action after an unbounded number of times in which he has not followed his strategy (see Rubinstein 1991).

My aim in this paper has been to shift the focus of theoretical bargaining models from "formulae" to "argumentation." Casual observation of real-life negotiations indicates that seldom does a bargainer simply make an offer. An offer is usually accompanied with arguments. The arguments may be concerned with the underlying interests ("If you disagree, you may lose the opportunity to make a deal") or with fairness concepts ("I gave up more than you did") or may just be rhetorical ("A taxi driver offered me a discount the size of the tolls on the fare"). A bargaining solution is taken to be an agreement for which no acceptable objection exists, given the arsenal of arguments available to the bargainers.

In this chapter, I have dealt with only one type of argument: "You should agree to x; if you demand the admittedly acceptable y you take the risk of breakdown and this is not worthwhile for you." The Nash bargaining solution is the agreement that survives this argument if the players identify what is acceptable after raising objections with the convention. All agreements between $x^*(p)$ and $y^*(p)$ are those for which any objection is credibly rejected by a counteroffer which is acceptable in an internally consistent sense and given that p is a fixed probability of breakdown whenever an offer is rejected.

This paper has dealt with the interpretation of old concepts and results. I believe that the approach presented in this paper can provide grounds also for new results. But like any other statement of this sort, its proof is only in the doing.

CHAPTER EIGHT

Analytical Barriers

Howard Raiffa

My CSCE Experience

*I*n mid-December of 1991 I joined my colleagues[1] of the not-for-profit firm Conflict Management Group (CMG) and the Harvard Negotiation Project (HNP) to give a negotiation workshop to diplomats of the foreign ministries of the thirty-five[2] nations of the Conference for Security and Cooperation in Europe (CSCE). The workshop was unofficial as far as the CSCE was concerned. The attendees were invited by the Foreign Ministry of Greece and held in a hotel on the Aegean south of Athens.

The CSCE members are all too aware that there are many disputes in their domain that should be, but are not, being settled by peaceful means— and this usually means by negotiations. As we discussed these problems in the workshop, we heard of the latest atrocities in Yugoslavia. Present in our midst were official representatives from both sides of the Cyprus conflict, of the Irish-English conflict, and on and on. Incipient problems for the CSCE were identified: internal ethnic conflicts, new territorial disputes, the overwhelming flow of people from country to country. Next, rather systematically we talked about the *barriers to negotiation,* and they are legion: internal political barriers, institutional barriers, cultural barriers. As the list grew longer, I kept thinking that the decision whether a country should negotiate or not is a complex one, to say the least, and probably little systematic analysis is done and, if done, done poorly. I did not articulate my concern to the CSCE audience but I wanted to add to their list the barrier of "not doing good analysis."

---

[1] Diana Chigas, Professor Roger Fisher, Alton Jenkins, Robert Rocigliano.

[2] Conference for Security and Cooperation in Europe: up to forty-eight nations as of February 1992, and climbing quickly.

As is my wont, let me abstract. Alba and Batia—we used Pulchra and Veritas with our CSCE audience—are two countries engaged in a dispute. Let's identify Alba as the recipient of our decision-analytical advice. Figure 1, in a schematic way, depicts Alba's choices. To start off, Alba must decide to negotiate (N) or not ($\bar{N}$). Let's assume that if Alba goes down the N-path, then Batia will also come to the negotiating table. It's easy to complicate the tree. If Alba decides to negotiate there are a host of benefits and liabilities. In Roger Fisher's terms, if Alba says yes to negotiations, what are the pluses and minuses and how does this net out? This analysis evokes the whole set of costs that can be identified with the barriers to negotiation. So in summary, let us evaluate the toll of going down the N-branch by $C(N)$, the symbol C being mnemonic for "cost." You can, if you wish, think of $C(N)$ as a multidimensional vector quantity, but I'm a bold utilitarian and I'm thinking of $C(N)$ as a scalar quantity summarizing all debits and credits, creatively rendered commensurable. For an indication how this might be done in practice, see Keeney and Raiffa 1976 / 1992a.

Next we come to node D. What will happen in the negotiation is highly uncertain. It entails interactive decision problems of enormous complexity with intricate game-theoretic interactions; working backward in the decision tree, let's say the certainty equivalent at being at D is $V(N)$—that does *not* include $C(N)$.

Backing up to the initial node A, a similar, and sometimes just as complex, story holds if Alba chooses the $\bar{N}$ branch. In this case there is also a $C((\bar{N})$ to consider. At node B, Alba faces an uncertain dynamic world with lots of uncontrollables. Alba at B may have a set of viable alternatives it can pursue, but it is prey to a lot of uncertainties of the actions of others as well as what may happen to other uncertainties in the environment whose outcomes will not be impacted by Alba's choice but which will affect Alba's well-being (e.g., what happens to the regional economy). The decision to choose N or $\bar{N}$ should depend on $C(N)$, $V(N)$, $C(\bar{N})$, and $V(\bar{N})$, and all these are highly uncertain and dependent—a formidable task for analysis. Of course, Alba's decision makers may be implicitly considering these entities without ever labeling them or without even conceptualizing the decision tree of Figure 1. But no matter what, the problem is horrendously complex and vitally important. The cost of systematic analysis, if it is done, is usually trivial in comparison to the stakes involved, but most countries don't engage experts to help them think through the intricacies of the problem. First of all, they don't recognize the problem as one being amenable to any analysis; second, if they thought about doing such analysis, who would be competent to do it, whom could they trust, and so on.

FIGURE 1

Decision Tree Schematic: To Negotiate or Not

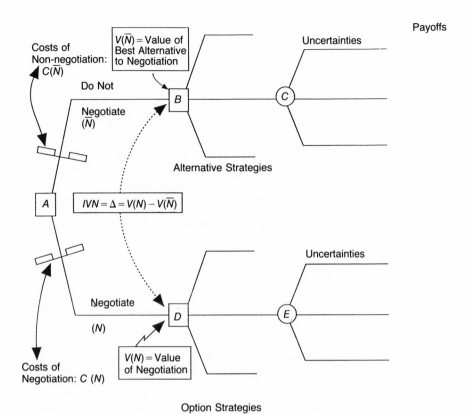

The Value of Perfect and Imperfect Information

In keeping with standard practice in decision analysis (DA) let us define the incremental value of negotiation as $V(N) - V(\bar{N})$, or symbolically Δ. Before doing any depth analysis, Alba can think of Δ as an uncertain quantity (or random variable). To flag this uncertainty I'll write it as $\tilde{\Delta}$, the super-tilde reminding us that Δ is uncertain. We (thinking of Alba's problem) start off with a probabilistic perception of $\tilde{\Delta}$, and Figure 2 depicts the perception that Δ is probably not large enough to overcome the cost disadvantage of negotiating (i.e., $C(N) - C(\bar{N})$). But we may be wrong; some probability is assigned that Δ will indeed be large enough to overcome the cost deficit. (See the shaded right tail of the distribution of $\tilde{\Delta}$.) The expected value of the broken line, called the *Conditional Value of Perfect Information* (CVPI), is labeled the *Expected Value of Perfect Information* (EVPI). (See Raiffa 1968, and Raiffa and Schlaifer 1961). In DA parlance, EVPI is the expected

FIGURE 2

Conditional and Expected Value of Perfect Information

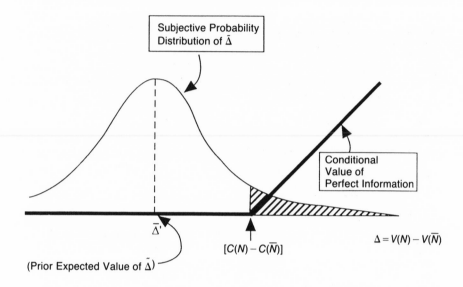

value of the perfect information to be learned from a clairvoyant who will unambiguously tell us what we want to know about the uncertainties of our problem: the true values of $C(N)$, $C(\bar{N})$, $V(N)$, *and* $V(\bar{N})$. It is my contention that in many problems when Alba refrains from negotiating, its EVPI value may indeed be very large. It is also my contention, which I'll develop later on, that Alba's EVPI is even larger than a first-cut analysis would indicate, if such analysis were indeed conducted.

A numerical example might be instructive. In classroom simulation exercises it is quite common to use scorable games in which a protagonist, such as Alpha, would be given a concrete scoring system that could be used to evaluate any final contract which provides a specific resolution of the many issues under contention. For the time being let's abstract out the cost of analysis. Let's suppose that Alpha scales the outcomes from 0 to 100, where 0 is disaster and would be completely unacceptable, and 100 would be nirvana. Let's suppose that if Alpha were to think hard about the uncertainties facing him—including exogenous uncertainties about the world and endogenous uncertainties that may arise from negotiating with Batia—he would assign a normal distribution (of possible ending scores) with a mean of 40 units and a standard deviation of 15 units—thus he would assign a roughly two-thirds chance that he would end up with a score from 25 to 55.

Continuing with this example, suppose Alpha thinks hard about his best alternative to a negotiated agreement, his BATNA (see Fisher and Ury

1981), and evaluates the possible outcomes as being normally distributed, with mean 50 and standard devation 10. Thus we assume that analysis shows that $V(N)$ is normal (40, 15) and $V(\bar{N})$ is normal (50, 10) and, if we assume for simplicity that $V(N)$ and $V(\bar{N})$ are independent, we could conclude that the uncertain quantity $\Delta \equiv V(N) - V(\bar{N})$ is normal, with mean 40−50 or −10 and standard deviation of 18 (which is $\sqrt{(15)^2 + (10)^2}$). So Alpha might conclude that it is just not worth the effort to go to the negotiating table. His certainty equivalent (CE) for the non-negotiating path might be 45, say, a value below his mean of 50 to reflect risk aversion; and his CE for the negotiating path may be 33, say (again this value may be below his mean of 40 to reflect risk aversion). And since his CE for N is below his CE for $\bar{N}$, he will not enter into negotiations. A clairvoyant would still be valuable, however, since although the uncertain quantity Δ has a mean of −10 it has a standard deviation of 18 and it could turn out that the clairvoyant would inform Alpha that indeed $\Delta > 0$, that $V(N) > V(\bar{N})$.

Given the above numbers, if negotiating costs are minimal, it still may be desirable for Alpha to enter into negotiations for the *option value* of the exercise: as negotiations proceed, Alpha will learn more about the true value of $V(N)$. If $V(N)$ looks sour, then Alpha can withdraw and get $V(\bar{N})$ minus the cost of effort; but if $V(N)$ turns out to be promising, then negotiations can continue.

I don't want to leave you with the impression that I believe the major error of the CSCE negotiations is that they don't quantify their uncertainties and values. That's not the point. Participants should, however, think intuitively about these uncertainties, about the expected value of perfect information, about the option value of getting information from starting negotiations even if they don't look promising.

Talks with CSCE members suggest they have a bias in thinking about $V(N)$ and $\Delta = V(N) - V(\bar{N})$. In the first place, many of them appear more certain than they should be about $V(N)$ and Δ. The tails of their probability distributions for the uncertain quantity Δ are too tight (I believe) and therefore EVPI is undervalued. In the second place, they don't think consciously enough about the option value of starting negotiations and most importantly about creative ways of collecting information about the uncertainties of their problem—e.g., by pursuing informal dialogues that precede formal negotiations.

Power Imbalances

Power imbalances were an often cited barrier to negotiation. Several members of the CSCE workshop believe that negotiations do not make sense if there are power imbalances between the contending parties. Why should the more powerful party negotiate? It is "winning" without negotiat-

FIGURE 3

*Feasibility, Efficiency, Equity and The Power of a Good
Alternative*

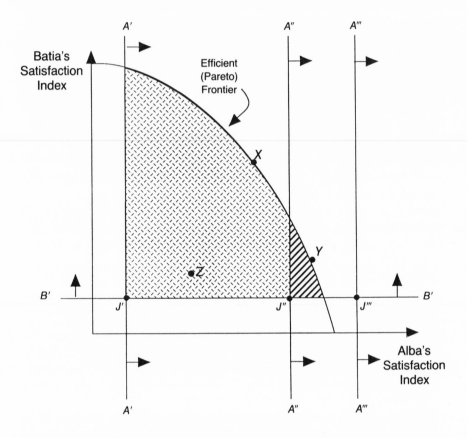

ing, so why risk "losing"? A zero-summish mentality. Their remedy is to
first correct these power imbalances if possible, to force both sides to
engage in voluntary but binding arbitration, the outcome of which sets up
legal precedence. Of course, this may be completely unacceptable to the
other side. I have addressed the problem of power imbalances in terms
shown in Figure 3.

Figure 3 depicts symbolically the standard two-party negotiation problem.
Each axis is poetically defined in terms of a composite satisfaction index for
the negotiating parties Alba and Batia. The line $B'B'$ depicts Batia's reservation value; Batia needs a value north of line $B'B'$ to meet what it could
accomplish with no negotiations. The line $A'A'$ is Alba's reservation value;
Alba needs a value east of line $A'A'$ to meet what it could accomplish with
no negotiations. (Actually what Alba can get outside of negotiations is that

uncertain quantity $V(\bar{N})$, and $A'A'$ is determined by Alba's certainty equivalent for that uncertain payoff.) Alba and Batia seek agreements depicted in the dotted region northeast of point J', but both Alba and Batia are only qualitatively aware of the realities of Figure 3 and lack knowledge of critical details. In looking for agreements, the parties might "satisfice" on a Pareto-inferior point Z without realizing that they are leaving potential joint gains on the table. Point Z is inefficient but perhaps equitable; X is both efficient and equitable; Y is efficient but not equitable. Now for power.

Power is a multifaceted concept. It could mean the added power of information about the other party's reservation value and trade-offs; or the power of better negotiation skills; or still other forms of power. But what the representatives of the CSCE countries had in mind was the power of an advantageous alternative to negotiations—a very good reservation value that could be backed by force. With such an attractive alternative to negotiation, why negotiate? Let's examine this question by assuming that Alba's fortunes have just changed and that now, instead of requiring an agreement to the east of reservation value line $A'A'$, it must be east of line $A''A''$ (or even east of $A'''A'''$) (see Figure 3). Of course if the reservation value line is $A'''A'''$, then the Zone of Possible Agreement (ZOPA) is empty and no acceptable negotiated agreement can be found.

But let us keep in mind that Alba (and Batia for that matter) does not know the details shown in Figure 3. Even though we now posit that Alba is a powerful player with a good reservation value, Alba may not know if the reality is of the type $A''A''$ or $A'''A'''$. If it is $A''A''$, it might be hard for the parties to find a mutually acceptable agreement—an agreement possibility northeast of point J''. But it may be worth the try. Incidentally if Alba has a strong reservation value (like $A''A''$), Alba might want to be quite open in order to convince Batia of its veracity, because otherwise Batia may be thinking that reality is like $A'A'$. If Alba postures as if the line is $A'''A'''$ rather than the reality $A''A''$, it may forgo the possibility of getting value added from the negotiation.

Equity and Legitimacy

Let's continue using Figure 3 with the assumption that the reservation value line $A''A''$ is the appropriate one. In searching for objective standards of legitimacy to be employed in negotiations, the weaker party Batia may prefer to ignore the reality that the no-agreement state leads to J''. Indeed, Batia might offer good legitimate rationales for a point such as X, but this, of course, will be rejected by Alba. With full disclosure, which rarely happens, Alba might argue that an agreement such as Y is fair, but this has the flavor of power politics. If the negotiation is public, Alba might appear to outsiders to be crass if it exploits its comparative advantages and pushes for Y. We will return to this problem when we consider the role of intermediaries.

Where Is the Efficient Boundary?

When parties contemplate the merits of starting negotiations, it is only natural to ruminate about the issues that divide them and the possible compromises that will have to be made to get an agreement. Little thought goes into contemplating visions about what the future could bring if only the dispute that confronts them can be surmounted. It's my impression, and I admit it is very subjective and biased by my notion that "negotiations" are good, that if the long-run future were appropriately factored into the analysis, the efficient boundary would be further extended northeasterly. I think the Greek and Turkish Cypriots, the Arabs and Israelis, and other pairs would do well to plan actively together what true peace might bring to their region in the long run. They should share visions.

To round up my argument, a strong Alba might refuse to come to the negotiating table because it perceives that its reservation value line, $A'''A'''$, falls outside the set of potential agreements. But often, I believe, Alba acts this way because it is undervaluing the long-run benefit of an agreement. Keep $J'''J'''$ where it is in Figure 3, but now move the efficient frontier northeastward to reflect long-run considerations.

If the Greek and Turkish Cypriots, or the Arabs and Israelis, or the Croatians and the Serbians could settle their affairs amicably—well, not "amicably," but peacefully through negotiations—the rest of the world would benefit, enough so that as an expression of their happiness these other countries, if properly engaged, would extend financial aid, trade, loans, gifts, etc., to the no longer bickering parties. This consideration should also push out the imagined Paretian frontier of the now bickering parties when they contemplate whether or not they should negotiate. This reality is not duly evaluated and, as such, this inadequate analysis is a barrier to negotiations.

Synchronization of Internal and External Negotiations

Countries are not monolithic. Almost any agreement with Batia will yield winners and losers on Alba's side of the table. The losers may be in a minority, but losers are gregarious and have motivation to forge a blocking coalition. Off the record, the CSCE representatives might say, "Yes, I can conceive of agreements with the other country that will be beneficial for my country, but it can't be done politically because of internal differences." Yes, we all know that agricultural barriers should fall, but the reality is that farmers would be losers. The barrier is not caused by poor external negotiations but by not very imaginative internal negotiations. The organized, blocking minority must be enticed to break ranks. How? By the internal winners' creatively compensating the internal losers (not necessarily all of them). Three ways occur to me for accomplishing this internal compensation: (1) monetary compensation through tax and subsidy arrangements; (2) linking this external negotiation to other external negotiations where the sets of losers and winners in each overlap in such a way that there are fewer losers in the combined deal; (3) linking the external negotiation to an internal negotiation where effectively the losers from the external deal became winners of the internal deal. The third means seems most promising and politically acceptable, to my way of thinking. When I consider barriers to negotiation, I put the inadequate synchronization of internal and external negotiations as being near the top of the list.

Negotiating without Negotiating

Let's return to the case where Alba is uncertain whether a Zone of Possible Agreement (the ZOPA) exists and where Alba assigns a sufficiently high probability to that case so that its expected value of perfect information is high. Alba would pay a lot to a clairvoyant who would tell it whether or not it should go to the negotiating table. This is a standard situation in DA, and the standard advice is to seek relatively inexpensive information that might be far from perfect but nevertheless is potentially powerful enough to alter initial action plans. In this case, how can Alba check whether it is indeed right that negotiations would be of no avail? It could do more solo analysis; it could engage in mock negotiations having its own team members play the role of Batia. It also could engage in exploratory, nonofficial dialogues with Batia—off-the-record pre-negotiation probes. The idea is to revise its prior probabilistic distribution of $V(N)$ (see Figure 1.) I am using standard DA jargon here, but the idea is simple, and at the country level this activity is done intuitively by diplomats who talk to each other and negotiate without *Negotiating*. This could be done very effectively without incurring the full cost of $C(N)$. It could also be done without the glare of the public media, thus decreasing to the cost of $C(N)$.

While pre-negotiating dialoguing is done, it often is not done seriously enough; and diplomats, I believe, need to be made more conscious of just what they are trying to do. It's the perfect place to probe each other's interests, to jointly explore options, and perhaps to create a negotiation template of what issues should be resolved if formal negotiations were to take place.

There are, of course, disputes that are so heated that even information dialoguing is precluded, or if it does take place it degenerates into an exchange of barbs. Here is where an intermediary might help.

INTERMEDIARIES

The Valletta Accord

In February 1991, at Valletta (Malta), the CSCE adopted a *Mechanism* for the peaceful solution of disputes. If the parties are unable, within a reasonable period of time, to settle the dispute in direct consultation or negotiation, any party to the dispute may request the establishment of a CSCE Dispute Settlement Mechanism which invokes a series of possible external interventions: mediation, conciliation, good offices, fact finding, arbitration, and adjudication. Within the CSCE, and the UN for that matter, these possible third-party[3] intermediary roles are well-defined, but in many ways that are not in accord with universal usage. Arbitration in the CSCE can be voluntary or nonvoluntary (mandatory), but it is always binding. In contrast, many states in the United States require mandatory, but not binding, arbitration as a step prior to full-court adjudication for civil liability torts.

Note that before the CSCE Mechanism is invoked the conflict has to mature or ripen, the parties must be frustrated by nonproductive, unassisted negotiations, and one disputant must trigger the Mechanism. For some steps in the Mechanism all disputing parties must agree. I'll return to this in a later section.

Roles of Intermediaries and Barriers

We, the CMG faculty at the Athens workshop, asked the CSCE participants to brainstorm about possible activities or roles of an intermediary (see Table 1.) Our intention was to expand on this list and to introduce possible helpful activities that did not conveniently fall into their standard vocabulary of good offices, mediation, facilitation, and so on. We followed this up with an exercise on the perceived barriers to intermediation and our audience enthusiastically brainstormed with us. (See Table 2 for the list that developed.)

---

[3] It is almost standard vernacular to refer to the intervening party who is extraneous to the dispute and who tries to assist the parties as the "third party" even if the dispute involves three or more parties. It would be more precise, but too pedantic, to talk about the "*n* plus first" party. The term "intervention," which I use occasionally, is shunned by many CSCE members as connoting "meddling," something to be guarded against.

TABLE 1

Roles of an intermediary

1. Help with informal exchanges (pre-negotiations, shuttle diplomacy)
   (Explore desirability of negotiations in low-key, unofficial way)
2. Help each party to better prepare for negotiations
   (Focus on interests; on creative options, etc.)
3. Help evaluate reasonableness of each party's best alternative to negotiation
4. Help with facilitation; good offices
   (Convener of meetings; rapporteur (keeping minutes); summarizer of arguments;
   drafter of public relations documents)
5. Help with ambience
   (Maintain rules of civilized debate; help reticent speakers)
6. Help relationships
   (Stabilize and control emotions of protagonists; help defuse personality conflicts;
   separate people from problem)
7. Help with information exchanges
   (Convey selected confidential material; use of shuttle diplomacy; help a party to back
   away from an unreasonable commitment; convey the seriousness of a commitment)
8. Help with fact-finding
9. Help with substantive expertise
   (about technical, legal, financial matters)
10. Help with the process of negotiation (as a teacher)
    (Encourage side-by-side joint problem solving; discourage positional bargaining;
    encourage joint creativity with excessive claiming; seek external standards of legitimacy)
11. Help with analytical interventions in problem solving
    (Exploration of uncertainties; predictions; use of (computer) modeling by
    neutral experts; have parties help structure models to be used privately and jointly)
12. Help in preparation of templates (listing issues and options) and single-negotiating texts
13. Help with generating efficient compromise agreements
    (Exploit differences in probabilistic assessments, in risk aversion; in temporal
    trade-offs (e.g., discount rates) in value trade-offs; in symbolic needs; etc.)
14. Help in jointly improving final contracts
    (Post-settlement settlements)
15. Help (if asked) with suggesting compromise proposals
16. Help (if asked) to adjudicate

A Role-Play Simulation on Early Intervention

The CMG faculty used a simulation, role-playing exercise, DS-30,[4] to illustrate the effectiveness of intervention in the early stages of a dispute. The relations between Veritas, a small industrialized country, and Pulchra, an agrarian country, have been sorely strained by a catastrophic industrial accident. A gaseous and concentrated form of chemical pesticide DS-30

---

[4]The case was developed from an earlier version by Robert Ricigliano of the Harvard Negotiation Project and Dr. Victor Issraelyan of the Diplomatic Academy, Ministry of Foreign Affairs of the USSR, with the help and revisions of Wayne Davis, Douglas Stone, and Diana Chigas.

TABLE 2

Barriers to intermediation
(Intermediary≡ IM)

- IM may not be neutral.
- IM may have interests of its own.
- IM may not understand the subleties of situation, be uninformed.
- Parties may lose control—no longer masters of their affairs.
- Inconsistent IM may escalate conflict.
- IM may add issues better left untouched.
- IM may not wish to explore linked problems.
- Parties accepting IM may feel they lose face; it is a sign of weakness;
  their pride suffers; reputation suffers.
- Confidential information may be leaked.
- IM may not be competent.
- Best solution may be the solution freely arrived at.
- Flexibility may be lost; IM may complicate interchanges.
- Parties may fear IM will insist on international legal standards only.
- IM may be judgmental.
- IM may not take into account power imbalances.
- IM may increase pressure to accept compromise worse than status quo.
- Parties may not want to resolve dispute.
- IM may be interested in keeping talks going.
- IM will increase uncertainty in outcome.
- Who selects? Who pays? etc.

leaked from a chemical plant in Veritas near the Pulchran border, adversely affecting large tracts of Pulchran farmland. Talks (negotiations?) between the contending parties started, quickly deteriorated, and were broken off; accusations escalated; linked, grieving animosities were injected into the caldron, and extremely provocative statements appeared in the media. Both Veritas and Pulchra are members of the Regional Organization of States (ROS) and an ROS representative arranges to have private communication with Veritas and Pulchra separately. End of background, beginning of the three-party simulation. (Actually we had two CSCE diplomats play the role of the ROS intermediary, so it was a four-party exercise.)

Not surprisingly, amicable accord was achieved through negotiation in these simulations. Most ROS intermediaries used several rounds of shuttle diplomacy, and assisted, face-to-face negotiations between the disputants were introduced only after the structure of an agreement was apparent. To the faculty's delight, the CSCE diplomats opined that there was substantial value added by the "good-office" role of the intermediary.

Several participants playing the ROS intermediary roles indicated that they would have liked much more information before they started. And this led to our next topic: What type of information?

Pre-mediation Briefing Reports (PMBRs)

Next I proposed the following topic for discussion: Suppose that you have been appointed to play an intermediary role in a specific complex, festering dispute in the CSCE. You have an analytical staff available to you and you have commissioned them to prepare an extensive Pre-Negotiation Briefing Report (PNBR) for your confidential purposes. Your staff has access, unofficially, to very knowledgeable partisans of each side of the dispute. What would be some chapter or section headings of such a report? The group participated vigorously and with some tweaking and editing on my part the listing in Table 3 emerged.

After brainstorming about what should go into a PNBR, I asked whether such an analytical staff should be a part of the CSCE secretariat or be commissioned from a private consulting firm. And here I met resistance. Several of the diplomats felt that while such reports, done in strict confidence, might help the intermediary—some said "only marginally"—they would object to institutionalizing this procedure. Too much central intrusion. But I remonstrated, "As an intermediary you wanted more information in the DS-30 case."

"Yes, but . . ."

I next asked whether a PNBR report would be of use to one of the disputants. "Yes, but only if it were available to that side only." Again, the zero-summish mentality to the fore.

I queried, "What if a Ph.D. student prepared a PNBR as part of a doctoral dissertation?" The response was, "Well it would not do much good or harm because it would just collect dust on the shelf." There was no real sense that the parties may be engaged in a difficult, joint-problem-solving activity, where one side may not be ready to start negotiating, and where information could possibly be gained from a PNBR. No recognition that a PNBR could be used to help lure a recalcitrant disputant to start negotiations. It is my strong contention that it is far easier to brainstorm creative options if one is not simultaneously trying to stake out commitments. The PNBR can effectively separate out the creating and claiming functions.

Early Identification of Conflicts and Unsolicited Offers of Help by Intermediaries

The Valletta agreement calls for the intervention of intermediary helpers only after negotiations have failed and one side has asked for such assistance. Roger Fisher and the CMG group invited the participants of the Athens workshop to address another possible approach. Incipient disputes may be easier to manage and to solve at an early stage before tempers flare into

TABLE 3

Table of contents of a pre-negotiation briefing report (PNBR)

1. History of the conflict
   (Past attempts at negotiation; partisan reviews)
2. Parties
   (Key biographies of the parties; how they negotiate)
3. Internal political structures
   (Who decides; who must influence whom; internal vulnerabilities)
4. Interests and values
   (Fundamental and derived; elicited from surrogates)
5. Visions of the future with agreement
   (Long-run advantages of a settlement; e.g., development)
6. Alternatives to negotiation
   (Scenarios if no agreement is reached; best alternatives to each party)
7. Exploring options
   (Joint devising with surrogates; creating options without claiming)
8. Template for negotiations
   (Listing of issues to be resolved and possible resolutions of these issues)
9. Objective standards of fairness; precedents
10. Trade-off analyses
    (Elicitation from surrogates of comparative importance of issues)
11. Possible appealing agreements
    (Derived from 4–9 above; possible lure to get parties to negotiate)
12. Benefits to external parties
    (Who are the outsiders who gain from an agreement? Possible subsidies)

the public, before escalatory actions are taken, before positions are frozen. "Wouldn't it be helpful," asked Fisher, "if dispute counselors could offer their process assistance in a very low profile, nonpublic, informal, strictly confidential, exploratory, nonbinding, nonjudgmental way to the disputants at an early stage?"

"Well, this could be done now using the good offices of the secretariat if assistance is requested," was the reaction of the audience. "But according to the Valletta agreement intervention cannot be initiated by the secretariat."

"But," insisted Fisher, "that's the way it is now, I know, but *should* it be that way? Is the CSCE missing an opportunity?"

The conversation deteriorated quickly because some of the participants were worried that unsolicited early intervention—even in the mildest form—would shift too much power to the central administration dominated by the big countries. The faculty caucused and suggested that the participants break up into three working groups to investigate (1) how early intervention could be implemented within the present Valletta guidelines, (2) how the Valletta agreement could possibly be modified to accommodate unsolicited dispute counseling, and (3) how the CSCE could work with other institutions and groups outside the CSCE framework.

The working groups were instructed to shift into a brainstorming modality in which suggestions would not be adversely criticized but rather positively nurtured. The diplomats enjoyed that experience and were both creative and productive. Unfortunately, since this discussion was off-the-record, I do not feel free to report on suggestions they made about how early intervention could be implemented within the present Valetta guidelines, or how the Valetta guidelines could be modified. But I would like to say a few words about how the CSCE could work with other institutions outside the CSCE framework.

Some enthusiasm was expressed for the creation of an international, non-governmental panel of distinguished dispute counselors who could identify embryonic problems among CSCE members and who could initiate without request constructive dialogues with the parties in the dispute. This panel would include distinguished ex-diplomats, ex-government leaders, judges, and academics who are recognized for their independence, creativity, and leadership qualities. The number of members of the panel could be large— on the order of twenty, say—but for a given embryonic dispute an executive committee could assign one, two, or three relatively impartial members of the panel to that particular dispute. The panel could be supported by a small staff of analysts and investigators who, among other activities, could prepare confidential, pre-mediation briefing reports for the panel members.

Funding for the panel should ideally come from outside the formal CSCE structure—say, from foundations. The panel might also choose to provide educational programs for diplomats and government officials promoting the peaceful resolution of disputes through negotiation.

CONCLUDING REMARKS

Poor and inadequate analysis is a barrier to the effective resolution of conflict through negotiations. From my partisan perception, negotiation theory has not adequately stressed the use of standard analytical techniques developed for decision making under uncertainty. A lot of emphasis, rightly so, has been given to altering the mind-set of negotiators from zero-summish, positional haggling to joint problem solving; but given that, how should those joint problems be solved? In this paper I have considered two key decision problems: whether or not to negotiate, and whether or not to introduce an intermediary to assist the disputants. I indicated that in both cases the assessments of uncertainties may be broadly distributed, causing the expected value of perfect information to be very high, and thereby suggesting that each disputant would be well advised to seek ways to obtain relatively inexpensive, partial or imperfect information about the value of negotiations. One way to achieve this is by the use of unofficial dialoguing or pre-negotiations of an exploratory nature where creative brainstorming is emphasized and claiming postponed. Such explorations could be assisted by outside helpers who not only possess interpersonal skills and are knowledgeable about process but are problem-solving experts. Intermediaries, acting as neutral negotiation counselors, might in turn be supported by an analytical backup staff who prepare briefing documents for their use. These briefing documents in some cases could also be used to lure the parties to the negotiating table by demonstrating that there are indeed potential agreements that jointly dominate the no-agreement state. Negotiation counselors may be more effective if they can identify conflicts in an early stage of development before positions harden in an escalating spiral.

CHAPTER NINE

Dealing with Blocking Coalitions and Related Barriers to Agreement: Lessons from Negotiations on the Oceans, the Ozone, and the Climate

James K. Sebenius

*T*o someone seeking to forge a multiparty negotiated agreement, those who are opposed may constitute a primary barrier. If opponents are numerous or strong enough, they may combine in what in parliamentary jargon is a called a "blocking coalition" and thwart the creation of a sustainable "winning coalition." This chapter takes the point of view of an advocate for a negotiated agreement and addresses the means for dealing with would-be blockers. It does not treat the problem of blocking coalitions in the abstract, but instead examines it in the context of an advocate for a negotiated international regime to control "global warming." This chapter was written shortly after the mammoth 1992 "Earth Summit" in Brazil at which virtually all the world's leaders signed a general climate convention—likely to be followed by years of on-and-off negotiations over specific strategies of global warming control. As such, its analysis of blocking coalitions is intended to remain of interest beyond the near term; ideally, the insights developed for climate negotiations will also find applications to problems well beyond this class of environmental issues.

The author is a professor at the Harvard Business School, and former member of the U.S. Delegation to the Third United Nations Conference on the Law of the Sea. As a result of the pleasant, persistent, and persuasive efforts of Professor Robert Mnookin, this chapter grew from an article of mine, Designing negotiations towards a new regime: The case of global warming, that appeared in *International Security* 15 (1) (spring 1991): 110-48; that article contains an extensive set of background and supporting citations that are incorporated by reference into the present chapter. I am indebted to the same people and organizations acknowledged therein, especially the Negotiation Roundtable at Harvard and the Salzburg Environmental Initiative, as well as to Kenneth Arrow's subsequent helpful suggestions. Support of the Office of Policy and Evaluation of the United States Environmental Protection Agency and the Charles Stewart Mott Foundation is gratefully acknowledged.

Popular and scientific concern has been rising about the possibility that human activities will result in damaging global climate change.[1] Along with recent weather extremes, a number of computer models suggest that a warming is in prospect that could change weather and crop patterns, cause sea-level rises that would inundate low-lying areas, and result in other unprecedented and adverse consequences. Apparent causes include greenhouse gases such as carbon dioxide, chlorofluorocarbons (CFCs), methane, and nitrous oxides, emitted as a result of worldwide modes of energy use, transportation, industry, farming, and forestry. Not only are these activities embedded in the very fabric of industrial and agricultural practice, but the atmosphere is a true commons, implying complete global interdependence with respect to both emissions and control measures. Further, while carbon-emitting activities in developed countries since the Industrial Revolution are largely responsible for present greenhouse gas concentrations, industrialization and population growth in developing countries will, over the next century, become the most important source of the problem. This challenge, therefore, is deep-seated, long-term, and worldwide.

There are many barriers to resolving the scientific, economic, and ideological conflicts that underlie the climate change issue. Negotiations to curb greenhouse gas emissions may ultimately produce few tangible results unless the negotiation process is designed pursuant to a farsighted strategy to craft and sustain a meaningful "winning" coalition of countries backing such a regime. Two centrally necessary, though not sufficient, conditions for this fundamental task are (1) that each member of the coalition see enough gain in the regime relative to the alternatives to adhere, and (2) that potential and actual "blocking" coalitions of interests opposed to the regime be prevented from forming, be acceptably accommodated, or otherwise be neutralized.[2]

In addressing these questions, this chapter will draw on concepts from the

---

[1] For solid evaluations of the global warming problem with special reference to the negotiation issues involved, see Grubb 1989, 1990; and Mathews 1991. For more general treatments, see Mintzer 1992; S. H. Schneider (1989), The greenhouse effect: Science and policy, *Science* (243): 771–81; Skolnikoff 1990; and D. A. Lashof and D. A. Tirpak, eds. (1990), *Executive summary: Policy options for stabilizing global climate* (Washington, D.C.: Environmental Protection Agency, Office of Policy, Planning and Evaluation.

[2] The terms "winning" and "blocking" coalitions are used in a looser sense than is common in a well-structured (e.g., parliamentary) context. In the climate case, "blocking" coalitions may include nonjoiners and free riders. However, peculiarities in the rules of conference diplomacy may allow such nonjoiners actually to block agreements that are widely desired. For traditional discussions of these coalitional concepts see Luce and Raiffa 1957; or Riker 1962. Here, "winning coalitions" are only defined with respect to a set of policy measures from the point of view of a particular actor or actors; such coalitions consist of sufficient numbers of adherents to render the policy effective (again from the

emerging prescriptive field of "negotiation analysis."[3] It is organized around key questions of "negotiation design" whose answers will influence whether and how these two barriers may be surmounted. For example, should negotiations following the general "framework" agreement proceed step-by-step with various specific control "protocols" to be dealt with independently? Or should a more comprehensive, "package" approach be employed? How about negotiating a small-scale agreement among a few key countries versus an agreement with virtually universal participation? How does an aspiration for decision making by consensus, as opposed to rules that permit majority voting, interact with these choices about issues and parties? Should agreements be relatively fixed or adaptive, permitting modifications without re-ratification? Is the most promising avenue to be found in traditional, formal negotiation processes—aimed at producing conventions that will be subject to sovereign ratification—or in less formal approaches?

In addressing these questions for the case of global warming, the analysis will often refer to past negotiations over the law of the sea (LOS) and over CFCs that harm the ozone layer. Like climate change talks, both these negotiations concerned global resources, and have been prominent reference points in global warming debates. In general, environmental diplomats have largely taken negative lessons from the comprehensive LOS model and positive ones from the step-by-step, "framework / protocol" model used for the CFC accords. This chapter's analysis will challenge that conventional wisdom.

In addressing the problems of winning and blocking coalitions, this essay does not seek to evaluate or resolve the considerable scientific and economic uncertainties that surround the global warming issue, nor does it analyze the merits of proposed policy responses. Instead, as a reasonable (but contested) assumption for purposes of analysis, this essay uncritically maintains that the prospect of a serious climate problem exists and it speaks from the perspective of a greenhouse control advocate.

---

point of view of the specific actor or actors.) "Blocking" coalitions are those opposing interests that could prevent a winning coalition from coming into existence or being sustained. The term "actor" should be contextually obvious and can include states, domestic interests, and transnational groupings of either as appropriate. Though the "necessary" conditions described above are extremely important, "sufficient" conditions do not in general exist for an agreement to reached and impasse or escalation avoided. See Lax and Sebenius 1986.

[3] "Negotiation analysis" is a prescriptive approach to negotiating situations that draws on game-theoretic concepts but does not presuppose the full "rationality" of the participants or "common knowledge" of the negotiating situation. For expositions, see, e.g., Raiffa 1982; Lax and Sebenius 1986; Sebenius 1992; or Young 1991.

A "FRAMEWORK-PROTOCOL" APPROACH TO CONTROLLING CLIMATE CHANGE

Negotiations toward agreement to restrict activities that emit greenhouse gases have figured on the international diplomatic landscape for some time and will undoubtedly continue to do so for years. The widely accepted goal for climate change negotiations has been for a general "framework convention," perhaps together with one or more "protocols" on specific subjects. A framework convention was indeed signed in Brazil though specific control protocols were not.[4] Of special disappointment to many greenhouse control advocates worldwide was the virtually single-handed opposition of the United States—among industrialized countries at least—to adopting binding targets and timetables for greenhouse gas stabilization in the convention. (Prior to the 1992 Earth Summit, the nations of the European Community and the European Free Trade Association, along with Japan, Australia, Canada, and others, adopted greenhouse gas stabilization or reduction targets.[5]) In part, this step-by-step, framework-protocol approach was a reaction against the years of negotiating the detailed and comprehensive LOS treaty that was ultimately rejected by the United States and opposed by other key powers. In part, the present approach to climate negotiations seeks to build on the perceived success of an analogous process that led to widely accepted control measures for CFCs. While a large number of other international negotiations have influenced the dominant course of climate change negotiations and contain useful insights, both the LOS and the CFC negotiations concerned global resources (like the atmosphere), embody valuable lessons in themselves, and served as especially salient examples for many informed observers.[6]

---

[4]Climate change was but one of the many subjects for the 1992 conference, which was timed to take place on the twentieth anniversary of the initial UN environmental conference held in Stockholm. The vast agenda of the 1992 conference also included other atmospheric issues (ozone depletion, transboundary air pollution), land resource issues (desertification, deforestation, and drought), biodiversity, biotechnology, the ocean environment, freshwater resources, and hazardous waste. UN General Assembly (1992).

[5]For a summary of the unilateral and small-group greenhouse gas reduction and stabilization targets adopted worldwide, see Cutter Information Corporation 1990, as well as subsequent issues.

[6]Other useful precedents range from the Limited Test Ban Treaty to the nonproliferation agreements, to the Basel convention on hazardous wastes, to the Convention on International Trade in Endangered Species, to the Antarctic Treaty, and to various regional environmental accords such as the Mediterranean Action Plan. For useful distillations of some of the lessons from these and many other related accords, see Young; Thacher 1990; and especially Sand 1990.

"Lessons" from the Law of the Sea Conference[7]

The Third United Nations Conference on the Law of the Sea, launched by the General Assembly in 1970, led in 1982 to a comprehensive treaty signed by 159 states (and other authorized parties) that was designed to enter into force once the sixtieth instrument of ratification was deposited (a requirement met in 1994). On the positive side, against the predictions of many knowledgeable observers, a broadly acceptable LOS convention—a "constitution for the oceans"—did result from this mammoth effort despite technical complexity, uncertainty, and ideological division. The negotiation process and the LOS treaty have reduced much of the ocean conflict that was burgeoning at the outset of the negotiations. Given these factors—and that the atmosphere, like the oceans, is a global resource—there were calls from some quarters for a loosely analogous, comprehensive "law of the atmosphere" to address global warming.

By contrast, many view the law of the sea as precisely the wrong way to negotiate a convention. The process was conducted at a level of detail that arguably should have been unthinkable in a treaty framework; moreover, twenty-two years after its inception, the result was barely scheduled to enter into force. In the views of skeptics, the result of this unwieldy process, especially with respect to deep-seabed resources, was unworkable, a dangerous precedent, and counter to Western interests. Just as the United States rejected this flawed treaty, goes this line of argument, so it should reject any analogous process or result on climate change.

"Lessons" from CFC Negotiations[8]

In 1977, the United Nations Environmental Programme (UNEP) and other UN agencies drew up an "Action Plan to Protect Stratospheric Ozone" that strengthened international efforts at research, monitoring, and assessment. Under the auspices of UNEP, a working group was established in May 1981 to try to come up with a global agreement, a "framework convention," to protect the ozone layer from chlorofluorocarbons. After seven rounds of negotiations, the compromise Vienna Convention for the Protection of the Ozone Layer was signed in March 1985 by twenty countries and the European Community. The convention created a framework for interna-

---

[7]The following LOS discussion generally relies on Hollick 1981; Sebenius 1984; Oxman, Caron, and Buderi 1983; and Richardson 1990.

[8]The following account draws generally on Benedick 1990b; 1990a; 1991; Doniger 1988; and Haas 1989.

tional cooperation on research, monitoring, and exchange of information, and provided procedures for developing "protocols" containing specific control measures. In 1987, twenty-four countries signed the Montreal Protocol on Substances That Deplete the Ozone Layer, calling for a 50 percent cut in the consumption of most CFCs by 1999. By mid-1990, over sixty countries had ratified the protocol or announced their date of ratification. This list included key developed countries, including the U.S., the former Soviet Union, Japan, and the EC countries. However, relatively few less developed countries (LDCs) had ratified the Montreal protocol; holdouts included potentially major CFC producers such as India, China, and Brazil. In a June 1990 London meeting, following some North-South pyrotechnics, ninety-three nations—including some vocal LDC holdouts such as India—signed a much strengthened CFC convention that would virtually ban CFC production and use by the year 2000. The new agreement also promised substantial financial and technical assistance to the developing world.

In direct contrast to the blunt U.S. rejection of the LOS treaty, President Reagan described the 1987 Montreal accord as "the result of an extraordinary process . . . of international diplomacy . . . a monumental achievement." In assessing the relevance of this approach for climate change negotiations, some of those involved with the CFC process—after noting that the complexity of climate issues makes it "impossible to deal with everything at once," recommended disaggregating the problem, and following a step-by-step framework-protocol process modeled after the CFC experience. Subsequent official action by both developed and developing countries endorsed the framework / protocol approach.

Though this chapter will often refer to the LOS and CFC processes, they should not be thought of as pure competing archetypes, such as "step-by-step versus comprehensive." Instead, each approach bundles several important negotiating characteristics from which designers of future negotiations to control climate change might selectively draw. Key features of the CFC process—which was widely seen as a model for climate negotiations—included formal negotiation of a general framework followed by (separate) specific protocols, aspirations for universal participation and decision making by consensus, and an agreement subject to significant modification without re-ratification. The LOS process was also formal, was universally inclusive both with respect to issues and participants, and virtually required consensus on a comprehensive "package deal."

CLIMATE CHANGE NEGOTIATIONS WILL BE
FAR MORE DIFFICULT THAN THOSE OVER
CFCS OR THE LAW OF THE SEA

To place the climate change negotiations in perspective, especially with respect to those over the oceans and the ozone layer, it is important to understand the nature of the issue. Consider four complementary dimensions along which to understand the sources of greenhouse gas emissions:

- In conventional scenarios, slightly less than half of the expected warming from emissions during the decade of the 1980s, for example, came from energy-related activities (coal, petroleum, and natural gas—used in industry, home heating, transportation, etc.), with nonenergy industrial activities delivering about a quarter, and land-use activities (deforestation, rice cultivation, fertilization, etc.) causing the rest.

- About 55 percent of the expected contribution to warming from emissions during this period is due to carbon dioxide, with CFCs (24 percent, or less depending on the effects of the Montreal protocol and of findings that the effective warming contribution of CFCs may be small), methane (15 percent), and nitrous oxides delivering the rest.

- About half of the expected warming will reflect global population growth and about half will reflect growth in per capita demand.

- About 40 percent of the expected warming now comes from activities in the developing countries, a figure that may rise to 60 percent by the end of the next century. (These proportions are reversed, of course, for the developed world.) Thus, both issues of economic growth for the industrial countries and development in the Third World will critically be at stake as possible responses to global warming are fashioned.

This examination of the present and future causes of the greenhouse effect reveals the manifold causes and range of policies that could make some difference in the amount or rate of expected warming. No approach that is narrowly focused on carbon dioxide, for example, or fossil fuels or conservation or deforestation can fully solve the problem. More importantly, this look at the vast scope of the greenhouse problem underscores just how deeply its causes are embedded in the central aspects of the world's economic and social activity: across transportation, industrial, agricultural, and forestry practices; from the developed to the developing world; and in the very growth of populations and economies. This carries an important implication: Although some expected a full solution to the climate change problem to emerge from the negotiations that culminated in the Earth Summit, these talks should be regarded at best as a first step in a series of greenhouse negotiations that will likely stretch over decades.

Thus, negotiating and sustaining serious actions to mitigate greenhouse gas emissions will be far more difficult than counterpart processes for either the law of the sea or the Montreal protocol. While the CFC model is often seen as appropriate, the number of significant CFC-producing countries was small. The economic costs, required institutional changes, and affected industries were relatively limited. Those firms that expected to be able to produce CFC substitutes could benefit compared with their competitors and thus could even gain from the treaty. Few of these conditions apply to limits on carbon and other greenhouse emissions. Further, negotiating a broad-scale convention on the apparent causes of global warming will be much more difficult even than negotiating the law of the sea.

A Convention of Limitation versus a Convention of Expansion

Much of the LOS accord granted or legitimated a series of previously tenuous new claims to ocean resources by many states. Devising an LOS "convention of expansion" involved the relatively easy problem of how to divide an expanding pie.[9] By contrast, climate change negotiations will likely focus on working out convention(s) of limitation, of shared sacrifice, and of painful transfers and compensation—requiring curtailments in energy use, more expensive LDC development paths, changes in agricultural patterns, cessation of currently profitable deforestation, and other such activities. To the extent that climate change negotiations are perceived as allocating sacrifices, they will be fundamentally more difficult than the happier LOS problem of allocating "new" resources. Of course, to the extent that the participants focus on the joint gains relative to feared climate disaster, the process will be so much the easier. And some groups that will directly benefit—such as vendors of renewable, cleaner, more efficient energy and the technologies that make such energy use possible—may join environmental advocates as vocal proponents of a greenhouse control regime.

A True Global Commons with Damaging Incentives

In a statement effectively about property rights, the UN General Assembly unanimously declared deep-seabed resources such as manganese nodules to be the "common heritage of mankind." By contrast, the global atmosphere is a true commons in that any greenhouse gas emissions from a single

---

[9]There were, of course, limitations on various activities (e.g., coastal state seaward territorial claims, marine scientific research) negotiated in the LOS context. Not surprisingly, they were among the most difficult aspects of the conference.

country eventually mix and adversely affect the entire world. True commons resources contain economic disincentives for individual initiatives to curb emissions since the full costs of efforts to mitigate harmful emissions by one state can be borne fully by that state—while the benefits of such actions are diffused throughout the global community. Moreover, any benefits of actions now that would slow the present rate of growth of greenhouse gases would only be felt decades hence by the inhabitants of a *future* world. Thus, facing full costs of abatement today but enjoying only a fraction of any future benefits, individual entities have powerful incentives to continue emitting and to "free ride" on any costly actions others might take to mitigate the problem. As such, strong political and economic forces can lead states and private parties to postpone any action absent a broad international agreement.

ENSURING SUFFICIENT JOINT GAINS WITHOUT BEING OVERWHELMED BY COMPLEXITY: SINGLE-ISSUE PROTOCOLS VERSUS COMPREHENSIVE PACKAGES

In the face of these substantive challenges, a successful accord on climate change calls for a process designed to achieve relatively expeditious results that can be sustained over time and modified as appropriate. In particular, the CFC process with independent protocols to be negotiated on a step-by-step basis was thought to have the advantage of speed and relative simplicity over a comprehensive LOS-like approach. This raises the more general question of how to deal with greenhouse issues: singly, comprehensively, or in intermediate-sized linked packages. The answer, most usefully explored in an LOS context, has a direct implication for ensuring enough gains in an agreement to attract a winning coalition.

Many factors contributed to the lengthy LOS process, but four procedural cornerstones virtually guaranteed its duration and could easily do the same if adopted for global warming negotiations. These included (1) virtually universal participation, combined with (2) a powerful set of rules and understandings aimed at taking all decisions by consensus (if at all possible), (3) a comprehensive agenda, plus (4) the agreement to seek a single convention that would constitute a "package deal" (Koh and Jayakumar 1985). The rationale for each of these components was understandable, but, in the extreme, *a universally inclusive process both with respect to issues and participants, together with the requirements of consensus on an overall package deal, would be very time-consuming—holding the ultimate results hostage to the most reluctant party on the most difficult issue.* In practice, the LOS conference was less constrained by absolute versions of these procedural choices, but the powerful bias toward a snail's pace was very real.

Reacting against the broad agenda / package deal LOS approach, climate change negotiators aimed for a framework convention to be followed by specific protocols. In line with the CFC experience, this retained the aims of universality and consensus, but dropped comprehensiveness and the goal of a package deal—in favor of single, separable protocols on limited subjects. This alternative has attractive negotiating features, but it is worth noting that it was the failure of precisely this approach—negotiation of separate "mini-conventions," analogous to protocols—in earlier LOS conferences (in 1958 and 1960) that indirectly led back to the comprehensive package approach of the 1973 LOS conference.

This experience suggests the nature of the problem. By 1958, for the First UN LOS Conference, the International Law Commission had suggested a negotiating structure with four separate conventions, concerning different issues such as the breadth of the territorial sea and the extent of the continental margin. With respect to the comprehensive agenda of the 1973 LOS talks, conference president Tommy Koh observed, "A disadvantage of adopting several conventions is that states will choose to adhere only to those which seem advantageous and not to others, leaving the door open to disagreement and confrontations. The rationale for this [comprehensive] approach was to avoid the situation that resulted from the 1958 conference which concluded four [separate] conventions" (Koh and Jayakumar 1985, 41).

Such an uneven pattern might also result from a framework / protocol structure on climate change. Imagine Libya signing a forestry convention while Nepal agreed to a transportation and automotive protocol. For individual countries or groups of similar ones, a single issue often represents either a clear gain or a clear loss. As with the early LOS conferences (with independent mini-conventions), countries sign the gainers and shun the losers. In a climate context, for example, China may resist a specific fossil-fuel protocol that would place restrictions on the development of its extensive coal resources. Such single-issue protocols may prove non-negotiable unless they can be combined with agreements on other issues that offset the losses (or at least seem to distribute them fairly). A package deal may offer the possibility of "trading" across issues for joint gain—thus breaking impasses resulting from treating issues separately.

For example, following the 1958 and 1960 LOS experiences, two *separate* negotiations were attempted; until linked, each proved fruitless. With deep-seabed resources the "common heritage of mankind," the "Seabeds Committee" undertook a negotiation over the regime for seabed mining. Developing countries wanted this convention to offer meaningful participation in deep-seabed mining and sharing of its benefits. Yet the developed countries whose companies potentially had the technology, the capital, and the managerial capacity ultimately to mine the seabed saw no reason to be forthcoming, and these negotiations were inconclusive. At about the same time, strenuous efforts by the United States, the Soviet Union, and other maritime powers—greatly concerned about increasing numbers of claims by coastal, straits, island, and archipelagic states to territory in the oceans—sought to organize a set of negotiations that would halt such "creeping jurisdiction." In effect, the maritime powers were asking coastal states, without compensation, to cease a valuable activity (claiming additional ocean territory). Not surprisingly, these discussions over limits on seaward territorial expansion in the ocean yielded scant results.

Seen as separate "protocols," these two issues taken independently were not susceptible to agreement. Yet—together with concerns over the fisheries and outer continental shelf hydrocarbons—it was ultimately the linkage of these two issues, navigation and nodules, in a bargaining sense that came to be at the heart of the comprehensive LOS conference negotiations. With respect to climate change negotiations, it is easy to imagine that separate protocols calling on different groups to undertake painful and costly measures will similarly be rejected unless they can be packaged in ways that offer sufficient joint gains to key players. Since any action on climate change will largely involve shared and parallel sacrifice, it is probably only by linking issues such as technological assistance and various forms of financial or in-kind compensation that many countries will be induced into joining. As such, despite the conventional wisdom about negotiating a framework followed by independent protocols, one should expect great pressure toward combining issues that might initially be conceived as separate (protocols) for purposes of negotiation.

Given this analysis, a central problem in greenhouse negotiation design would seem to be finding a constructive path between the Scylla of a comprehensive package agenda that risks LOS-like complexity and the Charybdis of independent, single-issue protocols (that may lack sufficient joint gain and risk very selective adherence).[10] Rather than trying to predict the appropriate linkages, the conference should be designed in such a way as to facilitate them as they become evident and necessary. It is generally preferable to deal with issues on their separate substantive merits as much as possible, yet be alert to potential linkages to break impasses. This suggests a conference design with independent working / negotiating groups, with a higher-level body seeking to integrate across the groups and facilitate valuable, but limited, "trades."

Yet issues should be linked with caution. It can be extraordinarily difficult

---

[10] For a general treatment of the underlying theoretical issues of issue linkage and separation, or "negotiation arithmetic," see Sebenius 1983; or chap. 9 of Lax and Sebenius 1986.

to "unpackage" them once they have been combined for bargaining purposes. For example, the United States was generally in favor of the navigational portions of the LOS treaty, but had obvious problems with the concessions demanded on a seabed regime. It exerted strenuous efforts at unlinking or separating these topics into "manageable packages," but to no avail. The "package deal" was too strong in the minds of many delegates, and ultimately the LOS convention contained both elements. To choose appropriately between separating and linking issues, the negotiating problem should also be examined from a very different perspective, that of potential blocking coalitions, to which the analysis now turns.

THE BASES OF ''BLOCKING COALITIONS'' IN GLOBAL WARMING NEGOTIATIONS: SCIENCE, INTEREST, IDEOLOGY, AND OPPORTUNISM

A natural way to think about concluding a treaty on global warming is to imagine creating a supportive and "winning" coalition of countries that see enough joint gains in the new regime that it can be sustained over time. Yet it is also useful in this instance to turn this approach on its head and inquire about the often underestimated capacity of opposing interests or potential "blocking coalitions"—nonjoining and opposing entities—to prevent agreement on or implementation of an otherwise desirable treaty. With respect to climate change negotiations, as various restrictions (e.g., on energy use, industrial processes, agricultural or forestry practices) are seriously contemplated, the dangers increase of blocking coalitions made up of parties with interests in these areas. As presently contemplated, the general-framework convention on climate change—setting forth an agreed definition of the problem, joint research, monitoring, and coordination—will be followed by specific protocols detailing restrictions to be placed on various sectors. *In such an approach, the choice of which specific protocols to pursue singly, in combination, or in sequence (e.g., transportation, energy, tropical forestry, etc.) will heavily determine which interests will arise to oppose action; in choosing one's issues, one chooses one's opponents.* As elaborated below, this "choice of potential opponents"—which can be expected to be both private and sovereign, and located both in the developed and developing worlds—should be a conscious and strategically sophisticated decision. Attention turns naturally enough to opposition based on economic self-interest. Yet this is too constricted a view; as the LOS and CFC experiences attest, scientific disagreement, ideology, and opportunism may also animate blocking coalitions.

Blocking Coalitions Based on Economic Interest and Ideology: The Cautionary LOS Experience

It is perhaps sobering to recall how the LOS treaty's burdens on seabed mining—for all intents and purposes a nonexistent industry segment—engendered tenacious and ultimately effective opposition, for pragmatic and ideological reasons. Major maritime establishments, especially in the Soviet Union and the United States, were powerfully motivated in the 1960s by the desire to stop so-called jurisdictional creep, or the tendency for territorial claims, especially by developing countries, to expand and cast an ever widening net of restrictions on submarine, ship, and aircraft mobility in what had traditionally been the high seas. Thus the developing world influenced something of high value to the maritime powers.

Emboldened by this genuine maritime interdependence, many developing countries effectively pressed for a seabed regime modeled on the precepts of the New International Economic Order (NIEO), including significant wealth redistribution, greater LDC participation in the world economy, and greater Third World control over global institutions and resources. Real LDC leverage meant that the maritime powers could not costlessly reject NIEO demands and just walk away. This perceived vulnerability to LDC coastal state power kept the United States and other maritime powers at the LOS bargaining table for years, but ideological disagreements ultimately spurred the treaty's rejection.

As the LOS seabed regime took on more of a NIEO-like character, industry opposition grew. The most effective vehicle the seabed mining industry found to oppose the treaty was less its economic self-interest than the ideological cast of the emerging regime. Elements included the declaration that seabed resources were the "common heritage of mankind" (seeming collectivist), seabed production controls (OPEC-like cartelization), mandatory technology transfer (seeming to ride roughshod over intellectual-property rights), financial requirements (that functioned as globally levied taxes), new voting schemes (more like the UN General Assembly), and the creation of international mining enterprises (worse even than state-owned enterprises). A number of these issues—such as LDC demands for technology and resource transfer, and demands for new institutions—were very similar to those now beginning to animate climate change negotiations.

Richard Darman, once the vice chairman of the U.S. LOS delegation and subsequently a senior policy adviser in the Reagan White House and director of the Office of Management and Budget during the Bush years, contended in an influential *Foreign Affairs* article that "the most important issues at stake in the deep seabed negotiations, however, are not merely questions of manganese nodule mining. What is fundamentally at stake is a set of precedents with respect to systems of governance." In particular, he distinguished between the "precedential elements of the *seabed regime* (as distinguished from *seabed mining*)" (Darman 1978). The Reagan administration generally concurred. Seabed mining was only a small part of the LOS treaty, but the blocking coalition of seabed miners and policy skeptics that it engendered in the United States was ultimately successful, prevailing over the defense and environmental interests that were the strongest supporters of the LOS convention.

Implications for Climate Negotiations

This history highlights a largely overlooked danger with which advocates of global climate change negotiations should be concerned. As with the law of the sea, long-term success is impossible without the cooperation of the developing world. Greenhouse gases in the atmosphere are now mainly due to past and present activities of developed nations. However, with projected population and economic growth in the developing world, the source of the greenhouse problem will rapidly shift over time, especially if India and China choose their least-cost development paths that rely on their vast coal resources. China, for example, now plans to expand its coal consumption fivefold by the year 2020, a result that would add nearly 50 percent to current worldwide carbon emissions (Grubb 1990, 75). Anti–global warming steps agreed and taken by the developed world alone could be heavily offset over time by inaction in the developing countries; by the year 2050, projected warming without developing-country cooperation would be 40 percent higher than with it (Lashof and Tirpak 1990, 40–43). Thus, the developed world cannot solve the climate problem in the long run without the cooperation of the LDCs.

Especially given prevailing levels of distrust—not to mention the steep energy requirements of vital development—a threat by key developing nations not to cooperate with an emerging climate regime—even if ultimately mutually destructive, and even if its effects might be more severe in the developing world—could have a clear rationale and a measure of credibility. No wonder that, in the words of a recent discussion of climate change and overall Third World concerns, "The problems presented by climate change also present opportunities to reexamine and correct many of the underlying problems of development that have led to the current dilemma . . . including trade issues, debt, technology transfer, technical assistance, and financial assistance" (Stone 1990). To southern diplomats with this view, the climate change issue may be a very potent bargaining lever with application well beyond the climate context. According to another observer, "this group sees environment as the same kind of issue in the 1990s that energy was in the 1970s. They hope that the developed countries' high interest in the environment can be used to wring concessions on economic and development issues from the North" (Stanley 1990, 8).

But fundamentally conflicting North-South agendas have found and will continue to find expression in climate negotiations. (See, e.g., Krasner 1985.) The underlying ideological template, also present in the LOS and Montreal negotiations, is that of the New International Economic Order. A great deal of the preparatory negotiations for the 1992 conference focused on generalized North-South concerns expressed in well-worn NIEO terms. The risk, to be assessed in more detail later, is that attempted use of real southern leverage on behalf of NIEO precepts might meet northern intransigence based on antipathy to the underlying ideology.

Blocking Coalitions Based on Science and Economic Interest: The CFC Negotiations

Though the CFC accords indeed represent important international coordinating steps, they illustrate complementary bases of potential blocking coalitions—scientific disagreement and economic interest—to those explored above in an LOS context. Despite periodically intense public concerns dating from the SST and aerosols, the actions of a relatively small number of industry players—DuPont and Allied in the United States, ICI and others in Europe—along with policy skeptics in the major countries were able to delay action on an ozone convention for a number of years. To understand why, it is critical to focus on "internal" (domestic) considerations along with that which is happening in the "external" (international) negotiating forum.

It is both instructive and sobering to see how this industry opposition was overcome by 1987. In part, it was a matter of science. Though predictions of individual scientists varied greatly, consensus estimates of the extent, likelihood, and danger of ozone depletion had declined from the early 1980s prior to the surprise discovery of the Antarctic ozone hole in 1985; thus industry opposition to regulation during this period had a scientific basis. However, DuPont was publicly committed by statements of company officials to Congress to the effect that if scientific evidence conclusively showed adverse health effects, it would no longer produce CFCs; this was a key factor in its "conversion."

But two other special dynamics may have been at work in overcoming DuPont's effective blocking actions. First, though it put the work on hold for a time in the early 1980s, DuPont had been intensively engaged in the search for CFC substitutes, and appeared to be well ahead of its global competitors in this regard. If this were so, international limits on the amount of CFCs that could be produced and consumed would both permit the price of the allowed production to be raised and place DuPont in a favorable competitive position. Second, as public concern culminated in tremendous concern about the Antactic ozone hole, prospects grew substantially for U.S. legislation that would have unilaterally restricted CFC production and use. From DuPont's point of view, while no regulation would have been the preferred alternative, international rules that constrained the entire global industry were far preferable to a U.S. law that singled out domestic companies. Thus, the unusual confluence of several distinct factors—scientific evidence coupled with prior public statements by the company, competitive dynamics within the industry driven by CFC substitutes, and the unusual effect of a threat of domestic legislation—were sufficient to turn DuPont around and open a split in global industry ranks.

Extent of Likely Blocking Coalitions in Anti-Greenhouse Negotiations

These LOS and CFC accounts warn of how potent greenhouse treaty opponents may be—on scientific, economic, ideological, and / or opportunistic bases. As noted, the LOS treaty was scuttled in the United States and in other important industrial nations by the economic and ideological concerns of an industry segment (seabed mining) that did not even exist. With respect to the ozone experience, the 1990 *Economic report of the president* estimates the U.S. costs of compliance with the Montreal accord at $2.7 billion—one measure, since reduced, of the costs motivating skeptical policy-makers and corporate opponents of the treaty.[11] Despite public concern over the ozone layer, the Montreal treaty was effectively delayed for several years by these groups until the scientific consensus shifted.

Now $2.7 billion is certainly a high cost, but the same report cites the U.S. costs of an anti-greenhouse 20 percent carbon dioxide cut at between *$800 billion and $3.6 trillion*.[12] *If these figures are even remotely accurate, they suggest that those concerned about the prospect of large-scale greenhouse control* (e.g., policy skeptics, coal and oil companies, auto makers, etc.) would have an economic motivation for opposition—regardless of the level of environmental benefits—literally hundreds of times stronger than that of the CFC industry. The battle throughout the 1980s over amendments to the Clean Air Act, with annual costs in the "mere" $25–35 billion range, gives another sobering point of comparison. Cost estimates of the magnitudes mentioned above are by no means universally accepted; respectable analyses suggest that some

---

[11] U.S. Congress, Joint Economic Committee 1990.

[12] See *Economic Report of the President*, 234, based on Manne and Richels 1990.

reductions may be achieved at low or even negative cost.[13] Yet it is the credible *prospect* of burdensome costs that will engender opposition, especially among risk-averse firms who fear that they will bear the costs. Further, since the benefits are uncertain and diffuse and will mainly accrue to future generations, today's opponents are likely to speak with the clearest voices.

Indeed, the powerful coalitions that will arise to resist major greenhouse action are now mostly asleep. Yet they will certainly awaken to the extent that the prospect of such action becomes more likely and the *feared* costs are large. Look for example to Canada, a country in the rhetorical vanguard of greenhouse concern. If serious actions are proposed, however, will the Canada that pumps oil, cuts forests, and builds cars really just go along? And are those Brazilians who profit from burning rain forests today readily going to buy arguments about future world benefits? More broadly, blocking coalitions are just as likely to arise in "southern" countries whose development could be impeded by anti-greenhouse measures as in developed countries whose industries and consumers could face heavy cost burdens. Likewise, the imperative for Eastern Europe to grow to consolidate its political gains will weigh against major greenhouse action. Such coalitions will likely be composed not only of traditional nation-states, but also of domestic interest groups and transnational alliances. In short, the potentially huge costs that are feared to result from significant anti-greenhouse policies offer one measure of the economic motivation for opposition to action—and a partial guide to the strength of likely blocking coalitions.

This implication has particular force with respect to negotiating national "targets," or reductions from given emission levels that would collectively be within an overall world reduction target. Emission targets and timetables have been the dominant theme in international discussions over a greenhouse control regime; environmental advocates and media observers have generally judged the seriousness of national governments by their willingness to endorse binding targets and timetables—and judged the Brazil framework a failure given its absence of binding commitments. Especially given the high level of public concern about the greenhouse issue, many environmental advocates expected quick negotiations and decisive agreement on targets. The significant number of industrial countries that unilaterally or in small groups had committed by early 1992 to greenhouse gas stabilization or reduction targets was in line with this optimistic view

---

[13] For a critique of the Manne-Richels estimates, see R. H. Williams (1989), Low cost strategies for coping with carbon dioxide emission limits (Princeton: Center for Energy and Environmental Studies, Princeton University). More generally, for a sophisticated review of various cost estimates, see Cline 1992.

(although there is a long road between target and result). Yet U.S. opposition to an overall target—limiting greenhouse emissions in the year 2000 to 1990 levels—effectively kept targets out of the climate change agreement that was signed at the Earth Summit.

U.S. opposition to targets may appear anomalous, especially given that all other Organization for Economic Cooperation and Development (OECD) countries except Turkey had agreed to stabilization by mid-1992. *Yet as the effects of targets become more specific and stringent, the more resistance will generally grow from those affected.* This implies that negotiating meaningful anti-greenhouse action is likely to take considerable time. The above analysis spells out the extent to which climate change negotiations could seriously impinge on a range of vital activities—far more than the twelve-year LOS negotiating process. The much simpler CFC negotiation process—from which specific country obligations emerged—took over *five* years from the start of negotiations and over *ten* years from the announcement of UNEP's 1977 Action Plan to Protect the Ozone Layer. Similarly, the twelve-nation European Community Large Combustion Plant Directive to limit acid rain took *five* years of negotiations, often twice-weekly, among a relatively homogeneous group to agree on targets.

Both more recently and ominously, although the European Community *as a whole* agreed to stabilize its *overall* greenhouse emissions at 1990 levels by the year 2000, its internal negotiations over which nations would be required to make what reductions—the "target-sharing" problem—utterly broke down. This should be especially sobering to proponents of targets, given the EC's high level of greenhouse concern and its relative homogeneity (especially compared with the broader UN membership that is charged with negotiating the next (protocol) phase of a global climate treaty). With this failure to negotiate country-specific targets, EC attention then shifted to a imposing a carbon-related tax. As this alternative was being developed, the *Economist* observed that "the proposed carbon tax has been subject to some of the most ferocious lobbying ever seen in Brussels."[14] Carlo Ripa di Meana, the EC environment commissioner, charged that the EC faced "a violent assault from industrial lobbies and the [oil-producing] Gulf countries, which even threatened to break off diplomatic relations" following the announcement of the energy tax.[15] Largely as a result of industry opposition, before the carbon tax was even proposed as a directive to the Council of Ministers, both energy-intensive industries and major exporters were preemptively exempted from the tax. Further, rather than apply the tax *unconditionally* as a means of reducing EC carbon emissions, as environmental advocates

---

[14] *Economist*, May 9, 1992, 19.

[15] *Financial Times*, May 15, 1992, 3.

urged, the tax was made *conditional* on comparable action by the EC's main trading partners. This episode attests to the power of potential blockers in the realm of climate negotiations.

At first blush, the acceptance of stabilization targets by all the OECD countries except Turkey and the United States might seem to contradict the above analysis arguing for the extent and power of potential blocking coalitions vis-à-vis targets. Yet another interpretation is possible: as illustrated by the EC experience, *targets may be relatively easy to adopt but difficult to implement*. One might even draw the analogy to the Gramm-Rudman antideficit law, which eerily resembles a climate "framework" convention in that it contained targets and timetables but left specific agreement on cuts and tax increases for later. As such, this law served for years as an expedient political "solution"—at a time of intense public deficit concern—allowing executive and legislative officials to declare the problem "solved" and return to budgetary chicanery. It is quite possible that the significant number of unilaterally adopted greenhouse gas control targets or a very weak framework convention that was politically touted as the "solution" to global warming could have analogous effects. In short, the more clearly identified the objects of antigreenhouse measures—such as targets or carbon-related taxes—the greater the likely opposition from affected parties and the more likely that, if adopted, the measures will not be implemented.

The Bases of Blocking Coalitions: Science, Interest, Ideology, and Opportunism

If climate woes strike with force, they will likely entail widespread harm. Yet the immediate costs of each preventive measure would mainly fall on a specific group. As to providing uncertain future benefits for all, such smaller groups will not want to pay the full tab now, and can be expected to mobilize to block action. These considerations suggest that those concerned with organizing effective international action to combat global warming should carefully anticipate, prevent, and prepare to deal with the potential blocking coalitions that may arise. Such coalitions will likely be composed not only of traditional nation-states but also of domestic interest groups and transnational alliances.

Though economic reasons are most often cited as the basis for opposition to greenhouse action, that is too narrow a view; scientific disagreement, ideological clash, and opportunistic use of apparent bargaining leverage are also likely to play roles. In principle, each type of blocking coalition might be dealt with according to its basis; in practice, the bases are likely to be intertwined. (These are not the only bases for opposition; for example, clashing values or different attitudes toward risk or the passage of time may engender opposition.) The seabed mining industry appealed to economic interest and ideology in opposing the LOS treaty; science and self-interest played complementary roles in delaying a CFC accord; ideological clash and opportunism may well combine in global climate talks. Opposition for one set of reasons will often masquerade behind another, perhaps more politically palatable, one.

Generic Approaches to Dealing with Blocking Coalitions

Further research on global warming carries the promise, though not the certainty, of reducing the scientific basis for opposing greenhouse control regimes. Of course, other approaches exist for dealing with potential blockers. An appealing option is to prevent their formation in the first place by procedural and / or substantive choice. As the earlier discussion on issue linkage for joint gain suggested, issues can be added as "side payments" to induce previously blocking parties into an agreement. Economic, ideological, and opportunistic opponents may sometimes be won over by appeal to shared interests, by at least partially meeting their separate interests, by providing them with selective incentives, by showing them how a new control regime would really be in their interest, or by inventing new options that sidestep their objections. Classic tactics include isolating and overwhelming them by political pressure, dividing and conquering them, lulling them, and so on. It is to a number of such specific suggestions that the analysis now moves.

DEALING WITH POTENTIAL BLOCKING COALITIONS I: PREVENTION

Evidently, the choice of protocols and the negotiating relationship that is envisioned among them is of central importance; after all, with the choice of a protocol comes a set of opponents (as well as supporters). Protocols have been suggested, seemingly without much explicit analysis of their implications for negotiating success, on a virtually endless number of potential subjects: targets for reducing national greenhouse gas or carbon emissions, credits for providing carbon "sinks," automotive transportation, industrial energy use, tropical forestry, agricultural practices, sea level rise, technology transfer, international funds to aid LDCs, population growth, a carbon tax, tradeable emission permits, methane, and so on.

While it is beyond the scope of this chapter to develop and justify a specific agenda for this process, at least three criteria should guide the choice of protocols: maximizing substantive desirability and the potential of the chosen issue to contribute joint gains to a broad-based group of adherent countries—while reducing the likely opposing interests that will be stimulated. Following substantive value, a prime consideration in the choice of protocols should be a clear-eyed view of the likely opposition. Is a proposed target concentrated or diffuse? Politically influential in key countries or not? Are the necessary changes inexpensive or very costly?

Sequential Approaches to Minimize the Risk of Energizing and Unifying Disparate Interests into a Large Blocking Coalition

A good way to guarantee an endless negotiating impasse would be to handle all the above-mentioned protocols in a "law of the atmosphere" package to be agreed by consensus. Comprehensive anti-greenhouse efforts that affect a number of potentially powerful interests risk energizing and unifying otherwise independent, blocking forces. A protocol that, for example, targeted oil companies, coal mining interests, or automobile manufacturing firms, as well as various agricultural concerns—let alone the full range of human activities that result in greenhouse gases—would almost certainly take a very long time to negotiate and might never surmount the solid wall of opposition it could raise.

An unlikely but illustrative U.S. domestic parallel involving the creation of an unusual and potent blocking coalition may be found in Michael Pertschuk's stewardship of the formerly sleepy Federal Trade Commission (FTC) in the late 1970s (See Heymann 1987). The FTC had recently launched a number of rule-making efforts directly affecting a range of small business interests in the United States, such as funeral homes, used car dealers, and optometrists. Further, the FTC decided to take on the issue of children's TV advertising, which not only threatened major media advertising revenues but also smacked of First Amendment restrictions. In effect, having energized and unified an enormous coalition of large and small business and media companies—many of whom had been bitter rivals before— the FTC engendered a hail of protest, had its budget and authority slashed, and was even shut down for a while. In part, Pertschuk's unintended legacy was a far more unified and politically effective business community.

In the greenhouse case, therefore, to avoid creating a potent unified opposing coalition, it may be wise to proceed *sequentially* with protocols. Perhaps it would be best to pick "easy" subjects first—protocols directed at greenhouse contributors that are politically weak, morally suspect, and concentrated in highly "green" countries—to generate momentum, with strategically chosen later protocols building on early successes.

In this connection, one of the more promising greenhouse control regimes involves allocating a number of "tradeable emission permits" such that the overall level of greenhouse gas emissions could be limited. Beyond the initial allocation, the ultimate distribution of the permits would not have to be negotiated or bureaucratically determined, since these permits could be bought and sold. In theory at least, they would end up in the hands of those entities that could reduce emissions most efficiently. An ongoing question with respect to such a tradeable permits regime is whether it should only cover carbon dioxide emissions or should extend to other greenhouse gases such as methane and nitrous oxides (in order that the *overall* least-cost control actions be chosen). A full answer to this question depends on issues such as source identifiability, monitorability, and negotiating complexity. Yet from the standpoint of blocking coalitions, it is clear that seeking to negotiate a more comprehensive regime would also risk unifying a much wider set of disparate, opposing interests. Analogous reasoning applies to other proposed anti-greenhouse regimes, such as outright emission limits and various forms of "carbon taxes."

DEALING WITH POTENTIAL BLOCKING COALITIONS II: INCREMENTAL AGREEMENTS AND "RATCHETS"

Beyond measures to prevent the formation of blocking coalitions in the first place, a number of other approaches can be characterized as incrementalist. The idea behind them is to gain agreement on a relatively weak or nonspecific treaty or plan of action in the expectation that over time it will progressively be strengthened. This approach may be a conscious, initial choice or may simply reflect the strength of opposing forces in the early negotiations. Advocates may "settle for what they can get" or "half a loaf" and hope that the stage is set for another round that will conclude more in line with their preferences. This section considers several such incrementalist approaches in rough order of how specific and heavy the commitments are that would be undertaken.

Voluntary Actions Short of Agreed Emissions Limits or Specific Greenhouse Control Regimes

Instead of immediately seeking a traditional control regime, other approaches can partly sidestep and prevent the problems of blocking coalitions as well as some of the time lags and sovereign difficulties characteristic of formal treaty negotiation, ratification, and implementation. For example, former UNEP deputy executive director Peter Thacher has argued *against* the conventional wisdom of waiting for a negotiated framework convention as a "first step," to be followed by specific protocols. Instead, in line with the experience of the Mediterranean and Ozone Action Plans, he suggested that as many countries as are now willing should first agree on a greenhouse "action plan" that contains *no* formal obligations but that offers the willing sponsors a vehicle within which to promptly commence valuable research, monitoring, and assessment programs as well as to offer developing countries needed assistance to participate in technical and negotiating forums (Thacher 1990). Such voluntary actions would support and may well speed up the conventional framework / protocol negotiation. Arguably, enough countries and environmental organizations are already supportive enough of such actions that they should not have to wait for the conclusion of a framework convention. (In effect, the climate convention agreed to at the 1992 Earth Summit—which contained no binding greenhouse gas reduction requirements for signatory nations—adopted this approach, postponing negotiations over actual restrictions to a later, "protocol" stage.)

There are also a number of "soft law" options—so called to distinguish them from "hard" treaty law—that function by joint declarations and resolutions. Given the potential of global communications technologies and the efforts of concerned governments and interested nongovernmental organizations, these actions can help to spur "informal" control regimes, in part by building on and influencing domestic opinion. In turn, stronger informal regimes may come to be embodied in more potent formal instruments that might earlier have been blocked by opposing coalitions.

A slightly "harder" option has been suggested by Abram Chayes by analogy to the launching of the International Monetary Fund.[16] By creating a postwar "transition" period during which treaty members could simply "maintain" various forbidden restrictions until they voluntarily relinquished them, the institutional apparatus could be developed, professional staffs and reporting practices established, and momentum built toward the result which was ultimately widely accepted. Applied to the greenhouse case, this would permit further collection of detailed statistical series on global emissions; facilitate technical assistance to environmental agencies, especially in the developing world; permit the development and empirical validation of more specific performance criteria; and help develop a technically competent and credible monitoring and compliance capability.

A "Baseline Protocol"

In the best of circumstances, a framework / protocol process on climate change is bound to take considerable time before any major substantive agreements are hammered out. Meanwhile, valuable time may be lost as countries wait until the international process concludes before taking actions to mitigate greenhouse problems. Some domestic opponents of action will cynically argue for delay; others will merely regard it as prudent bargaining

---

[16]A. Chayes, Managing the transition to a global warming regime or what to do until the treaty comes, in Mathews 1991, 61–68.

technique to hold off any unilateral action until an international accord is reached. Either way, their blocking (and delaying) potential can be damaging.

One approach to this problem would be the early negotiation of a protocol specifying an early baseline date—perhaps in the past—after which anti-greenhouse measures taken by individual countries would be credited against the requirements of a later international agreement (Moomaw 1990). With such a date agreed, states could promptly undertake unilateral or small-group initiatives to reduce greenhouse emissions in the confidence that these measures would "count" toward the reductions required by an ultimate regime. Such a "baseline year" agreement, perhaps negotiated as a protocol, could help to neutralize a major argument of domestic opponents of anti-greenhouse measures who hold that action absent overall international agreement is either unwarranted or foolish.

Given the likely time required for an overall agreement embracing substantive anti-greenhouse measures such as binding targets and timetables, a preliminary "baseline" protocol of this sort should prove far easier to negotiate quickly. Incidentally, such a baseline protocol need only assure states that their actions subsequent to the agreed baseline year would count; the question of the status of actions taken *prior* to the agreed date could be explicitly left for future negotiation.

"Ratchet Mechanisms"

Suppose that greenhouse gas reduction targets were set at extremely modest levels in an initial protocol. Likewise, imagine that an international tax on carbon emissions were initially set at a very low rate—for example, to collect resources for an international environmental fund. Given its low rate, this tax (or set of reduction targets) might not trigger concentrated opposition. Later, with the monitoring and collection structures in place, the tax rate (or targets) might be "ratcheted" up, if the state of the science merited it and if broad-based support existed for such a move.

Indeed, a review of the history of the ozone negotiations suggests the potential value of such a "ratcheting" device. When an agreement to set CFC limits proved unreachable in 1985, the United States and others pressed for the Vienna "framework" convention that collectively legitimated the problem, set in motion joint efforts at monitoring, coordination, and data exchange, and envisioned the later negotiation of more specific protocols.[17]

---

[17] Indeed, the legal discussions that led to the Vienna convention began in 1981, four years after UNEP had formulated a World Plan of Action on the Ozone Layer. See Thacher 1990, 108–9.

In 1987, after scientific consensus on the problem had solidified and industry opposition was largely neutralized, the Montreal protocol embodied an agreement to cut CFC production and use 50 percent by the year 2000. Many environmental activists harshly criticized these agreed targets as inadequate.

Yet the institutional arrangements set up by the Montreal protocol included provisions to facilitate a review of the agreed limits in the face of new evidence (or, effectively, with shifts in public opinion). In effect, these provisions functioned as a "ratchet," whereby later findings such as the direct link between CFCs and the ozone hole stimulated treaty parties to tighten up the limits over the 50 percent base. As UNEP's Mustafa Tolba put it, "By aiming in 1987 for what we could get the nations to sign . . . we acquired a flexible instrument for action. If we had reached too far at Montreal, we would almost certainly have come away empty-handed. . . . [The] protocol that seemed modest to some . . . is proving to be quite a radical instrument (Tolba 1989, 305). This assessment was borne out by the 1990 London negotiations that converted a 50 percent reduction into a virtual CFC ban. This model of settling for relatively modest restrictions on which early agreement can be reached, together with arrangements that facilitate reconsideration, may well be emulated in the climate context.

Yet there is a danger to partial agreements exemplified by the 1963 Partial Test Ban Treaty. A number of observers have criticized these accords as stopping too soon and bleeding off the intense public pressure for change—when, arguably, a *comprehensive* test ban treaty was then attainable with intensified negotiating efforts. By addressing the concerns about Strontium-90 from atmospheric testing in the food chain (particularly in mother's milk), this argument goes, the broader dangers of nuclear testing were not addressed and a valuable opportunity was squandered. Rather than acting as a stepping-stone to a larger accord, the Partial Test Ban Treaty became a stopping place. (Recall also the analogy to the Gramm-Rudman antideficit law that was drawn above.)

With respect to climate change negotiations in particular, it is quite likely that public concern will be cyclic, in part as a result of natural climate variability as well as unrelated environmental events (such as medical waste on beaches and the Exxon Valdez oil spill). Arguably, a naturally occurring period of climate calm, including milder summers and normal rainfall, will lead to reduced public concern and pressure for action. Moreover, scientific understanding will change over time. These prospects argue for more limited agreements with analogs to the ratchet mechanism in the Montreal protocol—if and as more stringent action appears warranted. Such agreements could constitute a "rolling process of intermediate or self-adjusting agreements that respond quickly to growing scientific understanding"

(Mathews 1989). And an even more fundamentally adaptive institution might be envisioned, better matching the rapidly changing science and politics of this issue area.

DEALING WITH BLOCKING COALITIONS III: REDUCING THE RISK OF A NORTH-SOUTH IMPASSE

As discussed above, there is an acute risk that a larger North-South agenda—some of it only loosely related to climate change and much of it highly contentious—will occupy center stage in greenhouse negotiations over time. Indeed, these talks have already been characterized by LDC demands for technology transfer and large resource commitments from the industrial world. It is clear that finance and technology, for example, are legitimate interests, but the extent to which developed countries will be forthcoming on them in the context of a climate change negotiation is far less clear—especially given ideological reservations about what could be seen as resurgent demands for a "discredited" New International Economic Order. Moreover, despite the keen concern in many nations about climate change, the greenhouse problem is speculative, contested, far in the future, and very costly to address now merely on its own terms—absent additional resources to mitigate generalized problems of developing countries. The uncertain prospect of global warming may not be a strong enough hook on which to hang a larger North-South agenda.

With the crumbling of socialist ideology in Eastern Europe and the Soviet Union, many Europeans are also becoming less receptive to formerly attractive NIEO precepts. Thus, if the language negotiated as part of a climate change convention invokes images such as central command, heavy-handed international bureaucracy, forcible technology transfer, blame-casting ideological declarations, guilt-based wealth transfers, and the like, the results of any such negotiation run substantial risk of being overturned. Indeed northern, especially U.S., opponents of a climate change convention may well base their negative stand on the actual or supposed adverse ideological cast of the regime.

As with the law of the sea, therefore, real mutual interdependence means that climate change talks have the ingredients for an inescapable, long-term, North-South engagement: southern insistence on NIEO-like measures met with U.S.–led northern resistance. Given that southern commitment to the NIEO per se has moderated considerably since the 1970s, the risk of an ideologically driven impasse is probably manageable with some conscious effort. As will be discussed below, creative steps are essential to meet legitimate LDC interests while reducing the risks that such an engagement results in endless delay and damaging ideological confrontation—with no action to address the greenhouse problem.

Informal Workshops

A number of well-publicized regional workshops in advance of the negotiations—presented by regional scientists and policy figures who focused on possible local impacts—could help spread the conviction that this is a common threat from a shared problem. Joint developing–developed country research and study should likewise be encouraged, perhaps building on the work of the UNEP-WMO–sponsored Intergovernmental Panel on Climate Change.

During the negotiations themselves, similar informal educational events could be helpful. One extraordinary element of the LOS experience that has been detailed by outside observers consisted of the influence of a computer model of deep ocean mining developed at MIT. This model came to be widely accepted in the face of the great uncertainty felt by the delegates about the engineering and economic aspects of deep-seabed mining. A critical point in the negotiations occurred during a Saturday morning workshop—held outside UN premises, under the auspices of Quaker and Methodist nongovernmental organizations—in which developed- and developing-country delegates were able to meet and extensively query the MIT team that had built the model. Indeed, the delegates over time came to make frequent use of the model for learning, mutual education, invention of new options—and even as a political excuse to move from frozen positions (Sebenius 1990).

Similarly, a series of informal, off-the-record workshops where diplomats and politically active participants in the negotiation gathered aided the Montreal protocol process. These events greatly increased mutual understanding, improved relationships, and contributed to a successful treaty. Despite its potential abuse by advocates, therefore, outside scientific information—when it can be seen to be objective and is accessible to the participants—can help move a complex negotiation, even one that is highly politicized and ideologically controversial, in the direction of mutual cooperation. (Of course, improved science might instead clarify winners and losers, thus polarizing the issue.)

Advisory Groups and Cross-Cutting Coalitions

Given the actual and feared adverse impacts of measures under discussion, conference leadership would be wise to make extensive use of broadly constituted advisory groups, composed of business and other multinational interests, to understand concerns, anticipate emerging problems, correct misapprehensions, and communicate about the issues and evolving negotiating responses. Not only could the two-way communication be useful in such settings, but cross-cutting coalitions might form. For example, industries that could gain from substantial anti-greenhouse action in the developing world (by, for example, supplying critical technology for energy efficiency) might make common cause with key LDCs and green advocacy organizations in arguing the case for more developed-country assistance for this purpose.

Mutually Beneficial Linkages

Just as in the LOS experience, mutually beneficial "manageable packages" of protocols under a framework climate convention might be cautiously extended to other environmental issues in the context of the 1992 conference. This might have the effect of bringing on board otherwise potential blockers from the developing world. For example, desertification and soil erosion issues may be more pressing to key developing countries than greenhouse questions. Many developed countries that are unwilling to make "bribes" to induce developing-country participation may nonetheless be genuinely concerned about and more willing to be forthcoming on these regional issues in the context of a larger agreement that promised global climate benefits. Similarly, more expansive versions of so-called debt-for-nature swaps may be explored. One of the most potent long-term steps that could be taken by developing countries to combat global warming (as well as a host of other environmental issues) would be significantly stepped-up population control programs.[18] Unlike, say, energy use restrictions, this course of action has the virtue of helping rather than hindering economic development objectives. For cash-strapped LDCs, relatively modest developed-country aid in this dimension could considerably enhance domestic population control efforts.

A New Ideological "Template"

The North-South conflict has been a staple of recent global negotiations—from the UN Conference on Trade and Development to debt and codes of conduct for transnational corporations—though the overt NIEO focus has moderated in the years between the LOS and Montreal talks.[19] Joint development of a new "ideological template" within which the climate question could be negotiated offers another means to escape impasse. Such a new conception could avoid lumping countries with vastly different climate interests—from coal-rich developing countries such as China and India, to sub-Saharan Africa, to the "Second World" of Central Europe, and to Norway

---

[18] See, generally, P. R. Ehrlich and A. H. Ehrlich (1990), *The population explosion* (New York: Simon & Schuster).

[19] See, e.g., Rothstein 1979 for an account of an earlier such engagement.

and the United States—into catchall categories such as "North" and "South." The most promising candidates to date are the principles of "sustainable development"—insisting on development that meets the needs of the present without compromising the ability of future generations to meet their own needs—articulated by the Brundtland Commission in *Our Common Future*.[20] Though in need of clearer definition, these widely discussed principles call for tight links between environment and development, for institutions that integrate environmental and economic decision making, for international cooperation on global issues, and for major efforts toward more sustainable paths of population, energy, and resources. Whether such principles can come to have the acceptance, weight, and specific implication needed to affect climate negotiations remains to be seen, but they are a promising possibility.

DEALING WITH BLOCKING COALITIONS IV: A SMALL-SCALE (EXPANDING) AGREEMENT

The complexities of a universal process, either in a stand-alone framework / protocol context or as part of a larger conference, may still threaten endless delay or impasse. In such cases, an alternative possibility will likely become more salient. But suppose that a smaller group of industrialized states—with potent domestic interests keenly interested in anti-greenhouse measures—were to negotiate among themselves a reduction regime—including timetables and targets, either voluntary or mandated. Presumably the core group would include major contributors to the greenhouse problem in which there was substantial and urgent domestic sentiment for action. A natural starting core would be the twelve nations of the European Community, the six member states of the European Free Trade Association, plus Japan, Australia, and Canada—all of which by late 1990 had unilaterally or collectively adopted greenhouse gas stabilization or reduction targets.[21] If and as the United States became more greenhouse-friendly politically, it would be a natural candidate for such a core group.

Agreement among such a group would likely prove far easier to achieve than a global accord, as a function of the smaller number of states involved as well as their greater economic and political homogeneity. The obvious

---

[20] World Commission on Environment and Development (1987), *Our common future* (Oxford, England: Oxford University Press).

[21] At present, the OECD countries account for approximately 45 percent of carbon emissions; with the addition of the Soviet Union and Eastern Europe, the total would rise to 71 percent. Manne and Richels 1990, 15.

umbrella for such an effort is the framework climate convention signed at the 1992 Earth Summit, but existing institutions (such as the UN Economic Commission for Europe or the OECD) might also facilitate the process. And while there would clearly be substantial negotiating difficulties involved, this smaller-scale process could avoid a protracted, inconclusive North-South clash that might characterize a larger forum.

To be effective in the longer term, of course, a smaller-scale agreement would have to be expanded later to include key developing countries such as China, India, Brazil, Indonesia, and Mexico, as well as additional developed nations, especially in Eastern Europe. In this sense, an agreement explicitly designed for an increasing number of adherents has strong parallels to agreements that "ratchet" to become increasingly stringent. The design of the smaller negotiation could anticipate and facilitate such an expansion in several ways.

First, the smaller agreement should seek to follow the negotiation of a widely accepted framework convention on climate, when the general problem will have been legitimated and accepted to the largest extent possible.

Second, it should be cast not as an alternative to the global process over protocols but as a complement to it—in which those nations that have evidently caused the present greenhouse gas problem so far are those that would take early actions to mitigate emissions. This would give the smaller group that had agreed to cuts a higher moral standing in soliciting later reductions from others.

Third, the smaller-scale group should structure its accord with the explicit expectation of collectively negotiating incentives, likely tailored to special circumstances, for key developing nations to join the accord. For example, the smaller group might agree to tax its members on their carbon emissions. All or part of those tax proceeds could be used to gain the acquiescence of other key countries to anti-greenhouse measures. The smaller group could create an entity that would carry out these negotiations with these key countries, rather than leaving such negotiations to ad hoc efforts by individual member countries.

Negotiations between the smaller treaty group and, say, China, could set a schedule of emission targets and offer China significant incentives to reach them. Or it could address a range of China's environmental and other concerns in return for less climate-damaging development (e.g., assistance with greater exploration for Chinese natural gas reserves, Chinese agreement to use CFC substitutes in refrigeration, and to make its coal development more greenhouse-friendly, perhaps by the transfer of more efficient electrical generating equipment). Such "customized" small-group negotiations—with China, India, Brazil, and others—should be more conducive to environmentally desirable results than would generalized North-South clashes in a full-scale UN conference.

Fourth, as the group of adherents to the smaller convention grew in size, it might choose to impose a tax on products imported into member countries from nonadherents, perhaps based on the direct or indirect carbon content of those products. The carrot (of providing individually tailored negotiated incentives for nonadherents to join) and the stick (of raising such a "carbon fence" around the anti-greenhouse group) might together lead to a much larger number of countries jointly taking measures to prevent climate change. Evidently, a price to be faced, deliberated, and accepted by the smaller group would be a substantial number of free-riding countries. With a large enough group of adherents, however, the smaller group could still be preferable to no agreement at all.

Ironically, though a number of developing countries have joined the Montreal protocol, it is quite possible to interpret this experience after the fact as strongly analogous to the smaller-scale convention just discussed. While carried out in the context of a widely accepted framework (the Vienna convention), a relatively small number of key CFC-producing countries ultimately acceded to the CFC reductions in the Montreal protocol. However, important LDCs (India, China, Brazil) did not go along until 1990. India, for example, demanded $2 billion—a number related to its cost of using more ozone-friendly technology in the future—as its price to join the 1987 protocol (Stone 1990). In 1990, a number of developed nations agreed to provide such assistance up to $240 million. This proved sufficiently attractive to representatives of states such as India and China that they indicated willingness to join. Yet as a result of the "smaller-scale" Montreal protocol, extremely significant ozone-protection measures are now under way even before the full resolution of important issues concerning financial aid and technology transfer to the developing world.[22]

It is important to note that the provisions in the Montreal protocol for LDC financial and technical assistance, while generally in favor of such actions, did not contain very specific commitments. Taking this frustrating experience as a lesson, LDC activists (e.g., India, Brazil, China) will likely press for far more specificity in a larger climate conference as early as possible. These questions must be addressed, but requiring their resolution before any climate action is undertaken could cause considerable delay.

---

[22]The experience of the Long-Range Transboundary Air Pollution Convention, in which groups of expanding size acceded to the later sulfur and nitrogen oxides protocols, is also generally in accord with this "small-scale" approach. For a summary, see C. I. Jackson (1990), A tenth anniversary review of the ECE Convention on Long-Range Transboundary Air Pollution, *International Environmental Affairs* 2 (3): 217–26.

The problem of negotiating a regime to control global warming amply illustrates powerful barriers to agreement, versions of which apply in a large number of contexts. This chapter has sought to clarify the nature of these barriers and suggest constructive responses to them. Environmental diplomats have largely taken negative lessons from the LOS negotiations and positive ones from the CFC accords in envisioning a framework / protocol process for global warming. Yet gaining significant action to curb greenhouse emissions will be a far more difficult task than dealing with either ocean resources or the ozone layer. Despite the apparent appeal of the step-by-step framework / protocol approach, a review of the evolution of the LOS process from separate "mini-conventions" into a comprehensive treaty illustrates the powerful forces that will likely operate on a climate change negotiation to combine protocols and to collapse what is seen as a many-stage process into a more unified effort. The trick will be to find smaller, more manageable packages that embody enough mutual gains to attract key players.

The power of the coalitions that will arise to block greenhouse action—not merely for reasons of economic interest, but also for reasons of science, ideology, and / or opportunism—must be taken into account in designing an effective negotiating process. Preventing and overcoming these forces could be aided by a sophisticated choice and sequence of protocols, as well as innovative devices such as "ratchet" mechanisms, negotiated "baselines," and voluntary actions short of negotiated targets. Even if these hazards are avoided, the possibility of a North-South impasse looms; a number of actions could mitigate it, including workshops, negotiation process choices, creative linkages, and advancement of new ideological "templates." If these measures are unsuccessful, attention may shift to a smaller-scale, expanding convention that could use incentives and penalties to later bring other states into its fold. Good candidates to start this process include those countries that have unilaterally committed to greenhouse targets.

In sum, to an advocate of a new greenhouse control regime, the fundamental negotiating task is to craft and sustain a meaningful winning coalition of countries backing such a regime. Two powerful barriers to this fundamental task are (1) that each member of the coalition fails to see enough gain in the regime relative to the alternatives to adhere, and (2) that potential and actual "blocking" coalitions of interests opposed to the regime are neither prevented from forming, acceptably accommodated, nor otherwise neutralized. The negotiation design recommendations developed in this chapter suggest that over time, as the science and politics warrant, there are many ways to surmount these daunting barriers for the climate, and, one hopes, in other areas.

PART FOUR

Institutional Perspectives

Cooperation and Competition in Litigation: Can Lawyers Dampen Conflict?

Ronald J. Gilson and Robert H. Mnookin

Most civil cases are settled before trial but not until years of legal wrangling have tied up the courts and run up large fees and expenses. Cases aren't settled sooner because lawyers, who benefit most from litigation, are in control—not the clients who pay the bill.

WHITNEY NORTH SEYMOUR, 1992

As a peace-maker the lawyer has a superior opportunity of being a good man. There will still be business enough.

ABRAHAM LINCOLN

*D*o lawyers facilitate dispute resolution, or do they instead exacerbate conflict and pose a barrier to the efficient resolution of disputes? A distinctive characteristic of our formal mechanisms of conflict resolution is that clients carry on their disputes through lawyers. Yet at a time when the role of lawyers in dispute resolution has captured not only public but political attention (See Margolick 1991), social scientists have remained largely uninterested in the influence of lawyers on the disputing process. This is not to say that academics have ignored the growth in civil litigation in the United States. (See Galanter and Rodgers 1991; Galanter 1988.) Economists have developed an extensive literature that models one or another aspect of the litigation and settlement process. (Cooter and Rubenfeld [1989] provide an excellent survey.) But the economic literature, with rare exceptions, shares a troublesome feature. Almost by convention, litigation is modeled as a two-person game between principals, thereby abstracting away the legal system's central institutional characteristic—that litigation is carried out by agents.

While any model must make concessions to tractability, this simplifying assumption is especially troublesome because lawyers have long been considered to have a special influence on how litigation is conducted, even if there has been no consensus on whether lawyers dampen or exacerbate conflict in litigation. Today, the dominant popular view is that lawyers magnify the inherent divisiveness of dispute resolution. Litigators, according to this vision, rarely cooperate to resolve disputes efficiently. Instead, shielded by a professional ideology that is said to require zealous advocacy, they end-

For an extension and elaboration of this chapter, more substantially referenced and with greater attention paid to strategies for increasing the level of cooperation in litigation, see Gilson and Mnookin 1994.

lessly and wastefully fight in ways that enrich the lawyers but rarely advantage the clients.

Within the legal profession, many share this pessimistic view, as suggested by the quoted comment of Whitney North Seymour, former United States attorney for the Southern District of New York and president of the New York Bar Association. Claims that the conduct of litigation has become uncivil and unprofessional, and that lawyers' conduct has deteriorated in ways that increase the contentiousness of civil litigation are now standard fare for lawyer convocations. Interestingly, the anguish at the current state of affairs is not over the behavior of a few disreputable lawyers who abuse litigation practices in ways that respectable lawyers from white-shoe firms would not. Rather, the concern is that, like Pogo, big-city commercial litigators have met the enemy in themselves: the perception is that litigators from the great national law firms are now very much part of the problem.

But the lawyer as purveyor of needless conflict is not the only vision of the lawyer's role in litigation. Over a century ago, Abraham Lincoln suggested that lawyers can play an extraordinarily constructive role in disputes—as peacemakers who facilitate efficient and fair resolution of conflict when their clients cannot do so for themselves. From this perspective, a central characteristic of the formal legal system—that clients carry on their dispute through lawyers who are their agents—has the potential for dampening rather than exacerbating the conflictual character of litigation. In this chapter we offer a conceptual foundation for this alternative perspective, a foundation that rests on the idea that lawyers may be able to cooperate with each other in circumstances where their clients cannot.

Our story involves a dialectic between game theory and agency theory. In section I we begin with the most abstract vision of the litigation process: a one-round, two-person prisoner's dilemma game in which the parties' inability to effectively cooperate results in dominant strategies that yield suboptimal results. Because a single lawsuit has a number of strategic interactions, in section II we complicate the analysis by allowing the clients to play a finite number of repeated games against each other.

The standard prisoner's dilemma and other game-theoretic models of the litigation process abstract away what we have noted as the central institutional characteristic of the legal system: that litigation is carried out by lawyers on behalf of their clients. In section III, we show that in contrast to principals who are unlikely ever to litigate against one another again, lawyers are repeat players who have the opportunity to establish reputations. Thus, at the core of our story is the potential for principals, by choosing lawyers with a reputation for cooperative behavior, to solve the prisoner's dilemma by selecting lawyers who credibly commit them to a cooperative strategy. The dialectic character of the process results from the fact that bonding cooperation by means of an agent inevitably introduces a principal / agent conflict that exacerbates the general difficulty of establishing a reputational equilibrium in the market for lawyers and law firms. The danger exists that the agents may "collude" to exacerbate conflict when their own interests are served by that behavior. Moreover, the requisite reputation may be difficult to establish and maintain for individual lawyers practicing alone.

Section IV explores whether law firms may be more effective repositories of reputation than individual lawyers. We show that the firm may ameliorate some principal / agent conflicts that might undermine cooperation. But like the introduction of individual lawyers to the basic prisoner's dilemma game, the introduction of firms of lawyers also adds a new level of agency conflict, now between the firm and the individual lawyers who compose it, that has the potential of undermining the ability of lawyers to dampen conflict in litigation.

In section V we draw on the accumulated insights from our analysis to address what changes in the market for legal services may account for the perception that commercial litigation (and lawyers) have become more conflictual, and to examine why there may be more cooperation in some areas of practice than in others.

We conclude by suggesting why further theoretical and empirical research concerning patterns of cooperation among lawyers will deepen our understanding of how the institutional environment might be altered to enhance dispute resolution.

I. LITIGATION AS A ONE-ROUND PRISONER'S DILEMMA

The prisoner's dilemma provides a useful heuristic for illuminating a common characteristic of dispute settlement through litigation. In many disputes, each litigant may feel compelled to make a contentious move in order to avoid being exploited and to take advantage of any weakness in the other side. Nevertheless, the net result of contentious moves by both may be an outcome that is less efficient than if the disputants had been able to cooperate.

This possibility is suggested by the following "litigation game," which has the required characteristics of a one-round prisoner's dilemma. Able and Baker have a dispute over how to divide $100 according to some legal standard. For the moment, we assume that litigation does not involve lawyers, but instead only the two parties and a judge. Each party has information, unknown by the other side, material to the dispute. Some of this information is favorable and some of it is unfavorable. Before the judge decides the case, there is a one-stage simultaneous disclosure process in which each party hands to the judge and the opposing party a sealed envelope containing information. Only two moves are possible, and neither player can know in

PAYOFF MATRIX

Player 1

		Cooperate	Compete
Player 2			
Cooperate		50 / 50	15 / 70
Compete		70 / 15	35 / 35

advance what the other will do. One move is cooperation. Cooperation involves a player's voluntarily (and at no cost to the other side) disclosing both to the other side and to the judge all information in its possession material to the dispute. Defection, on the other hand, involves the adversarial use of the disclosure process to hide unfavorable information. As a consequence, the other side will have to spend $15 to force disclosure of some but not all of the information withheld. After the envelope exchange, the judge resolves the dispute on the basis of the information disclosed.

With a payoff structure, such as the matrix that follows, this game poses a prisoner's dilemma. If both players cooperate, there are no disclosure expenses for either side and we will assume the judge awards $50 to Able and $50 to Baker. If both players defect, each will have to spend $15 to pry out some but not all of the unfavorable information possessed by the other side. While the judge lacks complete information, we will assume that she divides the $100 in the same ratio, but the net recovery to the parties is now $35 to Able and $35 to Baker. If one player defects while the other cooperates, this provides the defector with a higher payoff ($70) and hurts the "sucker" in two ways. First, because the cooperating player has disclosed all of his unfavorable information while the defecting party has only disclosed some of the information unfavorable to him, the judge awards the sucker a gross recovery of only $30. And second, the "sucker" has had to spend $15 to get less than all of the information unfavorable to the other side before the judge. This means his net recovery is only $15.

To what extent does the prisoner's dilemma represent an appropriate, albeit highly simplified, model of the litigation process? Let us first focus on the payoff structure of a prisoner's dilemma. The best payoff for each player must occur when that player defects and the other player cooperates. The sucker's payoff occurs when a player cooperates while the other player defects. The other two outcomes fall in between, with the reward for mutual cooperation better than the payoff for mutual defection. In other words, a prisoner's dilemma cannot be a zero-sum or purely distributive game: the total combined payoff from mutual cooperation must be greater than the total combined payoff from mutual defection.

How realistic is it to assume that in litigation the payoff structure takes this form? In many disputes the assumption that there are potential gains from cooperation seems entirely realistic. Mutual cooperation should usually involve lower total litigation costs than mutual defection. Moreover, when parties share information, reveal their true underlying interests, and engage in collaborative problem solving, they may sometimes be able to develop new options that "create value," or "expand the pie" for both disputants in comparison to the resolution flowing from mutual defection. (See Lax and Sebenius 1986.) Parties may sometimes both be made better off through a negotiated resolution that takes a form that a judge would not impose. It also seems plausible that in many disputes, because of the adversarial nature of litigation, cooperative moves by one litigant, if unreciprocated by the other, can lead to exploitation and something akin to a sucker's payoff.

Not every legal dispute involves the sort of payoff structure required by the prisoner's dilemma, and as we suggest later, this has important implications. In some disputes the very best payoff for one or both players may occur when both players cooperate. In other cases, mutual defection that causes delay may yield the best payoff for a defendant because interest earned by putting off the damage payment will exceed any differential in transaction costs. This suggests the importance of exploring in particular legal contexts whether the prisoner's dilemma's payoff assumptions are in fact appropriate.

In addition to an appropriate payoff matrix, a prisoner's dilemma requires that one player cannot know for sure what the other player will do before the actual move is made: enforceable commitments or contracts are not possible and this means that the parties cannot credibly bind themselves to cooperate.

At first glance, this restrictive assumption seems entirely inappropriate for the litigation process. Disputants in litigation can enter into enforceable agreements with respect to future conduct. The prisoner's dilemma would disappear if the parties could, at reasonable cost, spell out the terms of an enforceable agreement to cooperate in the litigation, to exchange all material information, and to dampen the litigation costs. The problem is that in many cases, particularly complex ones, the parties may not be able to specify fully the terms of such an agreement in advance. Agreements with respect to certain aspects of litigation—for example, limiting the number of depositions, or adopting a particular discovery schedule—may be easy to write and enforce, but it may be very difficult or expensive to specify fully a contract to "conduct a litigation cooperatively" or "to disclose all material information." Moreover, even if the terms can be specified, it may be very difficult to determine whether notwithstanding the agreement, a defection has occurred.

Even if a breach of such a contract were observable by the parties, a violation may be difficult to verify to a judge, thus making enforcement problematic. (See Kreps 1990a.) Discovery disputes in contentious cases reveal the seriousness of this problem. If one party claims that the other party has breached an agreement by engaging in abusive discovery practices, a judge often faces substantial evidentiary difficulties. Typically, the judge does not know a great deal about the information available to either the responding or the requesting party. "If the responding party were to produce fully the information sought and display it to the judge, the responding party would already have incurred all the costs that the responding party was trying to avoid. In the absence of such production, the responding party has some leeway with which to exaggerate the burden of response, and a wise judge will thus, to some extent, discount the protestations of that responding party. The requesting party provides no more reliable guidance, as that party possesses the incentive to exaggerate, in a complementary fashion, the ease with which the responding party can produce the information." (J. Setear 1989.)

This also suggests why a judge may be no more able to ensure cooperation by enforcing general rules of procedure than by enforcing a general contract between the parties. In our game, for example, if the judge could identify defection, then defection could be punished. Relying on the judge, the parties could avoid the prisoner's dilemma. Unfortunately, breaches of general rules of procedure—"don't engage in burdensome discovery"—are no easier to observe than breaches of a contract of similar specificity. Thus the judge would have difficulty verifying defection even when both parties know it has occurred. In sum, there remains a wide range of litigation conduct, including especially a general commitment to cooperative behavior, with respect to which the prisoner's dilemma game's assumption that binding commitments are impossible is descriptively accurate.

Thus, despite its restrictive assumptions, in our view the prisoner's dilemma game is a powerful heuristic for understanding the barriers to cooperation in litigation.

II. LITIGATION AS A MULTIROUND PRISONER'S DILEMMA GAME

At first glance, litigation between principals who are unlikely to sue each other again is a one-round game. However, if one views the lawsuit through a microscope it disaggregates: the one-round game becomes a series of repeated prisoner's dilemma games. Each dispute over the scope of a discovery request, or the scheduling of depositions, or the admissibility of evidence, is a separate game. (Indeed, in litigation, extending the process can be a form of noncooperation.) Each tactical choice during a lawsuit might be understood as having the structure of a prisoner's dilemma. Does the fact that principals play against each other on multiple occasions over the course of a single lawsuit provide an opportunity for cooperation not available to players in a one-round game?

The answer seems to be no, although the explanation is more complicated than it once appeared. Luce and Raiffa demonstrated some time ago that so long as the prisoner's dilemma game was played a known finite number of times, rational players still would have no incentive to cooperate. The reasoning is straightforward. In the last round, both players know that there is no incentive to cooperate because the final game is no different than the one-round game described in section I. Now consider the next-to-last round. Because the players know that both will defect in the last round, the next-to-last round is no different than the last. Reasoning backward round by round, the multiround game will unravel all the way back to the first. (See Luce and Raiffa 1957.)

More recent research, however, suggests that cooperative behavior can develop in a multiround prisoner's dilemma game under certain conditions. Suppose that instead of a finite number of rounds, there is only a known probability that the game will end. If there is a high enough probability in each round that an additional round will played, the prospects of future dealings can induce cooperation depending upon the payoff function. Indeed, Robert Axelrod's computer simulation suggests the possibility that cooperation may evolve because players who commit to a "tit-for-tat" strategy might over the long run do very well (Axelrod 1984).

Other research has suggested that cooperation may be sustained even in games of a known number of rounds, provided the number of rounds is large enough and there are at least a few players in the population who will always play cooperatively. (See Milgrom and Roberts 1982; Kreps, Milgrom, Roberts and Wilson 1982.)

Together, this theoretical work suggests that there may be circumstances under which the parties may be able to escape the prisoner's dilemma, provided there are significantly high prospects that they will have a large number of future dealings with each other. Unfortunately, the conditions necessary for the evolution of cooperation in the course of a single lawsuit, even decomposed into a series of subgames, are sufficiently rigorous that the prisoner's dilemma remains a useful heuristic with which to explore the potential for lawyers to facilitate cooperation.

First, the disaggregation of a single lawsuit into a series of subgames is not complete. Unlike the repeated prisoner's dilemma games considered in the theoretical literature, the aggregate payoff to the subgames in the disaggregated litigation remains fixed. Thus, the stakes change as the subgames are played out. Second, and more important, the number of subgames in the disaggregated litigation, while perhaps unspecifiable *ex ante*, has predictable finite limits. Thus, within a reasonably predictable range, the final round can be located and unraveling will begin. Finally, the strategies that induce cooperation in multiround games require that both parties know after each round whether their opponent cooperated or defected. For example, a shared strategy of tit-for-tat deteriorates into alternating defections if the parties with sufficient frequency mistake cooperation for defection. (See Bendor, Kramer, and Stout 1991.) In litigation, where even cooperative behavior occurs in the context of competition, the risk of misunderstanding an opponent's move is significant. One's opponent does not announce that she is cooperating or defecting, but merely takes an action that must be evaluated by degree: was the action *too* competitive and therefore a defection? In the prisoner's dilemma, each player has only two basic moves: cooperation or defection. In litigation, there are many gray tones between the black and white of these two pure moves.

III. CAN LAWYERS FACILITATE COOPERATION?

We are now ready to introduce individual lawyers into the clients' prisoner's dilemma litigation game. Each client would prefer to cooperate if only she were confident that her opponent also would cooperate. However, each lacks the means to credibly commit her good intentions. Can disputing through agents provide a means to make such a commitment? Do lawyers have the potential to solve the game-theoretic problem of assuring cooperation?

The Pre-litigation Game: Choosing Lawyers

Suppose that both clients are required to litigate through a lawyer (an assumption that, for a change, *is* descriptively accurate). Suppose further that there exists a class of sole practitioners who have reputations for cooperation which assure that, once retained, they will conduct the litigation in a cooperative fashion. Three final assumptions define our "pre-litigation game." First, clients disclose their choice of lawyer—whether they chose a cooperative lawyer—prior to the beginning of the litigation game. Second, if one client chooses a cooperative lawyer and her opponent does not, the client choosing a cooperative lawyer can change her mind without cost before the litigation game is played. Third, after the litigation game begins, clients cannot change lawyers.

Under these assumptions, disputing through lawyers provides an escape from the prisoner's dilemma because the choice of a cooperative lawyer allows clients to make a credible commitment to cooperation. As we have defined this game, each client's dominant strategy is to chose a cooperative lawyer. If client A chooses a cooperative lawyer and client B also chooses a cooperative lawyer, both clients receive the cooperative payoff. Alternatively, if client B does not choose a cooperative lawyer, client A is no worse off having initially chosen to cooperate. In that event, client A gets to replace her cooperative lawyer with a gladiator and is in the same position as if she had chosen a gladiator in the first instance. Thus, her dominant strategy is to choose a cooperative lawyer and switch if her opponent does not adopt a parallel strategy. Of course, client B confronts the same choices and has the same dominant strategy. The result is a cooperative equilibrium if the litigation game has the payoff structure of a prisoner's dilemma.

How realistic are these three assumptions about the pre-litigation game? Plaintiffs must typically disclose their choice of lawyer before the real litigation game begins: the lawyer's name is, quite literally, the first thing that appears on the complaint. Similarly, the defendant must have a lawyer to respond to the complaint, even to request an extension of the time in which an answer to the complaint must be filed. Again, the identity of the lawyer chosen is disclosed.

Can a plaintiff choosing a cooperative lawyer costlessly switch to a gladiator upon learning that her opponent has chosen a gladiator? In the real world, there are costs in switching lawyers, but these costs are likely to be low at the outset. A client will have expended little on her lawyer by the time the identity of her opponent's lawyer is revealed. Thus, for practical purposes, the game's assumption of a costless opportunity to switch lawyers on the disclosure of opposing counsel is consistent with real litigation patterns.

The third assumption—that clients cannot change lawyers during the litigation game—is more problematic. At first glance, the assumption seems patently false; a client is allowed to discharge counsel at any time. On closer examination, the presence of substantial switching costs may provide a reasonable proxy for a prohibition on discharging cooperative counsel once the litigation is well under way. As litigation proceeds, a lawyer expends substantial time becoming familiar with the law and especially the facts of the case. The client pays for the lawyer's acquisition of this knowledge. The client's investment in the lawyer's knowledge is relationship-specific in the extreme; that is, it is of *no* value to the client if the lawyer is fired. Thus, the price of firing the lawyer is the cost of bringing another lawyer up to speed in the litigation While not a prohibition on changing lawyers, substantial switching costs imposes a penalty on defection. (See Klemperer 1987 for a general discussion of how switching costs create market power.) Indeed, the longer the litigation continues, the higher the cost.

Thus, the special assumptions of our pre-litigation game by which clients credibly commit to cooperation by their choice of lawyer are not implausible. What remains, however, is the most critical of the assumptions on which lawyers' potential to facilitate cooperation depends: the existence of lawyers with reputations for cooperation. How and why are such reputations created and sustained? How do clients learn which lawyers are cooperative?

A Reputation Market for Lawyers

The preceding discussion suggests why there might be a demand for cooperative lawyers. Both parties to a lawsuit with a prisoner's dilemma payoff schedule would like to hire cooperative lawyers because that allows them to commit to a cooperative strategy. Clients should be willing to pay a premium for such lawyers, reflecting a portion of the amount by which the cooperative payoff exceeds the noncooperative payoff.

Establishing the supply side is also straightforward. Lawyers would be willing to invest in achieving a reputation for cooperation because they would receive a return on that investment by virtue of the premium fees clients would be willing to pay. As in standard reputation models, the lawyer's investment in reputation serves two functions. First, it identifies the lawyer as one possessing the desired, but otherwise unobservable, attribute; the client must be able to find a cooperative lawyer. Second, it represents the penalty that the market will impose if the lawyer treats his reputation as bait rather than as a bond by turning gladiator at the instance of an opportunistic client. A lawyer's investment in a cooperative reputation is forfeit if he once behaves noncooperatively. (For other applications of involving reputational intermediaries, see Klein and Leffler 1981; Gilson and Kraakman 1984; Diamond 1984.) Thus, so long as the lawyer's investment in reputation exceeds the size of the bribe an opportunistic client would be willing to pay, cooperative lawyers will not be suborned and a market for cooperative lawyers should be available for clients who find themselves in litigation with a prisoner's dilemma payoff.

However, establishing that clients would demand demonstrably cooperative lawyers and that lawyers would want to supply that service is not sufficient to assure that the market operates. The key word in the previous sentence is "demonstrably." The linchpin of this structure is that the lawyer's cooperative behavior be observable. What makes the client's commitment credible is that her lawyer will lose his investment in reputation if he behaves noncooperatively. But this penalty cannot be imposed if the noncooperative behavior cannot be observed. Thus, the structure fails if an erstwhile cooperative lawyer can behave noncooperatively and get away with it.

For this purpose it is critical to follow David Kreps and return to the distinction between observable and verifiable misconduct noted earlier (Kreps

1990a). That misconduct be observable requires only that the party suffering the affront know with confidence that it occurred. For that misconduct to be verifiable, in contrast, the party suffering the affront must be able to demonstrate to an enforcement agency such as a court that the misconduct occurred. The difference is important. Verification requires formal proof of misconduct sufficient to satisfy a standard specific enough for judicial application. It is commonplace that misconduct which is observable—known to the participants—nonetheless may not be verifiable either because there is no extrinsic proof and the misbehaving party can simply deny it, or because the cost of verifying the misconduct is too expensive, or because the legal standard is limited to extreme misconduct because of the difficulty of defining misconduct.

In our case, noncooperative conduct by one client's lawyer may not be verifiable, but it may nonetheless be readily observable. For a reputational market to be perfectly functioning, the costs of observability must be low at several levels. In the context of the repeated prisoner's dilemma, the costs of observability can be referred to as the costs of scrutiny (see Frank 1988), which consist of three elements: (1) the costs of clients in gauging the reputation of the lawyer, (2) the costs of a lawyer in gauging the reputation of the opposing counsel, and (3) the costs of each side in gauging the facts and the law necessary for litigation. In an adequately functioning reputation market all three costs must be low.

The institutional factors that determine the costs of scrutiny are diverse and beyond the scope of this chapter. They include, among other things, the sophistication of legal clientele, the complexity of litigation, and the speed with which information about reputation spreads in the legal community. Notice, however, that if any of these costs are high the reputational market will not function adequately. For example, if there are considerable costs borne by clients in gauging the reputation of their counsel, disputants will not know whether they have chosen a gladiator. The costs of scrutiny determine the functioning of the reputational market and can affect the ability of a reputational penalty to promote cooperation in the prisoner's dilemma game.

Agency Problems That May Subvert Cooperation

To this point we have concentrated on establishing the feasibility of individual lawyers with reputations for cooperation serving to bond the cooperation of their clients. Lawyers in individual practice do have the potential to facilitate cooperation in litigation. But their ability to fulfill that potential is limited by the fact that commitment to cooperation is bonded through agents. This gives rise to three possible agency problems.

First, the two lawyer-agents may "conspire" to maximize their income at the expense of their clients by noncooperative behavior that prolongs the litigation and increases legal fees. While each lawyer stands as gatekeeper against the other lawyer's individual noncooperative misconduct directed at the opposing client, what protects both clients from the lawyers' joint determination to behave noncooperatively, especially because most instances of joint noncooperative behavior by the lawyers are difficult for a client to observe?

Second, an agent with a reputation for cooperation may be subverted by her client. This second problem represents the converse of the first—because a lawyer in solo practice has a limited number of clients, a particular client may be so important that the threat of withdrawing his patronage may induce the lawyer to risk her cooperative reputation by behaving noncooperatively. When a dispute is large and complex, while there may be greater gains from mutual cooperation (compared to mutual defection), there may also be greater gains from a unilateral defection. If a large and complex matter represents a substantial percent of a sole practitioner's practice, this may mean that a client's threat to his own lawyer to change counsel will be more intimidating.

Third, lawyers are short-lived. Reputation models typically assume that the party whose reputation is relied upon has an infinite life. (See Rasmusen 1989 at 96–7.) Lawyers, however, do not.

The relation between the cooperative lawyer and the opposing client can itself be seen as a one-sided prisoner's dilemma game. The client is asked to choose cooperation (by not changing his cooperative counsel for a gladiator) in reliance on the cooperative lawyer's reputation. This reliance is warranted because if the lawyer behaves noncooperatively, she will be penalized by losing her valuable reputation. But if the lawyer is conducting her last trial, then the penalty cannot be imposed. When a repeated prisoner's dilemma game has a finite (and more or less) predictable end, theory tells us it may unravel. To be sure, common sense may counsel that a lawyer with years of practice before her will not destroy her investment in a cooperative reputation for the payoff available for defecting in a single case. However, individual lawyers are short-lived; they predictably retire, and this may well create "end-game" problems.

While it is beyond the scope of our efforts here to examine the manner in which lawyers might develop and sustain a reputation for cooperation, the problem of reputation formation is not straightforward in situations where reputations must be developed by behavior rather than by investment in reputation-specific assets like image advertising. (See, e.g., Diamond 1989.) Assume, not unreasonably, that a reputation for cooperation takes time to develop. Further assume that a lawyer's skills also take time to develop, so that it is only with age and experience that a lawyer is asked to represent clients in litigation involving both large amounts and large potential gains from cooperation. Both assumptions increase the plausibility of concern that a cooperative solution to the one-sided prisoner's dilemma game may unravel. The larger and more complex the cases handled by the lawyer, presumably the larger the gains from defection and the larger the bribe her own client would be willing to pay her to cheat on her investment in reputation. And because the lawyer is retained to handle larger and more complex cases only as her reputation and skills grows with time, she is ever closer to retirement. This pattern yields the perverse result that at the same time the size of·the bribe offered to the lawyer increases to reflect the increased size and complexity of her cases, the value of the lawyer's reputation decreases to reflect the fact that she is that much closer to retirement. Unfortunately, unraveling is not an unreasonable concern.

IV. LAW FIRMS AND REPUTATIONAL COMMITMENTS

In this section we examine how law firms may serve as reputational repositories that have the potential to mitigate the problems of self-interest, client pressure, and mortality presented by the use of sole practitioners as cooperative agents. Just as with sole practitioners, however, the game theory–agency theory dialectic will also plague a law firm solution to the problem of bonding cooperation in a prisoner's dilemma. Solving the cooperation problem through the use of a multiple-agent entity exposes the solution to a different set of agency problems that arise between the firm and its own agents—the individual lawyers comprising the firm.

How the Law Firm Might Bond Cooperation when an Individual Lawyer Cannot

Law firms increase the size of the bond and decrease the size of the bribe. In our story, clients rely upon a sole practitioner to observe defection by the opposing counsel because noncooperation—that is, more conflict than "necessary" in an admittedly competitive environment—is more observable to a professional. The client's reliance on the lawyer as a professional observer creates the potential for collusion between counsel. An increase in noncooperation jointly determined by counsel likely would not be observable by the clients themselves, and the lawyers would jointly reap the benefit of the resulting increase in legal work and fees. Because collusion reduces the likelihood that noncooperation will be detected, the deterrence calculation that supports the reputation model breaks down. To the extent clients expect this collusion, the pre-litigation game will not yield a cooperative result.

Using a law firm instead of a sole practitioner has the potential to mitigate this problem, for a firm may provide a larger repository of reputational capital. Additionally, law firms have a substantial amount of more or less firm-specific physical capital, composed of lease obligations, office equipment, and the like, that has much less value on the resale market than it does to the firm in support of the firm's practice. In effect, the firm pledges its reputation behind the cooperative commitment of *each* of its lawyers. Defection by any single lawyer in any single case may damage the entire firm's reputation for cooperation. The result is that the size of the penalty imposed on the firm for noncooperation in any single case may be larger than the penalty that can be imposed against a sole practitioner. In this way, the risk of non-detection is balanced by an increase in the penalty if the misconduct is observed.

Additionally, using a law firm to bond cooperation can directly reduce the potential for collusion. Precisely because the firm allows its entire reputation to be invoked by each lawyer, it has a substantial incentive to monitor the behavior of its own lawyers. Thus, in addition to relying on an individual firm lawyer to detect misconduct on the part of opposing counsel, the client can rely on the firm, acting in its own interest, to monitor the conduct of the particular firm lawyer actually doing the client's work.

Law firms may also mitigate the problem of observability of defection in a second, albeit indirect, fashion. In addition to facilitating cooperation among their clients, law firms also have the skills and capabilities to undertake sophisticated and complex litigation that is beyond the capacity of sole practitioners. (See Galanter and Paley 1991.) The clients who are parties to such litigation are large commercial concerns that typically have full-time in-house general counsel who increasingly were themselves partners in large law firms earlier in their careers. (See Gilson and Mnookin 1985.) As a result, noncooperation by opposing counsel is far more observable to the client and, as a result, the client is far less dependent on its lawyers to monitor opposing counsel. The opportunity for collusion between counsel declines as a consequence.

Law firms diminish the size of the client's threat. Using a law firm instead of a sole practitioner to bond cooperation also mitigates the danger that an individual lawyer will be susceptible to the economic pressure of her large clients to risk her reputation by behaving noncooperatively. Large law firms often have a diversified client base, with no single client or matter representing a material percentage of total firm revenues. As a result, the size of the threat posed by a client even in a large matter is reduced and so, correspondingly, is this danger to a cooperative outcome in the prelitigation game.

Law firms are long-lived. The problem with sole practitioners is that they predictably retire. As time passes and a lawyer develops the skills and reputation to handle the complex cases that have the greatest potential for gains from bonding cooperation between clients, he gets closer to his final round: retirement. Ironically, then, a lawyer-mediated cooperative solution to the prisoner's dilemma game experiences greater pressure to unravel as its potential for contribution increases.

The problem might be solved if the individual lawyer could sell his practice on retirement for a price that reflected the value of his reputation for cooperation. There would be no final period because any pre-retirement noncooperative behavior by the lawyer would result in the reduction in the sale price of his practice. (See Kreps 1990a.) The difficulty with this neat solution is that it is very hard to transfer so intangible an asset as a personal reputation.

Law firms can be understood, in effect, as allowing the intergenerational transfer of such personal reputations. Suppose that the reputation for cooperation attaches to the firm rather than to the individual lawyer. Then the lawyers in the firm earn a return on their contribution to that reputation during their productive lives from two sources: the extra income the firm earns during their active years, and the amounts paid by the young lawyers for the right to share in the future returns on the firm's reputation through a reduction in the amounts they receive for their labor in their early years with the firm. By retirement, a lawyer will have been paid for his interest in the firm's reputation for cooperation, essentially having sold it to the firm's next generation of lawyers.

The result of this intrafirm sale of reputation is that the pressure on the cooperative solution to unravel resulting from the fact that individual lawyers are short-lived is mitigated by the institution of the law firm. From this perspective, the law firm may eliminate or mitigate the final-period problem associated with using lawyers with a reputation for cooperation as a means to bond the cooperation of their clients.

Agency Problems with Bonding
Cooperation through Law Firms

Unfortunately, resort to law firms to diminish one set of agency problems between clients and solo practitioners creates a principal / agent problem of its own. Agency conflicts between the law firm and *its* agents—the lawyers acting on behalf of the firm—may threaten the use of reputational markets to create cooperative solutions. As with sole practitioners, these conflicts threaten the effectiveness of a lawyer-mediated cooperative solution to the prisoner's dilemma game.

Law firm income-sharing rules may increase the size of the client's threat. In the previous discussion we showed how a law firm's diversified client base diminished a client's ability to subvert a lawyer with a reputation for cooperation by threatening to withdraw its work. In many large law firms, no client represents a large enough percentage of the firm's revenue for its withdrawal to pose a credible threat. The problem is that the incentives created by the way a firm splits its income among its lawyers may alter this happy outcome.

Within a law firm, litigation decisions typically are made by the small team of individual lawyers actually doing the work. The organizational chart of a law firm's line operations is virtually flat. Suppose, as has become commonplace, a law firm divides its profits among its lawyers based on the productivity of individual lawyers (see Gilson and Mnookin 1985). Further suppose, as also has become commonplace, that the profit generated by a lawyer is treated as a proxy for her productivity because "real" productivity is unobservable. Finally suppose that a lawyer's profitability is largely a function of the number of hours billed to her clients. Under these circumstances, the power of a client's threat to withdraw business unless the lawyer risks the firm's reputation for cooperation must be measured not at the firm level, but at the level of the individual lawyer. Even if a client's work is quite small in relation to the firm's total revenues, it nonetheless may loom quite large with respect to the income of the individual lawyer who makes the actual litigation decisions on the firing line.

While the previous example illustrates how the firm's method of splitting profits can create a risk of increased noncooperation at the client's behest, the same phenomenon can occur even when the client wants to preserve a cooperative solution. This manifestation of the perverse incentives created by productivity-based profit splitting reflects the increased incentives for collusion between opposing counsel. If the lawyers on both sides of a case belong to firms that split profits this way, each has an interest in increasing the work done for her clients.

A final manifestation of this phenomenon yields the same result. Suppose that young lawyers in a firm are paid in two ways: current compensation in cash and deferred compensation through the promise of a performance-dependent probability of becoming a partner. Further suppose that the probability of becoming a partner depends in important part on the number of hours a young lawyer bills. In many large firms, lawyers whose partnership chances will soon be resolved—senior associates—have substantial authority to influence the extent and intensity of discovery, commonly a major source of litigation conflict. In this setting, the senior associate has an incentive to risk the firm's reputation for cooperation by creating conflict; conflict generates additional work and, therefore, an increased probability of making partner.

The three scenarios described here share a common core. In each, the individual lawyer is in a position to gain—whether through an increased share of current profits or an increased probability of a chance to share in future profits—from actions that risk the firm's reputational capital. And in each, the lawyer gets the bulk of the return from risking the firm's reputation, but bears only a small part of the loss if that risk is realized. The conflict of interest between the law firm and its lawyers, an agency cost of disputing through a multiple-agent entity, threatens the potential for a lawyer-mediated solution to the prisoner's dilemma game.

Client preferences may deconstruct the law firm. By shifting the reputation for cooperation from the individual lawyer to the firm, the size of the investment in reputation that supports any single lawyer's commitment to cooperation increases. The problem is that client preferences for deconstructing the firm may interfere. The catch phrase for large clients has become that they "hire lawyers, not law firms." Their goal is to maintain competition among firms for their business by avoiding what Oliver Williamson refers to as the "fundamental transformation"—the shift from market conditions characterized by many competing suppliers to market conditions characterized by one supplier's having a substantial advantage over potential competitors as a result of relationship-specific investment following the supplier's initial selection (Williamson 1985). Thus, the search for reputation shifts back to the individual from the firm, potentially offsetting the increase in the size of the reputational capital achieved by moving from individual to firm representation. If it is only the individual lawyer's reputation upon which the client relies, then the aggregate of the reputational capital of the lawyers in the firms does not bond the conduct of the individual lawyers. Moreover, to the extent that reputation reverts to being a lawyer-specific rather than a firm-specific asset, the potential for the cooperative solution to unravel because an individual lawyer's career is finite reappears.

That bonding cooperation through a law firm rather than an individual lawyer evokes its own set of agency problems is not to say that law firms may not remain more efficient repositories of reputation than do individual lawyers. It merely reflects the operation of the game theory–agency theory dialectic. Any solution to the problem of assuring cooperation in a competitive game that relies on agents generates agency costs. Like friction, they may be reduced but not eliminated. But understanding the ways in which agency costs can plague cooperative solutions does allow the analysis to take both a positive and, to a lesser extent, a normative turn. Can the prisoner's dilemma heuristic help us understand the institutional landscape of litigation that we observe? Far more tentatively, can the prisoner's dilemma heuristic suggest insights about how to strengthen those institutional elements that facilitate lawyer-mediated cooperative solutions? While the design of a reform agenda is well beyond the scope of our effort here, we offer in our concluding comments some suggestions about the kind of inquiries that might structure such an agenda.

V. UNDERSTANDING THE LANDSCAPE OF LITIGATION

Viewing litigation through a prisoner's dilemma perspective—in light of the potential for lawyers to facilitate cooperative solutions and the determinants of that potential—illuminates our understanding of the patterns and institutions of litigation. We focus our attention on two inquiries. First, can the prisoner's dilemma heuristic help us better understand the clear public and professional perception that the conduct of large commercial litigation has deteriorated to the point that lawyers liken it to Los Angeles freeway shootings? Second, can the prisoner's dilemma heuristic help us better understand the distribution of cooperative litigation across other practice settings? In each case, the inquiry centers on the characteristics that the prisoner's dilemma heuristic has identified as critical to a cooperative role for lawyers: the litigation payoff structure and a workable reputation market. With respect to the former, there must be gains from cooperation. With respect to the latter, the issues center around what might be called the costs of scrutiny—the ease with which both clients and lawyers can observe lawyers' reputations and, correspondingly, lawyers' difficulty in credibly establishing reputations for cooperation.

Understanding the Contentiousness of Commercial Litigation

Viewing the perceived deterioration in the conduct of commercial litigation through the lens of the prisoner's dilemma suggests two explanations for the increase in contentiousness: a change in the character of the litigation itself, and the impact of growth in the size of the legal community on the formation and maintenance of reputations for cooperation.

The changing payoff structure in litigation. Two conclusions about the character of large commercial litigation have emerged in recent years, the first empirical and relating to its frequency, the second subjective and relating to its conduct. Recent studies have documented a dramatic increase in the amount of commercial litigation after 1970. A nationwide study of federal court contract cases found that the annual number of filings, after remaining at a relatively constant level of about 14,000 during the 1960s, began rising in the 1970s and reached an annual rate of over 47,000 by 1986 (Galanter and Rodgers 1991). Similarly, a study of contract filings in the southern district of New York (Manhattan), the federal trial court with what is likely the largest commercial caseload in the country and certainly the largest commercial bar, found that contracts cases increased from an average of some 391 cases per year during the 1960s to an average of 1,272 cases per year during the period 1973 through 1990, with the number in some years exceeding 1,400 (Nelson 1990). At the same time, the involvement of large New York law firms in these cases also increased substantially.

The prisoner's dilemma heuristic suggests a link between the empirical fact of increased commercial litigation and the subjective fact, attested to by the lawyers conducting the litigation, that litigation behavior has become significantly more contentious. Recall that in order for lawyers to bond a cooperative solution, the payoffs in the lawsuit must take the form of a prisoner's dilemma; there must be gains from joint cooperation. Suppose that much of the increase in commercial litigation had payoffs in which there were no gains from cooperation. In that event, litigation would become more conflictual because the parties would choose gladiators in the pre-litigation game. At least some of the increase in commercial litigation appears to be lawsuits in which there were no gains from cooperation.

In his study of New York commercial litigation, Nelson notes that during the 1970s the statutory prejudgment interest rate—the amount a defendant would have to pay a plaintiff on a damage award from the date the damage was suffered to the date of judgment—was no higher than 6 percent. In contrast, the market rate of interest over the 1974–1980 period ranged from 10.5 percent at the end of 1974 to 21.5 percent at the end of 1980, a spread over the statutory rate of from 4.5 percent to 15.5 percent (Nelson 1990). Now imagine the payoffs to a litigation game in which one player owed the other money. In the face of such an interest rate spread, the defendant's dominant strategy is always noncooperative. The more conflictual the litigation, the longer the process takes. While the interest rate spread that drove the increase in noncooperative litigation during the 1970s has abated, the phenomenon of strategic litigation, which may have the same payoff pattern, may have replaced it. For this purpose, litigation is strategic when it seeks not to vindicate a substantive legal right but to secure a business advantage by imposing costs on the opposing party. (See Cooter and Rubenfeld 1989 at 1083–84.) Examples include litigation brought by a target company simply to delay a hostile takeover (Wachtell 1977), or trade-secret litigation, brought against former employees of a high-technology company who leave to form a start-up venture, with the goal of creating sufficient uncertainty that financing is unavailable and the venture fails (Silverman 1989). In this type of litigation, the payoff structure is such that for one party the dominant strategy is noncooperation.

Explanations for the increased incidence of such litigation are varied and still at the stage where the boundary between empirical evidence and speculation is blurred. Nelson points to the opening of management to new groups who felt less constraint in treating litigation as part of the competitive environment, as well as to the increased bureaucratization of management (Nelson 1990). Galanter and Rodgers stress the general increase in business instability resulting from such things as the internationalization of competition and increased business failures. From our perspective, however, the cause is less important than the fact that the prisoner's dilemma heuristic helps isolate the settings in which lawyers cannot serve to facilitate cooperation.

The impact of growth in the size of the legal community on the formation and maintenance of reputation for cooperation. Central to the potential for lawyers to bond a cooperative solution to a prisoner's dilemma litigation game is an effective reputation market for lawyers. Lawyers must be able to earn and maintain reputations for cooperation that are observable by other lawyers, and lawyers must be able to observe breaches of reputation by opposing counsel. There is reason to believe that the enormous growth in size of the large law firms that provide most legal representation in substantial commercial litigation has undercut the operation of the reputation market.

The first step in the analysis is to recognize the extraordinary growth of large law firms. In the late 1950s, only 38 law firms had more than 50 lawyers. By 1985, 508 firms had reached that size. Fewer than a dozen firms exceeded 100 lawyers in 1960; by 1986, there were 251 such firms. In 1968, the largest law firm had 169 lawyers; in 1988 the largest firm had 962 lawyers and 142 firms were larger than the 1968 leader (Galanter and Paley 1991).

Now consider how lawyers might develop a reputation for cooperation. Suppose that the primary vehicle of reputation formation is other lawyers who then communicate that reputation to the client community. As discussed earlier, this is a plausible assumption given that cooperation in litigation is not a bright-line concept; because litigation is inherently competitive, a reputation for cooperation will be based on the more ephemeral concept of not being *too* conflictual. This kind of standard requires professional application in the first instance.

In this setting, formation of a cooperative reputation is facilitated by repeated experience with the same lawyers so that the noise associated with the lawyer's conduct has the chance to factor out. The number of times one lawyer has the experience of litigating against another lawyer in the community is a function of the size of the community. Thus, the smaller the community, the easier it is to learn about the predilections of other lawyers toward cooperation. These circumstances are sufficient to predict a secular trend of decreased reputations for cooperation among law firm lawyers in a given community. Members of the older generation of lawyers will be perceived as having a reputation for cooperation, their reputations having been developed when large law firms had fewer than 50 lawyers and when, outside New York, only 17 firms in the entire country had more than 50 lawyers (Galanter and Paley 1991). Leading lawyers in a community dealt with each other every day. In contrast, the succeeding generations of lawyers would have found it much more difficult to develop reputations for cooperation, because the likelihood of their having sufficient dealings with a large enough segment of the bar to develop one is decreased by the continued growth in the legal community. In that circumstance, if a lawyer cannot develop a reputation for cooperation, then the dominant career strategy is noncooperation—to be a gladiator.

To be sure, many lawyers do not identify themselves as gladiators. Rather, they describe their personal strategy as, in effect, being tit-for-tat lawyers: cooperate until the other side defects and then retaliate. However, it is likely that a tit-for-tat strategy will frequently deteriorate to repeated defection that mirrors the conduct of gladiators. Litigation is a noisy prisoner's dilemma game. Distinguishing cooperation from defection is difficult in a competitive environment where cooperation is defined as not being *too* conflictual. Moreover, because some litigation will lack the payoff structure of a prisoner's dilemma, correctly identifying defection also requires correctly evaluating the litigation itself—noncooperation is not defection if gains from cooperation are not possible. Not surprisingly, the experimental literature suggests that playing tit for tat in a noisy prisoner's dilemma game deteriorates into gladiatorial mutual defection (see Bendor, Kramer, and Stout 1991). Thus, with the passage of time, as the older lawyers retire and are replaced by younger lawyers, the legal community becomes dominated by lawyers who, whether or not instrumentally, have developed a noncooperative style and conflict in litigation increases over time.

Indeed, the potential for law firms to develop a reputation for cooperation may not save civilization as the older generation knew it. As we saw in the previous subsection, only some litigation has a payoff structure that rewards joint cooperation, and there is reason to believe that the proportion of noncooperative litigation is increasing. If a large law firm represents clients both in litigation in which the dominant strategy is to cooperate and in litigation in which the dominant strategy is to compete, reputation formation becomes much more complicated because the observation of noncooperative behavior is compatible either with a noncooperative lawyer or noncooperative litigation.

The same problem also hinders the maintenance of reputations. For a reputation market to work, defections by cooperative lawyers must be observable. However, observability is complicated by a number of factors. First, if the population of litigation is mixed, lawyers may be expected to handle both kinds of litigation. Experience may be required to determine whether a lawyer's noncooperative behavior represents a breach of her existing reputation for cooperation or, alternatively, occurred in the context of noncooperative litigation. Second, even in cooperative litigation, it may be difficult to determine from a single observation whether a particular action is cooperative or not, because the standard is blurred: cooperation is defined as not being *too* competitive. The experience with a particular lawyer necessary to observe defections becomes less likely in a larger legal community.

Understanding the Distribution of Cooperation Across Practice Settings

We now consider whether the prisoner's dilemma also can be applied to help understand the distribution of cooperation across practice settings. Given the different institutional characteristics in, for example, commercial litigation and family law litigation, does the prisoner's dilemma heuristic suggest different levels of cooperation? In this subsection, we examine from this perspective two substantive practice settings—criminal practice and family law practice.

Cooperation in criminal practice. Much criminal practice lends itself to lawyers' facilitating a credible commitment to cooperation. The most difficult issue comes at the threshold: whether the payoffs in criminal litigation take the form of a prisoner's dilemma.

At first glance, the criminal litigation game seems arguably zero-sum. The defendant is either guilty or not guilty; if guilty, each additional year of the defendant's sentence may benefit the prosecutor and obviously hurts the defendant, and vice versa. Yet one can quickly think of circumstances where there are gains from cooperation. For example, consider the recent prosecution of Ivan Boesky or Martin Siegel for criminal securities fraud (see Stewart 1991). A noncooperative strategy would have been zero-sum: guilt or innocence and length of sentence. However, both sides had something to gain from cooperation: the prosecution could secure incriminating information about other potential defendants like Michael Milken, and the defense could secure a shorter sentence than would be possible without the prosecutor's recommendation for leniency. More generally, the potential for gains from cooperation may be pervasive in criminal litigation given its particular institutional structure. If prosecutors are typically concerned about court congestion, that can be avoided by a successful plea bargain, and if even clearly guilty defendants are at least risk averse concerning length of sentence, the potential for gains from cooperation will always be present: the defendant will trade a jury trial for a reduced sentence and both parties will be better off. These two examples are hardly exhaustive, but the point should be clear enough. The payoffs in criminal litigation frequently can take the form of a prisoner's dilemma.

The threshold issue of payoff structure thus resolved, the prisoner's dilemma heuristic suggests a high degree of cooperation between lawyers in criminal litigation. The circumstances of practice are well suited for a reputation model, thereby allowing lawyers to make credible commitments. The practice tends to be localized in particular jurisdictions; it is uncommon for out-of-town lawyers to defend even very high-profile criminal cases. Because only two firms practice on the prosecution side—the state attorney general's office or its local equivalent, and the United States attorney's office—defense lawyers will have repeated opportunities to observe the conduct of prosecutors, and reputations for cooperation (or conflict) can develop.

On the defense side, there is typically only one large firm (the public defender's office) and a number of private defense lawyers practicing alone or in small groups. Prosecutors would have the opportunity for sufficient interaction with particular defense lawyers for the latter to build and maintain reputations (see Mann, 1985). Moreover, the reputations of individual prosecutors and public defenders should spread very efficiently within the offices of their familiar opponents. And while communication about particular prosecutors' reputations outside the public defender's office would be somewhat more difficult, many private defense lawyers know each other through earlier career stints as public defenders or prosecutors, which also facilitates a network for the transmission of information about reputations.

Also facilitating cooperation in criminal litigation is the fact that the agency problems that grew out of using lawyers to bond cooperation in commercial litigation loom less large in criminal practice. Unlike commercial litigators public defenders and prosecutors lack the incentive to create fee-generating conflicts. To be sure, private defense lawyers are paid by their clients, but in much criminal practice compensation takes the form of an advance payment of a fixed fee. Thus neither side has an incentive to drag out a case unnecessarily.

Finally, the risk of a client's pressuring a lawyer not to live up to his reputation for cooperating should be comparatively weak in most criminal cases. For private defense lawyers, no single client ordinarily would be a source of a great deal of repeat business, and most would have a diversified portfolio of active cases.

Anecdotal evidence is certainly consistent with the prediction derived from the prisoner's dilemma heuristic that there is significant cooperation in criminal practice. The overwhelming majority of cases are disposed of through plea bargaining. To be sure, some cases are resolved by combat after a contested trial, and white-collar and mob prosecutions are sometimes very big cases. Interestingly, these are often cases in which defense lawyers are paid by the hour. However, as Stewart demonstrates in *Den of Thieves*, even in high-profile criminal prosecutions involving alleged securities law violations, there are defense lawyers with reputations for being good at negotiating pleas in a cooperative manner, and others with deserved reputations for being hardball litigators who spend a great deal of their time in court (Stewart 1991).

Family law practice. As with criminal law, the first step in applying the prisoner's dilemma heuristic to family law practice is analyzing the litigation payoff structure. For lawyers to have the potential to bond their clients' cooperation, there must be gains from cooperation (and the risk of loss if the other party defects). Put in context, divorce litigation must be more than a zero-sum game in which the couple's property and children are divided.

The opportunities for cooperation in divorce litigation are readily apparent. Division of property, such as a closely held business, presents the same opportunity for the parties to devise cooperative solutions that a court could not impose itself as does large commercial litigation that also seeks to determine the parties' rights in contested property. More contextually, the division of a couple's community property often involves circumstances where each individual attaches a very different subjective value to the same items of property. As a result, gains from trade are available that could not be achieved by a Solomon-like judicial division (see Mnookin and Kornhauser 1979). Finally, and most importantly, cooperation can result in very substantial gains to important third parties when the divorcing couple have children. The goodwill that is not squandered in retributive conflict benefits the children in the future by helping to create a postdivorce relationship that allows the parents to cooperate in raising their children (see Maccoby and Mnookin 1992).

Family law practice is also an area where lawyers should be able to develop and maintain reputations with respect to cooperation. Practice tends to be both localized and specialized. Usually the husband and wife hire attorneys in the same legal community, and in a given community there are typically lawyers that specialize in family practice. In all but the largest legal communities, specialized lawyers would deal with one another frequently. Thus, the conditions for reputation formation and maintenance should be satisfied.

Interestingly, the institutional structure of family law practice appears to facilitate reputation development and maintenance. Professional organizations, like the American Academy of Matrimonial Lawyers, a self-appointed elite of the family law bar, seem to exist for the principal purpose of providing an efficient reputational network among family lawyers. All of its members are specialists, who are frequently involved in divorces of high-income individuals.

We have been told that in the San Francisco legal community, for example, these lawyers rarely insist on formal discovery procedures with each other, but instead cooperate by trading information informally. However, there are a small number of the elite who have deserved reputations for making everything into an adversarial issue and being highly contentious. These noncooperative gladiators are not viewed as "cheats," because their behavior is consistent with their reputations. Moreover, they attract clients who want to play thermonuclear war. But so long as reputations are clear, the fact that the lawyer population is heterogeneous will not stop lawyers from facilitating cooperation so long as the difference can be observed.

VI. CONCLUSION

Our story weaves together three principal ideas: (1) The prisoner's dilemma represents a suggestive and powerful metaphor for some aspects of litigation; (2) a lawyer's reputation may serve to bond a client's cooperation in the litigation process, thereby resolving the prisoner's dilemma; and (3) principal / agent conflicts (whether between lawyers and clients or between lawyers in the same firms) create incentives that sometimes facilitate cooperation in litigation and at other times undermine cooperation. Our message is that the *relationship* between opposing lawyers and their capacity to establish credible reputations for cooperation have profound implications for dispute resolution: conditional on payoffs that establish cooperation as the most desirable strategy, lawyers may be able to dampen conflict, reduce transaction costs, and facilitate resolution.

The prisoner's dilemma metaphor also helps explain a feature of litigation that is anecdotally emphasized by lawyers—that clients often pressure their own attorney *not* to cooperate with the other side. An arguably increasing amount of litigation has a payoff structure which, unlike a prisoner's dilemma, establishes defection as one player's dominant strategy regardless of the other player's behavior—what we have called strategic. Such client pressure may be rational.

Our story rests fundamentally on the idea that lawyers develop reputations, and that the reputation for being a cooperative problem solver may be a valuable asset. When opposing lawyers know and trust each other, we believe that there often will be substantial opportunities to benefit both parties by reducing transaction costs. Further research might usefully explore a variety of empirical questions relating to the idea of reputational markets for lawyers.

A very basic question goes to how lawyers in fact cooperate in the litigation process. How do lawyers signal their willingness to cooperate? To what extent is a lawyer's reputation important in facilitating cooperation? In different practice settings, is there a consensus about a lawyer's reputation? How do these reputations develop? In choosing lawyers, how do clients secure information about the reputation of their own lawyer? To what extent do patterns of cooperation and the degree of cooperation vary across practice contexts and practice communities?

Theory suggests that a reputational market would operate most effectively when its size is comparatively small and therefore lawyers expect to do business together in the future. Our analysis certainly suggests why small-town lawyers may be less prone to exacerbate disputes with one another than big-city lawyers, and also why one might expect to see a greater degree of cooperation within certain specialities than within the general community of attorneys. These questions suggest opportunities for empirical research to see whether there are significant differences, and to what extent these differences can be explained by reputational markets.

It is also interesting to speculate about how the reputations of lawyers and law firms spread through a community. We would expect more cooperative behavior in areas of litigation where the behavior of counsel is both observable and can be confidently characterized as cooperative or defecting. Indeed, in contexts where cooperation is not only observable but verifiable to a judge, the judiciary may represent a powerful mechanism to ensure cooperation. Litigators are profoundly concerned about their reputation with judges, and are typically very hesitant about doing anything to damage their reputation with a judge before whom counsel is likely to appear many times in the future. But experience with Rule 11 sanctions—judicially imposed sanctions for some kinds of uncooperative behavior—raises serious questions concerning the verifiability of much misconduct.

We suspect that many lawyers would claim that they want a reputation or a capacity to cooperate when the other side is prepared to cooperate, but an ability to be tough when necessary. In other words, many litigators may describe themselves as behaving consistently with Axelrod's normative suggestions in *The Evolution of Cooperation*—i.e., they will play "tit for tat." This would suggest, of course, that a lawyer might seek to have a reputation for never defecting first (Axelrod 1984). How well does this work? Particularly in complicated cases, it may be difficult to know who defected first. If this is so, then we would predict that cooperation would often break down even in circumstances where both parties claimed that they wished to cooperate. This is an empirical question, however, and it would be interesting to explore in the context of actual cases the extent to which lawyers are able to develop reciprocal cooperative patterns.

We are intrigued by both the opportunities and the limitations in encouraging cooperation through contracts and rules, both formal and informal. Obviously there may be ways other than through reputation for lawyers to commit credibly to cooperation. Our analysis certainly suggests that to the extent that defection is observable and verifiable there may be substantial opportunities to improve the efficiency of dispute resolution. The explosion in interest in alternative dispute resolution and the increasing use of arbitration certainly suggest that parties and lawyers are actively exploring contractual ways of reducing the transaction costs of ordinary litigation.

Our analysis suggests that in evaluating the possibility of reform it would be very useful to explore whether the development of new institutions and various procedural changes might facilitate cooperation between opposing counsel and thus minimize transaction costs. It may be possible to encourage the development of informal norms that promote cooperation quite apart from formal legal sanctions (see Ellickson 1991). Alterations in professional socialization in law school certainly comes to mind. Reforms at both the state and federal level suggest the possibility of rules that affirmatively require the prompt exchange of material information between counsel. The hope is that such changes will avoid the expensive "hide-and-seek" game that often characterizes pretrial discovery practice in civil litigation today. Apart from formal rule changes, bar associations might propose model stipulations that permit lawyers who wish to cooperate to specify with more precision the ground rules which both will agree to play. In all of this, the question of whether defection is observable or verifiable remains critical. The distinction also serves as a helpful reminder that in many settings rule changes alone may be insufficient to ensure cooperation.

We began our inquiry with the question of whether lawyers facilitate dispute resolution or instead exacerbate conflict. Common sense and anecdotal observation together suggest that lawyers sometimes help and sometimes hurt. Our goal in this chapter has been to provide a theoretical framework to better understand why this is so. The analysis presented represents an early reconnaissance mission that suggests for ourselves (and we hope for others) the value of further exploration—both theoretical and empirical.

CHAPTER ELEVEN

Cooperation in the Unbalanced Commons

Edward A. Parson and
Richard J. Zeckhauser

I n June 1992, leaders of 178 nations met in Rio de Janeiro to conclude negotiations on a broad set of measures to protect the international environment, including treaties on climate change and biodiversity. Such multiparty negotiations are pervasive in modern international affairs, and many, like the Rio negotiations, involve the provision of collective goods, those from which all benefit but which states provide individually. Other examples include controlling weapons proliferation, supporting liberal trade policies, financing international organizations, and deterring aggression. Problems of similar structure also arise frequently in other contexts, for example, among individuals or among states within a nation.

In this chapter we consider how multiple negotiating parties pursue and reach agreement on distributing obligations to provide collective goods. Our analysis of the process of arguing and bargaining that brings parties to accept certain obligations in return for others' accepting reciprocal obligations is principally conceptual, and applies to most multiparty bargains. Our illustrations focus on international bargaining over the environment.

We argue that study of multiparty negotiations is too often stuck in an assumption of symmetry. In fact, environmental and other multiparty international negotiations typically involve substantial *asymmetry of interest:* negotiators differ sharply in the trade-off each perceives between the benefit of the collective good being provided and their costs in providing it themselves. Though nations may share a common purpose, such as containing climate change, such asymmetries can obstruct agreements by putting the nations at odds over which negotiated solutions are desirable.

There are three conceptually separable elements to the process of reaching agreement on a multiparty public-good bargain: who participates, what simplifying principles are used to define relative obligations, and what particular levels of provision are chosen within these principles. Asymmetries of interest complicate each of these three stages, principally by obscuring or eliminating the clear primacy that the simple focal points of unanimous participation and identical measures enjoy in the symmetric case. Instead, there can be one or more stable coalitions of contributors short of the set of all affected parties. There can also be multiple competing principles for allocating obligations, which impose different distributions of burdens but which all have plausible claims to fairness. Even after a simple principle is agreed on, asymmetric agents can differ strongly in their preferred level of stringency for enacting it.

We make three assumptions and exclusions in our discussion. First, we assume that negotiations are among unitary parties, with no supervening authority. Thus we exclude domestic politics and negotiations within a federal state, in which parties can be compelled to participate and a rich set of trade-offs across issues and over time is available (though some of our arguments apply here as well). Second, our focus on single-issue negotiations (with no side payments) excludes the ability to link issues, an important determinant of asymmetry in power. The pure public-goods character of a single pollution problem prevents even the largest agents from bringing targeted incentives to bear on others. Finally, we exclude consideration of negotiations over monitoring, enforcement, compliance, and institutional issues that would accompany any real collective-good negotiation, on the assumption that these functions could be provided cheaply enough not to obstruct otherwise acceptable agreements.

The chapter first discusses how the implicit assumption of symmetric interests makes the process of reaching agreement look too easy. We then present a simple formal model of asymmetric interests, and examine some of its implications in the two-agent case. Next, we discuss the elements involved in reaching agreement in multiparty negotiations. On the question of who participates, a ten-nation illustration shows how asymmetry can lead to stable coalitions of participants. Finally, on the question of what a particular coalition will do, we show how asymmetry complicates the process of bargaining over the simplifying principles that determine relative allocations of responsibility.

STANDARD APPROACHES ASSUME TWO PARTIES, OR SYMMETRY

Most formal analysis of international affairs employs two-person game models, even when the interactions studied involve multiple parties (Keohane 1984; Oye 1986; Snyder and Diesing 1977; Martin 1992). Some analyses, such as Axelrod's study of the repeated prisoner's dilemma (1984), justify this simplification by assuming that agents can discriminate in their choices toward particular others, thereby disaggregating an N-party interaction into a series of two-party ones. This disaggregation is not appropriate for multiparty collective-good negotiations, in which a party cannot limit the effects of its decisions to one other party.

Formal models of collective goods that do consider multiple agents most commonly assume that agents' interests are identical, typically by formulating the decision problem of a "representative agent" (Dasgupta 1982, 19–24; Schelling 1978; R. Hardin 1982; Cornes and Sandler 1983; Weitzman 1974). While the main result of these models—that without imposed controls or binding cooperation, public goods will be underprovided and commons overused—is robust to relaxation of the symmetry assumption, assuming symmetry makes the optimal point so simple that the process of negotiating to reach it looks too easy. Identical agents all pollute at equal, excessive levels in the absence of agreement, and at equal, lower levels in the optimal negotiated solution. These classic models do not address the negotiating process of agreeing to move from one point to the other, but it seems clear that identical agents would quickly focus their negotiations on equal reductions by all, and would then agree unanimously on the optimal level. Any reasonable principle used to argue for the required reductions would give the same, optimal result: equal absolute or proportional emission reductions, movement to equal levels, or equal measures per capita, per dollar of GNP, per square kilometer of land area, or relative to historical emissions.

Each agent would of course prefer an asymmetrical solution in which she reduces emissions less than others do. But any argument to support such a solution must be based on some unique characteristic of her situation. If all are identical and all know it, then any argument that justifies a lesser burden for one does so for all. Nor could any agent realistically hope to gain an advantage simply by convincing others of the firmness of her resolve; if one can be that stubborn, so can all. Since no one can expect to prevail decisively in either a principled argument or a contest of wills against a large number of identical copies of herself, the only plausible outcome in bargaining among truly identical agents is unanimous agreement on optimal equal reductions.[1]

Since agents would prefer to cheat if they could get away with it, even a

---

[1] One qualification is necessary. As Schelling (1960) points out, the availability of an external commitment mechanism may enable one agent (or some agents) decisively to secure an advantage, thereby creating asymmetry where none existed. But if all are identical in interest, resolve, and skill, the outcome of a race to commit can only be simultaneous incompatible commitments, a tie (to be broken by whatever rule applies), or a random process determining which lucky agent (or agents) succeeds in commiting first.

group of identical agents must monitor and enforce compliance. But in a symmetrical world, all other things being equal, even enforcement is likely to be easier. When any cheating represents a departure from otherwise completely uniform behavior, it is likely to be conspicuous and easy to detect. And if cheating is observed—even if no penalty can be applied—both cheater and noncheater will view it as threatening to bring down the agreement, as others imitate and seek equally favorable treatment.

A SIMPLE MODEL WITH ASYMMETRY

While symmetric models may be unhelpful because they make the process of reaching agreement look too easy, asymmetry of interest is difficult to model because it can be so diverse. In the environmental arena, for example, asymmetries of interest arise from several sources. Some nations may value the environmental good more highly than others, because they are wealthier, more vulnerable, larger, or have "greener" political values. Alternatively, some may find it costlier to reduce their emissions than others, due to differences in economic structure, capital stock, or technological capabilities. On some issues the harm may be asymmetrically borne, say, if one country's emissions blow or flow principally into another. Measures to control an environmental harm may also impose asymmetries, by limiting some activities more strictly than others or defining a new set of property rights. These forms of asymmetry can admit arbitrary variation in the functions that define nations' costs from providing, and benefits from consuming, an environmental good.

How significant are such asymmetries of interest on real issues? While it is not possible to measure comprehensive national environmental interests directly, a few measures of contributions, costs, and political attitudes on climate change illustrate how extreme asymmetries of interest might be. Carbon emissions per capita vary by more than a factor of 100 among countries worldwide, and by a factor of 8 even among the relatively similar countries of the European Community (EC) (World Bank 1992; World Resources Institute 1992; Subak and Clark 1990). One study of limiting EC carbon emissions found that marginal costs of a 10 percent cut would range from a few dollars to several hundred dollars per ton (Barrett 1991b). Estimated costs of protecting coastlines against a one-meter rise in sea level range from $40 to $1,800 per capita in various world regions (IPCC 1991). In a recent comparison of environmental attitudes across twenty-two countries, those considering climate change a "very serious" problem ranged from 33 percent to 73 percent (Dunlap et al. 1992).

We present a simple approach to modeling asymmetric interests that assumes that nations' interests vary only along a single dimension. In Figure

FIGURE 1

Benefit from National Emissions

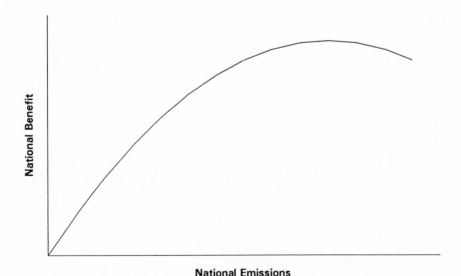

1, each nation derives a private economic benefit from its own emissions with diminishing and ultimately negative marginal benefits.

To compare benefits across nations, we assume first that nations comprise different numbers of individuals, but that all individuals in all nations are identical. All nations distribute their private product in the same way and use an additive social welfare function (or alternatively, they distribute their product equally among their citizens). With these assumptions, nations that emit at the same level per capita receive the same benefits per capita; one nation twice as populous as another will derive double the total benefits of the smaller one by emitting double the pollution (whereas the smaller nation could not double its own benefits by doubling pollution, due to diminishing returns). Benefit functions for different nations are thus scaled both horizontally and vertically in proportion to the size of the nation. Figure 2 shows this relationship for two nations, Alpha and Beta, where Alpha is three times larger than Beta.

Nations also suffer increasing marginal cost of environmental harm from the total of their own and others' emissions, as shown in Figure 3.[2] Harm begins with the first unit of world emissions; there is no threshold.

---

[2] A more general treatment would use a transport matrix, separately specifying the contribution of each agent to each other's harm. Our approach assumes full global mixing, equivalent to a unit transport matrix.

FIGURE 2

Emission Benefits for Two Nations
(Alpha three times larger than Beta)

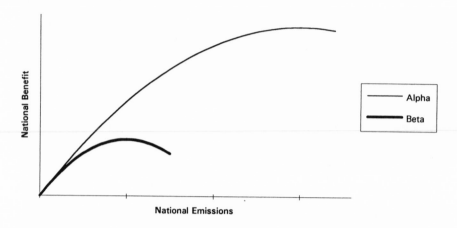

To compare harm across nations we assume that pollution is a pure public bad within each nation, so each nation's harm from a given global pollution level is proportional to its population. A nation twice as populous as another consequently suffers twice the harm from the same level of global pollution. Damage functions are scaled vertically, in proportion to national populations. Figure 4 illustrates this relationship of harms for Alpha and Beta (Alpha is three times the size of Beta).[3]

This structure yields three significant insights. First, it suggests a dual focus on the physical agreements undertaken, and the consequences in terms of each agent's benefits. Second, it identifies size with environmental concern. Because the largest nations subsume within their borders the largest fraction of the global harm emissions cause, they are willing to incur a proportionally higher cost to control emissions, at any global emissions level.

Third, it illustrates a three-stage structure of decision making that we contend realistically represents environmental issues: unconcerned, uncooperative, and cooperative decisions. Nations normally only learn of an activity's environmental harm after they have practiced it for some time.

------

[3] Vertical scaling of damage functions alone can also be used, representing differences in environmental sensitivity or concern (including, with a reversal of sign, nations who gain from pollution, as it has been suggested some may from climate change). Related approaches are found in Hoel 1990, Barrett 1991b, and Parson 1992, chap. 4.

FIGURE 3

Environmental Damage from World Emissions

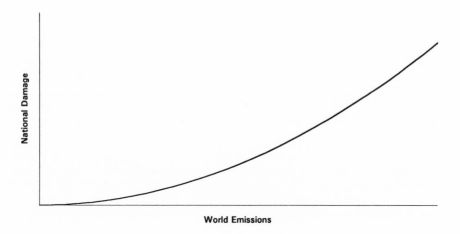

This was the case with ozone depletion, acid rain, and climate change. The delay may reflect advances in scientific knowledge or monitoring technology, or the increasing scale of an activity reaching previously unrecognized environmental constraints. The consequence of the delay is that agents initially optimize without concern for environmental effects, considering only the benefit functions of Figures 1 and 2, and not the cost functions of Figures 3 and 4. Agents in this "unconcerned" stage would emit at the top of their benefit functions, giving equal per capita emissions for all nations.

When agents recognize environmental harm and include it in their decisions they will cut back emissions unilaterally, but only to the point that equalizes their own marginal benefit and damage from their emissions. They thus achieve the uncooperative Nash equilibrium, where each takes the others' emission levels as given. Reductions at this "uncooperative" stage are suboptimal, since each neglects the harm its emissions cause others. Negotiations to pursue further emission reductions begin from this point of noncooperation. In this third, "cooperative" stage, each agent seeks advantageous conditional agreements to reduce emissions further, contingent on others' reducing theirs. These three stages, though conceptually separable, often overlap temporally in real negotiations.

FIGURE 4

Environmental Damages for Two Nations
(Alpha three times larger than Beta)

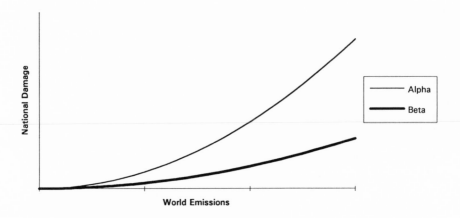

AN ILLUSTRATION WITH TWO PARTIES

Figures 5 and 6 illustrate this three-stage model with a simple example of bargaining between two nations Alpha and Beta. Alpha is three times larger than Beta. These figures use quadratic cost and benefit functions, requiring one arbitrary parameter that defines the relationship of costs and benefits for Beta, and with proportionality therefore for Alpha. The qualitative results apply with any concave functions.

Figure 5 graphs various possible emission decisions of the two agents. The horizontal and vertical axes measure Alpha's and Beta's emissions respectively (in arbitrary units, denominated so that at the unconcerned point, Alpha emits seventy-five units and Beta twenty-five). At the unconcerned point per capita emissions are equal, with Alpha's total three times Beta's. At the optimal point, per capita emissions are also equal (and lower). The optimization weights each person's welfare equally, so it is unaffected by the asymmetric grouping of more people into Alpha than Beta.

In the initial movement from unconcerned to uncooperative, however, the asymmetric grouping matters in two ways. First, Alpha makes larger unilateral reductions because it bears proportionally more environmental harm within its borders. That the larger country bears a disproportionate burden is an instance of a well-known result for other international public goods, such as alliance burden sharing or output reductions in OPEC (Olson and Zeckhauser 1966). Second, at this stage asymmetry promotes emission reductions. If a fixed total world population is split in some proportion between two countries, and each sets its emissions uncooperatively, then

FIGURE 5

Two-Agent Bargaining: Emissions

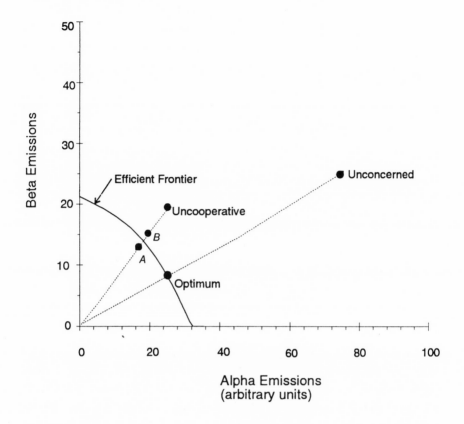

world emissions are largest when the two countries are equal in size, and decrease monotonically as they become more unequal. At the limit, with all people gathered in a single country, it makes the optimal level of reduction.[4]

In negotiations to move beyond the uncooperative point, however, asymmetry obstructs movement in two ways. First, the optimum is unlikely to be

---

[4]This simple consequence of convexity of cost and benefit functions is not the only case where asymmetry creates gains. For example, when some subset of a group is required for a task that cannot be shared—joining a small-town posse or a rescue party, for example—an obvious rank-ordering of ability to contribute would mitigate the problem of each waiting for others to join. In a quite different spirit, when negotiation concerns multiple issues (including issues of time and risk), it is asymmetric valuation that creates opportunities for joint gains (Raiffa 1982; Lax and Sebenius 1986).

FIGURE 6

Two-Agent Bargaining: Benefits

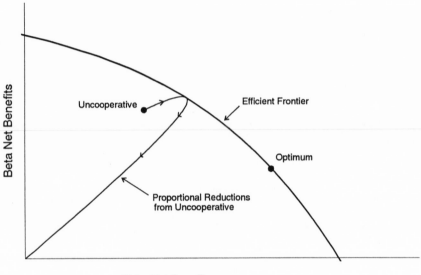

Alpha Net Benefits

achieved without side payments, since reaching it can require much larger reductions from Beta than from Alpha (proportionally, and perhaps in absolute terms). Figure 6 illustrates the consequences to each nation of the same set of possible emission decisions; the horizontal and vertical axes are net benefits to Alpha and Beta respectively. Figure 6 shows that Beta can be better off at the uncooperative point than at the optimal point, perhaps substantially so. With certain parameter values it is even possible for Alpha's emissions to be *lower* at the uncooperative point than at the optimal solution, so reaching the optimum would require Alpha to *increase* emissions.

Second, instead of trying to reach the optimum point, Alpha and Beta might agree on the "fair" rule of making equal proportional reductions from their uncooperative emissions—seeking a point on the dashed line joining the uncooperative point to the origin in Figure 5, or on the curved path marked with arrows in Figure 6. In this case, agents will disagree on how far to reduce, since their benefits are maximized at different reduction levels, marked *A* and *B* in figure 5. Solution concepts such as the Nash bargaining solution or the constrained joint optimum lie between their two preferred points.

The two-party negotiation illustrated above shows several effects of asymmetry on potential distributions of obligations. But in these examples there is no agreement unless all (i.e., both) affected parties choose to participate; the only negotiation is over how much each will do. In multiparty negotiations, in contrast, a cooperative agreement can be negotiated with less than full participation.

Consequently, in multiparty negotiations there are two distinct issues to settle: Who is in, and how much will each do? Asymmetry of interests can affect both issues. Complicating matters further is the fact that the two issues interact. Changing what the participants in an agreement will do can change the set of agents willing to participate, and changing the set of participants can change the stringency of measures they are willing to undertake.

We examine the two issues separately, however, considering two ideal types of bargaining situations: one in which the meaning of "participating" is somehow fixed and agents negotiate over who will participate, and one in which a fixed set of participants must agree on the distribution of obligations among them.

WHO PARTICIPATES?

First, we assume that what it means to participate in an agreement is fixed, so *who participates* is the only item for negotiation. In a real environmental negotiation this "fixed decision" case can arise in several ways. The object of discussion could be an intrinsically binary decision, such as nations deciding whether to require separated ballast tanks in oil tankers, or to prohibit hunting whales, or small-town citizens deciding whether to vote for property tax reductions. Even on matters that are not intrinsically binary, one specific proposal may so dominate debate that nobody discusses other measures, but only whether they will join or not. For example, negotiations over European acid rain control for many years only considered whether countries would make a proposed 30 percent sulfur dioxide reduction (Levy 1993). In formal models of bargaining, joining is often made into a binary decision by assuming that any fixed set of participants will reach some particular bargaining outcome, such as the Nash bargaining solution (Nash 1950).

In this situation each agent faces a binary decision: whether to participate or not. Since negotiation begins from the uncooperative point, nobody is willing to participate alone; but because of the public-good character of the issue (and assuming the meaning of participation has been sensibly chosen), all prefer unanimous participation to unanimous nonparticipation.

Between zero and full participation, however, each agent's willingness to join is conditional on others' joining as well, and on how their joining in turn depends on that agent's joining. Such conditionality relationships may take two forms. The first are *rules*, based perhaps on equity principles or politics. For example, agents may require that particular others join if they do: Canada may be unwilling to join an agreement unless the United States does, or the United States unless Germany and Japan do; the European Community may either all join together or not at all; or all agents may perceive a natural rank-ordering of decisions, requiring the biggest, the richest, the greenest, or those who benefit the most to join before others will.[5]

Agents' conditions for joining can also be driven by a *benefits calculation*. An agent will only join a coalition if the benefit of joining exceeds the benefit of staying out. Agents may perceive that other potential coalition members will not join unless they do, effectively raising the cost of not joining. An agent's choice is between the benefit of joining the proposed coalition and the benefit of not joining the smaller coalition that would form without her, from which all who require her participation have withdrawn (and all others who require theirs, and so on).

These two forms of conditions on individual participation allow us to define conditions for stable coalitions. A coalition C is stable if and only if: (1) no member requires the participation of somebody not in C as a condition of its participation, and (2) the withdrawal of any member would result, directly or indirectly, in other withdrawals whose effect would be to leave the original agent worse off. (Note that this condition does not require that *all* others withdraw, but only enough to offset the first one's gain from withdrawing.)

Stable coalitions comprise natural groups of cooperators that are likely to persist once established, for all members will recognize that if they withdraw they will end up worse off. In the case where agents act only on benefit calculations, not on rules, stable coalitions are the asymmetric equivalent of the "minimum viable coalitions" (MVCs) of identical-agent cooperation models. MVCs are participating subgroups of just sufficient size that their members are better off if all participate than if none do (Schelling 1978). Since anyone's withdrawal from an MVC leaves the rest worse off than if none participate, each member would reasonably expect all others' participation to depend on its own, and so stay in.

Whether stable coalitions are defined by benefit calculations, rules, or

---

[5] The experimental literature on individual decision-making shows clearly that such nonconsequential equity rules can be important. People *do* decline to make or accept advantageous offers that violate obvious fairness norms (Bazerman and Neale 1992). Of course, these empirical results are for individuals, not nations.

FIGURE 7

Stable Coalitions, Three Possible Configurations

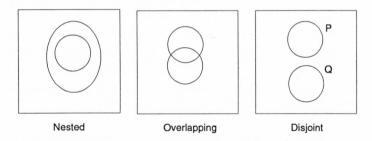

| Nested | Overlapping | Disjoint |

both, many potential stable coalitions can exist within any group negotiating. Whether a stable coalition can be expected to emerge in the first place depends in part on the number of stable coalitions and their relationships to each other.

If only one stable coalition exists, and negotiators have full knowledge, we expect agents to perceive their interests correctly (and each to perceive the consequences of attempting to free ride), so the stable coalition will form. If multiple stable coalitions exist, relationships among them can be of three kinds, as shown in Figure 7. Pairs of stable coalitions can be nested, overlapping, or disjoint.

If there is a natural ordering of agents joining an agreement, by size or environmental concern or net benefits, then stable coalitions will be nested. In this case we expect the largest to form, since all within the largest coalition are better off within it than with any other stable outcome.

If stable coalitions are overlapping or disjoint, strategic interaction between them can obstruct the formation of any of them, so the outcome is indeterminate. Disjoint stable coalitions, such as groups P and Q on the right of Figure 7, are each stable relative to the uncooperative starting point, but each would benefit at no cost if the other formed. If each group would no longer benefit from forming once the other already has formed (which depends on details of the payoffs), then each has an interest in delaying and in finding ways to press the *other* group to form. With overlapping coalitions, this tendency to delay may be partly offset by those agents in the intersection pressing those in the remainder of either stable coalition to join them.

It is each agent's *perception* of whose participation depends on her own that determines agents' perceived consequences of joining, and so for the agents collectively determines what coalitions are stable. Forming a stable coalition thus requires the emergence of a consistent set of expectations of whose participation depends on whose. If all the agents in some group come to perceive that they all depend on each other, and that nobody else is likely to join, then they all are likely to join. Any group would wish to resist the formation of such perceptions if the alternative is that some other group will bear the burden, but it may not be able to. A sufficiently large subgroup possessing some salient common characteristic, even if it is irrelevant to their benefits from cooperating (perhaps in a group of individuals some are Stanford graduates, or have red hair), could come to be identified by its members and others as a "natural" coalition. If each member of such a group comes to expect that enough others will join if she does, then all will. Their shared characteristic puts them at a disadvantage in the subtle struggle to push the responsibility onto some other group.

With strongly asymmetric groups, the process of identifying such characteristics will be difficult and contestable. When agents possess *many* varying characteristics, more or less conspicuous or relevant to their participation, each agent has an interest in maximizing others' perception that characteristics that *they* share (but she does not) are the "natural" bases for forming cooperative groups. With many overlapping stable coalitions, some characteristics will come to seem more salient and relevant than others, perhaps due to arbitrary artifacts of language, history, and context, as well as various agents' attempts to frame issues in ways that render their own participation inessential. Each agent's costs and benefits influence this struggle, affecting her ability to threaten credibly not to join, but do not by themselves determine the outcome.

AN ILLUSTRATION: COOPERATION IN A TEN-NATION WORLD

We illustrate the preceding argument with a specific model of ten-nation bargaining over carbon dioxide emissions that illustrates nested stable coalitions. The ten nations have quadratic cost and benefit functions as shown in Figures 1 through 4 above; their sizes are chosen so that their emissions at the "unconcerned" stage match those of the ten highest carbon-emitting nations of the 1980s, as shown in Table 1. Emissions are expressed in millions of metric tons of carbon, and are rounded.

The arbitrary calibration of costs and benefits is set so that movement from the unconcerned to the uncooperative (Nash equilibrium) point represents a reduction of somewhat less than 10 percent for the largest nations. Bargaining starts from this uncooperative point. From this point, no nation would undertake further reductions on its own, but nations will consider joint agreements to reduce together.

As in all bargaining models, restrictive assumptions are needed to generate unique outcomes. We invoke a particularly simple participation rule: Countries are arranged in order of size and environmental concern from biggest to

TABLE 1

Nations in the illustration

Nation Number	Corresponds to	Unconcerned Emissions (MT of carbon)
1	USA	1300
2	former USSR	900
3	China	450
4	Germany	275
5	Brazil	250
6	Japan	250
7	UK	150
8	Mexico	130
9	India	125
10	Colombia	120

smallest, and no country will consider joining an agreement to reduce emissions unless all larger countries, who also receive larger net benefits, have joined. The two largest consider joining first, then the third considers joining them, and so on. Beyond this rule, only a nation's net benefits determine whether it will join or not; if it will be better off by joining, it joins.

The meaning of "joining an agreement" is assumed to be fixed; all participants will make equal proportional reductions from their uncooperative emission levels, to a level given by the Nash bargaining solution. Nonparticipants continue to optimize uncooperatively, so as the cooperative coalition grows and cooperators decrease their emissions, noncooperators increase theirs slightly.

Figure 8 illustrates the result of this bargaining process. Cooperative coalitions make progressively larger emission reductions, and gain progressively larger benefits, as the coalition grows. Adding an additional cooperator makes each member of the original set of cooperators go further, given the Nash bargaining solution. Noncooperators increase their emissions by less than cooperators decrease theirs (a consequence of concave benefit functions), so total emissions decline as the cooperative group grows. In this figure, both emissions and benefits are scaled relative to their levels in the uncooperative equilibrium, which are assigned the value 100.

Table 2 shows each nation's net benefits when each size of coalition forms, illustrating the basis of nations' decisions to join or not join. Because all benefit figures are in arbitrary units, only comparisons between a nation's benefits under different coalitions are significant. The first column, headed "Uncoop", shows benefits to each nation at the uncooperative equilibrium, the last under a coalition of all ten nations, and the others under intermediate sizes of cooperative coalitions. With the assumptions and parameters used here, there are three points to note.

FIGURE 8

Cooperators' Emissions and Net Benefits as a Function of Coalition Size

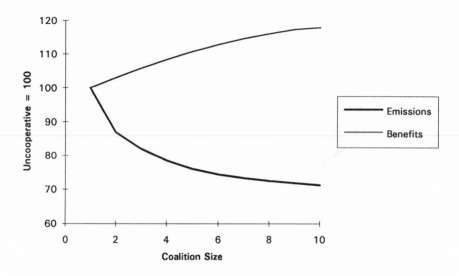

First, the largest two nations join to reduce emissions, even if nobody else joins them. This two-nation coalition is thus a stable cartel, in that no nation would unilaterally wish either to join or leave it (Donsimoni et al. 1986). The third nation would not benefit from joining this group, so it does not. But note that if the third and fourth nations both join, they—as well as all others—enjoy higher benefits than under the two-nation coalition. Here then is a coalition that can form if nations three and four know the relevant benefits and can come to expect that they will both move together. With full knowledge and no obstacles to communication, they are likely to join. Once formed, this group will likely be stable, since its marginal member, the fourth, will expect that if it withdraws so will the third, and so will evaluate its benefits relative to those under the two-nation coalition. Both nations three and four prefer to remain participating. Similarly, the nine-member coalition is stable because nations five through nine are all better off under the nine-member coalition than under the four-member one.[6] The ten-nation coalition is not stable, since nation ten prefers to be outside the nine-member coalition rather than inside the ten-member one.

The particular configuration of stable coalitions in Table 2 merely illustrates the range of possibilities. Other configurations can be obtained by vary-

---

[6]The apparent ties for nations five through eight are due to rounding. They are in fact strictly better off under the nine-nation coalition.

TABLE 2

Net benefits to each nation as a function of coalition size

| Nation | Uncooperative | Number of nations reducing below uncooperative level | | | | | | | | |
		2	3	4	5	6	7	8	9	10
1	573.2	573.6	574.2	574.6	575.1	575.6	575.9	576.2	576.5	576.8
2	397.2	**397.8**	398.3	398.7	399.1	399.6	399.8	400.1	400.3	400.6
3	198.7	199.6	199.6	199.8	200.1	200.3	200.5	200.6	200.8	200.9
4	121.4	122.0	122.5	**122.2**	122.4	122.5	122.6	122.7	122.8	122.9
5	110.4	110.9	111.3	111.7	111.3	111.4	111.5	111.6	111.7	111.8
6	110.4	110.9	111.3	111.7	112.0	111.4	111.5	111.6	111.7	111.8
7	66.2	66.5	66.8	67.0	67.2	67.4	66.9	67.0	67.0	67.1
8	57.4	57.7	57.9	58.1	58.2	58.4	58.5	58.1	58.1	58.2
9	55.2	55.5	55.7	55.8	56.0	56.1	56.2	56.3	**55.9**	55.9
10	53.0	53.2	53.4	53.6	53.7	53.9	54.0	54.1	54.2	53.7
Total Benefits	1743	1748	1751	1753	1755	1757	1758	1758	1759	1760

ing the parameters of the common cost and benefit functions, and the relative sizes of participating nations. Under different configurations the smallest stable coalition can contain either two or three members, various intermediate sizes can be stable, and the unanimous coalition can either be stable or not. This example illustrates two results: that cooperative coalitions short of unanimity can form and be stable; and that when stable coalitions are nested, the largest can be expected to form.

WHAT DO THE PARTICIPANTS DO?

The preceding analysis addressed what sorts of coalitions will form when the distribution of requirements to be imposed on any particular coalition is specified. We now turn to the other ideal type of multiparty negotiations, and inquire what sorts of agreements a specified coalition will reach.

We suppose that a fixed set of N agents has agreed to cooperate and must negotiate the magnitude of emission reduction each will undertake. They must accept an agreement unanimously, since we assume that nobody in the provisional set of participants opts out. This means deciding on the values for N numbers, that is, picking one point in an N-dimensional space.

How will they choose such a point? As in the two-dimensional case, there are many potential distributions of obligations that all would prefer to the uncooperative status quo, and all know it. Unlike the two-dimensional case, though, it seems unlikely that they will come to agreement through unstructured haggling. Such a negotiation would be too complex and take too long. The negotiation has too many degrees of freedom, and moreover would grant each agent unlimited license to argue (whether sincerely or not) that its special situation calls for a lower burden than others will bear.

Instead, agents will normally first negotiate over devices that simplify and restrict the space of possible agreements by fixing relationships among the obligations they undertake. We call such devices *principles*. They serve two purposes: an *informational* one, promoting a manageable negotiation by reducing the amount of information that negotiators must process in seeking and reaching agreement; and a *moral or rhetorical* one, providing support for claims that particular allocations of obligations are fair or not, and that particular bargainers are carrying their due burdens or not.

A principle, once chosen, reduces the bargaining space but not to a single point. Hence, choosing a principle does not end the negotiation, but simplifies it, leaving a restricted set of items still to be negotiated. Many often-used principles, such as equal proportional emission reductions or equal contributions per unit GNP, are so constraining that only a single degree of freedom remains to be negotiated: how much total reduction or contribution. Other principles could leave more. For example, industrial countries could cut to one level and developing countries to another, or emission entitlements could be defined as linear functions (to be negotiated) of population, current emissions, GNP, and land area.

By far the most common principle used in environmental agreements is equal proportional emission reductions. For example, more than seventy nations have ratified the Montreal protocol to protect the ozone layer, a 1987 agreement to cut chlorofluorocarbons (CFCs) by 50 percent, amended in 1990 to eliminate them entirely. Under the Convention on Long-Range Transboundary Air Pollution (LRTAP), twenty-one nations have agreed to cut sulfur emissions by 30 percent, and twenty-three to freeze emissions of nitrogen oxides (while a "club" of twelve nitrogen activists separately agreed to 30 percent cuts). The eight North Sea nations agreed to reduce pollution by dioxins and heavy metals by 70 percent and other chemicals by 50 percent, while the six Baltic nations pledged to cut chemicals and nutrients flowing to that sea by 50 percent. In two nonbinding declarations since eclipsed by the weaker climate convention signed in Rio, about a dozen industrial nations pledged to cut carbon emissions by 20 percent by the year 2005 (UNEP 1987; 1990; Levy 1993; Haas 1993; Toronto Declaration 1988; Hague Declaration 1989).

The few exceptions to equal proportional reductions almost all fall into two categories: grouping countries into two classes (industrial and developing), with identical measures for all members of each class; or specially negotiated, seemingly universal measures that in fact create special exceptions for one or a few parties (and everybody knows it). For example, the original 1987 Montreal protocol included a provision drafted to accommodate one Soviet CFC plant, which included the output of a new plant in a country's baseline if it met four conditions; only the Soviet plant met the conditions (UNEP 1987, article 2 para. 6; Benedick 1991, 83). In each case, large groups of countries are still subjected to equal proportional reductions.[7]

Principles other than equal percentage reductions could be effective simplifying devices for complex negotiations, but not just any constraint will do. There are a number of desiderata if a principle is to simplify negotiations. It should be easy to articulate, recognize, and agree upon; and it should be "sticky," resistant to incremental chiseling or renegotiation once adopted. It must tie together the contributions of different agents in a supportable manner, so that all perceive it to be stable, expect others not to chisel, and expect to be hurt if they try to chisel.

For example, consider the following principle: "Emission reductions of countries A, B, C shall be in the ratio 1 to 1.32 to 1.73." Such a principle, stating a crystal-clear algebraic relationship among parties' emission reductions, could in theory serve the function of reducing bargaining degrees of freedom. It could never do so in practice, though, since it appears utterly arbitrary and would be subject to participants' constant efforts to improve their positions just a little. It would take forever to negotiate, and would not be resistant to chiseling and renegotiation.[8]

Rather, an effective negotiating principle should be a *focal point* in the sense of Schelling (1960), commanding attention by virtue of salience, uniqueness, or discreteness. These characteristics are defined cognitively, relative to the perceptions of the particular agents negotiating; as both Schelling and Kreps (1990b) point out, different resolutions may appear salient or unique to different groups. Some principles are likely to be focal points for almost all groups, however; for example, setting some quantity equal for all participants; setting something to zero or another round number; or maintaining something at its status quo value.

The 1990 amendments to the Montreal protocol on the ozone layer illustrate the usefulness and power for negotiations of strong focal points. When it became clear from scientific and technical reports that "zero" (i.e., a complete phaseout of a broad class of chemicals) was feasible and environmentally desirable, the ninety-odd negotiating nations agreed on full phaseouts essentially without difficulty. "Zero" is a uniquely salient and powerful

---

[7] We know of only one recent environmental negotiation that proceeded by unstructured haggling, and yielded highly asymmetric assignment of obligations: the European Community's Directive on Emissions from Large Combustion Plants. This agreement's uniqueness, and its five-year, twice-weekly negotiating history, support our claim that this approach is difficult (Grubb 1989).

[8] Note, however, that a principle to cut back in proportion to GNP or to emissions excess over 1990 levels might be acceptable, and such a principle could yield contributions in the ratio 1 to 1.32 to 1.73.

negotiating outcome, but cases such as ozone where it is also the right (or a feasible) answer are rare. Consequently, this precedent is of limited use in current major international negotiations on issues such as climate change and species loss, where total elimination of the harmful activities is not possible.

How will a principle be chosen to serve this simplifying function? This is no problem at all with symmetric agents, for every reasonable principle is equivalent to equal reductions. When agents differ on many dimensions, however, the number of plausibly fair principles will be large (Young 1991). With many seemingly reasonable rules for reductions available, none can approach the salience that equal reductions have in the symmetric case.

Moreover, with asymmetric interests different principles will impose relatively lighter or heavier burdens on different nations. "Equal proportional reductions" favors countries with high emissions and low abatement costs, while "equal per capita emissions" favors populous countries. Different reasonable arguments may justify higher emissions for different countries: Japan may claim higher carbon emissions because its energy use to GNP ratio is already the lowest of the industrial countries, the United States because it defends the world, or Canada because it is so big and cold. Negotiators can be expected to favor, often sincerely, those "neutral" principles that advantage them (Messick and Sentis 1983).

But the same uniqueness that makes principles effective simplifying devices once adopted makes them hard to negotiate over. A compromise between two principles is likely to lack the sticky, discrete character that makes principles useful. When there are many candidate principles, different agents strongly favor different ones, and compromise is difficult, reaching agreement will be a challenge. Moreover, if failure to choose any principle means a breakdown or an impossibly cumbersome and drawn-out negotiation that all want to avoid, then the negotiation over *which* principle to use has the character of a chicken game, giving agents incentives to fabricate commitments to one principle or another.

How agreement will be reached in any real negotiation we cannot predict. As long as negotiators remain committed to incompatible principles, there will be no agreement. But the record of real negotiations suggests that parties usually do break this impasse, surprisingly often by agreeing on symmetric measures despite asymmetries of interest. Burtraw and Toman (1991) argue that a process through which perceptions of fairness change as negotiations proceed is likely to promote agreement. If the negotiating group includes some "neutrals" who initially lack strong preferences between the principles under contention, then persuading the neutrals may be a particularly effective way of forcing the group's expectations to converge on one principle rather than another.

Finally, the choice of a principle, while necessary, is but a first step toward concluding the negotiation. When, for example, parties have agreed on equal proportional emission reductions, they must still agree on the level. Moreover, the two negotiations we have treated as separable ideal cases—who participates and what they do—are in fact simultaneously determined. If those most concerned begin discussing an agreement among themselves, they may then need to change the measures they adopt to entice new members into their coalition. Alternatively, if more parties become interested in joining, the resulting gains may make it possible to adopt stronger measures.

The recent climate negotiations illustrate several of the phenomena we have described. A group of activist nations, led by the European Community, had pressed strongly for a convention with binding national emission limits. They perceived U.S. participation as essential to any successful agreement, however, so they accepted a much weaker treaty than they preferred in order to induce the U.S. to sign (rather than acting by themselves, or signing a convention in which some committed to limit emissions and some did not). The convention includes "principles," but they are so vague as to put scarcely any limits on possible future negotiations of specific emission limits. About the only clear implication is that developed countries will do the bulk of emissions limitation. The convention does include significant measures for the development of national plans, reporting of national emissions, and creation of institutions. Many hope that these hortatory and institutional measures alone will induce national actions sufficient to bring about whatever global emission reductions are required. We think it more likely that these measures and principles will simply serve as foundations for future negotiation of more concrete national emission obligations. If so, then most of the hard bargaining remains to be done (UN General Assembly 1992).

CONCLUSION

The usual analytic view of the world, which assumes symmetric interests, is not useful for most collective-good negotiations in the real world. In most important multiparty negotiations, the parties are highly asymmetric in their interests. This has several important consequences. First, there can be stable groups of participants in an agreement short of universal participation. Insistence on universal participation is rooted in symmetric thinking.

Second, most multiparty bargains will need to employ simple principles to distribute obligations among participants. With significant asymmetries of interest, however, there will exist multiple plausible candidate principles, each with its own distributional implications. Appealing concepts such as equal sacrifice in pursuit of a common purpose become ambiguous. Choosing a principle is likely to be contentious and difficult. Even with an agreed-upon principle, differences will remain, on questions such as how stringently it should be applied.

The principle of equal proportional emission reductions, widely employed in environmental agreements, can be highly inefficient and unequal in the distribution of burdens, given asymmetry of costs (Bohm 1990). But the requirements of salience, seeming fairness, and stickiness may mean that the choice is between a flawed agreement that can be reached and an efficient one that cannot. In such cases the political and informational advantages of a viable principle must outweigh its efficiency losses.

This trade-off may change as the stakes in a negotiation rise, particularly if the asymmetries among nations are considerable. On climate change, the most pessimistic projections of losses from high-cost emission abatement policies approach 10 percent of some nations' GNPs, while the most pessimistic projections of losses from climate change approach catastrophe (Broecker 1987; Manne and Richels 1990). If these projections have a chance to prove accurate, the potential environmental risks make an agreement to control emissions desirable, while the losses inherent in a simple agreement of equal proportional reductions would probably render such an agreement infeasible. Parties who would be willing to go along with symmetric deals if the stakes were low would likely be more sensitive to perceived unfairness in the burden they bear relative to the gains they reap when the sacrifices are significant. If nations are to achieve agreement on issues as consequential as climate change, significant creativity may be required in inventing and identifying focal points and principles of fair burden, enlarging the set of approaches to feasible agreement and thereby reducing the likelihood of sustained impasse.

Cooperation in the unbalanced commons will be more difficult than the consideration of symmetric models, or precedents of moderate-stakes agreements, would suggest. Such cooperation will be facilitated by understanding the conceptual lessons laid out here. Simple principles will play a salient role, in defining both the group of cooperators and the actions they take. Nations will be unlikely to participate if their peers, and those they perceive to have a greater responsibility, do not. The language of agreement will enshrine symmetric treatment, by some definition, within groups of fairly heterogeneous nations. This pursuit of symmetry, though sacrificing efficiency, will promote both the feasibility of agreements and their perceived fairness.

CHAPTER TWELVE

Strategic Uses of Argument

Jon Elster

I. INTRODUCTION

*I*n trying to reach agreement people can interact in two main ways. On the one hand, they can try to persuade each other by rational argument. On the other hand, they can try to induce agreement by threats and promises. In this chapter I consider the advantages and disadvantages of these two modes of communication, with respect both to the prospect of reaching agreement and to the quality of the agreement, if any, that is reached. The main empirical illustrations of the argument will be the debates of constituent assemblies, especially at the Federal Convention in Philadelphia in 1787 and the Assemblée Constituante in Paris 1789–91.[1] I shall also draw on some other empirical material, notably a few stylized facts about collective wage bargaining (see also Elster 1989, chap. 4) and some aspects of the allocation of scarce resources (Elster 1992).

When people argue, they make assertions with a claim to *validity*. To elucidate this notion, I shall draw on the writings of Jürgen Habermas (1984 / 1989, 1990). When they engage in bargaining, they make threats and promises with a claim to *credibility*. This idea will be developed in the spirit of Thomas Schelling (1960). But I'll try to do more than simply juxtapose the two approaches. I shall also consider *strategic uses of argumentation*, reading Habermas, as it were, through the lens of Schelling. On the one hand, bargainers often try to present their threats as warnings. Instead of uttering a threat, they substitute a *factual equivalent* of a threat. On the

---

[1] References to the American proceedings are given by Roman numerals I–III followed by a page number, corresponding to the three volumes of Farrand 1966. References to the French proceedings will be given by Arabic numerals 8–30 followed by a page number, corresponding to the volumes of the *Archives parlementaires, série I: 1789–1799*, Paris 1875–1888. The documents reproduced in Furet and Halévi 1989 are referred to by the letter "O," followed by a page number.

other hand, self-interested actors often try to ground their claims in principle. Their self-interest tells them to appeal to an *impartial equivalent* of self-interest. Much of the paper will be devoted to the constraints on these substitutions, the reasons for making them, and the consequences of doing so. The puzzle I want to illuminate can be stated very simply: *Why argue at all?*

As I said, I shall mainly look at constituent assemblies, in which both arguing and bargaining have a central role. Two situations closer to the extremes of pure argument and pure bargaining are, respectively, ordinary legislative debates and collective wage negotiations. Yet even in these cases both types of speech act are observed. In legislatures the government can threaten to resign or to dissolve parliament unless its proposal is adopted. Legislators may use the threat of filibustering and engage in logrolling. (Note, however, that all these forms of bargaining behavior are based on resources created by the political system itself. They do not involve threats to the adversary's life, reputation, or purse.) Conversely, even adversarial wage bargaining contains a good deal of rational argument. Professions that are prevented by law from striking nevertheless engage in wage negotiations. Even when the repertoire of the parties includes strikes and boycotts, bargaining over wages often includes discussion of purely factual matters, such as the wage increases of other groups, the financial health of the firm, or the expected rate of inflation. One cannot negotiate over such matters any more than one can negotiate over the weather.

Constituent assemblies are privileged, nevertheless, in that they often exhibit both arguing and bargaining in their most striking forms. On the one hand, the matters that have to be decided are far removed from petty, self-interested, routine politics. Because these assemblies are to decide the organization of the legal and political system for the indefinite future, there is a strong pressure to adopt an impartial stance. On the other hand, constitutions are often written in times of crises that invite extraordinary and dramatic measures. In Philadelphia, many of the states threatened to leave the union unless they got their way on specific issues, such as the maintenance of the slave trade or proportional representation of all states in the Senate. (The first threat was successful; the second was not.) In Paris, the deliberations of the assembly were conducted under the shadow of threats based, in an early stage, on the king's troops and, in a later stage, on the crowds in Paris. (The latter threat was successful; the former was not.)

In this chapter I shall not consider specific instances of arguing and bargaining in the two assemblies.[2] Instead, I shall discuss how apparent cases

---

[2] Such instances are adduced and discussed in my Arguing and bargaining in two constituent assemblies, given as the Storrs Lectures, Yale University 1991.

of rational argument about values (section III) or facts (section IV) may, on closer analysis, turn out to be guided by self-interest. I shall examine for what reasons, and with what consequences, the participants in collective decision-making make strategic use of the (nonstrategic) ideas of impartiality and truth.

II. MOTIVATIONAL ASSUMPTIONS

In the bulk of the chapter I assume that participants in collective decision-making processes are (1) rational and (2) motivated exclusively by self-interest or group interest (*interest*, for short). If they make arguments that seem to deviate from their interest, it is because of a rational calculation that it is in their interest to do so. Since this assumption is obviously unrealistic, I shall make a few comments on its shortcomings.

In the first place, the assumption rests on a simplistic view of the mechanism by which interest may generate noninterested arguments. As observed by Tocqueville (1893; 1990, 84), self-deception as well as deception may be at work: "party politicians . . . are often accused of acting without conviction; but my experience goes to show that this is much less frequent than is supposed. It is just that they have a faculty, which is precious and indeed sometimes necessary in politics, of creating ephemeral convictions in accordance with the feelings and interests of the moment."

In the second place, and more importantly, the assumption rests on an impoverished view of human motivations. We may distinguish among three types of motives: passions, interests, and impartial reason. These motives are often opposed to each other in a pairwise fashion. David Hume (1960, 415, first published 1739–40), when addressing the relation between *passion and reason*, argued that the latter was and ought only to be the slave of the former. Albert Hirschman (1977) has considered the changing attitudes toward *passions and interests* in the eighteenth century, arguing that the dominance of interest over passion in a commercial society constituted "a political argument for capitalism before its triumph." In the following discussion, interest should be understood as the pursuit of material advantage, whereas the passions not only are not oriented toward advantage, but are even capable of inducing people to act against their interest. As La Bruyère (1696, IV:71) noted, "Nothing is easier for passion than to place itself above reason: its real triumph is to win out over interest." Finally, the present chapter is to a large extent guided by the contrast between *reason and interest*. At the Federal Convention, in particular, these two principles are generally believed to have exhausted the motives of the framers (Jillson 1988, 193–94; Rakove 1987).

In the analysis of the constituent assemblies that are my main focus here, these three motivations enter twice. First, the founders had to make some assumptions about the motives that would animate the future legislatures for which the constitution was written. Second, observers and historians can try to sort out the precise mix of motives that operated among the framers themselves.

Case 1: Impartial, Rational Framers

As a first subcase, consider rational impartial framers who engage in damage limitation with regard to the passions of future generations. This idea has two aspects, related, respectively, to the machinery of constitutional amendment and the ordinary machinery of legislation. By making it hard to amend the constitution, the framers can restrain passionate majorities who might want to suppress the rights of minorities. By slowing down the ordinary legislative process, through bicameralism and executive veto, the constitution can reduce the dangers of reckless and fickle majority legislation. Madison's argument (I, 421) that the Senate is needed to protect the people against its predictable "fickleness and passion" falls into this category.

By and large, the records from the Federal Convention give little evidence that the framers were concerned with the passions of future generations, in the sense in which I use the term here. They were much more concerned with their tendency to pursue myopic or partisan interests. They assumed, roughly speaking, that motives are always and everywhere self-interested. The assumption was probably adopted for prudential reasons, not because it was believed to be literally true. According to Hume (1963, 42), "It is . . . a just *political* maxim, *that every man must be supposed to be a knave;* though, at the same time, it appears somewhat strange, that a maxim should be true in *politics* which is false in *fact*." Steeped as they were in Humean thinking, the framers naturally adopted the same outlook (White 1987).

In the Assemblée Constituante, the assumptions made about human nature were both nastier and loftier than the ones adopted at the Federal Convention. Although Hume's assumption of universal knavishness is often thought to represent a worst-case scenario, there are worse things than self-interest (Hirschman 1977; Holmes 1990). Foremost among them are envy, spite, pride, and vanity. Although there are a couple of arguments (I, 72, 176) at the Federal Convention that may be read as if the framers imputed envy to those for whom they were legislating, the passages are ambiguous and atypical. In the Assemblée Constituante, however, arguments from pride and vanity, *amour-propre*, played a considerable role. One should never place any agent in a situation in which his vanity might lead him to act against the public interest. Twenty-five years later, Benjamin Constant remained concerned with "the problem of *amour-propre*, a peculiarly French flaw," and argued that "institutional devices" were needed to counter it. He advocated, for instance, the British system that forbade written speeches in Parliament (Holmes 1984, 139–40).

In the Assemblée Constituante, Bergasse repeatedly argued the need to accommodate the vanity or pride of the agents whose behavior would be regulated by the constitution (9, 115). The prosecutor, he says, should not also serve as judge, because if the functions are combined, the *amour-propre* of the magistrate might bias him toward the guilt of the accused (8, 443). If the legislature accuses a minister of misconduct, he should not be judged by an ordinary court, as it might make this an occasion to "humiliate the pride" of the legislative body (9, 111). A suspensive veto for the king will not have the intended effect of making the assembly reconsider, because its *amour-propre* will prevent it from backing down (9, 116). Malouet (8, 591) discussed a similar argument that had been advanced against the proposal to give a veto to the senate which could only be overruled by a two-thirds' majority in the lower house. In his reply, Malouet did not deny the operation of *amour-propre*, but argued that it would be limited to those who had initiated the law and not extend to everybody who voted for it.

Consider next a second subcase: In addition to addressing themselves to the passions of future legislators, the framers can try to control and harness their interests. In the Assemblée Constituante, there were relatively few instances of such reasoning. By contrast, public-choice theory was well represented at the Federal Convention, where the framers constantly based their arguments on the incentive effects of various schemes. Let me cite three examples, all from Madison.

Madison was worried about requiring landed property for members of Congress. Looking back, he observed that "It had often happened that men who had acquired landed property on credit, got into the legislatures with a view of promoting an unjust protection against their creditors" (II, 123). Another instance of incentive-effect reasoning occurred in his comments on a proposal that in voting for the president, each elector should have two votes, one of which at least should be cast for a candidate not from his own state. Madison "thought something valuable might be made of the suggestion. . . . The only objection which occurred was that each citizen after having given his vote for his favorite fellow citizen would throw away his second vote on some obscure citizen of another State, in order to ensure the object of his first choice" (II, 114). A final argument is less convincing. Arguing against selection of the executive by the legislature, Madison asserted that "the candidate would intrigue with the legislature, would derive his appointment from the predominant faction, and be apt to render his administration subservient to its views" (II, 109). But it is not clear that a candidate's promise to favor his electors would be credible. Unless the executive can stand for reelection, we would rather expect the legislature to become subservient to its creature. The kingmaker, in fact, should beware of the king.

As a third subcase, consider the idea that rational framers can try to create the conditions under which future legislatures, too, will be able to exercise their reasoning powers. At the Federal Convention, this idea was never mentioned. In the French assembly it was central. In some respects, as I said, the members of the Assemblée Constituante thought more highly of their successors than did their American counterparts. They believed that an assembly existed to effectuate the transformation of preferences through rational discussion, going well beyond a simple process of aggregation. In the best-known statement of this view Sieyès argued (8, 595) that the *voeu national,* the desire of the nation, could not be determined by consulting the *cahiers* of complaints and wishes that the delegates had brought with them to Versailles. Bound mandates, similarly, could not be viewed as expressions of the national will. In a democracy (a term that was used pejoratively at the time), he said, people form their opinions at home and then bring them to the voting booth. If no majority emerges, they go back home to reconsider their views, once again isolated from each other. This procedure for forming a common will, he claimed, is absurd because it lacks the element of deliberation and discussion. "It is not a question of a democratic election, but of proposing, listening, concerting, changing one's opinion, in order to form in common a common will." In the debates over the revision of the constitution, d'André (30, 668) and Barnave (30, 115) similarly claimed that the idea of a constitutional convention with bound mandates from primary assemblies would be a betrayal of the representative system in favor of democracy. In Barnave's phrase, "a personal wish or the wish of a faction, which is not illuminated by a common deliberation, is not a real wish *(un voeu véritable)."*

Case 2. Impartial, Imperfectly Rational Framers

Turning now to the motives of the framers themselves, we may first consider the possibility of an imperfectly rational concern with the public good. Imperfect rationality—being weak, and knowing it—can induce actors to take steps to forestall predictable, undesirable behavior in the future (Elster 1984). Metaphorically, the constitution itself may be seen as a device by which "society" protects itself against "its" known or expected tendencies to behave imprudently. "Constitutions are chains with which men bind themselves in their sane moments that they may not die by a suicidal hand in the day of their frenzy" (John Potter Stockton, as cited in Finn 1991, 5). Although this idea of intergenerational self-binding soon unravels if taken too literally, it can have a more direct application in the analysis of the motives of the framers. The members of a constituent assembly can seek to structure *their own* proceedings so as to minimize the scope of passion and self-interest. Both eighteenth-century assemblies created institutional devices for this purpose.

At the Federal Convention, the sessions were closed and secret. As Madison said later (III, 479), "had the members committed themselves publicly at first, they would have afterwards supposed consistency required them to maintain their ground, whereas by secret discussion no man felt himself obliged to retain his opinions any longer than he was satisfied of their propriety and truth, and was open to the force of argument." Presumably, the fear was that the pride and vanity of the delegates, as well as pressure from their constituencies, might prevent them from backing down from an opinion once they had expressed it. However, Madison did not consider the other effect of secrecy—that of pushing the debates away from argument and toward bargaining. I return to this effect below.

Unlike the Federal Convention, the Assemblée Constituante functioned also as an ordinary legislature. That arrangement, however, may be undesirable. A main task of a constitutional assembly is to strike the proper balance of power between the legislative and the executive branches of government. To assign that task to an assembly that also serves as a legislative body would be to ask it to act as judge in its own cause. A constitution written by a legislative assembly might be expected to give excessive powers to the legislature. In the abstract, this problem could be solved by means similar to the ones used in legislative bodies, by checks and balances. A royal veto over the constitution might, for instance, have kept the legislative tendency to self-aggrandizement in check. The Assemblée Constituante adopted another solution, by voting its members ineligible to the first ordinary legislature. It was Robespierre (26, 124), in his first great speech, who won the assembly for this "self-denying ordinance."

Although sometimes viewed by posterity as a disastrous piece of populist overkill (Furet 1988, 104), Robespierre's solution did respond to a genuine problem. If framers have both the motive and the opportunity to write a special place for themselves into the constitution, they will do so. At the Federal Convention, the motive may have been lacking. Although the framers were guided by the idea that future voters and politicians had to be assumed to be knaves, as noted above, they viewed themselves as moved by loftier motives (White 1987, 114, 249; Lovejoy 1961, 52). More importantly, however, the opportunity was lacking. It was a given fact, outside the control of the delegates, that the convention would be dissolved forever once the constitution had been written. In the Assemblée Constituante, by contrast, the founders had to take active steps to remove the opportunity to give themselves a privileged place in the constitution.

Case 3. Interested and Passionate Framers

Much has been written on the relative importance of impartial ideas and interest as motives of the framers at the federal convention. Charles Beard (1986) argued that the framers were moved wholly by their self-interest. Calvin Jillson (1988, 16) claims that in the choice between two institutional arrangements, ideas mattered when and only when interest was neutral. R. A. McGuire (1988) finds that the economic interests of the constituencies of the various delegates have more power to explain voting patterns at the convention than the economic interests of the framers themselves, although the latter are not negligible. We should note, however, that given the need for downstream ratification of the constitution, the interest of the constituencies may have mattered by serving as a constraint on impartial framers rather than by defining an interest of the framers themselves. (Conversely, as I argue in the next section, the norms of rational discourse may serve as constraints on self-interested framers.)

Although scholars disagree about the exact mix of ideas and interests in Philadelphia, most agree that both motives mattered. Passions, by contrast, seem to have played a relatively minor role. In the Assemblée Constituante, the interests of the delegates (and of their constituencies) were relatively peripheral, if we except the diehard defenders of the old régime. Ideas and passions—ideas defended with passion and sometimes distorted by passion—dominated the proceedings. My strategy in this chapter will be to treat these differences between the two assemblies as endogenous to the institutional context. Closed debates permit the open expression of interest; open discussions force it to go underground. In closed proceedings among a small number of delegates, expressions of passion will be derided as cant. In a public forum, with large numbers of delegates, passionate argument serves both as a sword and as shield. I am not saying that this is all there is to the matter. We may assume that both assemblies contained their share of passionate and self-interested members. My concern here, however, is with the way in which the setting of the debates channeled, amplified, or muted the expression of these motives.

III. STRATEGIC USES OF IMPARTIAL ARGUMENTS

Participants in assembly debates often do no more than pay lip service to the idea of the common good or the public interest. Even when their arguments are phrased in terms of these goals, they are often mere disguises for partial or partisan ends. To understand the nature, causes, and consequences of such pseudoarguments, we must begin with an analysis of the genuine arguments on which they are parasitic. Here I follow Habermas

(1984, 75 ff; 1990, 58). He argues that a speaker who aims at achieving *understanding* rather than *success* is committed to three validity claims: propositional truth, normative rightness, and subjective truthfulness (sincerity). It follows that a speaker who wants to *appear* as aiming at understanding must also appear to be committed to these claims. Hence I shall discuss the conditions under which a speaker who is really aiming at success will find it in his interest to appear to be aiming at understanding, by a seeming commitment to truth or rightness. The commitment to rightness is the topic of this section. The commitment to truth is discussed in the following section. The commitment to truthfulness or sincerity, although important, can be disregarded for the present purposes.

The idea of normative rightness is difficult and controversial. At a minimum it must involve some idea of impartiality. People ought not to be treated differently simply because they live at a particular time and place or belong to a particular sex, race, or profession. Any differential treatment of such groups must be grounded in properties that could in principle apply to anyone. It was precisely at the time of the two assemblies that these ideas of impartiality and universality became generally recognized as the basis for political life. In the French assembly, they were memorably expressed in Clermont-Tonnerre's plea for recognizing "Jews, comedians and executioners" as full citizens (10, 754 ff.) The refusal of the right of vote to women might appear to be an exception. In Sieyès's argument, however, the refusal was grounded in women's lack of a universal property, namely that of "contributing to the public establishment" (o, 1014). In fact, those who argued against full citizenship for Jews similarly referred to their lack of a universal property, namely that of doing military service (10, 757). Nobody claimed that Jews had to be excluded simply because of their race.

It is crucial for my purposes that the general idea of impartiality can be spelled out in many different ways. By itself, the demand for impartiality does not amount to a theory of justice; rather it must be seen as a constraint on any such theory. Both utilitarianism and rights-based theories are impartial. Norms of distribution according to need, desert, or contribution are impartial, as are norms of equal distribution or distribution by lot. The idea that social arrangements ought to reflect what rational individuals would choose behind a veil of uncertainty (a notion that can be spelled out in several different ways) also reflects an ideal of impartiality. The ideal can be applied to individuals or to collectivities, and yield radically different conclusions in the two applications. At the Federal Convention, both those who defended proportional representation for the states in the Senate and those who defended equal representation appealed to impartial notions of fairness and justice (I, 151, 159), the former claiming impartial treatment of individuals and the latter impartial treatment of the states.

Consider now a group whose interest leads it to favor proposal A. The question then arises whether the group can appeal to an *impartial equivalent* of its self-interest, if for some reason (see below) it does not want to strike a purely self-interested stance. Is there, in other words, an impartial argument for A? Suppose there is not. We can then ask what impartial argument will favor a proposal as close as possible to A. In the first case, we have a *perfect* fit between partial interest and impartial arguments, in the second case a *maximal* fit. However, it is quite likely that neither a perfect fit (if one exists) nor a maximal fit will be *optimal* from the point of view of the group. An impartial argument that coincides too well with the interests of those who deploy it tends to arouse suspicion. If the well-off advocate tax breaks *for all the well-off and only for the well-off*, the impartial argument that such policies will benefit all by a trickle-down effect is probably not optimal. If, however, an impartial argument is made that supports a diluted conclusion, with tax breaks for most but not all who are well-off and for some of the badly off as well, it is more likely to be accepted. An argument that offers tax breaks only for the badly off may also have good chances of being accepted, but would clearly not be optimal from the point of view of the well-off. They need an argument that deviates enough from their self-interest to be accepted by others, while not deviating so much that nothing is gained if it is accepted.[3]

Some examples may be useful at this point. In the 1920s, Yale College wanted to limit the admission of Jews. Following a recent scandal at Harvard, they did not, however, want to use explicit quotas. Instead they adopted a policy of geographical diversity, ostensibly as a goal in its own right, but in reality as a measure taken to reduce the number of enrollments from the predominantly Jewish pool of applicants from New York City. The beauty of this last strategy, from the point of view of publicity-conscious admissions officers, was that it could be presented as unbiased. "Though many individual Jews (concentrated in the northeast region from which Yale received most of its applications) would be affected by this principle, it was not an innately anti-Jewish principle. A geographical policy applied without regard to religion that would help an individual Milwaukee Jew or Duluth Catholic as much as it would hurt a New York atheist or Hoboken Protestant could not appropriately be termed religiously biased." (Oren 1985, 198). The impartial criterion of geographical diversity served as a diluted and therefore more acceptable equivalent of race.

---

[3] Similarly, Marxists have argued that it is in the interest of the capitalist class to have a state apparatus or an ideological system that does not in each and every respect promote the immediate interest of that class. See Elster 1985, 411 ff., 472 ff. These arguments fail because no plausible mechanism is suggested to bring about the optimal deviation from immediate class interest. At the individual level, however, a simple intentional explanation suffices.

Another example concerns restrictions on the right to vote. In many societies, property has been used as a criterion for the suffrage. One may, to be sure, offer impartial arguments for this principle. At the Federal Convention, Madison argued (I, 421, 443) that the stringent property qualifications for the Senate, rather than protecting the privileged against the people, were a device for protecting the people against itself. But, as I said, there is something inherently suspicious about such arguments. They coincide too well with the self-interest of the rich. It may then be useful to turn to literacy, as an impartial criterion that is highly but imperfectly correlated with property. At various stages in American history literacy has also served as a legitimizing proxy for other partial goals, such as the desire to keep blacks or Catholics out of politics (Creppell 1989).

The strategic use of impartial arguments is a well-known fact of political life. We know less, however, about the reasons why individuals find it in their self-interest to substitute an impartial argument for their self-interest, and even less about the consequences of such substitution strategies. Let me return to the first and most important question: *Why argue at all?* Why not simply adopt a bargaining stance, or demand an immediate vote without prior debate? I can think of five answers, but there may be others.

First, if others believe that one is truly arguing from principle, they may be more willing to back down. The belief that a person is arguing from principle and is willing to suffer a loss rather than accept a compromise will make other, self-interested actors yield (Frank 1988; Elster 1989, 231 ff.). In this respect, adopting a principle is a form of precommitment. This strategy is especially likely to be adopted by actors who otherwise have little bargaining power. When the strong bargain from strength, the weak argue from principles.

Second, Jonathan Macey (1986, 251) has argued that legislative coalitions tend to use public-regarding language as a "subterfuge" for what is in reality a deal among special interests. "The reason special interest legislation is so often drafted with a public-regarding gloss is because this gloss raises the costs to the public and to rival groups of discovering the true effect of the legislation. This, in turn, minimizes the major cost to the legislator of supporting narrow interest group legislation—the loss of support from groups that are harmed by the legislation."

Third, by citing a general reason one might actually be able to persuade others. Let us accept, as a crude approximation to reality, Jillson's claim that speakers will listen to impartial argument if and only if their self-interest is not at stake. In an assembly, some speakers will favor a given proposal on the basis of their self-interest, others will oppose it, and some will be neutral. It is then obviously in the self-interest of each of the interested parties to argue for their view in non-self-interested terms, to persuade the neutrals to come down on their side. This strategy is fully compatible with the third party's knowing that the others are moved purely by their interest. Moreover, the strategy is also compatible with opportunistic and inconsistent use of impartial arguments. Consistency is required only for the purpose of deceiving others, not for the purpose of persuading them.

Fourth, in a very different line of reasoning, James Coleman (1990, 393) argues that if "members [of an assembly] appear hesitant to bring up self-interest and sometimes express disapproval when another member does so," it is because there is a social norm "that says that no one should take a position that cannot be justified in terms of benefits to the collectivity." Moreover, that social norm is not accidental. "Since such a norm is in the interest of all members of the collectivity, it can be expected to emerge and to have some strength" (ibid., 394). This is not intended to be a purely functionalist argument, although it sounds like one. Coleman argues that collectively beneficial norms emerge through individually rational behavior. Each individual finds it in his interest to give up some of his rights to control his own actions in exchange for the right to control the actions of others. In my opinion, the argument fails to go through. I agree that there is a norm of the type he describes, but I do not think it can be reduced to individual self-interest. However, the individual framer might follow the norm out of self-interest, if the sanctions imposed on violators are sufficiently strong.

Finally, it has been suggested to me by Stephen Bundy that a speaker might use an argument from fairness to avoid humiliating an opponent. If the stronger party does not pull his punches, the weaker party might be willing to engage in mutually destructive behavior rather than cave in. By contrast, if the stronger party comes up with an impartial reason that allows the weaker party to save face, both would gain. The results from ultimatum bargaining experiments (Güth et al. 1982) give some stylized support for this proposition.

An important common feature of these reasons should be noted. Although I am assuming here that the actors who make the impartial arguments are really moved by self-interest, the reasons for doing so are parasitic on the presence of some genuinely non-self-interested actors in the system. One cannot try to pass oneself off as committed to principle unless there is common knowledge that some individuals do in fact have such motivations, as well as uncertainty as to which individuals these are. There is no reason to put a public-regarding gloss on private deals unless one believes that the public demands impartial arguments. There is no reason to try to persuade others by impartial arguments if one believes that everybody is moved by self-interest all the time. And even if those who obey the norm against invoking self-interest do so out of self-interest and fear of sanctions, those who impose those sanctions must ultimately do so for non-self-interested reasons (Elster 1989, 132–33). Impartiality is logically prior to the attempt to exploit it (or the need to respect it) for self-interested purposes. This is not to say, however, that impartial concerns are necessarily very widespread. We know from other contexts that it may take only a tiny proportion of cooperators in a population to induce everybody to behave as if they were cooperators (Kreps et al. 1982). Similarly, a small group of impartially minded individuals might induce many others to mimic their impartiality out of self-interest.[4]

The strength of these reasons will vary with the context. The norm against self-interested claims can be expected to be stronger in constituent assemblies than in ordinary legislatures. The system of checks and balances is intended to ensure that the interest of one group in the legislature will be set up against the interests of other groups, so that the outcome may approximate the common interest. However, future generations have no spokesmen in the constituent assembly. Although the Federal Convention saw some blatant attempts to bias the constitution in favor of the founding states (II, 3), intertemporally impartial arguments (e.g. I, 578) that allowed future states equal influence won the day. Also, the norm against expression of self-interest will be stronger in public settings than if the debates are conducted behind closed doors. A public setting will also encourage the use of precommitment through principle, with the larger audience serving as a resonance board for the claim and making it more difficult to back down.

Let me now turn to the consequences of the strategic uses of impartial argument, assessing the impact on efficiency and equity. Let us first compare strategic impartiality and bargaining along the efficiency dimension. We know that bargaining is vulnerable to the problem of misrepresentation of preferences: for a given bargaining mechanism, the parties may have an incentive to report false preferences that yield Pareto-inferior outcomes in terms of their real preferences (Sobel 1981). In addition, bargaining may be inefficient because of the difficulty of making credible promises that, if believed and respected, would benefit all parties (Elster 1989, 272 ff.). Mutual precommitment to incompatible positions is a third source of inefficiency (Crawford 1982).

The strategic use of impartiality is also vulnerable to the problem of mutual precommitment. When both sides appeal to principle, neither may feel able to back down. However, there is no analogue to the first source of inefficiency in bargaining; and the second problem is also less likely to arise because the very same motives that make speakers adopt the arguing rather than the bargaining attitude in the first place will also induce them to keep

---

[4]This is mere speculation. Whereas Kreps et al. (1982) offer a rigorous proof (based, however, on somewhat artificial assumptions) for a large "multiplier effect" of cooperation, I have no idea whether a similar argument would go through in the present case. However, no proof is needed to assert a small multiplier effect.

their promises. However, public debates introduce an additional source of inefficiency by the autonomous dynamics of political life. The need to demarcate oneself ideologically from the opponent even when there is no real disagreement can lead to false polarization, creating an impasse. The attempt by the opponent to avoid this trap can lead to false consensus, yielding a decision that is inferior in the eyes of both sides to another feasible outcome (Tocqueville 1893; 1990, 99). The Assemblée Constituante of 1789–91 showed many striking instances of radical and egalitarian overbidding by which the parties became locked into attitudes that had originally been adopted merely for tactical purposes.

It follows, I think, that neither bargaining nor strategic use of impartial reasoning is unambiguously more efficient than the other. By contrast, I believe we can assert that argument—even when purely strategic and based on self-interest—tends to yield more equitable outcomes than bargaining.[5] For the reasons mentioned above, argument—especially in a public setting—will prevent the strong from using their bargaining power to the hilt. The optimal impartial equivalent will be one that dilutes their self-interest by taking some account of the interest of the weak. On the average, this will yield more equitable outcomes. We may think of this effect as the *civilizing force of hypocrisy*.

The preceding remarks are already perhaps too speculative for some readers. Yet I now want to go further in the same direction, by offering some conjectures about the overall effects of arguing and bargaining in private and public settings. By "overall effect" I have in mind some criterion that somehow takes account both of efficiency and equity (don't ask me how they are combined or what the trade-offs are). I then claim that according to this criterion private settings are always better than public settings, for a given mode of communication; and that arguing is always better than bargaining, for a given setting. Roughly speaking, arguing is better than bargaining because of the civilizing force of hypocrisy, and private settings are better than public settings because they leave less room for precommitment strategies and overbidding. I have already said something (although far from enough) about the first claim; let me now add a few words about the second.

At the convention, the sessions were closed and the deliberations subject to a rule of secrecy respected by all. There was little risk, therefore, of being

---

[5]To be sure, one may think of exceptions to this tendency. If the initial endowments, although unequal, have a clean pedigree, there is nothing objectionable in an unequal outcome of bargaining. If the better-endowed adopt the optimal impartial argument they may get less than their fair share. I believe, however, that in most actual cases greater initial endowments are due to luck or unfair exploitation rather than to hard work, saving, or risk taking. Needless to say, this is not a statement for which proof can be offered. It is based on a rough overall assessment of historical trends, not on quantifiable analysis.

prematurely locked into one opinion—and few opportunities and temptations, therefore, to exploit such lock-in devices for strategic purposes. The trick of transforming the convention into the "committee of the whole" also made it possible to have preliminary votes that did not commit the delegates to premature decisions.

In the Assemblée Constituante, the debates were not only open to the public, but constantly interrupted by the public. It was initially envisaged that the assembly would meet two days a week, and work in subcommittees on the other days. However, the moderates and the patriots had very different opinions on these two modes of proceeding. For Mounier, leader of the moderates, the committees favored "cool reason and experience," by detaching the members from everything that could stimulate their vanity and fear of disapproval (o, 926). For the patriot Bouche (8, 307), committees tended to weaken the revolutionary fervor. He preferred the large assemblies, where "souls become strong and electrified, and where names, ranks and distinctions count for nothing." On his proposal, it was decided that the assembly would sit *in plenum* each morning and meet in committee in the afternoon. Soon there were only plenary sessions. The importance of this move, which constituted the beginning of the end for the moderates, was perfectly understood at the time (Egret 1950, 120). It was reinforced by the move to voting by roll call, a procedure that enabled members or spectators to identify those who opposed radical measures, and to circulate lists with their names in Paris.

Many of the debates at the Federal Convention were indeed of high quality: remarkably free from cant and remarkably grounded in rational argument. By contrast, the discussions in the Assemblée Constituante were heavily tainted by rhetoric, demagoguery, and overbidding. At the same time, the convention was also a place where many hard bargains were driven, notably the deal between the slaveholding and the commercial states (Finkelman 1987). The delegates from the southern states did not really try to argue that slavery was morally acceptable, with the exception of a lame remark by Charles Pinkney to the effect that "If slavery be wrong, it is justified by the example of all the world" (II, 371). Instead, they simply stated their position, using as leverage either the threat to leave the union or a warning that a constitution unfavorable to the slave states might not be ratified. If the proceedings had been held in public, they might have been forced to pull their punches.

Figure 1 ranks the possible cases according to the mixed criterion stated earlier. Note that the claims that arguing is superior to bargaining and secrecy to publicity *(ceteris paribus)* are compatible both with secret bargainings being superior to public argument and with the opposite ranking. If the two dimensions were independent of each other, this ambiguity would not matter, since one would always go for the first-best arrangement of

FIGURE 1

	Arguing	Bargaining
Secret	1	2 (3)
Open	3 (2)	4

arguing in private. However, as indicated by the arrows (and explained above), secrecy tends to induce bargaining, and publicity to induce argument. The real choice, therefore, may be between the second-best and the third-best options.[6] I do not want to extend my speculations to the relative merits of private bargaining and public argument. In specific cases it may be possible to be more precise, and to make an argument for opening or closing the debates to the public.

IV. STRATEGIC APPEALS TO TRUTH

I have tried to show how strategic actors may find it in their interest to substitute an impartial argument for a direct statement of their interest. I shall now argue that they may also find it useful to substitute truth claims for credibility claims. Instead of making a threat whose efficacy depends on its perceived credibility, they may utter a warning that serves the same purpose and avoids the difficulties associated with threats.

First, let me say a few words about credible threats. If a threat has to be carried out, this is ipso facto a sign that it has not worked. The event that the threat was supposed to prevent has already happened, and cannot be undone by executing the threat. At the same time, executing it typically involves some risks or costs to the actor. A rational actor would not carry out an action that involves no benefits and some costs; if he believes others to be rational, and believes them to believe him to be rational, he will not, therefore, threaten to do so either. Following Schelling, many authors have discussed various ways of overcoming this problem (Dixit and Nalebuff 1991 is a recent survey). Here I shall discuss strategies that amount to substituting warnings for threats, thus making the issue one of truth rather than credibility.

The terminology on this point is not settled. I use "warning" to denote utterances about events that are not within the control of the actors and

---

[6]This is an instance of the *pseudo-dominance effect*, described by Kahneman and Tversky (Chapter 3 in this volume).

"threat" to denote utterances about those that are. Threats are statements about what the speaker *will do*, warnings about what *will (or may) happen*, independently of any actions taken by the speaker. Thus understood, warnings are factual statements that are subject to the normal rules of truth-oriented communication. Disregarding a warning is more like disbelieving a statement about the past than it is like calling a bluff.

The idea of substituting warnings for threats can be illustrated by a look at wage negotiations. Sometimes a union leader will say things like, "If you don't give us what we ask for, I won't be able to stop my members from going on strike," or "If you don't give us what we ask for, the morale of my members will fall and productivity will suffer." Formally, these are warnings rather than threats. Needless to say, managers will not always take them at face value. They may suspect that the effects cited in the warnings are actually within the control of the union boss. At the same time, they can't be sure that the leader doesn't have access to information which they lack. Perhaps his members are in fact as recalcitrant as he makes them out to be. Perhaps, indeed, he has made sure, before coming to the bargaining table, that they are so heated up that he won't be able to stop them, turning them in effect into a doomsday machine. Note the difference between the latter strategy and other pre-bargaining ploys. Often, unions invest in the *credibility of threats*, e.g., by building up a strike fund. Alternatively, they can invest in the *truth of warnings*, e.g., by irreversibly stirring up discontent among the members.

Let me now turn to some examples from the two constituent assemblies. In the debate over the representation of the states in the upper house at the Federal Convention, delegates from both the large and the small states played on the ambiguity between threats and warnings. On June 30, Gunning Bedford, Jr. of Delaware asserted that "The Large States dare not dissolve the confederation. If they do the small ones will find some foreign ally of more honor and good faith, who will take them by the hand and do them justice. He did not mean by this to intimidate or alarm. It was a natural consequence; which ought to be avoided by enlarging the federal powers not annihilating the federal system" (I, 492). The statement is most plausibly seen as a threat, with the reference to the "natural consequence" serving to underline its credibility.

On July 5, Gouverneur Morris counterattacked:

Let us suppose that the larger States shall agree; and the smaller refuse: and let us trace the consequences. The opponents of the system in the smaller States will no doubt make a party and noise for some time, but the ties of interest, of kindred & common habits which connect them with the other States will be too strong to be easily broken. In N.Jersey particularly he was sure a great many would follow the sentiments of Pena. & N.York. This Country must be united. If persuasion does not unite it, the sword will. He begged that this consideration might have its due weight. The scenes of horror attending civil commotion can not be described, and the conclusion of them will be worse than the term of their continuance. The stronger party will then make traytors of the weaker; and the Gallows and Halter will finish the work of the sword. How far foreign powers would be ready to take part in the confusion he would not say. Threats that they will be invited have it seems been thrown out. (I, 530)

Here Morris states that he had understood Bedford's statement as a threat. His own reference to the sword and the gallows is more ambiguous. It can be taken as a threat or as a mere warning. Some of the other delegates undoubtedly took it as a threat, as indicated by the following retreat by Williamson on his behalf: he "did not conceive that Mr. Govr. Morris meant that the sword ought to be drawn agst. the smaller states. He only pointed out the probable consequences of anarchy in the U.S." (I, 532). In other words, Williamson sought to make it clear that Morris had been uttering a warning, not making a threat.

On the same day, Bedford also retreated, by making it clear that

he did not mean that the small States would court the aid & interposition of foreign powers. He meant that they would not consider the federal compact as dissolved until it should be so by the acts of the large States. In this case the consequence of the breach of faith on their part, and the readiness of the small States to fulfill their engagements, would be that foreign nations having demands on this Country would find it in their interest to take the small States by the hand, in order to do themselves justice. (I, p. 531)

Again, what was initially made (or understood) as a threat is restated as a warning. In a moment I shall discuss the reasons speakers may have for making such restatements. First, however, I want to look at some examples from the French context. The Assemblée Constituante was, as I said, suspended between the king's troops at Versailles and the crowds in Paris. Both extraparliamentary actors came to play an important role in the proceedings of the assembly, as the basis for threats or warnings.

In the first days of July 1789 the king reinforced the presence of troops near Versailles. The implied threat to the assembly escaped nobody. In his replies to the king's challenge, Mirabeau played on the threat / warning ambiguity. In his first speech on the subject he limited himself to a warning: "How could the people not become upset when their only remaining hope [viz. the assembly] is in danger?" (8, 209.) In his second speech he became more specific. The troops "may forget that they are soldiers by contract, and remember that by nature they are men" (8, 213) The implied threat to help nature along by stirring ferment among the troops is clear. Furthermore, the assembly cannot even trust itself to act responsibly: "Passionate movements are contagious: we are only men *(nous ne sommes que des hommes)*, our fear of appearing to be weak may carry us too far in the opposite direction" (ibid.). In this argument, Mirabeau presents himself and his fellow delegates as subject to a psychic causality not within their own control. If the king provokes them, they might respond irrationally and violently. Formally, this is a mere warning. In reality, nobody could ignore that it was a threat. (In some cases, though, predictions about one's own future behavior may be uttered as genuine warnings. See Frank 1988, 55 and passim.)

In his brief intervention in the same debate, Sieyès (8, 210) mentioned that in all deliberative assemblies, notably in the Estates of Brittany, the assembly refused to deliberate if troops were located closer than twenty-five miles from where it was sitting. However, when the assembly asked for the removal of the troops, the king in his response (8, 219) pretended that they had been brought to control Paris rather than to terrorize the assembly. If the assembly took objection to the presence of troops in the vicinity of Paris, he would be perfectly happy, he said, to move the assembly to Noyon or Soisson, and to move himself to Compiègne so as to facilitate communication between them. However, the assembly could not accept a proposal that would deprive them of the threat/warning potential of Paris. It was decided (8, 229) to send a delegation to the king, asking him to recall the troops "whose presence adds to the desperation of the people (*dont la présence irrite le désespoir du peuple*"). If the king agreed, the assembly would send a delegation to Paris "to tell the good news and contribute to a return of order." There was no need to say what they would do if he failed to accommodate them. The next day the Bastille fell, and the king agreed to send the troops away.

The Assemblée Constituante went on to debate the basic institutions of the state (Mathiez 1898; Egret 1950, 139 ff.). In private meetings between Mounier (the leader of the moderates) on the one hand and the radical "triumvirat" Barnave, Duport, and Alexandre Lameth on the other, the three came up with the following proposal: they would offer Mounier both an absolute veto for the king and bicameralism, if he in return would accept (1) that the king gave up his right to dissolve the assembly, (2) that the upper chamber would have a suspensive veto only, and (3) that there would be periodical conventions for the revision of the constitution. Mounier refused outright. According to his own account (o, 926), he did not think it right to make concessions on a matter of principle; also he may have been in doubt about the ability of the three to deliver on their promise. According to later historians (e.g., Mathiez 1898), he refused because he was so confident that the assembly was on his side that no concessions were needed. At the last meeting, the three responded by threatening to mobilize public opinion against him. Their utterance was probably neither meant nor understood as a threat to mobilize Paris against the assembly. Nevertheless, the defeat of bicameralism on September 10 and the adoption of a merely suspensive veto for the king on September 11 were in large part due to the fact that some delegates feared for their lives.

We may reasonably ask, therefore, whether the patriots in Versailles, through their contacts with journalists and pamphleteers in Paris, deliberately sought to raise the temperature so that they could say to the moderates, truthfully, that their lives were in danger if they voted for bicameralism and the absolute veto. The views of the actors and of later historians differ on this issue. My own opinion, for what it is worth, is that it is hard to believe that the thought of acting in this way did not cross somebody's mind. And if some members of the Assemblée Constituante were indeed stirring up things in Paris, we may also ask, in retrospect, whether they were not playing the sorcerer's apprentice.

There are two reasons why a speaker might find it to her advantage to substitute warnings for threats. First, as emphasized above, she does not have to worry as much about credibility. Even though her adversaries know that the events referred to in the warning may in fact be within her control, they must also take account of the possibility that she may have access to relevant private information. It is not unreasonable to think that the union leader knows more than the management about the state of mind of her members. Similarly, Mirabeau might be expected to know more than the king about the psychology of the delegates to the assembly. Second, as discussed in the previous section, warnings belong to the realm of argument and hence enable the speaker to avoid the opprobrium associated with naked appeals to bargaining power. At the Federal Convention, the restatement of threats as warnings allowed the proceedings to stay within the rules of the debating game. Similarly, Mirabeau could warn the king about his soldiers without risking the accusations of seditious talk that would have been made had he threatened to stir up unrest among the troops.[7]

Among the consequences of this substitutional strategy, two stand out. First, it can shift the balance of power, because not all actors may have available to them plausible warning equivalents of their natural threats. Whereas union leaders can and do warn about the unruly behavior of their members, management cannot similarly disguise their threat of a lockout as a warning. Second, it induces the risk, already cited, of setting in motion a

---

[7]We may note at this point the possibility of *self-fulfilling warnings*, which are, in this respect, intermediate between ordinary warnings and threats. By publicly telling the king that his troops were unreliable, Mirabeau may in fact have ensured the truth of that statement.

process that goes further than its instigators intended. If a leader stirs up unrest and discontent among his followers for the purpose of being able to make true warnings about what will happen if their wishes are not heeded, he may get more than he bargained for. The action of a crowd does not lend itself to fine-tuning.

V. SUMMARY

In this chapter I have deployed evidence from two constituent assemblies to discuss two questions. First, what reasons might induce self-interested actors to adopt an impartial public stance? Second, what are the consequences of such substitutional strategies, notably with respect to conflict resolution?

The various answers I suggested to the first question all presuppose that the actors in question interact with others who are genuinely committed to the ideals of impartiality and truth. In this connection I referred to a *multiplier effect* of impartiality, by which the presence of some genuinely impartial actors may force or induce self-interested others to behave as if they, too, were swayed by such motives.

My answers to the second question are more tentative. I have argued that the effects of substituting impartial arguments for self-interest are, on the whole, beneficial. The *civilizing force of hypocrisy* will lead to more equitable conflict resolutions. A similar claim cannot be made, however, about the consequences of substituting warnings for threats. If anything, the overall effect can be expected to be negative. There is no reason to think that the shift in balance of power caused by unequal availability of warning equivalents will lead to more equitable outcomes. And when both sides can and do invest in the truth of their warnings, efficiency will suffer. Moreover, the tendency for induced popular ferment to get out of hand can easily lead to outcomes that nobody had intended or desired.

CHAPTER THIRTEEN

Information Acquisition and the Resolution of Conflict

Kenneth J. Arrow

*T*he conflicts that motivate the following analysis are those arising from environmental issues. There are several classes of these. One consists of disputes over the formation of environmental policies. The outcomes of the conflicts, if they are resolved at all, take the form of legislation and administrative decisions. Another class of environmental disputes arises in judicial proceedings, particularly in damage assessments arising from torts. Location of hazardous waste disposal sites and administrative determination of risky substances for regulatory purposes are other examples of the issues to be discussed here.

I will start from concrete action situations, in which information and decision have had interesting and in some ways unexpected interactions. It is common to say that conflicts can be resolved more easily under full information, when all parties concerned understand the consequences of the alternative possible policies or other decisions. In particular, it is commonplace to hold that better measurement of the consequences of pollution will enable a more rational policy to be formulated and to be convincing. Clearly, this conclusion is true for a single individual making a decision, provided of course that the gain in outcome is sufficient to compensate for the cost of acquiring the information. But environmental problems are social problems. The conclusion that more information is better (apart from cost considerations) does not follow so readily from the usual assumptions of rationality. There are in fact a number of problems. Here, I stress one in particular, the problems in the social organization of information acquisition.

My aim is to outline the problems to enable an intellectual dialogue. We are not ready yet to formalize the issues and set them forth in terms of explicit models.

There are several common features in the use of information in different environmental disputes, along with, of course, many differences.

1. The underlying allocation problem involves a public bad, that is, one affecting many individuals, so that the costs imposed may be large in the aggregate but small to any one individual.
2. There are conflicting interests, in that remedies for the environmental costs require imposing costs on others.
3. Typically, there is a good deal of uncertainty in some or all aspects of the problem: the quantitative relation between the level of an activity and the level of the negative externality produced by it, possibly even the existence of such a relation; the costs of reducing the externality; the possibilities for the recipient of the externality to take action to avoid or minimize the negative effect; and the cost to the recipient of a given level of externality.
4. The uncertainty is in good measure reducible by the acquisition of information, particularly by methods that are usually thought of as scientific inquiry but that have some resemblance to facts and knowledge, full or partial, gathered in the course of judicial proceedings.

Although this whole field will need much more study, I wish here at least to characterize the issues and indicate the lines along which information gathering can help or hinder in the resolution of environmental conflicts and to discuss the institutional arrangements and incentives governing the collection of information.

In section I, I sketch very quickly the standard economic theory of information and some of the problems of applying it in a social context. Section II illustrates the complexity of gathering and using information in some environmental conflicts. Section III seeks to give a more extended general characterization of the class of environmental conflicts I am studying and the role of the information which might be useful in their resolution. Finally, in section IV, I discuss the alternative possible social organizations for accomplishing the relevant information gathering, with due regard for the costs as well as the benefits.

I. A BRIEF SKETCH OF THE ECONOMICS OF INFORMATION

Suppose a decision has to be made under conditions of uncertainty. The decision yields a benefit (net of costs), denoted by U, which depends on the act, a, chosen, and on the unknown facts about the world ("state of the world," in the standard terminology, denoted by $\underline{X}$; in symbols, $U = U(a,\underline{X})$. Since the outcome of an action is unknown, the value ascribed to it can be taken to be *expected* value (in the sense of probability theory, i.e., the average over all possible values of $\underline{X}$ weighted by their respective probabilities) of net benefit; in symbols, $E[U(a,\underline{X})]$ is the value ascribed to the action, a. Hence, among the available actions, the decision maker should choose the one with the highest values of $E[U(a,\underline{X})]$.

Now suppose that some information about $\underline{X}$ can be obtained, possibly at a cost. Formally, we consider making some observations, to be denoted as the *signal* (from nature). The signal will be useful if, after observing the signal $\underline{S}$, the probabilities of different values of $\underline{X}$ change. Let $c(\underline{S})$ be the cost of observing the signal, so that the benefit net of information as well as other costs is $U(a,\underline{X}) - c(\underline{S})$. Hence the value ascribed to the action a, after observing $\underline{S}$, is $E[U(a,\underline{X}) \mid \underline{S} - c(\underline{S})$, where $E[U(a,\underline{X}) \mid \underline{S}]$ means the expected value of U calculated using the probabilities of different values of $\underline{X}$ conditional on observing $\underline{S}$. Given the actual observation $\underline{S}$, we choose the action to maximize this expression; this means that the action is a function of the actual observation.

It is easy to see that the expected benefit, gross of information costs but net of all other costs, will be increased by the use of a signal, that is, making the action depend on the outcome of observations or research. However, the gain might or might not exceed the cost of the information.

In application, the signal is taken to be the outcome of research on the relation between activity levels (e.g., combustion) and damages. The legislation or the rules for damage claims should reflect the optimal choice given the outcome of the research.

The story told is convincing for a single individual. But matters get more complicated when there are many individuals involved, for two reasons. One is that there is already a good deal of information in the system, but it is dispersed. Any individual, including legislators and courts, knows only a little part of it initially. In total, however, there may be a considerable amount of knowledge. The acquisition of knowledge may be as much a question of transferring knowledge among individuals as of acquiring knowledge new to society as a whole, though both processes are involved.

Second, the net benefits of an action are peculiar to individuals. In general, one action may be beneficial to some or even most but sharply adverse to some, as compared with another action (such as continuing with the status quo).

The transfer of information interacts with the multiplicity of individual aims, for individuals may have some control over the information they reveal and consult their interests in doing so. These problems have been elaborated at great length in modern economic theory, under the rubric "games of incomplete information," but even to sketch the theory would be too diverting here.

One social solution has been to develop social conventions for presenting information in such a way as to impose at least the appearance of a common aim for society. Benefit-cost analysis (adding up individual gains and losses) is one such code. An overwhelming presumption for environmental integrity is another.

II. ENVIRONMENTAL CONFLICT AND INFORMATION: ILLUSTRATIONS

Let us take a typical area of environmental conflict in the field of legislation, the successive Clean Air Acts. I remind the reader only of the general attributes of the discussions, arguments, and upshots. It was becoming widely perceived that the air was dirtied by the wastes from industrial combustion, with particular emphasis on sulfur dioxide, and from automobile exhausts. More specifically, there were problems of irritation in breathing and to eyes, with special harm to those suffering from respiratory diseases. In some cases, the worst being in Europe, periods of accumulation of wastes in the air in periods of unusual atmospheric stability were accompanied by significant rises in mortality as well as morbidity. Any of the facts and beliefs were matters of common observation, but causal analysis also played its role. Chemists had ascertained the role of automobile exhausts in producing ground-level ozone concentrations.

The first steps then were taken under a general pressure of public opinion, driven by generally available knowledge and some elements of research. The all-important questions of implementation were not given much analysis. Controls were imposed in the naive way, restricting emissions by individual polluters in a way more or less proportional to original usage. Economists almost immediately urged the use of more flexible controls, such as emission taxes and transferable permits, designed to minimize the economic loss which accompanied the environmental gains as measured by volumes of emission. But these had very limited political appeal and almost no effect until very recently. Hence, knowledge of economic means for control was not used and its further development not encouraged.

On the other hand, it was quickly recognized that the implementation of many of the decisions required much technological knowledge, including predictions as to the feasibility of new technological developments. This came up particularly with regard to standards for catalytic converters in new cars and, later, in setting standards for gasoline mileage in cars and lead content in gasoline. One had to predict the possibility of redesigning cars and gasoline, the two, of course, interacting. Hence there was a deliberate attempt to create a new pool of knowledge, to a large extent through committees of the National Research Council.

In this effort, new strains began to appear, though they were in many ways well contained. Obviously, what appeared to be factual issues had very significant economic implications for many of the actors: automobile companies; manufacturing firms of all kinds and sizes; automobile users, who had to pay more for their new cars; and the public, which had to pay more for products, especially for electricity. Considerable fact-finding studies were made; it is not clear how much the final decisions made by Congress and administrative agencies depended on them.

An additional environmental cost from air pollution was perceived only after another decade: the acidification of precipitation (rain and snow) and its impact on lake acidity and forest growth. In part, the acid precipitation problem illustrates an intrinsic difficulty in information gathering for environmental purposes. One partial solution to local air pollution is higher smokestacks, so that the pollution is spread over a wider area. Conservation laws of nature should, however, suggest that the problem is only being transferred, and that is just what happened. Acid precipitation was increased. More distant points became polluted. The adverse consequences took different forms. Industrial areas are heavily populated, and health implications dominate. The diffusion of pollutants should, on the average, decrease the amount affecting individuals directly, but of course it had the effect of increasing the load on natural targets.

This story illustrates one of the intrinsic difficulties in information processing in this area. A problem is observed as a byproduct of daily activities. Causes are sought, possibly by relatively difficult research, and then policies are proposed on the basis of the given analysis. The policies may have consequences other than those in the problem at hand. But these are not likely to be studied. No doubt, experience with some problems will suggest looking out for side effects, as is now standard in the analogous situation of seeking pharmaceutical remedies for disease.

The identification of acid precipitation and its possible implications for lakes and forests led in fact to probably the most elaborate turn to information gathering as a means of resolving environmental disputes, the National Acid Precipitation Assessment Program. The expenditures reached $700 million over the ten-year span of the program. It was planned to engage in a multistep program: first, to settle by scientific research the extent to which pollutants (mainly sulfur dioxides and nitrogen oxides) contributed to acidification of lakes and consequent depletion of fish, to damage to forests, and to other forms of injury, such as health and material damage; and, second, to publish the results in the form of an integrated assessment which could be used by Congress to make final decisions.

Before the study, there was an extreme degree of uncertainty. While the increasing acid content of rain and snow was not in dispute, the effects on lakes and forests were. Certainly, some lakes in the Adirondack Mountains were acidified to the point that there were no fish, but it was not so clear that the acidity levels in these lakes had gotten worse in recent times as a result of the acid rain. The effects on forests were even more debatable. The contrary view, that the acidity already observed was merely the precursor of a rapidly growing disaster, was also widespread. In this case, the evidence was not confined to the United States. There was considerable concern in Europe, particularly in Norway, Sweden, and Germany. The deterioration of the Black Forest was clearly seen, but the causes were less clear.

The results of the study considerably reduced the range of the uncertainty. It was clear that local soil conditions mattered greatly in determining the effects of acid precipitation on the acidity of a lake. Some lakes were acid for reasons having nothing to do with precipitation; the soil surrounding others was sufficiently alkaline that it would buffer all possible acidity in the rain and snow. But other lakes were affected. Similarly, in the United States at least, the effects on forests were limited to certain marginal areas and species.

A participant would correctly argue that these remarks are a most inadequate summary of twenty-odd volumes of findings. There was a great deal of contribution to knowledge. The process by which pollutants are transported in the atmosphere has been studied in great detail. In some large areas, the possibility of acidification of lakes has been ruled out; in others, the risks are now known to be considerable. But the ability to predict the vulnerability of any given lake on the basis of easily available specific soil conditions remains poor. Other possible effects, such as those on health and materials, have been identified, but virtually no quantitative estimates can be done.

As is usual, the uncertainty in the aggregate is reflected by considerable diversity of judgment among experts. Indeed, one characteristic of risk assessments here as elsewhere is that the subjective certainty of any one expert seems to be excessive when one considers the differences among them. But it is also true that the institutional affiliation of the expert was correlated with his or her opinion. In this case, the information gathering was basically publicly financed, so simple self-interest in the collection and presentation of information is not at stake. But in a pluralistic government which, in its structure, reflects the diverse interests in society at large, the experts from different agencies had systematically different judgments. I do not imply literal distortion. Clear-cut scientific results were not disputed. But when it comes to expressing informed judgments in a situation of uncertainty, there is room for differing judgments without contradicting existing evidence, and these judgments do depend on institutional and doubtless other biases. These may arise from biases in the selection of experts among agencies (both self-selection and agency selection) or from institutional pressures.

The massive information-collecting effort was imposed by Congress to provide a better basis for revisions in the Clean Air Act. In fact, it was not completed in time to be useful for that purpose. (To be sure, the available data was summarized in some form, and the general flavor of the results was used. But none of the controversial aspects were given much consideration, though some of them leaked to the press. If there had been clear results contraindicating the proposed legislation, they would have emerged.) The president recommended legislation, which was enacted by Congress before the integrated assessment was written. Indeed, not all the reports integrating the scientific results had been prepared. The primary problem is that the study fell behind schedule. I do not know the full story. There were allegations that at an earlier stage there were political interferences with the process, to minimize the extent of damage found, and this produced enough discord and controversy to delay the process.

There was clearly another reason for delay: the scientific values of the participants. Precisely because there were so many uncertainties, there was always the perception (indeed, probably correct) that additional research could resolve them. The scientific point of view conflicted with the needs of decision. There was a conflict between professional values for defensible conclusions and the value of time in making decisions. The professional values are certainly real and socially desirable in many ways. We do not want, from the viewpoint of making better decisions, to encourage shortcuts and inadequately based conclusions; there is too much at stake. Yet in policy-making, there has to be a trade-off between accuracy and speed. Indeed, in complicated analyses of real-world phenomena in highly open systems, there is no guarantee that uncertainties will be resolved in any reasonable time, no matter how much effort is expended; the frustrations of medical research in understanding and treating cancer or AIDS or even common colds, or the difficulties of weather forecasting, provide ample evidence of this proposition. But policies still have to be made. Sometimes a policy can take the form of doing little or nothing until uncertainties are resolved; but sometimes the risks are such that such a policy is too dangerous—a dilemma we are facing in the global warming issue.

Still, it may be asked, why was not the decision on further reductions in emission postponed a year or two until the National Acid Precipitation Assessment Program could at least produce an integrated assessment on the basis of which the president and Congress could form better conclusions? We find another dilemma in the use of scientific information for the formulation of public policy. The political timetable is driven by considerations other than the availability of information, just as the research timetable is driven by internal motives and needs in addition to the imperatives of meeting policy-making needs. In this case, there was, among other things, a problem of international relations, specifically, the perception in Canada that its lakes and forest were suffering from emissions originating in the United States (particularly, the Ohio Valley). Delay to await the integrated assessment was being interpreted as unwillingness to act. In addition, once a process of decision making had started based on an assumption of availability of information at a given date, stopping it to match the delayed pace of scientific progress would have been too costly.

III. ENVIRONMENTAL CONFLICT AND INFORMATION: GENERAL CHARACTERIZATION

As noted in the introductory remarks, the essential analytic characteristics of environmental conflicts are the following: (1) There is an allocation issue involving a *public* good or bad; (2) there are *conflicting* interests in the sense that different possible policies have different implications for the individuals, firms, and governments concerned; (3) the consequences of the policies are likely to be highly *uncertain* for lack of basic scientific knowledge as well as for lack of knowledge of economic and social consequences; and (4) it at least appears to be true that the uncertainties can be resolved or at least reduced by acquisition of *information*, possibly by assembling already available knowledge or possibly by further research.

Environment as Public Good

The public-goods aspect of environmental issues is too well known to need elaboration. The essential point is that some steps in productive activities cause or are believed to cause injuries to others for which they are not compensated in the market. Typically, there are effluents from the activity which enter into the atmosphere or hydrosphere and therefore cross property lines; the adverse effects of the effluents are usually referred to by economists as *externalities*. As a result the scale of these environmentally adverse activities is socially excessive. In a world of conflicting goals, the term "socially excessive" is not so easy to clarify. Broadly speaking, it means that there is some alternative level of activity and a set of side payments among the economic agents involved such that everyone would be better off. If we substitute nations for individuals, we see the implication that externalities across nations, as in the diffusion of chlorofluorocarbons and possibly of carbon dioxide as instrumental in global warming, might be defined in terms of obligations to reduce effluents accompanied by compensation to the losers.

The definition of externalities in terms of compensation does not necessarily define the policies to be undertaken. Economists think naturally in terms of trying to approximate the market as well as possible. Hence, there are proposals for taxes measured by the externalities. Alternatively, and so far much more common, there are quantitative restrictions or even prohibitions, with some tendency to modify them by permitting sale and purchase of the licenses to emit. Still other policies are possible, for example, publicly operated cleanup, especially for water pollution. (It has even been proposed to offset global warming by releasing sulfur dioxide into the stratosphere to reduce solar radiation!)

Clearly, policy choices will (or at least should) depend on a great deal of knowledge. The typical question for scientific research is to estimate the amount and nature of damage per unit level of the activity in question: how much acidification of lakes for each additional amount of sulfur dioxide, nitric oxides, and other pollutants emitted? This apparently simple question is in fact a compound of a large number of questions relating to very different fields of science: What is the relation between emissions at a smokestack and transport of the pollutant over varying distances; to what extent do the pollutants enter into rain and snow; how much dry deposition is there; what is the effect of precipitation and dry deposition on the acidity of the soil; what is the effect of soil acidity on the acidity of lakes into which local streams enter? Further along in the chain of effects, we want to know the effect of acidity on fish and biota, and the effects of the acid lakewater and acid rain on health and on the durability of materials. In short, the knowledge needed is not only extensive but very varied in nature.

Besides the scientific information on effects, there is a need for economic and technological information to measure the possibilities and costs for alleviation of the problem. What are the technical possibilities of reducing sulfur dioxide and nitric oxide emissions, and how much do they cost? Since theoretically optimal policies will not and usually cannot be used, there are in addition what economists call "deadweight losses," inefficiencies resulting from the policy measures. Thus, if each firm is given permission to emit a fixed fraction of its previous emissions, we will have a situation in which some firms who could reduce emissions cheaply have no incentive to expand, while others who find it very expensive remain in business, though it might be more profitable individually and better for the economy to give up their rights to those who can expand with less pollution. Thus, the given reduction in pollution is being obtained at an unnecessarily high cost. But estimating these deadweight losses requires very considerable knowledge about the economic system.

Conflicts of Interest

That alternative public policy proposals have differing implications for different groups in society is hardly a unique characteristic of environmental issues. The regulations and taxes just discussed put the cost burden of clean air on one group to achieve a benefit to others. It may even be a benefit to all in some cases, but if the costs fall on a limited group, they may be net losers. (Actually, the analysis of costs is more complicated still. The firms on which the taxes or regulations fall may not, in the end, bear the costs, since they will raise prices and try to shift the costs to their consumers. This is particularly evident in the case of public utilities, which, as regulated industries, are entitled to raise their prices to pass on the additional costs of compliance with environmental restrictions, such as scrubbers. They lose only to the extent that the demand for their product is reduced by the higher prices. This may explain why they have generally been less determined in their opposition to emission controls and, therefore, why so much of the burden has tended to fall on them.)

Perhaps the one special feature of interest conflict in environmental issues is that the "interests" are to such a large extent noneconomic in origin. The political force for controls does not come from those affected in any very direct sense, but rather by a perception of public interest divorced from private concerns. The number of individuals directly concerned with acidification of lakes—say, sports fishermen—is very small, yet the political force behind changes is obviously very considerable. The *case* for taking special steps to abate pollution is that it causes damage, but the political force for taking steps does not come from the victims. On the other hand, the opposition to changes does come from parties that are interested in a fairly direct sense.

Certainly, the same role of public interest groups is not confined to environmental issues. Advocacy of public education or of civil rights or welfare draws much support from nonbeneficiaries. But the role of public interest groups seems to be even stronger relative to directly interested parties in environmental issues than in almost any other branch of policy formation.

Uncertainty

Most environmental issues take place in very complex environments with many factors at work. Reading the past to uncover causal relations can be very difficult when there is so much noise in the system. Atmospheric pollution occurs in the context of weather, and the difficulties of predicting weather are proverbial. Modern computing power and newer observations have led to only mild improvement in our abilities. Thus, when the possibility of ozone depletion through catalytic reactions was first raised on the basis of laboratory experiments, it was observed that testing an effect in the actual stratosphere would be very difficult because its ozone already had a large variation from year to year for other reasons.

In general, large complex systems are very difficult to understand. Observing them is unlikely to yield any strong knowledge about causal relations. But the choice among policies depends critically upon causal relations, for it requires making statements of the form "if such-and-such is done, then the reduction in some end-effect is so much."

In the presence of uncertainty, there are many possible strategies. One is to put up with the uncertainty and simply take steps to minimize its impact, i.e., choose policies which give satisfactory performance under a wide variety of possibilities. Thus, it is argued that in the present state of our knowledge about global warming, we should take significant steps to reduce carbon dioxide emission, because the costs are relatively low while very serious temperature changes are within the range of possibility.

Another approach is to seek to resolve the uncertainty by learning further. In environmental issues, where so much depends on scientific knowledge, this has taken the form of scientific research in many different areas—physics, chemistry, and biology, as well as social sciences.

Information is valuable; it is also costly, both in resources and in time. Value in improving decisions must be balanced against cost. In a diversified society, with varying interests, one has to ask how the amount and direction of information investment is determined. Since the environmental concern is, as has been noted, a public good, the information about the environment is also to a large extent a public good. Hence, it cannot be properly collected without government policy. We expect also that interested parties will be motivated to collect information, though in directions dictated by their interests.

Information always has a public-goods aspect, even if it were not directed to decisions about a public good. To collect the same information twice is clearly inefficient. To put the matter more formally, the cost of reproducing information is low compared with the cost of producing it.

IV. SOCIAL ORGANIZATION FOR THE ACQUISITION OF INFORMATION

In designing a system of collecting information for arriving at decisions to meet environmental issues, it must be recognized that two basic questions have to be faced. One is creating the incentives to supply the relevant information; the second is providing a mechanism for coordinating information from different sources. "Coordinating" may be a mild word in the context of vigorous disagreement. These generalizations hold whether the information is generated by diverse private (nongovernmental sources or by governmentally organized processes or, as is frequently the case, both.

Typically, in environmental issues, the research process not only is directed to social ends but is itself a social process, requiring extensive organization. This is necessitated partly by the scale of the project, but even more by the great variety of disciplines typically involved in any environmental issue. The design of a coordinated research effort is very much in the mold of an integer programming problem, since each part has to have a certain minimum scale to be of any use, and yet the different parts have to be related to each other.

The coordination is complicated by the fact that the investigators come from different institutional backgrounds and therefore differ in both values and beliefs. Indeed, in many cases, the values and beliefs are those of the agency, firm, or other institution rather than those of the individual, though there is inevitably a sorting mechanism which introduces some congruence between the two.

What creates incentives for the individual researchers to supply correct and relevant information? What incentives induce those organizing and financing the information-gathering effort to search out all the relevant areas to be studied? There are no easy answers to these questions, especially in view of all the pressures that have been brought up earlier in this chapter. There are two polar models, though they are not mutually exclusive.

The first is the model of adversary proceedings, as in judicial and, to a lesser extent, regulatory processes. Some environmental need is felt, and private organizations, profit-making and otherwise, are left with the task of bringing up the relevant information. They are motivated by self-interest or, in the case of public interest groups, by a sense of conviction, to bring up relevant but one-sided information. The assumption, as in a court of law or in a democratic political system, is that all the necessary information will be generated because all interests will strive to present their cases.

The adversary model is a form of "invisible hand" argument. The force in terms of incentives is clear. But the problems and deficiencies with this approach are also clear. In the first place, adversary proceedings require a sufficiently well organized venue, a court or a legislative committee or whatever, to make sure that standards of truth can be met and conflicts of interpretation confronted. (Analogous requirements are also needed for commodity markets.) Further, the problem of economies of scale and public goods is not well met by such a scheme. In theory, as Ronald Coase has argued, externalities can be handled by contracts. Thus, if there is a public interest in acquiring information about relatively small costs to a large number of people, in principle each could agree to give a small amount to finance the research. Obviously the organizational costs needed to create this contractual arrangement will usually be excessive. Class action suits in effect provide an entrepreneurial substitute for this contractual arrangement, but while they may be useful when there is a reasonable basis in expert testimony, they cannot serve as the basis for a large information-seeking effort whose outcome may be adverse to the proposed suit.

The alternative model is that of neutral experts, supported by the government. Here, as well as in the adversary culture, one of the main incentives to good performance is the scientific ethos. Reputation for observation of facts, skillful interpretation, and the like has been developed as a powerful motive and instilled by training. There are adverse effects to this ethos in a decision context. It may lead to excessive caution, manifested by delay and by conclusions which preserve scientific value by being ambiguous. The latter problem could in principle be taken care of by associating definite statements of uncertainty to conclusions for which scientific evidence is conflicting. Unfortunately, while we have objective bases for deriving definite conclusions when the evidence is present, we do not have nearly the same degree of objectivity in statements of uncertain conclusions. The Bayesian formulation to some extent exhibits this subjectivity in the arbitrariness of the prior. But actually the situation is worse. The models used to formulate likelihood functions (the Bayesian updating) are usually stated in statistical practice with much more precision than can be justified, because otherwise statistical analysis becomes impossible.

There is one final difficulty in the performance of large-scale research efforts to increase our knowledge of environmental processes, a point illustrated by the preceding sentence. The scale and specialization of research introduces communication problems. The results are complex, by any of the usual criteria found in computer science. Specialization increases efficiency of research, but also increases the costs of communication. This is seen most spectacularly in the problem of summarizing the information for the benefit of the ultimate decision makers—Congress, the executive, regulatory commissions, or the courts. But it also occurs in dialogues among the scholars from different disciplines. Certainly, communication between natural and social scientists is difficult, but even that among natural scientists is not easy.

During the course of this chapter, a long list of difficulties with the use of information to aid in the resolution of environmental conflicts has emerged. Information acquisition and transfer are subject to a variety of barriers: the costs of communication and complexity in a world of specialized knowledge; the interests of the parties, including the researchers, in communicating or withholding relevant information; the social structure of the information-gathering process itself; and the difficulties of acquiring any useful information by research on a natural and social world which is an open system not usefully subject to experimental control. Further, there is a problem in society's effective use of whatever knowledge is acquired. The timing of the political process is governed by its own laws and by unpredictable exigencies and may ill accord with the uncertainties of timing and reliability inherent in the process of uncovering knowledge in sequential steps.

I do not have any ready answers to these difficulties. We cannot and should not aim to avoid conflict within the information-gathering process. Just as in the market or in competition among scientists, the energy generated by the conflict can be a source of value increasing the final amount of information available to decision makers. It is more important to remove special pressures on leadership and coordination roles while preserving them in the development of expert opinions. Uncomfortable as it may be for those with scientific background, rigid deadlines for research findings need to be observed; they are essential for time coordination of the information-gathering and decision-making processes. Fuller analysis of past uses of research oriented to social problems will undoubtedly be a guide to better uses in the future.

PART FIVE

Contextual Explorations

CHAPTER FOURTEEN

The Creation of New Processes for Conflict Resolution in Labor Disputes

John T. Dunlop

I. INTRODUCTION

1. The conflict resolution paradigm as applied to labor and management disputes is not, in my view, an analytically significant perspective to understand or to predict the performance or output of an industrial relations system. The economic efficiency of enterprises, the quality of product, the competitiveness of the sector, the rating of human resources policies, even the satisfaction of employees or survival may have little direct relationship to the extent of overt conflict or its absence. Categories such as open conflict, armed truce, arm's-length bargaining, and full cooperation provide little understanding of substantive processes, quality of performance, or the operation of labor or management organizations and their interactions over time (Harbison and Coleman 1951; Selekman 1948).

The resort to the conflict-harmony dimension to interpret industrial relations is further demeaned by the fact that it is conventional wisdom that some conflicts, even bitter ones, have contributed materially to industrial peace. The conflict resolution perspective also has difficulty in dealing with internalized conflict, below the surface, that affects performance and attitudes of both organizations.

Long ago I eschewed these categories of war and peace as helpful tools of industrial relations analysis (Dunlop 1958). Conflict may lead parties, or those affected, to consult an "industrial relations doctor"—and far too many "patients" come to see me—but the "doctor" should treat conflict only as a crude symptom that reveals little as to the real problems and is only the beginning of diagnosis. Further, there are a lot of nonconflicted parties walking around who feel no current pain, but have real serious maladies.

If the focus of attention, however, is comparative methods and approaches to dispute resolution among various fields—as is the purpose of this volume—then less attention is appropriate to the "basic science" of industrial relations and more is required on the processes of diagnosis and treatment. Techniques of dispute resolution, however, without the underlying analysis, will not often generate basic improvement, although the "patient" may get over the current symptoms or feel better for a spell. Then there are "terminal conflicts" in which some "prolongation of life" or temporary palliatives may be administered.

2. The conflicts in the labor field of concern here are defined to involve organizations and their representatives (and members). Typically these are management (business, government or nonprofit) organizations and labor unions or employee associations. The essential characteristic is that organizations be involved, recognizing that many personal disputes or altercations in the work environment or outside of working hours may arise that do not involve the organizations. Some of these disputes may bring in the organizations. A further limitation is that the discussion is confined to this country. Conflict resolution in labor disputes in other countries involves distinctive institutions and is quite another matter.

3. At the outset it also needs to be recognized that most disputes between management and labor organizations take place in "the shadow of the law," to use a phrase Professor Robert H. Mnookin has felicitously introduced (Mnookin and Kornhauser 1979). At times the influence of the law or government agencies is largely controlling, while in other circumstances they have only a faint role. Then there are the cases in which governments are the employer organization, with varying specifications of the terms and conditions of employment by legislation or administrative fiat rather than by collective bargaining, although the political process often involves complex multiparty bargaining.

4. Conflict in labor-management relations potentially arises at almost every point in the interaction of a labor organization and a management. A listing of the major points of interface establishes a very large canvas and the need in this discussion to focus attention on a few areas. Conflict and dispute resolution may arise in:

> the recognition process
> negotiations of an agreement
> reducing an agreement to writing
> ratification process
> strike settlement in contract disputes or "wildcat stoppages"
> grievances over the meaning or application of an agreement
> unfair labor practices
> inter-union rivalry and conflict
> multi-employer and multi-union issues
> legislative conflicts
> community activities

These categories abstract from substantive areas such as wages, benefits, or rules which would multiply the listing of potential conflicts and the opportunities for dispute resolution many fold.

5. My experience suggests that a fundamental distinction needs to be made

between the resolution of a labor-management dispute (with government more or less in the shadows) through an established procedure and the resolution of a dispute through the creation of new processes or a major revision in an established procedure (Dunlop 1992). The first process involves the administration, maintenance, or routine working of a given industrial relations system, or some parts of it, as in the grievance process and arbitration or as procedures apply to an incentive system, fringe benefits, work jurisdiction, or some other element of the relationship. At times there may be choices to be made among alternative and even conflicting routes for jurisprudence, such as resolving a dispute through a grievance procedure and arbitration, equal employment opportunity processes, or litigation before administrative agencies or in the courts. The second and less frequent process, which is the focus of this chapter, involves the creation of a new system of dispute resolution or a major alteration and transformation of an existing system. This innovative step necessarily includes the test runs, balancing modifications, and stabilization of the new arrangements for a period of time in a dynamic environment.

The first and more routine activity is work assigned to journeymen and mechanics, with the involvement of some apprentices in the dispute-settlement business. The second involves elements of the activity of artist, inventor, architect, engineer, and manager in varying proportions. In these creative activities administrative law judges and most grievance arbitrators are useless or even dangerous. There are many labor, management, and government organizations, moreover, looking for assistance in creative problem solving today rather than for certainty, predictability, or a learned opinion in a rapidly changing environment.

Section II identifies some of the barriers and impediments to effective conflict resolution that are associated with the creation of new processes and procedures to settle disputes involving labor and management, including government as the employer or as a presence casting legal shadow on the parties.

In this field cases are essential to communications and to analysis, but they present an enigma. Each of the five cases outlined below would ideally require many pages, but this chapter can only outline a few elements of each case. The reader will have many more questions about a case than can be answered here. Citations to reference materials may be helpful for some issues.

Section III seeks to identify the factors that account for the development of the new processes described in section II, noting some common elements and some disparities in conflict resolution.

Section IV briefly calls attention to negotiations involving labor organizations, business, and governmental agencies over legislation or over regulations in the process known as negotiated rule-making that constitutes a relatively new focus of dispute resolution.

Section V draws some generalizations and conclusions from these reports.

II. BARRIERS TO CONFLICT RESOLUTION AND THE CREATION OF NEW PROCESSES

1. There may be literally no established or recognized process to resolve a dispute between a management, other parties, and a labor organization. You may regard that as most unlikely, given the penchant of American management to sue, to hire consultants, or to seek redress in the political process. Yet what follows is an account of working to establish a new industrial relations and dispute settlement system involving a migratory farm labor organization, farmers, and food processors where none previously applied. The shadow of the government is almost nonexistent for industrial relations and only shows as it relates to pesticides, housing inspections, the age of working children, health clinics, immigration agents, and the critical status of these migrants as owner-operators established by the courts in cucumber-harvesting in a region.

Migratory agricultural labor, northwest Ohio and southern Michigan. A report issuing from an office visit by a vice president of Campbell Soup Company, a complete stranger, in the fall 1984 complained of a boycott by Catholic bishops and the Council of Churches growing out of a dispute over the harvesting of tomatoes by Hispanic migratory labor from Texas and Florida on farms with contracts to supply products to the company. The suggestion was that I be hired as a consultant to resolve the controversy. I declined, explaining that my preferred role was that of a neutral; I had never heard of the dispute but would look into it. Fortunately, in my current view, neither the National Labor Relations Act nor any state statute constricted the problem solving. But a circuit court had created additional areas for dispute resolution by ruling that cucumber pickers were owner-operators, not employees.[1]

After an extended period of getting acquainted with the major participants, including many hours in the kitchens of farmers and their wives, it was possible to work out a procedure for voluntary elections on the farms with the aid of Harvard students, to use Spanish and English, to declare the Farm Labor Organizing Committee (FLOC) an appropriate representative on some farms, and to negotiate a first agreement for the 1986 season. With the approval of the parties, I appointed a commission comprised of Monsignor Higgins and Douglas Fraser with knowledge of labor organizations and Tom Anderson and Don Paarlberg with farmer and management backgrounds to assist in the process. The arrangements were also applied to Vlasic Foods, the pickle subsidiary. There is much more labor involvement in cucumber hand harvesting than in tomato harvesting—the latter is performed by machines introduced by Campbell Soup Company after an unsuccessful strike in 1978.

---

[1] *Donovan v. Brandel* 736 F.2d 114 (1984), *rehearing denied*, 760 F.2d 126 (1985). The status of these workers was changed to employees by voluntary agreement for the 1993 season. The agreements were then between FLOC and the growers, and were endorsed by the precessors.

Subsequently a mail ballot procedure was designed during the winter season for Heinz, U.S.A., outside the role of the commission, but with my involvement as neutral. An agreement with cucumber farmers, Heinz, and FLOC was signed, and in 1991 another procedure with a mail ballot resulted in agreements with farmers for Dean Foods, the other major processor of cucumbers in the area. Thus, three-way collective bargaining agreements, involving FLOC, the farmers, and the major processors, govern the harvesting of cucumbers in the area by migratory workers. There are about five thousand migrants covered by these agreements.[2]

2. Labor and management organizations may prefer to develop their own private machinery to handle a class of disputes rather than accept the procedures established by public policy, and government in turn may explicitly encourage such private machinery rather than the resort to government-mandated dispute-settling processes. Issues of a conflict of choice in forums inevitably arise, and in the absence of cooperative coordination the private machinery will be eroded or destroyed.

Jurisdictional disputes in the construction industry. Under the Labor Management Relations Act of 1947, it became an unfair labor practice for a labor organization to force or to require "an employer to assign particular work to employees in a particular labor organization or in a particular trade, craft, or class rather than to employees in another labor organization or in another trade, craft, or class. . . ." (8)(b) (4) (D). In cases of threats or work stoppages in such jurisdictional disputes an injunction under 10(1) could be sought to restore work operations and the NLRB was empowered under 10(k) to "hear and determine" the dispute unless the parties agree "upon methods for the voluntary adjustment of the dispute."

In 1947 the labor and management organizations in the construction industry engaged in collective bargaining were all distrustful of the government processes and much preferred to establish their own machinery. Government procedures, lawyers, and the absence of established rules for making work assignments combined to constitute a barrier against the newly established government processes and to create a new private machinery in the immediate shadow of the law. That shadow was largely to undermine the private machinery after twenty-five or thirty years and to leave only a minor private operation today.

I mediated an agreement creating private machinery among the parties that began to operate May 1, 1948. The plan was blessed by Robert Denham, general

---

[2] See Migrant farmworkers in the Midwest, Harvard Business School, Case 9-586-073, 1985; Migrant farmworkers in the Midwest (B), Case N9-592-031, 1991. Collective bargaining agreement between Farm Labor Organizing Committee and Vlasic Foods, Inc. and growers under contract to Vlasic Foods, Inc. [(for Ohio delivery), January 1, 1990–December 31, 1993.] Collective bargaining agreement between Farm Labor Organizing Committee and Heinz U.S.A. cucumber growers, March 1, 1990–February 28, 1994.

counsel, and Paul Herzog, chairman of the NLRB. I served as chairman of the National Joint Board for almost a full decade and then as chairman of an Appeals Board in the 1960s (Dunlop 1984). Both bodies contained an equal number of union and contractor members. The contractors were in turn equally divided between general and specialty contractors and the union representatives between the basic and specialty trades. In that period procedures and relations were developed so that there were no unresolved conflicts between the private machinery and the NLRB public processes. The private machinery handled several thousand cases a year involving the eighteen national unions and the fifteen national contractor associations in the industry, and in the period I mediated fifty national agreements involving the contesting international unions and contractor associations.

But the NLRB and the courts have largely destroyed the usefulness of the private machinery by several policies.

- The NLRB representatives who have heard the jurisdictional disputes under section (10)k are unschooled in the industry or in these complex disputes. They have almost invariably reached the decision to support the assignment of work made by the contractor. Their criteria do not relate to the experience of the industry. Any contractor accordingly had the incentive to withdraw from the private machinery with the assurance that his assignment would be supported by government with an injunction, if necessary. This is not the outcome the legislation envisaged.
- The NLRB and the courts required the private machinery to show that in any case that came to the government each contractor had clearly currently agreed to be bound by the private decision. (All the international unions and their locals were bound by the constitution of the Building and Construction Trades Department.) But the administrative task of keeping all the contractors under collective agreements explicitly bound to the plan, with paper to prove it, was impractical. The escape of contractors bound by collective bargaining agreements from the plan has proved its undoing as an effective and universal machinery.

The procedural rules for work assignments, developed by the National Joint Board in the late 1940s, however, have remained an effective device for much dispute resolution. The governmental machinery remains effective to restore work on a single project that is shut down by a strike, but these public procedures do little to resolve in a timely fashion any specific disputes or to establish national agreements or decisions to serve as precedents for future work assignments. Only a revitalized private machinery involving national unions and national contractor associations with cooperation from the public agency can resolve substantively this genre of disputes in the construction industry.

The case illustrates the limitations of the original governmental machinery designed for this category of disputes and the barriers to an effective private machinery under the law.

3. The federal government as customer or owner has designed specialized machinery to resolve a class of disputes, eliminating resort to previously established procedures applicable to labor and management parties generally. The preexisting machinery simply did not work, and the government as customer could not tolerate the delay or interruption of work.

Missile sites and space facility disputes. In 1961 President John F. Kennedy and Secretary of Labor Arthur Goldberg established the Missile Sites Labor Commission to resolve all labor-management disputes on missile or space sites. A no-strike pledge was secured from top labor leadership and a commitment from government contractors (through the agencies) was readily achieved to comply with decisions. The missile and space program had been plagued by all types of disputes and stoppage over jurisdiction, contract disputes, high costs, labor shortages, and grievances. The commission and the program established by Executive Order 10946 were criticized as extralegal activities of government (Northrup 1966).

I served as a public member of this special-purpose commission throughout its six-year existence, 1961–67. It got the job done, far faster and more equitably than the previously established law and agencies could possibly have, in my view (Howard 1968).

Let me provide an illustration of the need for diagnosis that escaped the proponents of the ordinary procedures. There were many jurisdictional disputes, not only among construction unions and contractors but also between construction and industrial unions and contractors. In fact, these disputes had received great attention in congressional hearings and affected the structure of the commission as established by Secretary Goldberg. The basic source of difficulty was really the disputes and lack of coordination between the Corp of Engineers that let contracts to construction contractors and the Air Force that let business to the airframe companies. Where should be the dividing line in the manufacture and installation of a missile in a hole in the ground between the contract let to airframe contractors (and their unions) and the construction contractors (and their unions)? This interface was new terrain for the government agencies and they did not know how to write or integrate the contracts for the purchase of services and equipment. The commission arranged for detailed specifications of a dividing line and for site committees to work out any difficulty. The government (Defense Department) had an interest to work out the problem with the commission that the NLRB and the courts would not likely have undertaken nor performed expeditiously.

As I reflect on my experience, a number of other cases come to mind in which specialized machinery has been developed by the federal government, to serve either its own operations or the public interest in private operations more generally. I served for five years (1948–53) on the Atomic Energy Labor Relations Panel handling disputes between enterprises managing atomic energy–producing facilities, weapons plants, and test facilities and the labor organizations of their employees.[3]

The railroad industry is also replete with cases in which the long-established procedures of the Railway Labor Act have not resolved a dispute, despite mediation and recommendations of an emergency board. The Congress and the president, in a long line of cases, have simply adopted as law the recommendations of the emergency board or have required that the dispute between labor and management be arbitrated.

An illustration in the private sector is represented by the Joint Labor-Management Committee in the Retail Food Industry. The previous mechanism of simple resort to the Federal Mediation and Conciliation Service resulted in too many work stoppages and no coordination in bargaining among localities or on occasion among crafts in the same area. The Joint Committee was established in 1974 as a condition for early release of the industry from wage and price controls, and this joint private machinery celebrated its fifteenth anniversary in 1991. The committee includes the leadership of the international unions—Food and Commercial Workers, Teamsters and Bakers—and the top officers of the major chain stores. It received an award in 1991 from the Federal Mediation and Conciliation Services (FMCS).

The labor and management of the retail food industry, under collective bargaining agreements, has concluded that private mediation with those fully knowledgeable of the industry should be able to coordinate concerns over relative differentials among areas. Private mediation would also provide a continuing forum for dispute resolution on an industrywide basis to resolve issues of OSHA regulations, health care costs, the introduction of technological change, and other common problems superior to isolated locality negotiations with ad hoc FMCS mediation. The parties, of course, pay for their private mediation and select their neutral. The Joint Committee was a new procedure to reduce old concerns.

In all these cases the preexisting and general procedures were not regarded as effective to resolve disputes as the special-purpose machinery that was created by the parties or with the government.

4. There is a large class of cases in which labor and management are unhappy with the formalism, the expense, the length of time, and the extent of control of the process by lawyers, and individually one party or the other sees little opportunity to change or escape the barriers to more direct agreement making.

Joint Labor-Management Committee for Municipal Police and Fire (Massachusetts). At the request of the Cambridge city manager in 1977 I met with statewide firefighters and municipal association representatives, all complete strangers. They were concerned with the problems arising under the compulsory arbitration statute for municipal fire and police collective bargaining.

---

[3] See Department of Labor (1957), *Report of the Secretary of Labor's Advisory Committee on Labor Management Relations in Atomic Energy Installations*, Washington, D.C.

An agreement between the parties was achieved in a few sessions to remove these collective bargaining disputes from an all-public-member arbitration board, with last-best-offer form of arbitration, and to set up instead a joint labor-management committee. The joint committee was to have a small staff to mediate the disputes with the assistance of fire, police, and municipal committee members and a neutral chairman selected by the parties, with general powers of arbitration in any form reserved as a last resort. The agreement was quickly and almost without opposition enacted into law (Brock 1982).

The new objective was to avoid routine resort to arbitration and to enhance the role of the statewide organizations of firefighters, police, and municipal officials in helping to settle disputes over the terms of collective bargaining agreements involving local parties and their lawyers. It was also agreed that the committee should constitute a forum to address continuing underlying issues such as training, health care, and civil service questions affecting the parties on a statewide basis.

The machinery and the processes continue after seventeen years despite some limitations on the role of arbitration. Our authority to arbitrate was eliminated in 1980 with Proposition 2½ and restored in a limited way in 1987.[4] An arbitration award now binds only the municipal executive, not any legislative body that needs to appropriate funding. Accordingly, the procedures do not constitute binding arbitration. In approximately 580 cases involving the terms of collective agreements handled between 1987 and 1993 we fully used this limited authority in no more than 13 cases. We use internal and external fact-finders and arbitrators. From the beginning there has scarcely ever been cast a divided vote on the committee; all procedural and substantive actions are unanimous (Lester 1984, 1989).

This dispute-settlement machinery has resolved about seventy-five contract disputes a year, largely by specialized mediation, with greater satisfaction and at lower costs to the parties, in the process denying business to scores of arbitrators.

5. There is another type of situation in which labor and management representations may seek to mitigate a visible problem, only to discover in the course of time that the issues are different, or need to be approached by other means, or that still other questions are more significant or tractable. There is at times a good deal of experimentation and adaptation in the design of new labor-management-government machinery.

The Textile / Clothing Technology Corporation [TC]². Following the negotiations in the shirt branch of the men's clothing industry, in October 1976, the Amalgamated Clothing and Textile Workers Union and shirt companies requested me to study the current extent and the likely prospects for imports. Added freedom to import, proposed by the companies, had been a significant issue in the negotiations, and the agreement to study the issue has been a part of the end-game that resolved the dispute and settled the contract. The study

---

[4]Chapter 589 of the Acts of 1987.

forecast a substantial expansion in imports for all men's clothing items and led to proposals for improved training and employee selection for greater quality control and for a genuine research and development program, all to enhance competitiveness (Dunlop 1984).

In 1980, a nonprofit corporation, now Textile / Clothing Technology Corporation [TC]², was established to develop new technology for the industry with contracts to the Charles Stark Draper Laboratory, Inc. My Harvard colleague Professor Frederick H. Abernathy of the Division of Applied Sciences provided the technological leadership. The organization included both union and non-union companies from the full chain of production and distribution, including retailers. Half of the funding has come from the Department of Commerce and the other half from the members (Salter 1987).

In 1992 [TC]² had more than ninety company members and the two national unions, the Amalgamated and the International Ladies Garment Workers Union. Its annual budget is $7 million; it owns and operates a model factory in Raleigh, North Carolina; it supports selected research and development projects and exhibits its products at the annual show of the industry (Kazis 1989). It has developed and sells interactive training videos for operators, mechanics, and supervisors. In recent years for many products it has come to recognize the critical relationships between retailers or mass distributors and manufacturers for inventories, stockouts and markdowns. It promotes flexible and modular manufacturing and quick response as means to enhanced competitiveness of the domestic industry. The problem of competitiveness initially approached as a training and labor cost issue was recast into a technological issue and is now seen as having many facets, including the integration of production and distribution. I serve as a member of the [TC]² board of directors.

In this discussion of new processes to resolve disputes I have sought to identify a few types of barriers and to illustrate the new or modified machinery that has emerged with case illustrations. To summarize:

1. There may be literally no previously established procedure.
2. The government-designed processes may be anathema and the parties may seek to establish their own.
3. The government as customer or owner may prefer specially designed machinery to that generally applicable to a class of disputes. In particular, the regularly prescribed machinery may not get the job done or may be too slow compared to the special-purpose procedures.
4. The parties are unhappy with the formalism, the expense, the time expended and the role of lawyers in the dispute resolution processes, and they may make major changes in the design of the conflict resolution arrangements.
5. The initial design of new machinery may evolve or be refocused to encompass a wider range of issues and participants as the nature of the problems and the opportunities for action are better understood in a changing world. It might be said that [TC]², whatever its origins, is not a dispute-settling machinery in

the ordinary sense except that international competitiveness, tariffs, and quotas are a major source of political and economic conflict among some businesses, labor, and government with respect to a sector that has among the highest of tariffs for manufactured imports (Cline 1990).

III. THE PROCESSES OF CONFLICT RESOLUTION

This section seeks to identify certain common elements in the cases described in the previous section that account for the acceptability and preference for the new processes, despite the great differences in problems and setting. Consider the cases as a group, labeled for shorthand as Tomatoes and Cucumbers, Jurisdiction, Missile Sites, Fire and Police, and Textiles and Clothing. In each case the disputes involve a variety of formal or less structured groups. There are numerous players. The leadership of all organizations in each case is scarcely monolithic. Public processes impinge on the problems and issues in a variety of ways. Four of the cases involve private employment and one public employment; the government is the sole purchaser of the "product" in two cases while in the other three the markets are highly competitive. The previous arrangements for dispute resolution were unsettled by events, or a new set of issues had intruded.

In these cases a neutral plays a catalyst role, although previous knowledge of the sector or association with the parties was absent in three of the five cases. These cases do not comport with traditional arbitration, although several of the processes use the form. Decisions or solutions are worked out by joint agreement and consensus. Procedures are mediatory and informal rather than akin to litigation with lawyerlike forms.

1. Dispute resolution in these cases confronts parties (sides) that may not be very cohesive. An agreement in Tomatoes and Cucumbers requires a three-way convergence among the farmers, the processor, and the migrant organization. Additionally, the agreement at the outset needed to be acceptable to the religious groups supporting a boycott. Any agreement requires four congruent agreements—one within each group to achieve a form of ratification and the agreement to be signed by representatives of all three organizations. Similarly, the Fire and Police machinery must deal with the internal politics of many cities, mayors versus city councils, and the internal conflicts between statewide and local union officers. "In two party negotiations, it takes an agreement within each side to reach an agreement across the table; that is, it takes three agreements to make one" (Dunlop 1984).

The differences within and among such organizations, often without effective internal control or discipline, require a form of mediation within each organization to achieve both internal agreement and consensus across the groups.

There are risks for a neutral to operate within one party, in that the levers of influence and power at any one time are not always unambiguous or well-known, and it is possible to alienate key players in an organization and, indeed, one of the parties requisite to an agreement. One device to lessen that risk is to use assessors of a tripartite commission or a panel with the members drawn from each side having a role to explore the positions within organizations with which they may have a special relationship. These "wingmen" may be voting or non-voting members of a panel or commission. This procedure may be effective in dispute resolution, or it may on occasion turn the dispute inward into a negotiation within the panel or between the assessors and the neutral. This result is not ideal, since the parties are absolved in part from the responsibilities and the "joys of settlement."

2. In working with diffuse organizations on a new approach to problem solving, a neutral may encourage a fact-finding state which may well lead to a greater common understanding of issues. In Fire and Police a continuing statewide database of wages, benefits, and other contract provisions is a significant tool in dispute resolution not ordinarily available in ad hoc cases. Mutual respect for a set of data is often an important step in the process of dispute resolution that saves time. But respect is not likely established solely by academic experts; it helps to have the parties work together to develop a data set.

A more complete picture of the relative position of Ohio in the output, quality, and costs of tomato or cucumber production is likely to be assembled for local parties with a neutral commission than would be forthcoming in the settlement of a single dispute. While a data set or a factual report seldom, if ever, resolves a labor-management-government dispute, a discussion grounded in mutually accepted or respected facts can be a productive tool toward reaching a settlement.

3. Government officials are likely to be more available and to pay more serious attention to labor and management parties if approached in the setting of a continuing machinery and a neutral chair. The Department of Commerce and the Congress, over presidential opposition, have been working for a decade to provide matching funding for [TC]^2 on the showing of significant private-sector initiatives, and funding to improve productivity and competitiveness in Textiles and Clothing. The Defense Department was much more willing to review its internal processes to resolve a succession of vital disputes with a Missile Sites commission than it had been dealing with individual work stoppages by conventional means.

The role of governmental impact on private-sector labor-management disputes and their resolution is a frontier that is not well understood in many circumstances. All governments may exacerbate or mitigate many private-sector labor-management disputes by policies or administrative arrangements, often without conscious intention (See also section IV below.)

4. The five new machineries described in the section II all provide an enhanced opportunity for the leadership of the respective labor or management organizations to be more effective in dispute resolution in a number of ways. At

times this added effectiveness is derived from the structure of the new dispute-settling mechanism, and at times it arises from the participation of a neutral.

Communications within an organization and across the groups included in the dispute-settling machinery typically take place through the leadership whose status may be at times reinforced by the neutral. Some of the static and ambiguity in the conversation may be reduced in these circumstances with a neutral in charge.

Top officials in the organizations tend to receive more recognition in the process than subsidiary officers who may be challenging. The presence of the neutral may share some responsibility in the ratification process by muting the opposition to a degree (Simkin 1971).

In tough internal conflicts the presence of the machinery and the neutral can always be blamed for a result regarded as untoward by an element of the constituency. A neutral needs to be sensitive to these internal differences and conflicts and the potential for upheaval that may also destroy any agreement or settlement. The tenure of the neutral in the cases cited lasted many years with changes in organizational leadership and in governmental officials and administration.

5. Although the problem may arise infrequently, a neutral and formal machinery is equipped to deal effectively with the press and media and other community concerns, particularly in times of crisis. There have been occasions in which the release of positions to the press or premature announcement by one side has intensified a dispute or materially complicated a sensitive settlement. The leaders of the organization have an easy and effective response that they would not otherwise have in referring all inquiries to the neutral.

It is instructive to understand the nature of negotiations and the barriers to settlement that public discourse creates. Negotiators want to explain the concessions, or departure from public positions they make and what they received in return, to their constituents directly through their internal processes rather than have the press or media make that explanation and appraise the advantages or disadvantages of the settlement. Negotiations are a major feature of the performance of leadership in the political life of a union, or an association of employers, and the leadership wants to do its own communicating. Press leaks make it more difficult to change positions; moreover, typically the understanding in negotiations is that there is no agreement until all items are agreed upon. Word on particular proposals and counterproposals is not very meaningful and certainly not helpful to agreement making.

In the public sector most open-meeting laws provide that a meeting may be closed for purposes of collective bargaining.

6. One of the most important ways in which a formal machinery and a neutral may influence dispute resolution is to utilize the meetings of the parties as a strategic planning meeting for the future, to report on factual studies on the sector, to identify problems on the horizon, to consider a variety of alternatives, and to use these discussions subsequently to inform their own internal constituencies. This process reduces future surprises, encourages reflection on alterna-

tive courses, and facilitates informal discourse and planning. It may well lead to new areas of agreement and new institution building (Salter and Dunlop 1989).

7. A direct application of this planning activity is the practice of pre-negotiations conferences and discussions over the state of the environment and the problems likely to arise in the forthcoming negotiations. These sessions are designed to take place before any party has formulated demands and placed them on the table, thereby climbing out on a limb with constituencies. Although an old idea (Taylor 1948), the procedure is invoked far too infrequently, and the overarching machinery of these cases encourages parties to engage in such periodic discussions in advance of actual negotiations over the terms of agreements. This process has been invoked in Tomatoes and Cucumbers, Missile Sites, and Fire and Police when deemed appropriate.

IV. NEGOTIATED RULE-MAKING

It would be remiss not to call attention to a growing area of negotiations involving labor and management organizations with government, either legislative bodies or regulatory agencies. The topic is a large one, and only brief reference and illustrations are appropriate to identify the terrain. In mid-1975 it naturally occurred to me, faced with the obligation to sign and issue numerous regulations as Secretary of Labor, that there were other choices than regulation by the established methods of the Administrative Procedures Act or deregulation. I sought to develop the option of regulation through the processes of negotiated rule-making. I used the process to implement section 13(c) of the Urban Mass Transportation Act and to develop an OSHA standard for coke oven emissions. An initial agreement between labor and business organizations would then be placed in the Federal Register for general comments and final decision. A history and analysis of negotiated rule-making has been provided by Professor H. Perritt, Jr., who worked with me in government (Perritt 1986). The Administrative Law Conference has approved the process, and in 1990 the Administrative Dispute Resolution Act was enacted.[5] Among federal agencies EPA has probably made the most extensive use of negotiated rule-making.

Brief reference should also be made to negotiations with the legislative branch. In a number of states, unemployment insurance provisions have been worked out in structured negotiations between labor and management representatives and committees of the state legislature. In the field of local governmental pensions in Massachusetts, I chaired a working group of private and public employers and labor organizations, legislators, and state gov-

---

[5] Public Law 101-552; November 15, 1990.

ernment officials over four years to work out three pieces of legislation introducing major changes in the local government pension system.[6]

The impediments to agreement in these negotiations with government multiply complexity.

V. GENERAL COMMENTS

From some perspectives it might be helpful to classify all barriers to conflict resolution in negotiating collective bargaining agreements into three categories: those internal to the labor and management organizations, those that are in the negotiating process, and those that are rooted in the encompassing environment of the parties. But such a scheme does not appear, at least to me, to advance the task of dispute resolution.

The growth of dispute resolution as a field in recent years involves some mixed blessings. I have applauded the promotion and growing recognition of certain simple fundamentals in dispute resolution. It is important for negotiators and mediators to learn to listen and to listen perceptively not only to what the other side says, but also to what it does not say or omits in a series of conversations. It is important to keep one's cool and learn to handle difficult people (as if there were any one way). It is helpful to think in terms of priorities among competing proposals. And phrases like "step to their side," "don't reject . . . reframe," and "bring them to their senses . . . not to their knees" may all be helpful to the relatively inexperienced. It is good pedagogy, and there is a real hunger in the population for these ideas (Fisher and Ury 1981; Ury 1991).

I am particularly pleased to pass accolades to those instructing law school students and lawyers in the arts of negotiations. Anything that reduces the litigious qualities of the legal profession and enhances its interest in good-faith negotiations is to be commended, because the country on average will get better solutions, faster and at lower costs than at present. I also believe there is something to be gained from specialists in various fields meeting occasionally and exchanging experiences.

But I am not persuaded that it is possible to be, or to train, a general-purpose resolver of all disputes. It is my experience that although there is some small carryover beyond certain general approaches, there is too much to the substance of disputes, at least labor-management disputes, to have them yield to general-purpose negotiators or mediators. Moreover, until one

---

[6] Chapter 630 of the Acts of 1982 creating the Public Employee Retirement Administration; Chapter 661 of the Acts of 1983 creating the Pension Reserve Investment Management Board; and Chapter 697 of the Acts of 1987.

has developed an understanding of industrial relations systems, either analytically or intuitively, I do not believe those with experience in other fields, such as broker-stockholder or landlord-tenant relations, are likely to make much of a contribution to industrial relations. As Henry H. Perritt, Jr., has written me, "You cannot help settle a labor dispute if you don't know anything about the way unions make decisions and the way labor relations officers interact with other functions within an employing institution."

I would hope that the barriers to conflict resolution in labor-management relations that lead to the creation of new systems, such as those that have been sketched above, provide some insight into the difficulties that a generalist in dispute resolution would encounter representing labor or management organizations or seeking to serve as a mediator. I also do not believe that a specialist in resolving labor-management disputes can readily transfer to settle marital disputes or international disputes among countries.

CHAPTER FIFTEEN

Barriers to Effective
Environmental Treaty-Making

Lawrence Susskind

O ne of the key obstacles to international cooperation on environmental resource management has been the long-standing tension between the developed countries of "the North" and the developing nations of "the South," particularly over issues such as technology sharing, compensatory economic aid, debt renegotiation, and the definition of sovereignty. Almost all environmental treaty-making negotiations, such as the 1992 Rio Earth Summit (United Nations Conference on Environment and Development), have snagged on these conflicts. Indeed, international negotiations on other issues, such as trade, have often run afoul on the same North-South disagreements.

The rigid institutional arrangements and norms governing the formulation, adoption, and implementation of international agreements have also hindered international cooperation on environmental management. It is difficult enough to build agreement among multiple negotiators on any issue. When the issues are scientifically complex and negotiators must struggle with a formal and unwieldy system that allows for few, if any, of the prerequisites of multilateral problem solving, it is not suprising that progress has been so limited.

The Earth Summit at Rio illustrates the difficulties that negotiators encounter as they struggle with this system. As with many international environmental negotiations, the cast of characters (both governmental and nongovernmental) demanding a role in the negotiations was enormous. The Earth Summit organizers faced the task of facilitating a dialogue among as many as five thousand official delegates. To make matters more difficult, upwards of twenty thousand observers from nongovernmental organizations sought to participate by holding parallel meetings in the same venue. Unfortunately, the traditional treaty-making system did not offer a process for taking account of all the interests and concerns of these multiple actors. With almost perpetual North-South confrontation and escalating demands from an ever-widening circle of nongovernmental organizations, it is remarkable that the Rio negotiators made any progress at all. Against all odds, they did manage to produce "broad-gauged" agreements, or what are called conventions, aimed at limiting the emission of "greenhouse gases" and protecting biodiversity.

These agreements add to the list of major environmental treaties signed since the Stockholm conference (the 1972 precursor to the Rio conference.) This list includes the 1973 Convention on International Trade in Endangered Species of Wild Flora and Fauna (CITES), the 1989 Basel Convention on the Control of Transboundary Movements of Hazardous Wastes and Their Disposal, and the 1985 Vienna Convention for the Protection of the Ozone Layer (which led to the subsequent 1987 Montreal protocol and further amendments banning chloroflourocarbons—CFCs).[1] Unfortunately, most of these treaties took a long time to negotiate, and in the end many countries did not sign them.

Some environmental treaty-making efforts have not even been minimally successful. The Law of the Sea (LOS) negotiations fell apart when a number of countries, including the United States, Britain, and others, refused to sign after more than a decade of international give-and-take. The LOS negotiations did in the end produce important "soft law" results that have reshaped common practices. However, many other environmental treaty negotiations—including some that have actually produced signed agreements—have, to a great extent, proven entirely ineffective. The International Convention for the Regulation of Whaling set a "zero quota" on the commercial harvesting of great whales, but did not stop the big whaling countries, which simply opted out of the convention when it failed to serve their purposes. Taking a different approach, the Rio negotiators refused to set timetables or targets for CO^2 reduction. The resulting agreement falls far short of its potential to effectively address the problem of global climate change. Even under the best of circumstances—with countries taking relatively painless actions that suit their needs—the rate of global warming could be somewhat slowed, but certainly not reversed. The treaty-making system must be designed and managed differently if global environmental problems are to be addressed effectively.

In this chapter, I want to review the reasons why it is so difficult to achieve agreements that address transboundary environmental problems effectively. There are four, in particular, that I think are most significant: (1) too few opportunities for regional coalition building, (2) inappropriate responses to

---

[1] For a list of countries which have signed some of the most important environmental treaties see World Resources Institute 1994–1995: 1994, 376.

scientific uncertainty, (3) a troubling separation of benefits and costs in formulating policy objectives, and (4) unworkable concepts of sovereignty. These barriers are, I believe, relevant to all kinds of multiparty conflicts. Strategies for overcoming them, however, must be sensitive to the particularities of the institutional settings in which they occur. So, I will focus exclusively on global environmental treaty-making and the reforms that might overcome the obstacles enumerated above.

THE ENVIRONMENTAL TREATY-MAKING PROCESS

Before I describe these barriers and what might be done to overcome them in more detail, I will sketch the steps in the typical treaty-making process.[2] The formulation of all international environmental agreements is governed by the Vienna Convention on the Law of Treaties. Although the United States is not a party to this convention, it is nevertheless considered binding by all American courts. Most multilateral environmental treaty negotiations are initiated by some international organization like the United Nations Environment Programme (UNEP). For example, UNEP called the two conferences that produced the Convention on the Protection of the Ozone Layer in 1985 and the Basel Convention on the Control of Transboundary Movements of Hazardous Wastes and Their Disposal in 1989.

Once a conference has been called and the negotiating committees for each nation have been convened, the participants are free to formulate ad hoc rules regarding how they want the negotiations to proceed. They must decide how long the conference will last, who will be allowed to participate, who will present scientific evidence, how proposals will be made, and how the participants will produce draft agreements. The Vienna Convention does not specify exact procedural rules, except that the adoption of the text of a treaty requires a vote of two-thirds of the countries present and voting (unless that same majority decides to apply a different rule).

Procedural decisions are important. The choice of ground rules can have a major impact on the prospects for reaching agreement. For example, the use of a "single text" approach (in which there is only one draft of a proposed agreement and all the parties suggest changes to it) has been credited with a number of successes in instances in which the traditional approach—using multiple versions of the proposed treaty put forward by different parties—would not have worked. Similarly, rules governing the participation of nongovernmental organizations in the proceedings are important since these

---

[2]This is an abridgement of the discussion that appears in Susskind 1994. My thanks to Eric Reifschneider, a student at Harvard Law School who helped to develop this description of the environmental treaty-making process.

groups often provide critical technical information on which official delegates rely.

Once the parties have adopted the text of an agreement, the next step is to secure signatures. Signature is not a trivial step, because parties unhappy with the final text may refuse to sign. This is especially true when the text is adopted by majority vote rather than by consensus. Once a party signs an agreement, that country must—according to the Vienna Convention—refrain from acts which would defeat the objectives of the agreement (even before the treaty takes effect). The Vienna Convention provides that an agreement takes effect, or "enters into force," when all the parties have agreed to be bound by it.

Multilateral agreements can be modified after they have entered into force. Unless a treaty provides otherwise, the general rule is that all parties must be notified of any proposed modification.

The typical treaty, or convention agreement, begins with articles defining the terms used in the agreement and specifying its geographic scope. Next, there are articles calling on the parties to take all appropriate measures, individually and jointly, to address the problem and to cooperate with one another in carrying out the provisions of the treaty. Sometimes the agreement expressly calls for the parties to formulate follow-up accords, or protocols, that address specifics not covered in the convention. In such cases, the convention outlines the provisions for establishing these protocols.

Additional articles usually call for periodic meetings or follow-up conferences. At these meetings, delegates may review new scientific information and establish joint research programs; assess the effectiveness of their individual and joint efforts to combat the problem; and propose, discuss, and vote on amendments. Such meetings typically occur once every few years. Extraordinary meetings can be called at the request of a certain number of parties (sometimes one-third, sometimes half).

Other articles may establish a secretariat. The primary duty of the secretariat is to call and supervise the meetings of the parties. The secretariat is often an international organization such as UNEP.

Proposed protocols or amendments to a treaty must be sent out by the secretariat well in advance of scheduled meetings. The parties try to reach agreement by consensus, but if they fail, amendments can be adopted by a vote of those present. Many amendments pertain to modification of annexes to the treaty. Annexes spell out technical definitions and specify actions appropriate to various circumstances. For example, the annexes to the CITES convention indicate which species are accorded various levels of protection. The annexes to the London Dumping Convention (aimed at regulating disposal of nuclear and toxic waste in the ocean) categorize various substances that may or may not be disposed of in the ocean. Annexes are often designed to be modified without the need to amend the treaty itself.

Responsibility for periodic updating of annexes may be assigned to a sub-group of signatory countries or to their technical representatives.

Finally, most treaties contain articles defining how the agreement will enter into force. Some of these articles specify when and how long the agreement will remain open for signature. Others designate a depository whose duties are to receive notices of ratification and, when enough parties have ratified, to inform the parties that an agreement is entering into force. (The depository is usually the government of the nation that hosted the meeting at which the convention was signed.) Further articles can specify the number of countries that must ratify for an agreement to enter into force, and how long the agreement is expected to remain in force.

THE CONVENTION-PROTOCOL APPROACH TO ENVIRONMENTAL TREATY NEGOTIATION

Since Stockholm, most multilateral environmental treaties have been developed using the two-step process I call the convention-protocol approach. This approach is the natural outgrowth of an environmental treaty-making system that provides few guidelines. Its procedures allow countries to sign fairly vague statements acknowledging the existence of a problem without requiring them to agree on specific actions that must be taken.[3] For example, the Barcelona convention (which established an agreement among sixteen countries aimed at protecting the Mediterranean Sea) established procedures for monitoring various sources of pollution without ordering specific pollution controls or reduction levels. Most countries were able to agree that further documentation of pollution levels would be desirable. However, commitments to specific targets would have been difficult to achieve because of domestic opposition to what many viewed as unacceptable short-term economic impacts. The CO^2 negotiations at Rio also produced vague and unenforceable commitments for the same reason.

The signing of environmental conventions produced by the convention-protocol approach can create momentum and encourage continued scientific

---

[3] This critique of the convention-protocol approach is drawn from L. Susskind and C. Ozawa, Negotiating more effective international environmental agreements, in Hurrel and Kingsbury 1992. Both the critique and the prescriptions for reform are contained in *The Salzburg Initiative*—an action agenda prepared in 1990 by an international team of more than one hundred diplomats, environmentalists, negotiation specialists, and international relations experts. The initiative was prepared with support from the Dana Greeley Foundation in the United States and the Salzburg Seminar in Salzburg, Austria. Copies of the *Salzburg Initiative* and progress reports on efforts to implement its recommendations can be obtained from The Secretariat of the International Environmental Negotiation Network (IENN) at the Program on Negotiation at Harvard Law School, Cambridge, MA. 02138.

inquiry. Groups within a country concerned about environmental protection can point to the signing of a convention as proof that further action is needed. In some cases, the accumulation of scientific evidence can reduce political resistance to remedial action. In other cases, the force of world opinion may create sufficient pressure to induce reluctant countries to sign follow-up protocols. And, sometimes, with the mere passage of time, domestic opposition may weaken, making it easier for national leaders to build support for specific actions outlined in follow-up protocols.

While the signing of a convention may create momentum that can propel subsequent action, the two-step process can also backfire. The signing of a convention can take the heat off political leaders, allowing symbolic but empty promises to substitute for real improvements. Nations and leaders with absolutely no intention of working to improve environmental quality can sign a convention and claim credit for doing something, while reassuring their supporters that nothing has, in fact, been promised.

Often the dynamics of the convention-protocol approach reinforce the tendency to seek lowest-common-denominator agreements. The Basel convention incorporates vague language and avoids the politically difficult task of defining key terms. While this made it possible for reluctant countries to sign, it probably undermined the chances of successful implementation. For instance, the agreement calls for the disposal of hazardous waste in an "environmentally sound manner." It does not, however, say what this means. Setting standards for environmental soundness is left entirely up to each country.

Most international environmental treaties impose the same requirements on all signatories. Indeed, this is why the lowest-common-denominator solution is often the only viable option for securing agreement. For example, the Basel convention regulates the movement of hazardous wastes between signatory countries, but allows bilateral agreements between signatory countries and nonsignatory countries. This explicitly contradicts an earlier provision of the agreement that states that signatory countries cannot ship hazardous wastes to nonsignatory countries. The provision allowing future bilateral agreements watered down the treaty; however, its inclusion was politically necessary to hold the agreement together.

Obviously, all treaty negotiations require some give-and-take among the countries involved. In the case of environmental agreements, however, merely satisying the demands of the countries is not enough to ensure an effective result. The dynamics of the natural systems involved must be respected, regardless of political resistance. Otherwise, nothing of substance will be accomplished.

Another key problem is that agreements produced by the convention-protocol approach sometimes neglect important scientific and technical information or incorporate requirements that are not technically feasible. When a convention is negotiated, agreements may be made that do not bear up under close technical scrutiny. Unfortunately, when it comes time to work out specific protocols, the terms of the convention—spelled out before the real costs and benefits of alternative courses of action were clear—may actually get in the way of producing effective agreements. The convention-protocol approach needs to be modified if we are to overcome these barriers to effective environmental treaty-making.

FOUR KEY BARRIERS TO EFFECTIVE ENVIRONMENTAL TREATY-MAKING

In a study of ten environmental treaty-making efforts, we were surprised to learn that the best that can be said about the agreements reached in recent years is that they *may* slow the rate of environmental degradation, but they will not reverse the destructive processes that triggered the need for action nor repair the damage already done.[4]

It is worth re-emphasizing, I think, that numerous environmental treaty-making efforts are typically under way at any time. Thus, environmental treaty-making involves not only multiple rounds of negotiation (i.e., conventions, then protocols, and then amendments in light of new data), but also simultaneous and in some cases interlocking negotiations that influence each other. The convention-protocol approach does not take account of this complexity. Each treaty negotiation has been treated as a zero-sum game. Moreover, by the time countries come together to negotiate treaty language, they have locked in (at home) to certain fixed positions. Thus, little if any creative problem-solving is possible. When agreements do emerge, they are usually the result of small compromises by the most powerful parties rather than of creative brainstorming or trading across different treaty regimes.

Based on our studies, we have concluded that the convention-protocol approach fails to come to grips with the weaknesses inherent in the UN-sponsored system of international environmental treaty-making. Our measure of success, by the way, is not how many agreements are signed, or even how many countries ratify treaties that are signed (although we were surprised to learn that dozens of nations have signed only two or three of the most important environmental treaties and that many treaties have been signed by fewer than half the countries of the world). Rather, our focus is on the speed and effectiveness with which the nations of the world produce tangible environmental improvements. Typical is the fact that the 1973

---

[4]L. Susskind, E. Siskind, and W. Breslin (1990), *Nine Case Studies of International Environmental Negotiation*, Cambridge, Mass.: Program on Negotiation, Harvard Law School.

CITES convention was not signed until ten years after the International Union for the Conservation of Nature and Natural Resources (IUCN) first called for regulation of the export, transit, and importation of endangered animal and plant species and their products. During that intervening period, many animal and plant species disappeared.

Following is a more detailed discussion of the reasons why the convention-protocol approach makes it difficult to produce international agreements that effectively address transboundary environmental problems.

Inadequate Opportunities for Coalition Building

The formality of the convention-protocol approach encourages the "hard bargaining" tendencies of most countries. It does little to discourage misrepresentation or exaggeration. Demands, followed by counter demands and concessions, form a typical pattern. Most treaty-making processes devote little or no time to encouraging countries to create options for mutual gain. There are few exploratory meetings of informal coalitions once treaty negotiations have officially begun (and prior to that, too few countries are paying attention to the issue to permit useful dialogue).

Because of the underlying suspicion that the South has of the North, it is almost impossible to call informal pre-bargaining sessions to which all countries are not invited. Certainly, a secretariat could not call such meetings. Indeed, the preparatory committees for the Earth Summit were hamstrung by the very requirement that all countries (and nongovernmental organizations) be invited to every preparatory session. With everyone present, it is impossible to go off the record. Moreover, few developing countries are likely to risk the wrath of their allies by indicating a willingness to explore common interests with developed nations. There is a strong feeling among the developing countries that continued solidarity is necessary to gain concessions from the North.

"Second track" or unofficial diplomacy, often used to explore options in treaty-making of other kinds, has been used sparingly in international environmental negotiations.[5] Indeed, many countries have strongly discouraged both their governmental and nongovernmental "team" members from meeting with counterparts from other countries. The United States, for example, was very concerned that "trial balloons" sent up by unauthorized delegates might be viewed as official American policy contradicting the publicly stated

---

[5] For a more elaborate analysis of the role of unofficial intermediaries in international dispute resolution, see L. Susskind and E. Babbit, Overcoming the obstacles to effective mediation of international disputes, in Berovitch and Rubin 1992.

positions of the Bush administration. Thus, if official country representatives are sent to informal meetings at all, it is usually to push the party line.

Besides suspicion and concern about being misinterpreted, many countries operate as if it is unlikely that they could have common environmental interests with countries that are not their typical allies. Indeed, many nations have made no attempt to identify potential allies among countries that they have not worked closely with in the past. Alliances among countries with shared environmental interests could surely bridge the North-South gap. For instance, many developed and developing countries have forests that are threatened in similar ways. Countries that have coastline along the same oceans will, at some point, have to work together to combat pollution, regardless of past political relationships. The Mediterranean Action Plan required cooperation among countries that did not even have diplomatic relations, proving that such unlikely coalitions are possible. Strong political rivalries, however, and a willingness to let past political relationships take precedence over shared environmental concerns, tend to inhibit bioregional cooperation.

Most secretariats for international environmental negotiations are neither empowered nor equipped to act regionally. UNEP, for instance, does not have widespread regional representation, although it shares space in some parts of the world with United Nations Development Programme (UNDP) offices. Without an active secretariat to convene or moderate, informal meetings are much less likely to happen. When one country, particularly a nation with strong views, proposes to host an off-the-record meeting, others are likely to view this as a lobbying effort and opt to stay away (or send very low-level observers).

Nontraditonal clusters of countries are neither assisted nor encouraged to caucus ahead of formal negotiations, even though there are many "small bargains" and working alliances that might be made. For example, the USA, China, Russia, and the European Community probably should have met prior to Rio to review possible strategies for stabilizing the emission of greenhouse gases. Since these are the chief emitting countries, what they might have said about the desirability of various control strategies could have carried substantial weight. By including China, the usual North-South split might have been avoided.

Nontraditional clusters of countries, meeting in exploratory sessions prior to the initiation of formal negotiations, could also forestall the formation of traditional blocking coalitions. The primary objectives of such sessions would be to encourage a clearer understanding of the interests of all sides before countries announce formal positions.

Bringing together nontraditional clusters of countries should not depend on the UN system for approval or support. While this recommendation flies in the face of tradition, it does not require major institutional adaptation. Informal alliance building, joint fact finding, and creative brainstorming by countries with shared environmental interests ought to be encouraged.

To date, efforts to use these processes have not been entirely successful. For example, the Intergovernmental Panel on Climate Change (IPCC), the international panel created to organize the scientific evidence for the climate change negotiations, represented an attempt to conduct joint fact-finding. It operated, though, in ways that undermined this objective. Subcommittee membership was structured to ensure balanced geographic representation. Countries with shared interests were not explicitly assigned to work together to gather information of greatest concern to them. Too many participants assumed that what they were involved in was "instructed science" (i.e., generating facts to substantiate already announced positions). The executive summary of the IPCC read, to many observers, as if the conclusions were reached in spite of the findings.

For many countries it is difficult to prepare for and participate in international negotiations. What time and money they have is devoted to hammering out internal positions. Few resources are devoted to researching how other countries might be thinking about the issues. Very little information-sharing occurs. Thus, few countries have a sense of who their allies might be.

Some countries do not have the legal and scientific resources to ensure that their delegations are adequately briefed, particularly on the scientific and technical aspects of environmental matters. They would benefit enormously from off-the-record, informal briefings by expert advisers of their own choosing. Conceivably, panels could be assembled to provide "seminars-on-demand" for interested countries. It is important to provide access to this kind of advice before countries lock into draft treaty language. By that time, countries are worried about "outsiders" learning what their official positions are, or what their negotiating strategies will be.

While it may be preferable, in some circumstances, to begin formal negotiations with a single text in hand—especially one that focuses on a relatively small number of bracketed points—it is a mistake to move too quickly to developing formal treaty language. Instead, conference leaders should encourage the preparation of multiple proposals that do not represent official commitments of any kind. The widest array of representatives should be involved in developing these early conceptual options. By relying on cross-cutting clusters of countries (including nongovernmental interests) in the preparation of multiple proposals, official national position-taking can be avoided for as long as possible. It is also conceivable that UNEP could designate ambassadors-at-large (not secretariats) to convene cross-cutting working groups. After gathering numerous preliminary proposals, the conference secretariat could produce a single text on which to focus formal negotiations. This would involve attempting to mediate the preparation of a draft that seeks to accommodate the conflicting interests of all the parties.

Nongovernmental interests have key roles to play in this process. International agreements must be implemented by individual countries, and unless there is a constituency in each country willing to push for implementation, the results are likely to be disappointing. Nongovernmental interests can help to push environmental concerns higher up domestic political agendas and provide continuity during periods of political change.

To sum up, because there are few opportunities for informal coalition-building (and exploration of interests), the environmental treaty-making system often reaches impasse more quickly than would otherwise be the case. There are various ways in which unofficial interaction among nations with shared environmental interests could be encouraged. This would lead to multiple treaty drafts from groups with shared interests, which could then be blended into a single text by an activist secretariat.

Inappropriate Responses to Scientific Uncertainty

Environmental questions almost invariably involve uncertainty that complicates decision making. Our understanding of the biosphere is incomplete. Forecasting tools provide only crude approximations, and are often based on unverifiable assumptions. It is not surprising, therefore, that disagreements among technical experts on complex issues are pervasive. If one country thinks it will be disadvantaged by a particular set of forecasts or findings, it taps sympathetic experts to raise doubts about the adequacy of the evidence put forward by others. If a country wants to delay implementation of costly pollution abatement measures, for instance, it is not hard to argue that further study would be desirable before long-term commitments are requested.

Rarely can scientists find the environmental equivalent of a "smoking gun" that proves that their causal explanations are correct or that their long-range forecasts are likely to be accurate. In the case of the stratospheric ozone negotiations, the discovery of a "hole" in the ozone layer over Antarctica (and more recently over the Northern Hemisphere) prompted action, but this was quite unusual.

The global warming debate is more typical. In a recent poll, atmospheric scientists from around the world were asked if the greenhouse effect, caused primarily by the burning of fossil fuels, could reach a "point of no return, after which global warming would continue to increase no matter what measures were later taken to combat it." Thirteen percent of the scientists said that an unstoppable "runaway" greenhouse effect was likely, and another 32 percent said it was possible. Forty-seven percent said it was unlikely.[6] In other words, about half thought that such an effect was likely and half did not. Such disagreement is not unusual. This stems, in large measure, from the fact that scientists lack the knowledge they need to explain and predict complex ecological interactions. For example, the depletion of the ozone layer—usually thought to be a totally separate problem from global warming—could increase the greenhouse effect by damaging plankton in the world's oceans and thus reducing their ability to remove carbon dioxide, the principal greenhouse gas, from the air. Such feedback loops are not well understood; indeed, they are not currently included in most CO_2 forecasting models.

When negotiations are conducted without a clear agreement on what is known, negotiators have a tendency to select explanations that serve their political needs. In the 1992 round of CO_2 negotiations, for instance, representatives from the United States argued that there was too much uncertainty about the timing and impacts of global warming to merit taking costly preventive action. They were so intent on defending this position that they were unwilling to admit publicly that there might be "no regret" policies the United States could adopt (like working toward greater fuel efficiency of the automobile fleet) that would both meet the country's interests *and* contribute to the stabilization of worldwide CO_2 levels.

The integrity of scientific analysis is undermined when technical studies are used (or ignored) primarily to justify politically expedient positions. Data must be generated that are credible to all parties regardless of their political biases or priorities. Credible data are more likely to be generated by international collaboratives than by national institutes or even independent scientific societies. All nations must share in the design and implementation of joint fact-finding if they are going to accept and use the results.

Many diplomats and politicans have the mistaken notion that once the scientific and technical community has defined a problem, the views of experts ought to give way to the political judgment of elected officials. In fact, though, ongoing scientific involvement is essential. Although elected officials must bear the final responsibility for resolving whatever contradictory claims remain, wise decisions and successful policy implementation can only result from the continued interplay of scientific and political perspectives. The technical evaluation of possible "solutions" is as important as the definition of the problem—scientific experts have a role to play in both. And the nonobjective judgments that are part of all technical analysis should be scrutinized by the policy makers and not left entirely in the hands of technical experts.

Negotiations almost always start before conclusive scientific evidence is in

---

[6] Fears expressed of runaway greenhouse effect, *Boston Globe*, February 10, 1992, 3.

hand. Indeed, environmental problems are rarely fully understood at the time political decisions must be made; additional research is always required. Once a baseline is obtained—a significant challenge in itself—it is usually appropriate to monitor ongoing results to determine whether policies are working as intended, and what adjustments in standards or procedures might be needed. Successful implementation of environmental treaties, therefore, depends on constant readjustment of goals and methods. This can only be accomplished by trial and error.

It is not just scientific analysis that is plagued by uncertainty. In evaluating the economic implications of various responses to environmental problems, we must realize that economic effects are often as hard to predict as ecological impacts. Every effort to forecast hard-to-quantify costs and benefits is surrounded by the same uncertainties that plague scientific forecasting. We know as little about the long-term mechanics of social and economic systems as we do about natural systems.

In light of the uncertainties and the difficulties of predicting the effects of alternative policies, it probably makes sense to rely more on *contingent agreements*. Instead of working to forge consensus on one "best estimate" of the future, alternative courses of action based on various possible future conditions should be negotiated. Even parties that disagree on the likelihood of a certain event's occurring should be able to agree on what ought to be done *if* that event transpires. Of course, this means that continuous monitoring must be built into all negotiated agreements. The Montreal Protocol is an example of an agreement that incorporates periodic reassessment and recalibration of treaty objectives in light of new scientific understanding. Earlier conventions, like the London Dumping Convention, included similar mechanisms.

As we have stated, uncertainty is likely to be misused to advance preconceived national positions. Joint fact-finding can minimize this behavior. Mere collaboration, though, is not enough; parties with conflicting interests must be encouraged to use models they have jointly built to formulate and test contingent commitments that do not require agreement on what the future holds.

A Troubling Separation of Benefits and Costs

The convention-protocol approach to international environmental negotiations as presently practiced fails to take full account of the longtime horizons for most environmental problem-solving. Many of the costs of combating pollution will be experienced now, while the full range of benefits of pollution control may not be realized in our lifetime.

Many environmental treaty negotiations focus only on the allocation of the economic costs associated with environmental regulation, and pay little or no attention to the intergenerational benefits associated with wise natural resource management. Indeed, most environmental treaties aim to curtail pollution or regulate the use of common resources by restricting all development activities in participating countries rather than by offering incentives for the adoption of different development patterns that would be more economically sustainable over a longer time frame. The time frame for environmental problem solving must be intergenerational to ensure a fair balancing of costs and benefits. Unfortunately, the time frame for most political decision-making is much shorter.

Many environmental issues hinge, in part, on the problem of how best to manage common-pool resources, or, conversely, how to penalize free riders. Presumably, if the benefits of regulated development or pollution control are diffuse, and accrue to all nations irrespective of their behavior, some nations will feel little or no incentive to accept restrictions. These we call free riders. For example, nations such as India and China have been hesitant to sign the Montreal protocol since reductions in the use and production of CFCs by other nations (especially bigger users) will slow down the rate of ozone depletion. India, as well as the rest of the world, will benefit without having to shoulder any of the short-term economic costs.

Most social scientists, particularly economists, believe in the inevitability of this "tragedy of the commons." However, there is counterevidence. Elinor Ostrom, a political scientist, has written a book called *Managing the Commons* describing hundreds of circumstances in which individuals and groups with competing interests have (without the imposition of rules by a higher authority) acted collaboratively to manage common-pool resources wisely (Ostrom 1990). So, while the game theorists assume that countries can be expected to act to maximize their own short-term interests by resisting restrictions aimed at meeting the common good, this is not always the outcome. How else could we explain why the countries of the European Community have unilaterally adopted voluntary targets for CO_2 reduction? In my view, national leaders in the EC have acted because they perceive the problem of global warming to be serious. They are being pressed by internal environmental-advocacy groups to take action, regardless of what the rest of the world decides to do. Indeed, the EC has also moved into a leadership position in defining the terms of the international debate by taking unilateral action. My point is that while there is uncertainty about how atmospheric forces will behave over time, there is also uncertainty about how individuals and nations will behave. The most likely way to motivate action by countries is to allow them to share the benefits and not just the costs of implementing environmental-protection strategies.

More creative linkages connecting costs and benefits that would otherwise be separated in time and place are needed for another reason as well. The impacts of environmental problems and the costs of combating them will not be distributed equally. Some countries do indeed stand to lose more than they will gain—even in the long run. Unless other negotiations, in which these net losses are guaranteed victories, are linked together, loser countries will have good reason to remain on the sidelines or even to sabotage international environmental treaty-making efforts. Thus, short-term economic incentives for acting to protect the global environment must be sought. While the institutional obstacles to linkage may seem insurmountable at first, the advantages are worth the trouble. Linking environmental improvements to the provisions of the General Agreement on Tariffs and Trade (GATT), for example, or to bilateral foreign aid agreements would put more benefits on the table for the nations of the South that find the North's arguments for rain forest protection, for instance, unattractive. Traditional side payments (i.e., cash transfers) are not enough; trades of other kinds (and not just taxes on the gainers) can generate additional value.

One set of countries might be willing to work toward greater energy efficiency (and thereby achieve carbon dioxide reductions) as long as it receives, in return, access to energy-efficient technologies on a subsidized basis. The countries providing this incentive might well benefit by creating new markets for their emerging technologies. Such linkages offer the best prospect for achieving synergistic results. However, all such trades should take account of the fact that each country must be free to follow a development path that it finds suitable. Newly industrialized nations need not replicate the energy choices or the inefficient patterns of development that other nations chose before them.

Up to now, environmental negotiations have been conducted largely in isolation from negotiations on other international issues such as debt, trade, or security. Negotiations sponsored solely by UNEP cannot adequately address linkages between environmentally related actions and other important economic and security-related considerations. Recently, some developing nations have raised the desirability of making such linkages. For nations facing dire poverty, malnutrition, mounting foreign debts, and rampant illiteracy, the long-term and uncertain consequences of environmental deterioration do not carry a sense of urgency. In such instances, linking development opportunities and environmental considerations may provide the needed incentive to cooperation. From a negotiation perspective, the linking of issues can increase the potential for mutual gain. Since the goal of a well-structured negotiation is not to encourage compromise but to find ways of ensuring that all parties are better off if they cooperate, issue linkage ought to be encouraged. Only in this way will there be an opportunity to make convincing connections between benefits and costs in the short term.

Unworkable Concepts of Sovereignty

Most environmental agreements worked out through ad hoc international negotiations include only weak monitoring and enforcement provisions. For example, the International Convention for the Regulation of Whaling (one of the longer-standing international environmental treaties) established a commission to oversee the provisions of the treaty, but failed to give the commission any enforcement powers.

Without effective monitoring and enforcement, implementation of treaties is much more difficult. However, monitoring and enforcement are difficult to achieve because they appear to conflict with the prerogatives of national sovereignty. Countries which otherwise comply with most existing international agreements may have difficulty meeting the kinds of standards set in environmental treaties and thus, may be tempted not to sign.[7] Sovereignty is often used as a shield by countries which fear that they may not be able to meet their treaty obligations.

The involvement of nongovernmental interests both within and separate from official delegations can help to overcome traditional sovereignty arguments against monitoring and enforcement. Environmental stewardship or similar concepts that call for worldwide and multigenerational commitments that transcend national sovereignty are more likely to be supported by nongovernmental interests than by political officeholders who fear encroachment on the prerogatives of nationhood. An approach to treaty making that hangs on the single thread of formal, nation-to-nation interaction will not be as strong as a more elaborate set of interactions that weave together governmental and nongovernmental interests.

An international league of nongovernmental organizations (NGOs) might organize environmental monitoring efforts along the same lines as Amnesty International monitors human rights violations. It could sponsor and instruct monitoring groups within every country. An environmental version of the Red Cross (i.e., the "Green Cross") might play a fact-finding role when ecological disasters occur, as former Soviet leader Gorbachov has suggested. Such roles for NGOs would address concerns about sovereignty since only people *within* each country would monitor that country's compliance with international environmental treaties. The key is to create transparency, as

---

[7] I would not assert that the most important reason for monitoring is that it legitimizes external enforcement. There are many examples of compliance when only self-monitoring is involved. But environmental treaty implementation requires constant readjustments of targets and methods in light of actual results. If reliable indicators of results can not be obtained on a regular basis, environmental treaties are not likely to produce the outcomes intended.

Abram and Antonia Chayes have argued, through publication and dissemination of periodic monitoring results (even if they are self-reported).[8]

Traditional notions of sovereignty conflict with efforts to push each country toward taking greater responsibility for the effects of its actions on the rest of the ecosphere. But these notions are, to some extent, eroding all the time. As countries find themselves increasingly economically interdependent, their sovereignty diminishes. As new satellite technologies allow for global monitoring without direct access to territory, traditional notions of sovereignty are softened.

Although notions of national sovereignty over the management of natural resources within a country's borders are evolving in response to technological and economic change, they still pose a substantial obstacle to effective environmental treaty-making. Only by providing benefits for joining a treaty regime that exceed the costs of remaining apart will concerns about encroachments on sovereignty be overcome. Moreover, through an international network of NGOs it would be possible to increase the transparency of compliance efforts. This, in turn, could eliminate the need for the top-down approach to enforcement that is typically the source of concern about sovereignty.

BROADER APPLICATIONS

I have tried to identify the key barriers to effective environmental treaty-making and to suggest possible ways of overcoming them. To the extent that multilateral cooperation for environmental action shares certain characteristics with other multiparty, multi-issue negotiations, these prescriptive suggestions may have broader application as well.

My primary prescriptions are as follows:

1. Encourage informal information sharing and coalition building among nontraditional allies and networks with shared interests (to bridge the long-standing North-South gap)
2. Use contingent agreements in the face of uncertainty or scientific disagreement
3. Encourage broad-gauged issue linkage (not just side payments) to increase the level of benefits available to those who would otherwise end up as losers
4. Build new networks (inside-outside coalitions) to bring greater internal pressure to overcome parochial conceptions of sovereignty and self-interest.

---

[8] See Chayes and Chayes 1994 and 1993.

CHAPTER SIXTEEN

Barriers to Negotiated Arms Control

Wolfgang Panofsky

INTRODUCTION

S overeign nations should have a common overriding interest in providing for their national security at minimum cost, risk, and other burdens. Therefore, arms control should be an ideal vehicle for resolving potential conflicts of interest between two or more parties through negotiations. National security is not a zero-sum game in that gains in the national security of one nation are attained at the expense of loss of national security of others. Rather, there is an emerging consensus that in the future multipolar world the national security of any one country, such as the United States, cannot be increased at the cost of national insecurity of other countries. Arms control is designed to provide for international management of military activities with these principles in mind.

The fundamental objective of arms control is to draw a boundary between allowed and forbidden military activities. Arms control can be divided into three categories: *quantative, qualitative, and operational.* The first category encompasses those agreements which set numerical ceilings on permitted classes of weaponry, numbers of military personnel, and the like. Qualitative limits can relate to performance of classes of weaponry, restrictions on innovation or modernization, and similar measures. Operational arms control might restrict permissible areas of operation of military forces or the type of maneuvers which may be carried out, and provide for advance notification concerning military exercises, and similar measures.

While there have been some recent successes in negotiated arms control, the overall record has not been encouraging. Agreements which can be

---

This chapter was submitted in final form in April 1992. Therefore the substantive information on arms control status is cut off as of that date. There have indeed been many additional substantive developments which do not affect the principles discussed here.

described by the term "arms control" have paralleled the entire course of military history; the number of such agreements in which the U.S. is a party since World War II is about ten. Nuclear weapons stockpiles have grown from the few weapons of World War II to over fifty thousand, with only a small recent reversal downward. Conventional armaments have grown apace, as have military exports; only the last year (1991) has shown a significant decrease. Thus increased understanding of the barriers to success in negotiated arms control is of clear value.

Negotiated arms control is a *process* comprising many stages. The process involves *internal decision making* on each country's national interest. Then there is the *negotiating process*, followed by the process of *coming into force* of the agreement resulting from negotiation. There is no higher authority which can be charged with *enforcement* of such agreements. Therefore a requirement for *compliance* results which in turn encompasses two major components: *verification* of the conduct of each signatory and the *decision process* for action to respond if doubts about a signatory's compliance arise.

Barriers to success can arise at each of these stages. Moreover, the success of an arms control regime can be impaired by changing political context (note, e.g., the impact of the breakup of the Soviet Union, which previously functioned as a single negotiating "party"), technological obsolescence of treaty provisions, and changes in the political will within each country. Ultimately, no arms control agreement can endure if a major party to the agreement no longer believes that the agreement serves its national interest.

One should recognize that *formally negotiated arms control*, i.e., negotiated by instructed delegations in face-to-face discussion, is not the only mechanism of achieving limits or decreases in armaments, or in controlling other military activities. There can be controls arrived at *without formal process* on weapons by mutual example, or they can be limitations generated by *internal forces* of a political or economic nature. For instance, while some of the mutual force reductions between the former Soviet Union and the United States have been achieved through formal negotiation, others—e.g., the recent withdrawal of short-range ground-based nuclear missiles—have taken place without explicit agreement. A recent example of unilateral but mutual steps was the initiative of President Bush on September 27, 1991, followed by a similar but even more incisive initiative of President Gorbachev on October 5, 1991. Subsequently, President Bush and Boris Yeltsin, the president of the Russian Republic (the legal heir to the former Soviet Union in respect to obligations assumed under arms control agreements) have made further, even more incisive declarations. These initiatives went beyond the formally negotiated treaties signed previously, but some gaps between the reciprocal declaration remain to be narrowed.

Historically, such reductions by mutual example have not generally proven to be durable. In the late 1960s, for example, the U.S. and the Soviet Union agreed to reduce their production capability of fissionable materials for nuclear weapons. But that reduction proved ephemeral because there was no clear agreed basis from which these reductions were to take place; furthermore, without an explicit agreement, the mutually expressed desire for reductions was soon forgotten. We can hope that the recent unilateral, but reciprocal, initiatives of Presidents Bush, Gorbachev, and Yeltsin will fare better.

There is an interesting middle ground between formally negotiated and informally agreed arms control: some arms control agreements are enacted for a fixed period of time (e.g., the Interim SALT I agreement on offensive strategic weapons). Yet after lapse of that period the parties have generally continued to adhere to the provisions, notwithstanding the lack of a legal obligation. A signed but unratified treaty obligates the parties not to violate the treaty in an irreparable fashion, as long as all parties continue to work toward ratification. However, even after President Reagan declared that the U.S. would not pursue ratification of SALT II signed by President Carter, SALT II remained unviolated for all practical purposes until superceded by START.

World military activity is also controlled by internal conditions in each country, notably by budgetary pressures in relation to perceived threats to security. It is the result of such internal forces rather than explicit agreement that world military expenditures have declined by 5 percent in 1990—the first such decrease in decades.

One should be clear to distinguish real arms control from arms transfer restrictions which are tuned to serve perceived national interest. Arms sales to one's friends in parallel with arms transfer restrictions to potential adversaries is not arms control. On the contrary, the increasing use of selective arms sales as a major instrument of foreign policy is an unfortunate development. Nothing illustrates this conflict better than the reaction of the U.S. administration in the aftermath of the Gulf war. On the one hand, the president announced his intent to work toward "arms control" in the Middle East. At the same time, arms sales were announced to some of the Arab states that had collaborated with the United Nations in its action against Iraq. Similarly the various arms transfer control mechanisms such as Coordinating Committee on Multilateral Export Control (COCOM) do not serve genuine arms control, since they selectively applied to the Warsaw Treaty Organization countries during the Cold War era and to some extent even beyond. The excessive use of arms sales as a tool of foreign policy is an example of a major barrier to effective arms control, as are the arms sales driven by economic interest or even necessity. Note that the economic collapse and the demise of centralized control in the Soviet Union have driven independent entrepreneurs into promiscuous arms sales.

In the discussion that follows I will largely restrict myself to *formally negoti-ated* arms control leading to documented agreements among sovereign nations. I will distinguish between those barriers which are inherent to the *process* of negotiated arms control and those which are inherent to the *content* of specific agreements.

TENSIONS—PROCESS

"Solemnity" of Commitment versus Complexity and Delay of the Enactment Process

It is important that agreements on arms control be enshrined at as high a level of solemnity as possible, since throughout the process of enactment and compliance agreements are expected to be opposed by some within each country that is a party to the treaty. Agreements can be either *formal treaties* or *executive agreements*, or they can be *declaratory* on the part of each country after prior informal consultation.

Under the U.S. Constitution the provisions of a treaty are internally and externally binding on the U.S. and preempt all federal, state, or local laws as well as state constitutions. Only the federal Constitution stands above the provisions of an international treaty. Corresponding to the preeminence of a treaty, its enactment has to pass several hurdles. The steps are *position for-mulation* within each country, *negotiation, signature,* and *ratification*. Only after the "instruments of ratification" are deposited is a treaty "in force."

In the United States, ratification of a treaty by the president takes place only with the advice and consent of a two-thirds' majority of the Senate. That consent is often difficult to attain. Opposition is generated both by specific interests which might be impacted adversely by the treaty and by the ideological conviction that covenants with potential adversaries are ill-advised. That opposition is frequently not explicit but focuses on proclaimed treaty defects, such as alleged inadequate verifiability, excessive U.S. con-cessions, etc. Historically it has been easier to obtain ratification of a treaty under a conservative executive branch government than under a liberal one. Once a treaty has been signed by a conservative president, most senators of the same party as the president will support the treaty out of discipline, while liberals will vote out of conviction. Under such conditions, obtaining two-thirds' majority is facilitated. Let me add that to the best of my knowl-edge the U.S. is the only country where ratification requires a two-thirds majority of a branch of the legislature.

The complexity of the ratification process as described raises barriers to agreement in the negotiation itself. Each side is forced to take positions designed to circumvent anticipated future difficulties in ratification. This, in turn, tends to make adoption of more flexible provisions more difficult for each side.

Because of the difficulty of securing ratification, an attempt can be made to lower the barrier to agreement by negotiating an executive agreement rather than a treaty. Such an agreement between heads of state would still be binding on subsequent governments, but would not preempt conflicting laws. Moreover, in order to discourage efforts by the executive branch to bypass the formal treaty-ratification process, the United States Congress has legislated that specifically in the area of arms control, executive agreements must be approved by a simple majority but by *both* houses of Congress. Moreover, use of an executive agreement rather than the treaty process by the executive branch is resented by the U.S. Senate, since it bypasses its constitutional prerogative; therefore in general the executive branch is discouraged politically from pursuing that route.

Almost all treaties conclude with an abrogation provision which states that if one side or the other considers its "supreme national interests" endangered by continued adherence to the treaty, then it may abrogate the treaty after having given advance notice, usually specified as six months. Such a provision is intended to give an explicit prescription for abrogation, thereby discouraging forces on each side opposed to continuation of the treaty from gradually eroding adherence to the treaty by progressive disregard.[1] At the same time potential abrogation makes it necessary that each side complete a thorough "breakout analysis," that is, a conservative examination of the state of its security if the treaty were abrogated on short notice. Such breakout analysis may lead to negotiating positions which create additional barriers to agreement.

The interests of arms control can also be served by formal declarations of intent without either explicit negotiations or demonstrable military measures. Prominent in this respect in recent times have been the "no first use" declarations, specifically in regard to nuclear weapons. Both the former Soviet Union and China have formally declared that they would not be the first to use nuclear weapons, and paradoxically Israel has declared they would not be the first to "introduce" nuclear weapons into the Middle East (!). The United States has resisted such a "no first use" declaration; it has been NATO policy to threaten the first use of nuclear weapons in case a Warsaw Pact invasion with conventional forces threatened to become suc-

---

[1] An interesting historical example is the Rush-Bagot Treaty enacted in 1817, which limited warships on the Great Lakes. This early arms-control treaty was progressively violated and threatened with abrogation; it was modified by executive agreement but in its total impact caused a great deal of friction between the United States and Canada without significantly limiting naval deployments in the Great Lakes. It has never been abrogated.

cessful. With that threat gone, arguments for a "no first use" declaratory policy have been strengthened. However, there are problems. The first is credibility. One can reasonably doubt that in case of war such a declaration would be binding in any way. The second is the possibility of misunderstanding: Might a nuclear "no first use" declaration also signal to those countries to which the U.S. has given security guarantees a weakened U.S. resolve to provide nonnuclear military assistance when needed?

The Negotiating Process: Narrow versus Broad Delegation to Negotiators

Formal negotiation of arms control agreements is the task of instructed delegations, usually headed by an individual given ambassadorial status. Official instructions to the delegation are generally the product of an interagency process within each government. That interagency process, in turn, requires the taking of positions by each of the agencies of government involved in national security. In the U.S. these are the Department of State, the Department of Defense, the Joint Chiefs of Staff, the Central Intelligence Agency, the Arms Control and Disarmament Agency, and the Department of Energy if nuclear weapons issues are involved. These agencies view potential treaty provisions as they relate to their particular mission.

Frequently, differences among agency positions at home are at least as difficult to resolve as differences in position across the negotiating table among the nations concerned. The resolution of differences among agencies takes various forms: under different administrations a variety of interagency "backstopping" groups are constituted, and interagency studies are commissioned with one of the agencies in the lead, with the goal to generate agency consensus. The National Security Council attempts to reconcile remaining interagency differences to the maximum extent possible; failing that, the national security adviser, acting in his capacity as chief of the staff of the National Security Council, identifies residual differences and submits them to the president for resolution. Only after this process has been completed can instructions to the delegations be issued. Moreover, in recent times the delegations themselves include members nominated by and reporting to the diverse government departments; the staff supporting the work of the delegations also has representatives from government agencies. Such divided loyalties of the "backstopping" staff at home and the delegation abroad can and frequently do inhibit the process, but they are a necessary consequence of the U.S. pluralistic political process.

In parallel with the internal formulation of policy leading to instructions, there must be consultation with other countries whose interests are affected by the negotiations, but who are not parties to the negotiations. For example, although the other members of NATO were not parties to the START treaty, their interests were definitely involved and in fact some of them were "basing countries" for the U.S. forces affected by START. Thus consultation with nonparties is frequently essential, and such consultation can and frequently does generate serious obstacles, or at least delays to the process of generating instructions to delegations. A choice has to be made between the increased complexities of a multilateral negotiation and a bilateral process requiring extensive consultation.

The instructions generated through this complex process can span the range from very narrow to quite broad. If they are very narrow, in effect the delegations are reduced to a mere channel of communication between the home governments of the parties, with little room for actual negotiation. If instructions are broad, there is indeed room for negotiation, but then there is a risk that negotiation will result in a product which may ultimately be unacceptable to one or the other home government. Thus, barriers to the success of the negotiation can result, through instructions which either are too narrow or too broad. There is a further danger (which has only rarely become a reality) that the negotiators may exceed their instructions, leading to an agreement which is subsequently disowned by the home government (and at times leading to recall of the negotiator!).

In practice, ostensibly formal negotiations have both a formal and an informal component. In addition to the plenary sessions involving the appointed delegations, there are working groups charged with ironing out treaty details or with supplying detailed technical substance. In addition, there is deliberate use of conversations in the corridors or at social occasions for exploratory "feelers" in search of flexibility among the parties. Each delegate tends to forward memoranda documenting such conversations to its instructing agency at home, and such memoranda are factors in formulating revised positions.

The above gives a rough overview of the formal negotiating process. The factors enumerated clearly indicate that the process can become extended in time and can generate obstacles as well as overcome them.

The "Endgame" in Negotiations

Frequently the core provisions of a treaty are agreed upon early in the negotiations, but subsequent agreement on the more detailed provisions proves elusive. Disagreement on details tends to elevate the importance of such details beyond their true military significance; the process then becomes a contest of political will as to which side makes concessions on them. A criticism frequently raised during the treaty-ratification process accuses the home negotiating team of having made too many concessions; there is of course no objective way to assess the "concession balance" during negotiations. In consequence, the need to resolve details has made some treaty negotiations take many years. To shorten that process, agreement is frequently sought at higher levels, for instance at the level of the secretary of state or minister of foreign affairs (the ministerial level), or at the level of the president or prime minister (summit meetings), which strengthen the will to agree. The scheduling of ministerial meetings, and even more so summit meetings, constitutes a de facto deadline by which agreement has to be reached to make it possible for the principals to have something to sign.

This again raises a tension of values. Negotiating under a deadline generates a need to compromise, a compromise which with the benefit of hindsight might be inadvisable. A deadline also may lead to errors in detailed technical substance. Yet without such a deadline it would frequently have been impossible to obtain reasonable closure on a timely basis. Thus the dynamics of this "endgame" in negotiations are the principal tools available to overcome ultimate barriers to agreement.

Barriers to Agreement Due to External Factors

It would be naive to assume that the enactment of an arms control agreement was controlled entirely by the intrinsic merit of that agreement as it affects the national security of the parties. Arms control is intertwined with the entire political process. Thus, many barriers to agreement arise from factors which do not have a logical connection to the content of the agreement but which nevertheless play a major role.

It is obvious that if the general political relations among the nations negotiating conditions for arms control deteriorate, then reaching agreement is much more difficult or impossible to reach, even if it were in the national interest of each party to agree. As a minimum there have to be civil relations among the parties; at best there can be a climate of mutual trust and commonality of interest. A classical example is the situation at the end of the Carter administration. The United States and the Soviet Union had signed the SALT II agreement; shortly thereafter the Soviets invaded Afghanistan. This led to a profound deterioration in relations, and President Carter withdrew the SALT II treaty from the Senate for further consideration of giving advice and consent on ratification. Analytically, the merits of the SALT II treaty were hardly affected by the Afghanistan invasion, yet politically it became infeasible to proceed.

Similar disruptions of the arms control process have occurred throughout the U.S.–Soviet relationship. Negotiations on the Nuclear Test Ban were halted when Khruschev "dropped the shoe" after the U-2 was shot down over the Soviet Union. The fluctuation of relations among negotiating partners, together with the complexities of the negotiating process, has been and is expected to continue to be an obstacle to reaching agreement.

Today we are facing the opposite situation: enmity and conflicting interests between the U.S. and the remaining structures in the former Soviet Union have disappeared. Therefore the U.S. has been willing to proceed more rapidly and to drastically lower its standards of verification. Yet the breakdown of centralized government in the former Soviet Union has generated a new barrier: While legally the United States and Russia have agreed that Russia is inheriting all arms control obligations incurred by the former Soviet Union, there is lack of clarity on many details. For example, the ratification process of START at the time of this writing (end of April 1992) is being delayed. The reason is that there is no agreement as to whether the non-Russian republics in which nuclear weapons nominally under the control of the Commonwealth of Independent States (CIS) are located should sign an agreement on the future of these weapons with Russia as a precondition of bilateral ratification, or whether these three republics (Ukraine, Belarus, and Varokston) should be independent parties to such an agreement also involving the United States. The issue here is that in essence the fate of important steps in arms control is becoming hostage to the settlement of disputes among republics of the former Soviet Union.

TENSIONS—SUBSTANCE OF ARMS CONTROL AGREEMENTS

Balance between the Assets and Liabilities of Weapons

Possession of weaponry and military forces implies both assets and liabilities. The assets are their potential value to the military mission, meaning the threat of force and the ability to use it in furtherance of national objectives. The liabilities are economic costs; diversion of skilled manpower; environmental and other impacts of the infrastructure needed to produce, store, and deploy the weapons systems; and the potential escalatory effect of weapons in inducing adverse responses by other nations.

Recently, further costs have been recognized. If in the future, either through negotiated arms control or for other reasons, existing weapons stockpiles are to be reduced, then the cost of the effort to destroy weapons may exceed that of their acquisition. A case in point is the chemical weapons stockpiles of the U.S. and the Soviet Union. Both countries have stockpiled vast quantities of chemical military stockpiles and munitions, containing thirty thousand and forty thousand tons of agents for the U.S. and Russia, respectively. The countries have now agreed to destroy their stockpiles, but technical obstacles to doing so have turned out to be much larger than estimated; costs for each country will exceed several billion dollars. A further cost stems from the need to safeguard excess existing stockpiles and critical raw materials and to protect existing weapons systems to prevent them from falling into unauthorized hands, or to prevent escape of noxious substances into the environment. A case in point here is the huge nuclear weapons arsenals, more than fifty thousand nuclear warheads worldwide, of which over 95 percent are in the hands of the United States and four republics of the former Soviet Union. While any valid mission for numbers of weapons this large appears even more remote, their very existence constitutes a threat in that they have to be protected against unauthorized use, hostile takeover, loss of control (such as is perceived to have occurred during the recent Soviet coup), proliferation of independent control as the Soviet Union disintegrates into autonomous states, and capture by terrorists or by insurgent groups. Major environmental problems from the vast nuclear-fuel-cycle complex required to support this large an inventory have recently been uncovered in the United States which may require remedial actions costing in the $100 billion range; similar, probably even larger, problems exist on the Russian side.

A balance between the assets and liabilities of weapons systems is required for formulating reasonable goals for negotiated arms control. However, a proper balance is naturally a subject of a wide spectrum of opinion. The temptation must be resisted to consider it "conservative" to acquire or retain weapons in excess of numbers corresponding to that balance. Conversely, the temptation must also be resisted to necessarily assume that a smaller number of weapons would make war less likely. A balance means just that; while judgments differ as to where the correct point of balance may be, there is no a priori reason to assume that deviating from that point in any one direction is preferable.

Naturally, the optimal balance point changes in time with political, economical, and military developments. There is little question that the splintering of the Soviet Union has lowered the value of justifiable nuclear weapons stockpiles, or of troop deployments overseas. New qualitative technical developments can compensate for decreased numbers of troops and weapons. Yet the social inertia and the political and economic power of institutions tends to induce a substantial time lag for readjusting the balance to new realities. This inertia has proven to be a difficult barrier to the formulation of an arms control agenda matching changing circumstances.

The Tensions between Narrow and Broad Provisions in an Agreement

The most recently signed arms control treaty, the START agreement, is seven hundred single-spaced pages in length. It could well be criticized as being excessively specific and detailed, in particular in the specificity of its verification provisions. In contrast, other agreements may be judged excessively broad. For instance, the Biological Weapons Convention, which was signed in 1972 and entered into force in 1975, fails to provide any specific verification measures. It permits biological weapons research activities while forbidding stockpiling and deployment of weapons, without, however, specifying quantities of biological agents which might correspond to either allowed or forbidden activities.

Whether treaty provisions may be narrow or broad, there will always be a gray area where differences in interpretation are expected to arise. This phenomenon is of course common to domestic law; in that case it is the function of the courts to interpret ambiguities of law. In the case of treaties no strictly analogous institution exists. If the negotiation process attempts to reduce the gray areas to a minimum, a very detailed treaty may result. Excessive detail of the treaty then increases the risk of the treaty's obsolescence either through technical or scientific developments or through political changes in the world. Excessive ambiguity defers unresolved issues into the future. Thus a tension exists between the extremes of creating excessive ambiguity and excessive precision, and this tension in turn can result in barriers to agreement.

In case ambiguity in treaty language generates a subsequent dispute, barriers to successful compliance can arise. In order to resolve such disputes, a hierarchy of additional factors will have to be considered in interpreting the treaty. These are the negotiating record, the patterns and practices of the parties since enactment of the treaty, and the testimony given by government officials during the ratification process. The full negotiating record is often not publicly available and its usefulness is impaired by the fact that the negotiators may have changed their positions, often dramatically, during the negotiating process. This hierarchy came into public view through the attempt by the Reagan administration to "reinterpret" the ABM Treaty of 1972 by introducing its so-called broad interpretation; some early Soviet positions in the negotiating record were selected in support of that interpretation. Opponents of the "broad" interpretation pointed out that government witnesses, when submitting the treaty for ratification, submitted testimony which clearly supported a "narrow" interpretation. The Senate rightfully invoked that such government testimony should preempt out-of-context quotations from the negotiating record, since otherwise the Senate would in fact be deceived about the treaty content for which it gave advice and consent for ratification.

Recognizing the fact that gray areas in treaty provisions will necessarily exist, most treaties include provisions for the establishment of a consultative commission. Such commissions cannot have binding judiciary functions; they are charged with resolving differences in interpretation of treaty language or of the compliance record whenever ambiguities arise or whenever charges of perceived noncompliance are filed. What actions to take in case of disagreements on interpretation or in response to charges of noncompliance has to be determined politically in each country; that decision ultimately must choose between living with the ambiguity or alleged noncompliance and abrogating the treaty. Such consultative commissions are essential to lowering the barriers to arms control success during the "compliance" phase.

Compliance

An arms control agreement constitutes an international covenant binding on the parties to the agreement. Assuring compliance with that covenant generates tensions not dissimilar to those inherent to law enforcement subsequent to enactment of domestic legislation. There is, however, an essential difference: in the case of domestic law, compliance can be enforced by the courts, which can ascertain the facts regarding alleged transgressions or resolve ambiguities in interpretation of law and can then order enforcement. Such a binding adjudicatory mechanism is absent in the case of arms control and must be replaced either by a consultative process or by unilateral response in the face of political realities. Thus the judgment whether a proposed arms control agreement serves the interest of national security has to be based on an assessment of whether national security would be better off with or without enactment of the agreement, *taking a realistic anticipated level of compliance into account*. That level of compliance, in turn, will be related to the means of verification of compliance which are available to each nation, or which are specifically provided for in the arms control agreement.

Indeed, verification has been probably the largest *ostensible* barrier to enactment of arms control agreements. Yet the issue of verification has been greatly abused by those who wish to bolster their respective positions on the substantive provisions of the agreement. We even hear voices objecting to arms control agreements because verification cannot detect any and all violations. Yet it would indeed be paradoxical if on the domestic scene objections were raised against having murder be illegal because not all murderers can be brought to trial!

There has been much debate about "adequacy" of verification. The *standards* of verification cannot be established on absolute principles but should be related to the military significance of potential transgressions. In general, "adequate"[2] verification implies that a transgression which would invalidate the arms control objectives of the agreement or which would constitute a major risk to national security should not remain undetected and unidentified for a sufficiently long time to prevent effective remedial action. Once such standards are understood, there is still tension between the costs and

---

[2] or "effective," to use the term introduced in the Reagan administration.

efficacy of various methods of verification, similar to the debate on how much police protection or how many jails the nation should afford in the domestic context.

Costs for verification are measured not only by economic burdens but also by *intrusiveness*. Again, this is similar to the tension in domestic law enforcement, where we have the tension between the effectiveness of peace officers and the civil liberties and privacy of the citizen. Verification can be by "national technical means (NTM)," which refers to technical measures such as satellites, radars, air sampling, etc., outside the national boundaries of the country to be inspected. Such systems may be costly, but they are viewed as nonintrusive. However, many arms control provisions cannot be "adequately" verified by NTM only, and various classes of inspection measures must be provided for.

Before the Gorbachev revolution, inspection measures were heavily resisted by the Soviet Union. More recently the former Soviet Union has been more flexible in accepting inspection measures, at times even more so than the Western countries. A reason why inspection constitutes a problem for the West is that not only military but also commercial secrets may be in need of protection. In addition, "anytime, anyplace" inspections raise profound constitutional issues. Should a foreign inspector be permitted to search for treaty violations without a warrant requiring "reasonable cause," while searches by domestic law enforcement agents are restricted under constitutional guarantees?

For all the above reasons, discussions on verification have been contentious. In fact verification issues have become so prominent that at times they have become more visible politically than the actual substance of arms control agreements. A prominent example is the debate about restrictions on nuclear testing, which has continued from the 1950s until today. Serious negotiations commenced in 1958 when the Soviets and Americans convened a Conference of Experts to discuss verification issues associated with cessation of nuclear tests; characteristically, verification was placed on the negotiating agenda prior to substantive provisions. Attainment of a comprehensive nuclear-test ban ostensibly foundered on a disagreement between the United States and the Soviets in the early 1960s as to whether three or seven inspections a year would be acceptable; this was clearly a pretense to cover deeper disagreements. In 1963 the United States, the Soviet Union, and the United Kingdom signed a treaty prohibiting nuclear tests under water, in the atmosphere, and in outer space, but left underground testing unrestrained. This agreement was to be verified by national technical means only, and thus exacted no costs in terms of intrusiveness; but it also did not result in any significant impediments to the development of nuclear devices. In other words, ostensibly driven by verification difficulties, an agreement was reached which was hardly any arms control at all, although it was benign as an environmental measure in that worldwide radioactive fallout from nuclear weapons was reduced by two orders of magnitude.

The recently ratified Threshold Test Ban Treaty limits the explosive power of underground nuclear test explosions to a maximum yield of 150 kilotons. Interestingly enough, that agreement, signed in 1972, remained unratified until 1990, with the barrier to agreement ostensibly being the precision with which the 150kt threshold could be measured. The accuracy of such measurements has steadily improved, but U.S. administrations continued to judge that accuracy to be insufficient unless much more intrusive observations at the test site could be made. The Soviets finally agreed to these measures, and the treaty was ratified. There is no question that the issue of precision of measurement of the threshold was simply a pretense put forward by those in the U.S. who were opposed to its provisions.

The Establishment of Quantitative Limits

Precise numerical specifications for the numbers of weapons or troops required for a specific mission cannot be established based on rigorous analysis. Outcomes of potential military conflict are sensitive not only to such numbers but also to other factors, most of them not predictable—among them political context; morale of troops; adequacy of logistic support, terrain, and weather; incidental presence of civilian populations; etc. Yet in the face of this imprecision, quantitative arms control frequently requires specified numerical limits. As a result, the negotiating process gives a political significance to the numbers which their military importance does not deserve. In other words, the numerical content of an arms control proposal becomes a political object of negotiation in itself. This situation in turn, can lead to verification issues. Once numbers are specified, then demands are raised to verify compliance with the exact numbers, even if this may have little significance militarily. The controversy about the precision of measurement of the yield threshold of underground explosions mentioned above is a case in point.

Total elimination of a whole class of systems is easier to deal with in an arms control context than specification of numbers. One of the great advantages of the Intermediate Nuclear Force (INF) Treaty was that it eliminated a whole class of missiles, rather than specifying a numerical legal limit. START eliminates no categories entirely, but sets numerical limits for categories and subcategories. Therefore the complexity of verification provisions in the INF Treaty are a great deal less than those provided for in the recently signed START Agreement.

Whether specified numerical limits are zero or not, the problem of *categori-*

zation of the classes to which such limits apply can become a source of controversy. The boundaries between intermediate-range nuclear forces, short-range nuclear forces, and strategic nuclear forces are usually given in terms of range. Yet the range which a given delivery vehicle can attain depends on technical factors, in particular the payload carried. Thus categorization frequently requires negotiated technical specifications or specific designation of permissible vehicles by type, rather than specifying a performance parameter like attainable range. In specifying numbers of permitted systems, ancillary information frequently must also be given. For example, does the numerical limit apply only to systems deployed, or also to those available for rapid reload, or in stockpile? How much modification within each category is permissible? Defining such boundaries has proven to be a significant barrier to agreement in several past treaty negotiations.

The Establishment of Qualitative Limits

Military effectiveness can depend as much on qualitative performance as on total numbers and numerical specifications of deployed systems. Such items as reliability, accuracy, the interaction between people and military equipment, and other such factors can become crucial. Most arms control provisions tend to permit what is called "modernization" of existing systems—that is, steps designed to improve qualitative performance without affecting basic mission. Yet this generates the problem of distinguishing between "modernization" and creation of "new types" of equipment of fundamentally different performance.

An additional complication is that limits on qualitative upgrade of performance are generally impossible to verify and therefore difficult to incorporate into an arms control agreement. The problem of distinguishing new types from modernization has led to much controversy and delay in bringing arms control negotiations to a satisfactory conclusion. Both in START and in the signed but never ratified SALT II treaty, new types were defined by restricting the variation of linear dimensions of missiles and their warheads and the throw weight carried by such missiles. The establishment of such limits is not free from controversy. For instance, what is to be included in throw weight? How does one account for possible instrumentation and diagnostic packages carried with the usual missile payload? What defines the dimensional limits? Is it verifiability—that is, the ability to measure such quantities with available technical means? Or should verification be based on mutual trust that declared parameters are correct?

There is a similar and even more fundamental issue associated with *multipurpose* systems. The START and SALT treaties restrict *nuclear* weapon systems but leave systems capable of delivering conventional high explosives or chemical munitions unaffected.[3] But how about systems capable of delivering either? Can they be distinguished, and can one prevent easy convertibility from one mission to the other?

I will not attempt here to outline the various means devised to respond to the gamut of questions listed. They have been addressed to a more or less satisfactory extent in recent treaties. In some cases answers have actually resulted in the requirement to introduce specific modifications in delivery vehicles which restrict the easy convertibility from one mission to the other, or which generate external observables through which other parties can distinguish the various types. However, in this field possibly more than in any other there is a danger of impeding agreement by insistence on excessive detail. Judgment is needed to cut off such detail when the military importance of further specificity is recognized to be less than the political and military value of reaching agreement.

Operational Arms Control

Operational arms control is intended to restrict operational practices of the parties to the agreement and to provide for exchange of communication in order to build confidence and to avoid misunderstandings and escalatory responses to operational practices. Codes of conduct for this type of activity can at times lend themselves to formal agreements. Items in the communications category have been formally agreed upon; this includes the establishment of the so-called hot line which provides for rapid communication among parties in the former Soviet Union and the United States in case of crisis who can, in turn, communicate with the heads of state. Another example is the agreement on the establishment of crisis management centers which permit communication among high-ranking military officers of all sides to assist in resolving misunderstandings in time of crisis.

An interesting issue is whether operational arms control should be negotiated directly on a military-to-military basis, rather than through State Department / foreign ministry channels, which are normally charged with the conduct of foreign affairs. Since much operational arms control deals with details of military conduct, there is much advantage to having such negotiations carried out directly by military officers. The 1990 agreement on avoiding dangerous military incidents was negotiated directly by general officers of the Soviet Union and the United States. Those negotiations resulted incidentally in great personal rapport between the principal officers

---

[3] Note, however, that the INF Treaty forbids nuclear *and* nonnuclear Ground Launched Cruise Missiles (GLCMs) alike.

involved (General Bolatko on the Soviet side and General Butler on the American side) in addition to providing a long list of measures conducive to avoiding military incidents which have bedeviled relationships of the super-powers in the past. A fundamental issue arises here: Do formal negotiations among senior military officers compromise civilian control of the military in some respects, or undermine the authority of the president for the conduct of foreign relations? Because of such concerns, the range of agreements which may be negotiated through the direct military-to-military channel is limited.

Operational arms control is a positive measure. Yet it also generates opposition by those who feel that secrecy and surprise yield an essential military advantage. Operational arms control produces just the opposite: it increases what in modern terminology is designated as "transparency," that is, making the intents of the potential adversarial parties more open to one another. It is this tension of values which may generate a barrier, depending on the wisdom of its resolution.

CONCLUSIONS

This chapter deals with identifying "barriers" to negotiated arms control, and therefore its purpose is to identify *negative* factors in arms control process and substance. Yet that identification leads to a number of *positive*, more optimistic recommendations designed to lower such barriers.

Multiplicity of Process for Pursuing Arms Control

In the preceding discussions a number of methods for the pursuit of arms control were identified. They should not be viewed as competing; rather, there can be a symbiotic relationship among all of these methods. The declaration of President Bush in September of 1991 included *both* unilateral withdrawals of tactical nuclear forces (with hopes for reciprocity) and a call for negotiated agreements on such items as improved control of nuclear forces. Successful enactment of formal arms control improves the climate for imposing further limitations by mutual example or agreements on the operational level. All such measures improve the political atmosphere. Moreover, there exists a whole class of activities generally described as "confidence-building measures" which are designed to signal potential adversaries that the intent of the parties is to minimize the risk of military conflict. The totality of all such activities is considerably more valuable than the sum of their parts.

Governmental Organization

Arms control is an integral part of the national security process; it is not "disarmament" as conventionally understood. Just as the function of the Defense Department is to increase national security by greater military preparedness and as the function of the State Department is to increase national security by improved foreign relations, it is the function of the U.S. Arms Control and Disarmament Agency (ACDA) to enhance national security by minimizing the dangers and burdens of armaments. It is essential that these voices—and similar voices in other countries—feed into the presidential decision-making process on a coequal basis. ACDA was created in this spirit, but more recently its role has in practice become ancillary to either the Department of Defense (in the Reagan administration) or the State Department. It would be helpful in overcoming the internal institutional barriers toward arms control if the independent voice of ACDA could be restored.

The Use of Existing Mechanisms

There has been a tendency to reinvent new mechanisms for the enactment of each specific agreement; methods for dealing with arms control issues have changed substantially among succeeding U.S. administrations. Barriers would be easier to overcome if existing mechanisms were more fully exploited than they have been in the past. Each treaty enacted in recent times provides for a *consultative commission* established under distinct formats in connection with each agreement. These commissions are to undertake mutual consultation with the goal to resolve ambiguities in treaty interpretation and address charges of noncompliance. The consultative commissions generally also have limited powers to amend treaty provisions. No U.S. administration has used the consultative commissions for significant treaty amendments or additions. These consultative commissions should be used more extensively; they have been underutilized.

It is unavoidable that compliance issues will arise. Addressing these in a nonconfrontational manner but in a problem-solving spirit is clearly desirable in the interest of enhancing the effectiveness of the arms control process. Public accusations of noncompliance or unilateral reinterpretation of treaty language are counterproductive. Some of the identified problems would be easier to overcome within the framework of the consultative commissions than in more public forums.

An example of a counterproductive process is the annual "Report on Soviet Noncompliance with Arms Control Agreements" submitted by the president under congressional mandate. That report, of which the latest version is dated April 9, 1992 (when there was no longer a Soviet Union!), publicly recites a "worst case" interpretation of alleged conduct—hardly a constructive process in overcoming barriers to agreement.

The agencies charged with enhancing national security will by their nature have adversary interests, at least from their respective parochial stances. As a result, formulation of arms control positions within each government is a difficult and time-consuming process. Effectiveness of the process would be enhanced if more use were made of independent groups advising the head of state. In the U.S. the General Advisory Committee (GAC) was established for just that purpose, but it has fallen into disuse for its intended function. Similarly, past Presidential Science Advisory Committees have dedicated substantial efforts to arms control, but recently this has not been the case.

The above discussion has related primarily to the hurdles encountered in bilateral or multilateral negotiations. There exist international bodies which can and do serve as forums for arms control discussions to supplement specific dedicated negotiations. The United Nations has a Disarmament Commission which meets periodically. This commission has been used primarily as a forum for national leaders to state their position on pending disarmament issues; it has rarely been used as a forum for negotiations to solve problems. At times such public statements have hardened the parties' positions rather than laying down a path to solutions. Following the recent strengthening of the UN, this pattern could well change for the better.

Easing the General Political Context

It is obvious that the significance of all the barriers cited in this discussion would diminish with overall easing of international tensions. National security has many dimensions—economic, political, ecological, as well as military. The change from a bipolar to a multipolar world brought on by the collapse of the Warsaw Treaty Organization led by an authoritarian Soviet Union has lessened the global importance of any one potential confrontation, and has deflated the relative military dimension of national security. This, in turn, should lower the severity of the level of conflicting interests, which has constituted the prime barrier toward achieving meaningful arms control. The recent changes should facilitate successful arms control. The importance of negotiated arms control is not lessened by these recent developments, since solemnity of commitment offers protection against the impact of a future potential deterioration of relations.

REFERENCES

Abelson, R. P. (1981). Psychological status of the script concept. *American Psychologist* 37(7): 715–29.

Abelson, R. P., and Rosenberg, M. J. (1958). Symbolic psycho-logic: A model of attitudinal cognition. *Behavior Science* 3: 1–13.

Adams, J. S. (1963). Toward an understanding of inequity. *Journal of Abnormal and Social Psychology* 67(5): 422–36.

——— (1965). Inequity in social exchange. In L. Berkowitz, ed., *Advances in experimental social psychology*, vol. 2. New York: Academic Press.

Akerlof, G. (1970). The market for "lemons": Qualitative uncertainty and the market mechanism. *Quarterly Journal of Economics* 84(3): 488–500.

Alpert, M., and Raiffa, H. (1982). A progress report on the training of probability assessors. In D. Kahneman, P. Slovic, and A. Tversky, eds., *Judgment under uncertainty: Heuristics and biases*. Cambridge, England: Cambridge University Press.

Arnold, III, J. (1986). Assessing capital risk: You can't be too conservative. *Harvard Business Review* 64(5): 113–121.

Aronson, E. (1969). The theory of cognitive dissonance: A current perspective. In L. Berkowitz, ed., *Advances in experimental social psychology*, vol. 4. New York: Academic Press.

Arrow, K. (1963). *Social choice and individual values*. New York: John Wiley.

Austin, W. (1980). Friendship and fairness: Effects of type of relationship and task performance on choice of distribution rules. *Personality and Social Psychology Bulletin* 6(3): 402–8.

Axelrod, R. M. (1984). *The evolution of cooperation*. New York: Basic Books.

Ball, S. B., Bazerman, M. H., and Carroll, J. S. (1991). An evaluation of learning in the bilateral winner's curse. *Organizational Behavior and Human Decision Processes* 48(1): 1–22.

Barley, S. (1991). Contextualizing conflict: Notes on the anthropology of dispute and negotiation. In M. H. Bazerman, R. J. Lewicki, and B. H. Sheppard (eds.), *Handbook of research in negotiation*, vol. 3. Greenwich, Conn.: JAI Press.

Barrett, S. (1991a). Economic analysis of international environmental agreements:

Lessons for a global warming treaty. In *Responding to climate change: Selected economic issues.* Paris: Organization for Economic Cooperation and Development, Environment Committee.

——— (1991b). Reaching a CO_2 emission limitation agreement for the community: Implications for equity and cost-effectiveness. Mimeo. Commission of the European Communities, Directorate-General for Economic and Financial Affairs, September 1991.

Bartlett, F. C. (1932). *Remembering: A study in experimental and social psychology.* Cambridge, England: Cambridge University Press.

Bazerman, M. H. (1994). *Judgment in managerial decision making,* 3rd ed. New York: John Wiley.

——— (1993). Fairness, social comparison, and irrationality. In J. Murnighan ed., *Social psychology in organizations: Advances in theory and research.* Englewood Cliffs, N.J.: Prentice-Hall.

Bazerman, M. H., and Carroll, J. S. (1987). Negotiator cognition. *Research in organizational behavior* 9: 247–288.

Bazerman, M. H., Loewenstein, G. F., and White, S. B. (1992). Psychological determinants of utility in competitive contexts: The impact of elicitation procedure. *Administrative Science Quarterly* 37: 220–40.

Bazerman, M. H., Magliozzi, T., and Neale, M. A. (1985). The acquisition of an integrative response in a competitive market. *Organizational Behavior and Human Performance* 34: 294–313.

Bazerman, M. H., and Neale, M. A. (1982). Improving negotiation effectiveness under final offer arbitration: The role of selection and training. *Journal of Applied Psychology* 67(5): 543–48.

——— (1983). Heuristics in negotiation: Limitations to effective dispute resolution. In M. H. Bazerman and R. J. Lewicki, eds., *Negotiating in organizations.* Beverly Hills, Calif.: Sage Publications.

——— (1991). Negotiation rationality and negotiation cognition: The interactive roles of prescriptive and descriptive research. In H. P. Young ed., *Negotiation analysis.* Ann Arbor: University of Michigan Press.

——— (1992). The role of fairness considerations and relationships in a judgmental perspective of negotiation. In Arrow et al, eds., *Barriers to the negotiated resolution of conflict.* New York: W. W. Norton.

——— (1992). *Negotiating rationally.* New York: The Free Press.

Bazerman, M. H., Schroth, H., Pradham, P., Diekmann, K., and Tenbrunsel, A. (in press). Inconsistent preferences in job acceptance: The role of social comparison processes and procedural justice. *Organizational Behavior and Human Decision Processes.*

Beard, C. (1986). *An economic interpretation of the Constitution of the United States.* Reprinted with a new Introduction by Forrest McDonald. New York: The Free Press.

Bell, D. E., Raiffa, H., and Tversky, A. (1988). Descriptive, normative, and prescriptive interactions in decision making. In D. E. Bell, H. Raiffa, and A. Tversky, eds., *Decision making: Descriptive, normative, and prescriptive interactions.* 9–30. New York: Cambridge University Press.

Bendor, J., Kramer, R. M., and Stout, S. (1991). When in doubt . . . Cooperation in a noisy prisoner's dilemma. *Journal of Conflict Resolution* 35(4): 691–719.

Benedick, R. E. (1990a). The Montreal ozone treaty: Implications for global warming (Symposium on International Environmental Law). *American University Journal of International Law and Policy* 5(2): 227–34.

———— (1990b). Ozone diplomacy. *Issues in Science and Technology* 6(1): 43–50.

———— (1991). *Ozone diplomacy: New directions in safeguarding the planet.* Cambridge, Mass.: Harvard University Press.

Berkowitz, L., and Walster, E. (1976). Equity theory: Towards a general theory of social interaction. In L. Berkowitz and E. Walster, eds., *Advances in Experimental Social Psychology*, Vol. 9. New York: Academic Press.

Bernstein, A. (1990). *Grounded: Frank Lorenzo and the destruction of Eastern Airlines.* New York: Simon & Schuster.

Bercovitch, J., and Rubin, J. Z. (eds.) (1992). *Mediation in international relations: Multiple approaches to conflict management.* New York: W. W. Norton.

Bies, R. J. (1987). The predicament of injustice: The management of moral outrage. *Research in organizational behavior* 9: 289–319.

Bies, R. J., and Moag, J. S. (1986). Interactional justice. In Lewicki, R. J., Sheppard, B. H., & Bazerman, M. H., eds., *Research in negotiation in organizations.* Greenwich, Conn.: JAI Press, Inc., vol. i.

Binmore, K. (1987). Nash bargaining theory II. In K. Binmore and P. Dasgupta, eds., *The economics of bargaining.* New York: Basil Blackwell.

Binmore, K., Rubinstein, A., and Wolinsy, A. (1986). The Nash bargaining solution in economic modelling. *Rand Journal of Economics* 17(2): 176–88.

Bohm, P. (1990, September). Efficiency issues and the Montreal protocol on CFCs. Environment Working Paper 40. Washington, D.C.: World Bank.

Boles, T. L., and Messick, D. M. (1990). Accepting unfairness: Temporal influence on choice. In K. Borcherding, O. Larichev, and D. M. Messick, eds., *Contemporary issues in decision making.* Amsterdam: North Holland, 375–90.

Bolton, G. E. (1991). A comparative model of bargaining: theory and evidence. *American Economic Review* 81(5): 1096–1136.

Brehm, J. W. (1966). *A theory of psychological reactance.* New York: Academic Press.

Brehm, S. S., and Brehm, J. W. (1981). *Psychological reactance: A theory of freedom and control.* New York: Academic Press.

Brock, J. (1982). *Bargaining beyond impasse.* Boston: Auburn House Publishing Company.

Brenner, L., Koehler, D., and Tversky, A. (1992). *On the evaluation of one-sided evidence.* Working Paper. Stanford: Stanford University Press.

Broecker, W. S. (1987). Unpleasant surprises in the greenhouse. *Nature* 328 (6126), 123–26.

Bruner, J. S. (1957a). Going beyond the information given. In H. Gruber, K. R. Hammond, and R. Jesser, eds., *Contemporary approaches to cognition* (a symposium held at the University of Colorado). Cambridge, Mass.: Harvard University Press.

———— (1957b). On perceptual readiness. *Psychological Review* 64: 123–52.

Burtraw, D., and Toman, M. A. (1991). Equity and international agreements for CO_2 containment. Energy and Natural Resources Division, Discussion paper ENR91-07, April. Washington, D.C.: Resources for the Future.

Carroll, J. S., Bazerman, M. H., and Maury, R. (1988). Negotiator cognitions: A descriptive approach to negotiators' understanding of their opponents. *Organizational Behavior and Human Decision Processes* 41(3): 352–70.

Chayes, A. H., and Chayes, A. (1993). On compliance. *International Organization* 47:2.

———— (1994). *The new sovereignty: Compliance with treaties in international regulatory regimes.* in press.

Clark, M. S., and Mills, J. (1979). Interpersonal attraction in exchange and communal relationships. *Journal of Personality and Social Psychology* 37(1): 12–24.

Cline, W. R. (1990). *The future of world trade in textiles and apparel*, rev. ed. Washington, D.C.: Institute for International Economics.

——— (1992). *Global warming: The economic stakes*. Washington, D.C.: Institute for International Economics.

Coase, R. (1960). The problem of social cost. *Journal of Law and Economics* 3(1): 1–44.

Cohen, D., and Knetsch, J. L. (1992). Judicial choice and disparities between measures of economic value. *Osgoode Hall Law Review, 30*, 737–770.

Coleman, J. S. (1990). *Foundations of social theory*. Cambridge, Mass.: Harvard University Press.

Cooper, A. C., Woo, C. Y., and Dunkelberg, W. C. (1988). Entrepreneurs' perceived chances for success. *Journal of Business Venturing* 3(2): 97–108.

Cooter, R. D., and Rubenfeld, D. L. (1989). Economic analysis of legal disputes and their resolution. *Journal of Economic Literature* 27(3): 1067–97.

Cornes, R. C., and Sandler, T. (1983). On commons and tragedies. *American Economic Review* 73(4): 787–92.

Crawford, V. P. (1982). A theory of disagreement in bargaining. *Econometrica* 50(3): 607–37.

Creppell, I. (1989). Democracy and literacy: The role of culture in political life. *Archives européennes de sociologie* 30: 22–47.

Crocker, J. (1981). Judgment of covariation by social perceivers. *Psychology Bulletin* 90: 272–92.

Cutler, D. M., and Summers, L. H. (1988). The costs of conflict resolution and financial distress: Evidence from the Texaco-Pennzoil litigation. *The Rand Journal of Economics* 19(2): 157–72.

Cutter Information Corporation (1990). *Global environmental change report* 2(19): 1–5. Arlington, Mass.: Cutter Information Corporation.

Darman, R. G. (1978). The law of the sea: Rethinking U.S. interests. *Foreign Affairs* 56(2): 373–95.

Dasgupta, P. (1982). *The control of resources*. Oxford, England: Basil Blackwell.

Davis, D. (1985). New projects: Beware of false economies. *Harvard Business Review* 63(2): 95–101.

Dawes, R. M. (1980). Social dilemmas. *Annual Review of Psychology* 31: 169–93.

——— (1988a). *Rational choice in an uncertain world*. San Diego: Harcourt, Brace, Jovanovich.

——— (1989b). Statistical criteria for establishing a truly false consensus effect. *Journal of Experimental Social Psychology* 25(1): 1–17.

——— (1990). The potential non-falsity of the false consensus effect. In R. M. Hogarth, ed., *Insights in decision making: A tribute to Hillel J. Einhorn*. Chicago: University of Chicago Press, 179–99.

——— (1991). Social dilemmas, economic self-interest, and evolutionary theory. In D. R. Brown and J. E. K. Smith, eds., *Recent research in psychology: Frontiers of mathematical psychology: Essays in honor of Clyde Coombs*. New York: Springer-Verlag.

Dawes, R. M., McTavish, J., and Shaklee, H. (1977). Behavior, communication, and assumptions about other people's behavior in a commons dilemma situation. *Journal of Personality and Social Psychology* 1: 1–11.

Dawes, R. M., Orbell, J. M., Simmons, R. T., and van de Kragt, A. J. C. (1986).

Organizing groups for collective action. *American Political Science Review* 80: 1171–85.

Diamond, D. W. (1984). Financial intermediation and delegated monitoring. *Review of Economic Studies* 51(3): 393–414.

—— (1989). Reputation acquisition in debt markets. *Journal of Political Economy* 97: 828.

Dixit, A. and Nalebuff, B. (1991), Making strategies credible. In R. Zeckhauser, ed., *Strategy and choice*, Cambridge, Mass.: MIT Press.

Doniger, D. D. (1988). Politics of the ozone layer. *Issues in Science and Technology* 4(3): 86–92.

Donsimoni, M. P., Economides, N. S., and Polemarchakis, H. M. 1986). Stable cartels. *International Economic Review* 27(2): 317–27.

Dun and Bradstreet (1967). *Patterns of success in managing a business*. New York: Dunn and Bradstreet.

Dunlap, R. E., Gallup, G. H., Jr., and Gallup, A. M. (1993). *Health of the planet: Results of a 1992 international environmental opinion survey of citizens in 24 nations*. Princeton, N.J.: George H. Gallup International Institute.

Dunlop, J. T. (1958/1993). *Industrial relations systems*. New York: Henry Holt; rev. ed., Boston: Harvard Business School Press.

—— (1984). *Dispute resolution, negotiation and consensus building*. Dover, Mass.: Auburn House.

—— (1992). *The neutral in industrial relations revisited, proceedings of the forty-fourth annual meeting, National Academy of Arbitrators*. Washington, D.C.: Bureau of National Affairs, Inc.

Dunning, D., and Ross, L. (1992). Unpublished manuscript. Stanford: Stanford University.

Dunning, D., and Ross, L. (1992). Overconfidence in individual and group prediction: Is the collective any wiser? Unpublished manuscript. Stanford: Stanford University.

Egret, J. (1950). *La révolution des notables: Mounier et les monarchiens*. Paris: Armand Colin.

Ellickson, R. C. (1991). *Order without Law: How neighbors settle disputes*. Cambridge, Mass.: Harvard University Press.

Elster, J. (1984). *Ulysses and the sirens*, rev. ed. Cambridge, England: Cambridge University Press.

—— (1985). *Making sense of Marx*. Cambridge, England: Cambridge University Press.

—— (1989). *The cement of society: A study of social order*. Cambridge, England: Cambridge University Press.

—— (1992). *Local justice: How institutions allocate scarce goods and necessary burdens*. New York: Russell Sage Foundation.

Farrand, M., ed. (1966). *The records of the Federal Convention of 1787*, (rev. ed.) New Haven: Yale University Press.

Festinger, L. (1957). *A Theory of cognitive dissonance*. Stanford: Stanford University Press.

Finn, J. E. (1991). *Constitutions in crisis: Political violence and the rule of law*. New York: Oxford University Press.

Finkelman, P. (1987). Slavery and the constitutional convention: Making a covenant with death. In R. Beeman, S. Botein, and E. C. Carter II, eds., *Beyond con-*

federation: Origins of the Constitution and American national identity. Chapel Hill: University of North Carolina Press, 188–225.

Fischhoff, B. (1982). Debiasing. In D. Kahneman, P. Slovic, and A. Tversky, eds., *Judgment under uncertainty: Heuristics and biases*. Cambridge, England: Cambridge University Press.

Fisher, R., and Ury, W. (1981). *Getting to yes: Negotiating agreement without giving in*. Boston: Houghton Mifflin Company.

Fisher, R., Ury, W., and Patton, B. (1991). *Getting to yes: Negotiating agreement without giving in* (2nd ed.). New York: Penguin.

Fiske, S. T., and Taylor, S. E. (1990). *Social cognition*. Reading, Mass.: Addison-Wesley.

Forsythe, R., Horowitz, J., Savin, N. E., and Sefton, M. (1988). Replicability, fairness and pay in experiments with simple bargaining games. Working paper.

Frank, R. H. (1988). *Passions within reason: The strategic role of the emotions*. New York: W. W. Norton.

Fry, W., Firestone, I., and Williams, D. (1983). Negotiation processes and outcome of stranger dyads and dating couples: Do lovers lose? *Basic and Applied Social Psychology* 4: 1–16.

Furet, F. (1988). *La révolution 1770–1870*. Paris: Hachette.

Furet, F., and Halévi, R. (1989). *Orateurs de la révolution française*. I: Les Constituants. Paris: Gallimard.

Galanter, M. (1988). The life and times of the big six; or the Federal courts since the good old days. *Wisconsin Law Review* 1988: 921.

Galanter, M., and Paley, T. (1991). *Tournament of lawyers: The transformation of the big law firm*. Chicago: University of Chicago Press.

Galanter, M., and Rodgers, J. (1991). A transformation of American business disputing? Some preliminary observations. Unpublished manuscript. Madison: University of Wisconsin (Institute for Legal Studies Working Paper No. DPRP 10-3, 1991.)

Gauthier, D. P. (1986). *Morals by agreement*. Oxford, England: Clarendon.

Gigerenzer, G., Hoffrage, U., and Kleinbolting, H. (1991). Probabilistic mental models: A Brunswikian theory of confidence. *Psychological Review* 98(4): 506–28.

Gilson, R. J., and Kraakman, R. H. (1984). The mechanisms of market efficiency. *University of Virginia Law Review* 70: 549–644.

Gilson, R. J., and Mnookin, R. H. (1985). Sharing among human capitalists: An economic inquiry into the corporate law firm and how partners split profits. *Stanford Law Review* 37: 313, 381–83.

——— (1994). Disputing through agents: Cooperation and conflict between lawyers in litigation. *Columbia Law Review* 94: 509.

Gilovich, T. (1991). *How we know what isn't so*. New York: The Free Press.

Granovetter, M. (1973). The strength of weak ties. *American Journal of Sociology* 78: 1360–79.

Griffin, D. W., and Ross, L. (1991). Subjective construal, social inference, and human misunderstanding. In M. P. Zanna (ed.), Advances in experimental social psychology, vol. 24, 319–59). New York: Academic Press.

Griffin, D., and Tversky, A. (1992). The weighing of evidence and the determinants of confidence. *Cognitive Psychology* 24(3): 411–35.

Grubb, M. J. (1989). The greenhouse effect: Negotiating targets. London, England: *Royal Institute of International Affairs*, Energy and Environmental Program.

———— (1990). The greenhouse effect: Negotiating targets. *International Affairs* 66(1): 67–89.

Güth, W., Schmittberger, R., and Schwarze, B. (1982). An experimental analysis of ultimatum bargaining. *Journal of Economic Behavior and Organization* 3(4): 367–88.

Haas, P. M. (1989). Ozone alone, no CFCs: Ecological epistemic communities and the protection of stratospheric ozone. Wellesley, Mass.: Conference on Knowledge, Interests and International Policy Coordination, Wellesley College.

———— (1993). *Protecting the Baltic and North Seas*. In P. M. Haas, R. O. Keohane, and M. A. Levy (eds.), *Institutions for the earth: Sources of effective international environmental protection*. Cambridge, Mass.: MIT Press.

Habermas, J. (1984/1987). *The theory of communicative action*. vols. 1 (1984) and 2 (1989) Boston: Beacon Press.

———— (1990). Discourse ethics. *Moral consciousness and communicative action*. Cambridge, Mass.: MIT Press.

Hague Declaration Report of the Ministerial Meeting (March 11, 1989).

Harbison, F. H., and Coleman, J. R. (1951). *Goals and strategy in collective bargaining*. New York: Harper and Brothers.

Hardin, G. G. (1968). The tragedy of the commons. *Science* 162(3859): 1243–48.

Hardin, R. (1982). *Collective action* (published for Resources for the Future). Baltimore: Johns Hopkins University Press.

Heath, C., and Gonzales, R. (in press). Interaction with others increases decision confidence but not decision quality: Evidence against information collection views of interactive decision making. *Organizational Behavior and Human Decision Making*.

Heath, F., and Tversky, A. (1991). Preference and belief: Ambiguity and competence in choice under uncertainty. *Journal of Risk and Uncertainty* 4: 4–28.

Heider, F. (1958). *The psychology of interpersonal relations*. New York: Wiley.

Heymann, P. B. (1987). *The politics of public management*. New Haven: Yale University Press.

Hirschman, A. O. (1977). *The passions and the interests: Political arguments for capitalism before its triumph*. Princeton, N.J.: Princeton University Press.

Hoch, S. J. (1987). Perceived consensus and predictive accuracy: The pros and cons of projection. *Journal of Personality and Social Psychology* 53(2): 221–34.

Hoel, M. (1990). Properties of international environmental conventions requiring uniform reductions of emissions from all participating countries. Presentation at conference, Environmental Cooperation and Policy in the Single European Market, Venice, April 16–20.

Hofstadter, D. (1983). Mathematical themes. *Scientific American* 248: 14–28.

Hogarth, R. M., and Einhorn, H. J. (1990). Venture theory: A model of decision weights. *Management Science* 36(7): 780–803.

Hollick, A. L. (1981). *U.S. foreign policy and the law of the sea*. Princeton, N.J.: Princeton University Press.

Holmes, S. (1984). *Benjamin Constant and the making of modern liberalism*. New Haven: Yale University Press.

Holmes, S. (1990). The secret history of self-interest. In J. J. Mansbridge, ed., *Beyond self-interest*. Chicago: University of Chicago Press.

Homans, G. C. (1961). *Social behavior: Its elementary forms*. New York: Harcourt Brace & World.

Howard, W. E. (1968). *The missile sites labor commission, 1961 thru 1967*. Washington, D.C.: Federal Mediation and Conciliation Service.

Howell, W. (1971). Uncertainty from internal and external sources: A clear case of overconfidence. *Journal of Experimental Psychology* 89(2): 240–43.

Hume, D. (1960). *A treatise of human nature*. Edited by L. A. Selby-Bigge. Oxford, England: Oxford University Press. First published 1739–40.

——— (1963). *Essays: moral, political, and literary*. London: Oxford University Press. First published 1903.

Hurrel, A., and Kingsbury, B., eds. (1992). *International politics of the environment*. Oxford, England: Oxford University Press.

Intergovernmental Panel on Climate Change (1991). *Climate change: The IPCC response strategies*. Washington, D.C.: Island Press. World Meteorological Organization / united Nations Environmental Program, Intergovernmental Panel on Climate Change.

Janis, I. L. (1972). *Victims of groupthink*. Boston: Houghton Mifflin.

Javine, D. (1988). A gender comparison: Cooperation for the public good. Unpublished doctoral dissertation. Reno: University of Nevada.

Jervis, R. (1992). Political implications of loss aversion. Unpublished manuscript. New York: Columbia University.

Jillson, C. (1988). *Constitution making: Conflict and consensus in the Federal Convention of 1787*. New York: Agathon Press.

Kahneman, D. (1992). Reference points, anchors, herms, and mixed feelings. *Organizational Behavior and Human Decision Processes* 51: 296–312.

Kahneman, D., Knetsch, J. L., and Thaler, R. H. (1986). Fairness as a constraint on profit seeking: Entitlements in the market. *The American Economic Review* 76(4): 728–41.

——— (1990). Experimental tests of the endowment effect and the Coase theorem. *Journal of Political Economy* 98(6): 1325–48.

——— (1991). The endowment effect, loss aversion, and the status quo bias. *Journal of Economic Perspectives* 5: 193–206.

Kahneman, D., and Lovallo, D. (1993). Bold forecasting and timid decisions: A cognitive perspective on risk taking. *Management Science* 39: 17–31.

Kahneman, D., Slovic, P., and Tversky, A. (1982). *Judgment under uncertainty: Heuristics and biases*. Cambridge, England: Cambridge University Press.

Kahneman, D., and Tversky, A. (1973). On the psychology of prediction. *Psychological Review* 80: 237–51.

——— (1979). Prospect theory: An analysis of decision under risk. *Econometrica* 47(2): 263–91.

——— (1979a). Intuitive prediction: Biases and corrective procedures. *TIMS Studies in Management Science* 12: 313–27.

——— (1979b). Prospect theory: An analysis of decision under risk. *Econometrica* 47(2): 263–91.

——— (1982). Psychology of preferences. *Scientific American* 246: 160–73.

——— (1984). Choices, values and frames. *American Psychologist* 39: 341–50.

Kazis, R. (1989). Rags to riches? One industry's strategy for improving productivity. *Technology Review* 92, (6): 42–53.

Keeney, R., and Raiffa, H. (1976 / 1992). *Decisions with multiple objectives: Preferences and value tradeoffs*. New York: Wiley (1976); reissued 1992 by Cambridge University Press.

———— (1991). Structuring and analyzing values for multiple-issue negotiations. In Young, H. P., ed. *Negotiation analysis*. Ann Arbor: University of Michigan.

Keohane, R. O. (1984). *After hegemony: Cooperation and discord in the world political economy*. Princeton, N.J.: Princeton University Press.

Kennan, J., and Wilson, R. B. (1989). Strategic bargaining models and interpretation of strike data. *Journal of Applied Econometrics*, (Supplement) 4: S87–S130.

———— (1993). Bargaining with private information. *Journal of Economic Literature*, 31(1): 45–104.

Klein, B., and Leffler, K. B. (1981). The role of market forces in assuring contractual performance. *Journal of Political Economy* 89(4): 615–41.

Klemperer, P. (1987). Markets with consumer switching costs. *Quarterly Journal of Economics* 102(2): 375–94.

Knetsch, J. L., and Sinden, J. A. (1984). Willingness to pay and compensation demanded: Experimental evidence of an unexpected disparity in measures of value. *Quarterly Journal of Economics* 99(3): 507–21.

Koh, T. B., and Jayakumar, Shanmugam (1985). The negotiating process of the Third United Nations Conference on the Law of the Sea. In M. H. Nordquist, ed., *United Nations Convention on the Law of the Sea 1982: A commentary*, 29–134. Boston: Martinus Nijhoff Publishers.

Kramer, R., Pradhan-Shah, P., and Woerner, S. (in press). Why ultimatums fail: Group identification, moralistic aggression, and noisy communication in coercive bargaining. In R. Kramer and D. M. Messic, eds., *Negotiation in its social context*. Newbury Park, CA: Sage Publications.

Krasner, Stephen D. (1985). *Structural conflict: The third world against global liberalism*. Berkeley: University of California Press.

Kreps, D. M. (1990a). Corporate culture and economic theory. In J. E. Alt and K. A. Shepsle, eds., *Perspectives on positive political economy*. Cambridge, England: Cambridge University Press.

———— (1990b). *Game theory and economic modelling*. Oxford, England: Oxford University Press.

Kreps, D., Milgrom, P., Roberts, J., and Wilson, R. (1982). Rational cooperation in the finitely repeated prisoners' dilemma. *Journal of Economic Theory* 27(2): 245–52.

La Bruyère, J. de (1696). *Les caractères de Theophraste*.

Langer, E. J. (1975). The illusion of control. *Journal of Personality and Social Psychology* 32: 311–28.

Lax, D. A., and Sebenius, J. K. (1986). *The manager as negotiator: Bargaining for cooperation and competitive gain*. New York: The Free Press.

Lepper, M. R., Ross, L., Tsai, J., and Ward, A. (1994). Preference reversal in the reactive devaluation of concessions. Unpublished manuscript. Stanford: Stanford University.

Lester, R. A. (1984). *Labor arbitration in state and local government: An examination of experience in eight states and New York City*. Princeton, N.J.: Industrial Relations Section, Firestone Library, Princeton University.

———— (1989). Analysis of experience under New Jersey's flexible arbitration system. *The Arbitration Journal* 44: 14–21.

Levy, M. (1993). European acid rain: The power of tote-board diplomacy. In P. M. Haas, R. O. Keohane, and M. A. Levy, eds., *Institutions for the earth: Sources of effective international environmental protection*, Cambridge, Mass.: MIT Press.

Lewinsohn, P. M., Mischel, W., Chaplin, W., and Barton, R. (1980). Social competence and depression: The role of illusory self-perceptions. *Journal of Abnormal Psychology* 89: 203–12.

Lichtenstein, S., Fischhoff, B., and Phillips, L. (1982). Calibration of probabilities: The state of the art to 1980. In D. Kahneman, et al., eds., *Judgment under uncertainty: Heuristics and biases*. Cambridge, England: Cambridge University Press.

Lincoln, A. (1942). Notes for a Law Lecture. In Philip Van Doren Stern, ed., *Life and writings of Abraham Lincoln*. New York: Modern Library.

Lind, E. A., and Tyler, T. R. (1988). *The social psychology of procedural justice*. New York: Plenum Press.

Lindskold, S. (1978). Trust development, GRIT proposal, and the effects of conciliatory acts on conflict and cooperation. *Psychological Bulletin* 85: 772–93.

Loewenstein, G., Thompson, L., and Bazerman, M. H. (1989). Social utility and decision making in interpersonal contexts. *Journal of Personality and Social Psychology* 57(3): 426–41.

Loewenstein, G., White, S. B., and Bazerman, M. H. (1991). The role of elicitation procedure in the ultimatum game. Dispute Resolution Research Center working paper. Evanston, Ill.: Northwestern University.

——— (1992). An inconsistency in revealed preferences for fairness. Dispute Resolution Research Center working paper. Evanston, Ill.: Northwestern University.

Lord, C. G., Lepper, M. R., and Preston, E. (1984). Considering the opposite: A corrective strategy for social judgment. *Journal of Personality and Social Psychology* 47: 1231–43.

Lovejoy, A. O. (1961). *Reflections on human nature*. Baltimore: Johns Hopkins Press.

Luce, R., and Raiffa, H. (1957). *Games and decisions: Introduction and critical survey*. New York: Wiley.

Macey, J. (1986). Promoting public-regarding legislation through statutory interpretation: An interest-group model. *Columbia Law Review* 86: 223–68.

Maccoby, E. E., and Mnookin, R. H. (1992). *Dividing the child: Social and legal dilemmas of custody*. Cambridge, Mass.: Harvard University Press.

Mann, K. (1985). *Defending white collar crime: A portrait of attorneys at work*. New Haven: Yale University Press.

Manne, A. S., and Richels, R. G. (1991). Global CO_2 emission reductions—The impact of rising energy costs. *Energy Journal* 12(1): 87–107.

March, J., and Shapira, Z. (1987). Managerial perspectives on risk and risk taking. *Management Science* 33(11): 1404–18.

Margolick, D. (1991). Address by Quayle on justice proposals irks Bar Association, *N.Y. Times*, Aug. 14, 1991, p. 1, col. 1.

Martin, L. L. (1992). Interests, power, and multilateralism. *International Organization* 46(4): 765–92.

Maruyama, M. (1963). The second cybernetics: Deviation amplifying mutual causal processes. *The American Scientist* 51: 164–79.

Mathews, J. T. (1989). Redefining security. *Foreign Affairs* 68(2): 162–77.

———, ed. (1991). *Greenhouse warming: Negotiating a global regime*. Washington, D.C.: World Resources Institute.

Mathiez, A. (1898). Étude critique sur les journées des 5 and 6 octobre 1789. Part I. *Revue Historique* 67: 241–81.

McGuire, R. A. (1988). Constitution making: A rational choice model of the Federal Convention of 1787. *American Journal of Political Science* 32: 483–522.

Merrow, E., Phillips, K., and Myers, C. (1981). *Understanding cost growth and performance shortfalls in pioneer process plants*. Santa Barbara, Calif.: Rand Corporation.

Messe, L. A., and Sivacek, J. M. (1979). Predictions of others' responses in a mixed motive game: Self-justification or false consensus? *Journal of Personality and Social Psychology* 37: 602–7.

Messick, D. M. (1991). Equality as a decision heuristic. In B. Mellers, ed., *Psychological issues in distributive justice*. New York: Praeger.

Messick, D. M., and Sentis, K. (1983). Fairness, preference, and fairness bias. In D. M. Messick and K. S. Cook, eds., *Equity theory: Psychological and sociological perspectives*, 61–94. New York: Praeger.

——— (1985). Estimating social and nonsocial utility functions from ordinal data. *European Journal of Social Psychology* 15: 389–99.

Miller, J. H. (1987). The co-evolution of automata in the repeated prisoner's dilemma. Working paper of the Santa Fe Institute Economics Research Program.

Milgrom, P., and Roberts, J. (1982). Predation, reputation, and entry deterrence. *Journal of Economic Theory* 27(2): 280–312.

Mintzer, I., ed. (1992). *The challenge of responsible development in a warming world*. Cambridge, England: Cambridge University Press.

Mnookin, R. (1993). Why negotiations fail: An exploration of barriers to the resolution of conflict. *Ohio State Journal on Dispute Resolution* 8(2): 235–49.

Mnookin, R., and Kornhauser, L. (1979). Bargaining in the shadow of the law: The case of divorce. *Yale Law Journal* 88: 950–97.

Mnookin, R., and Wilson, R. (1989). Rational bargaining and market efficiency: Understanding *Pennzoil v. Texaco*. *Virginia Law Review* 75: 295–334.

Moomaw, W. R. (1990). A modest proposal to encourage unilateral reductions in greenhouse gases. Unpublished paper. Medford, Mass.: Tufts University.

Myerson, Roger B., and Satterthwaite, Mark A. (1983). Efficient mechanisms or bilateral trading. *Journal of Economic Theory* 29(2): 265–81.

Nash, J. F. (1950). The bargaining problem. *Econometrica* 18: 155–62.

——— (1953). Two-person cooperative games. *Econometrica* 21: 128–40.

Neale, M. A. (1984). The effect of negotiation and arbitration cost salience on bargainer behavior: The role of arbitrator and constituency in negotiator judgment. *Organizational Behavior and Human Performance* 34: 97–111.

Neale, M. A., and Bazerman, M. H. (1983). The effects of perspective-taking ability under alternate forms of arbitration on the negotiation process. *Industrial and Labor Relations Review* 36: 378–88.

——— (1985). When will externally set aspiration levels improve negotiator performance? A look at integrative behavior in competitive markets. *Journal of Occupational Behavior* 6: 19–32.

——— (1991). *Cognition and rationality in negotiation*. New York: The Free Press.

Neale, M. A., Huber, V. L., and Northcraft, G. B. (1987). The framing of negotiations: Context versus task frames. *Organizational Behavior and Human Decision Processes* 39(2): 228–41.

Neale, M. A., and Northcraft, G. B. (1986). Experts, amateurs, and refrigerators: Comparing expert and amateur negotiators in a novel task. *Organizational Behavior and Human Decision Processes* 38(3): 305–17.

Nelson, William (1990). Contract litigation and the elite bar in New York City, 1960–1980. *Emory Law Journal* 39: 413–62.

Northcraft, G. B., and Neale, M. A. (1987). Expert, amateurs, and real estate: An anchoring-and-adjustment perspective on property pricing decisions. *Organizational Behavior and Human Decision Processes* 39(1): 84–97.

Northcraft, G. B., and Neale, M. A. (1990). Dyadic negotiation: The two-person game. In M. Bazerman, R. Lewicki, and B. Sheppard, eds., *Research in bargaining and negotiating in organizations*, vol. 3. Greenwich, Conn.: JAI Press.

Northrup, H. R. (1966). *Compulsory Arbitration and Government Intervention in labor disputes: An analysis of experience*. Washington, D.C.: Labor Policy Association.

Ochs, J., and Roth, A. E. (1989). An experimental study of sequential bargaining. *American Economic Review* 79(3): 335–84.

O'Donnell, P., and McDougal, D. (1992). *Fatal subtraction: The inside story of Buchwald v. Paramount*. New York: Doubleday.

Okun, A. M. (1981). *Prices and quantities: A macroeconomic analysis*. Washington, D.C.: The Brookings Institution.

Olson, M. (1965). *The logic of collective action: Public goods and the theory of groups*. Cambridge, Mass.: Harvard University Press.

Olson, M., and Zeckhauser, R. (1966). An economic theory of alliances. *Review of Economics and Statistics* 48(3): 266–79.

Orbell, J. M., and Dawes, R. M. (1991a). A "cognitive miser" theory of cooperators' advantage. *American Political Science Review* 85: 515–28.

———— (1991b). A reply to McLean. *American Political Science Review* 85: 1418–20.

———— (1993). Social welfare, cooperators' advantage, and the option of not playing the game. *American Sociological Review* 58: 787–800.

Orbell, J. M., van de Kragt, A. J. C., and Dawes, R. M. (1988). Explaining discussion-induced cooperation. *Journal of Personality and Social Psychology* 54(5): 811–19.

Oren, D. A. (1985). *Joining the club: A history of Jews and Yale*. New Haven: Yale University Press.

Osborne, M. J., and Rubinstein, A. (1990). *Bargaining and markets*. San Diego: Academic Press.

Osgood, C. E. (1962). *An alternative to war or surrender*. Urbana: University of Illinois Press.

———— (1980). GRIT: A strategy for survival in mankind's nuclear age? Paper presented at the Pugwash Conference on New Directions in Disarmament, Racine, Wis.

Osgood, C. E., and Tannenbaum, P. H. (1955). The principle of congruity in the prediction of attitude change. *Psychological Review* 62: 42–55.

Oskamp, S. (1965). Overconfidence in case-study judgments. *Journal of Consulting Psychology* 29: 261–65.

Ostrom, E. (1991). *Managing the commons*. New York: Cambridge University Press.

Oxman, B. H., Caron, D. D., and Buderi, C. L. O. (1983). *Law of the sea: U.S. policy dilemma*. San Francisco: Institute for Contemporary Studies Press, Council on Ocean Law.

Oye, K., ed. (1986). *Cooperation under anarchy*. Princeton, N.J.: Princeton University Press.

Parson, E. A. (1992). Negotiating climate cooperation: Learning from theory, simulations, and history. Unpublished doctoral dissertation in public policy. Cambridge, Mass.: Harvard University.

Perritt, H. H., Jr. (1986). Negotiated rulemaking before federal agencies: Evaluation of recommendations by the Administrative Conference of the United States. *Georgetown Law Journal* 74(6): 1625–1717.

Perritt, H. H., Jr. (1986). Negotiated rulemaking and administrative law. *Administrative Law Review* 38(4): 471–506; 74(6): 1625–1717.

P'ng, I. (1983). Strategic behavior in suit, settlement and trial. *Bell Journal of Economics* 14: 539.

Polzer, J. T., Neale, M. A., and Glenn, P. O. (1993). The effects of relationship and justification in an interdependent allocation task. *Group Decision and Negotiation* 2(2): 135–48.

Pratt, J. W., and Zeckhauser, R. J., eds. (1985). *Principals and agents: The structure of business*. Boston: Harvard University School Press.

Pruitt, D. G. (1981). *Negotiation behavior*. New York: Academic Press, Inc.

——— (1983). Achieving integrative agreements. In M. H. Bazerman, and R. J. Lewicki, eds., *Negotiating in organizations*. Beverly Hills, Calif.: Sage Publications.

Pruitt, D. B., and Rubin, J. Z. (1986). *Social conflict: Escalation, stalemate, and settlement*. New York: Random House.

Rachlinski, J. J. (1994). Prospect theory and the economics of litigation Doctoral thesis, Stanford University.

Raiffa, H. (1968). *Decision analysis: Introductory lectures on choices under uncertainty*. Reading, Mass.: Addison Wesley; reissued by Random House, forthcoming.

——— (1982). *The art and science of negotiation*. Cambridge, Mass.: Belknap Press of Harvard University Press.

Raiffa, H., and Schlaifer, R. (1961). *Applied statistical decision theory*. Harvard Press. Reissued by MIT Press, forthcoming.

Rakove, J. N. (1987). The great compromise: Ideas, interests, and the politics of constitution making. *William and Mary Quarterly*, 44: 424–57.

Rapoport, A. (1967). Optimal policies for the prisoner's dilemma. *Psychological Review* 74: 136–145.

Rapoport, A., and Chammah, A. M. (1965). *Prisoner's dilemma: A study in conflict and cooperation*. Ann Arbor: University of Michigan Press.

Rasmusen, E. (1989). *Games and information: An introduction to game theory*. Oxford: Basil Blackwell.

Richardson, Elliot L. (1990). Law of the sea: a reassessment of U.S. interests. *Mediterranean Quarterly* 1(2): 1–13.

Riker, W. H. (1962). *The theory of political coalitions*. New Haven: Yale University Press.

Ross, L., Greene, D., and House, P. (1977). "False consensus effect": An ego-centric bias in social perception and attribution processes. *Journal of Experimental Social Psychology* 13: 279–301.

Ross, L., Lepper, M. R., and Hubbard, M. (1975). Perseverance in self-perception and social perception: Biased attributional processes in the debriefing paradigm. *Journal of Personality and Social Psychology* 32: 880–92.

Ross, L., and Stillinger, C. (1991). Barriers to conflict resolution. *Negotiation Journal* 7(4): 389–404.

Ross, L., and Ward, A. (1994). Psychological barriers to dispute resolution. In M. Zanna, ed., *Advances in experimental social psychology*, vol. 27. San Diego: Academic Press.

——— (in press). Naive realism: Implications for social conflict and misunderstanding. In T. Brown, E. Reed, and E. Turiel, eds., *Values and Knowledge*. Hillsdale, N.J.: L. Erlbaum Associates.

Roth, A. E. (1991). An economic approach to the study of bargaining. In M. H. Bazerman, R. J. Lewicki, and B. H. Sheppard eds., *Handbook of negotiation research: Research in negotiation in organizations*, vol. 3. Greenwich, Conn.: JAI Press.

Rothstein, R. L. (1979). *Global bargaining: UNCTAD and the quest for a new international economic order*. Princeton: Princeton University Press.

Rubinstein, A. (1982). Perfect equilibrium in a bargaining model. *Econometrica* 50(1): 97–109.

——— (1991). Comments on the interpretation of game theory. *Econometrica* 59(4): 909–24.

Rubinstein, A., Safra, Z., and Thomson, W. (1992). On the interpretation of the Nash bargaining solution. *Econometrica* 60(5): 1171–86.

Salter, M. S. (1987). *[TC]² and the apparel industry*. Boston: Harvard Business School, 9-387-160.

Salter, M. S., and Dunlop, J. T. (1989). *Industrial governance and corporate performance*. Boston: Harvard Business School, 9-390-032.

Samuelson, W. F. (1991). Final-offer arbitration under incomplete information. *Management Science* 37(10): 1234–47.

Samuelson, W. F., and Bazerman, M. H. (1985). The winner's curse in bilateral negotiations. In V. Smith, ed., *Research in experimental economics* 3: 105–37. Greenwich, Conn.: JAI Press.

Samuelson, W., and Zeckhauser, R. (1988). Status quo bias in decision making. *Journal of Risk and Uncertainty* 1: 7–59.

Sand, Peter H. (1990). *Lessons learned in global environmental governance*. Washington, D.C.: World Resources Institute.

Saunders, M. (1991). *The other walls*, rev. ed. Princeton: Princeton University Press.

Schelling, T. C. (1960). *The strategy of conflict*. Cambridge, Mass.: Harvard University Press.

——— (1978). *Micromotives and macrobehavior. Fels Lectures on Public Policy Analysis*. New York: W. W. Norton.

Schoeninger, D., and Wood, W. (1969). Comparison of married and ad hoc mixed sex dyads negotiating the division of a reward. *Journal of Experimental Social Psychology* 5: 483–99.

Sebenius, J. K. (1983). Negotiation arithmetic: adding and subtracting issues and parties. *International Organization* 37(1): 281–316.

——— (1984). *Negotiating the law of the sea: Lessons in the art and science of reaching agreement*. Cambridge, Mass.: Harvard University Press.

——— (1981). The computer as mediator: Law of the sea and beyond. *Journal of Policy Analysis and Management* 1(1): 77–95.

——— (1992). Negotiation analysis: A characterization and review. *Management Science* 38(1): 19–38.

Selekman, B. M. (1948). Some implications and problems of collective bargaining. In L. M. Hacker et al., eds., *The new industrial relations*. Ithaca: Cornell University Press.

Seligman, M. E. P. (1991). *Learned optimism*. New York: A. A. Knopf.

Sen, A. (1977). Rational fools: A critique of the behavioral foundations of economic theory. *Philosophy and Public Affairs* 6: 317–44.

Setear, J. K. (1989). The barrister and the bomb: The dynamics of cooperation, nuclear deterrence, and discovery abuse. *Boston University Law Review* 69: 569, 593.

Seymour, W. (1992). Cheaper, faster civil justice. *New York Times*, January 7, 1992, p. A15, col. 2.

Sherman, S. J., and Presson, C. C. (1984). Mechanisms underlying the false consensus effect: The special role of threat to self. *Personality and Social Psychology Bulletin* 10: 127–38.

Siegel, S., and Fouraker, L. E. (1960). *Bargaining and group decision making: Experiments in bilateral monopoly.* New York: McGraw-Hill.

Silverman, A. E. (1990). Symposium report: Intellectual property and the venture capital process. *High Technology Law Journal* 5: 157–92.

Simkin, W. E. (1971). *Mediation and the dynamics of collective bargaining.* Washington, D.C.: Bureau of National Affairs.

Simmel, G. (1955). *Conflict: The web of group-affiliations.* New York: The Free Press.

Skolnikoff, Eugene B. (1990). The policy gridlock on global warming. *Foreign Policy* (79): 77–93.

Snyder, G. H., and Diesing, P. (1977). *Conflict among nations: Bargaining, decision making, and system structure in international crises.* Princeton, N.J.: Princeton University Press.

Sobel, J. (1981). Distortion of utilities and the bargaining problem. *Econometrica* 49: 597–617.

Solow, R. M. (1980). On theories of unemployment. *American Economic Review* 70: 1–11.

Sondak, H., Pinkley, and Neale, M. (1994). Negotiating norms of justice. Working paper. Dallas, Texas: Southern Methodist University.

Sonnenschein, H. (1991). Presidential address to the Econometric Society. Mimeo.

Stanley, R. H. (1990). *Environment and development: Breaking the ideological deadlock.* Report of the 21st UN Issues Conference. Muscatine, Iowa: The Stanley Foundation.

Stewart, J. B. (1991). *Den of thieves.* New York: Simon & Schuster.

Stillinger, C., Epelbaum, M., Keltner, D., and Ross, L. (1990). The "reactive devaluation" barrier to conflict resolution. Unpublished manuscript. Stanford: Stanford University.

Stone, C. D. (1990). The global warming crisis, if there is one, and the law. *American University Journal of International Law and Policy* 5(2): 497–511.

Subak, S. E., and Clark, W. C. (1990). Accounts for greenhouse gases: Toward the design of fair assessments. In W. C. Clark, ed., *Usable knowledge for managing global climate change.* Stockholm: Stockholm Environment Institute.

Susskind, L. (1994). *Environmental diplomacy: Negotiating more effective global agreements.* New York: Oxford University Press.

Taylor, G. W. (1948). *Government regulation of industrial relations.* New York: Prentice Hall.

Taylor, M. (1987). *The possibility of cooperation: Studies in rationality and social change.* Cambridge, England: Cambridge University Press.

Taylor, S. E. (1989). *Positive illusions: Creative self-deception and the healthy mind.* New York: Basic Books.

Taylor, S. E., and Brown, J. D. (1988). Illusion and well-being: A social psychological perspective on mental health. *Psychological Bulletin* 103(2): 193–210.

Tesser, A. (1978). Self-generated attitude change. In L. Berkowitz, ed., *Advances in experimental social psychology*, vol. 11. New York: Academic Press.

Thacher, P. S. (1990). Alternative legal and institutional approaches to global change. *Colorado Journal of International Environmental Law and Policy* 1(1): 101–26.

Thaler, R. (1980). Toward a positive theory of consumer choice. *Journal of Economic Behavior and Organization* 1(1): 39–60.

——— (1985). Mental accounting and consumer choice. *Marketing Science* 4(3): 199–214.

Thibaut, J. W., and Walker, L. L. (1975). *Procedural justice: A psychological analysis.* Hillsdale, N.J.: L. Erlbaum Associates.

Thompson, L. L. (1991). Information exchange in negotiation. *Journal of Experimental Social Psychology* 27(2): 161–79.

Thompson, L., and DeHarpport, T. (1990). Negotiation in long-term relationships. Paper presented at the International Association of Conflict Management, Vancouver, B.C.

Thompson, L., and Loewenstein, G. F. (1992). Egocentric interpretations of fairness and interpersonal conflict. *Organizational Behavior and Human Decision Processes* 51(2): 176–97.

Tilly, C. (1978). *From mobilization to revolution.* Reading, Mass.: Addison Wesley.

Tocqueville, A. de (1990). *Recollections: The French Revolution of 1848.* New Brunswick: Transaction Books. Originally published 1893.

Tolba, M. (1989). A step-by-step approach to protection of the atmosphere. *International Environmental Affairs* 1(4): 305.

Toronto Declaration (1988). The changing atmosphere: Implications for global security. Conference Statement, June 27–30, 1988. Toronto, Ontario: Environment Canada.

Tversky, A., and Fox, C. (1995). Weighing risk and uncertainty. *Psychological Review*, in press.

Tversky, A., and Kahneman, D. (1973). Availability: A heuristic for judging frequency and probability. *Cognitive Psychology* 5: 207–32.

——— (1974). Judgment under uncertainty: Heuristics and biases. *Science* 185: 1124–31.

——— (1981). The framing of decisions and the psychology of choice. *Science* 40: 453–63.

——— (1986). Rational choice and the framing of decisions. Part 2. *The Journal of Business* 59(4): S251–S78.

——— (1991). Loss aversion in riskless choice: A reference-dependent model. *Quarterly Journal of Economics* 106(4): 1039–61.

UNEP. (1987). Montreal protocol, final act. Montreal.

UNEP. (1990). Report of the second meeting of the parties to the Montreal protocol [UNEP / ozL.Pro.1 / 5.6]. London.

UN General Assembly (1992). *United Nations Conference on Environment and Development.* General Assembly Resolution 228, 44 UN GAOR Supp. (no. 49) at 300, UN Doc. A / 44 / 49.

Ury, W. (1991). *Getting past no: Negotiating with difficult people.* New York: Bantum Books.

U.S. Congress, Joint Economic Committee (1990). *The 1990 economic report of the president.* 101st Congress, 2nd sess. Washington, D.C.: U.S. Government Printing Office.

Vanberg, V. (1991). Rationality, morality, and exit. Presentation. New Orleans: Public Choice Society Meetings.

Valley, K. (1992). Relationships and resources: A network exploration of allocation decisions. Unpublished dissertation. Evanston, Ill.: Northwestern University.

Valley, K., Moag, J., and Bazerman, M. H. (1992). Relationships as the solution to the winner's curse. Dispute Resolution Research Center working paper. Evanston, Ill.: Northwestern University.

Valley, K., and Neale, M. A. (1992). Relationships among negotiations: The success of integrative agreements. Working paper. Evanston, Ill.: Northwestern University.

Vanberg, V. J., and Congleton, R. D., (1992). Rationality, morality, and exit. *American Political Science Review*, 86(2): 418–31.

Viscusi, W. K., Magat, W. A., and Huber, J. C. (1987). An investigation of the rationality of consumer valuations of multiple health risks. *Rand Journal of Economics* 18(4): 465–79.

Wachtell, H. (1977). Special tender offer litigation tactics. *Business Law* 32: 1433, 1437–38.

Walster, E., Berscheid, E., and Walster, G. W. (1973). New directions in equity research. *Journal of Personality and Social Psychology* 25: 151–76.

Weitzman, M. L. (1974). Free access vs. private ownership as alternative systems for managing common property. *Journal of Economic Theory* 8(2): 225–34.

White, M. (1987). *Philosophy, The Federalist, and the Constitution*. New York: Oxford University Press.

White, S. B., and Neale, M. A. (1994). The role of negotiator aspirations and settlement expectancies in bargaining outcomes. *Organizational Behavior and Human Decision Processes* 57(2): 303–17.

Wicklund, R. A. (1974). *Freedom and reactance*. Potomac, Md.: John Wiley.

Williamson, Oliver (1985). *The economic institutions of capitalism: firms, markets, relational contracting*. New York: The Free Press.

Wilson, R. (1993). Design of efficient trading procedures. Chap. 5 in D. Friedman and J. Rust, eds., *The Double auction market: Institutions, theories, and evidence*. Reading, Mass.: Addison-Wesley.

World Bank (1992). *World development report 1992*. New York: Oxford University Press.

World Resources Institute (1992). *World resources 1994–95: A guide to the global environment*. New York: Oxford University Press.

Young, H. P. (1991a). Sharing the burden of global warming. Mimeo. University of Maryland, School of Public Affairs.

———, ed. (1991b). *Negotiation analysis*. Ann Arbor: University of Michigan Press.

Zeuthen, F., (1930). *Problems of monopoly and economic warfare*. London: G. Routledge and Sons.

Index

environmental treaty-making, 292–309
  broader applications of, 309
  coalition-building and, 300–303
  convention-protocol approach to, 297–99
  four key barriers to, 299–309
  major examples of, 294
  process of, 295–97
  scientific uncertainty and, 303–5
  separation of benefits and costs in, 305–7
  sovereignty and, 308–9
Epelbaum, M., 15, 28
equal proportional reductions vs. equal per capita emissions, 232, 234
equity, 11–13, 65, 139–40
  see also fairness
European Community, 154, 155, 169, 179, 216, 233, 301, 306
  Large Combustion Plant Directive of, 168, 231n
European Free Trade Association, 154, 179
Evolution of Cooperation, The (Axelrod), 210
exchange goods, three types of, 56
exchange vs. communal relationships, 97
executive agreements, 314
exogenous sanctions, 111
expanding (small-scale) agreements, 179–81
Expected Value of Perfect Information (EVPI), 135–36
extensive game strategy, 129
externalities, 266

fairness, 65, 86–106
  gains and losses and, 57–59
  inconsistency and, 92–96
  irrationality in judgments of, 88–96
  Pareto optimality and, 90–92
  social relationships and, 96–106
  supply / demand violations and, 89–90
fair value, 17
family law practice, 208–9
Farm Labor Organizing Committee (FLOC), 278–79
Federal Mediation and Conciliation Service, 282
Federal Trade Commission (FTC), 171
Ferrara, Pam, 63n
Festinger, L., 18, 34
final-offer arbitration, 115–18, 119
Financial Times, 168n
Finn, J. E., 242
Fire and Police case, 282–83, 285, 286, 288
Firestone, I., 97, 104
Fischhoff, B., 40
Fisher, Roger, 8, 13, 41, 133n, 134, 136, 145–46, 289
Fiske, S. T., 13
FLOC (Farm Labor Organizing Committee), 278–79
focal points, 231
Foreign Affairs, 163
forewarning, 40
formal treaties, 314

Forsythe, R., 91
Fouraker, L. E., 16
Frank, R. H., 69, 81, 195, 247, 255
Fry, W., 97, 104
FTC (Federal Trade Commission), 171
fundamental transformation, 201

GAC (General Advisory Committee), 329
gains in trade, 27
Galanter, M., 185, 198, 202, 204, 205
game theory, 6, 22n, 24, 186
  criticism of, 121–22
Gauthier, D. P., 67, 69
gender, 68, 72, 83
General Advisory Committee (GAC), 329
General Agreement on Tariffs and Trade (GATT), 307
General Motors, 32
Getty Oil, 4
Gilovich, T., 106
Gilson, Ronald J., 6, 184–211
Glenn, P. O., 101
global warming, 151, 152, 267, 303–4
  bases for blocking coalitions in, 162–70
Goldberg, Arthur, 281
Gonzalez, R., 18
Gorbachev, Mikhail, 29, 30, 41, 308, 312, 313
Gramm-Rudman antideficit law, 169, 175
Granovetter, M., 96
Greece, 133
"Green Cross," 308
Greene, D., 18
greenhouse gases, 154, 168, 182
  examples of, 152
  sources of, 157, 164
  voluntary actions on, 172–73
Griffin, D. W., 13
"groupthink," 18
Grubb, M. J., 152n, 164, 231n
Gulf War, 125, 313
Güth, W., 11, 90, 91, 248

Haas, P. M., 155n, 230
Habermas, Jürgen, 237, 244–45
half-dilemmas, 81
Harbison, F. H., 275
Hardin, R., 215
Harvard University, 151n, 246
Heath, C., 18
Heider, F., 34
Heinz, U.S.A., 279
Herzog, Paul, 280
Heymann, P. B., 171
Hirschman, Albert, 239, 240
Hoch, S. J., 81, 82
Hoel, M., 218n
Hofstadter, D., 64
Hollick, A. L., 155n
Holmes, S., 240, 241
Homans, G. C., 11, 27

Rapoport, Amnon, 64
Rapoport, Anatol, 63, 64
Rasmusen, E., 196
ratchet mechanisms, 174–76
rational fools, 69
reactive devaluation, 26–42, 56
  avoidance of, 23
  definition of, 15–16
  overcoming, 38–42
  summary of empirical research on, 29–33
  underlying mechanisms of, 34–38
Reagan, Ronald, 29, 30, 41, 85n, 156, 313
Reagan administration, 163, 164, 321, 322n, 328
Red Cross, 308
Reifschneider, Eric, 295n
"Report on Soviet Noncompliance with Arms Control Agreements," 328–29
representative agent, 215
restricted channels of information and communication, 19–20
Richardson, Elliot L., 155n
Richels, R. G., 166n, 167n, 179n, 234
Riker, W. H., 152n
Rio, see Earth Summit
Ripa di Meana, Carlo, 168
Roberts, J., 191
Rocigliano, Robert, 133n, 143n
Rodgers, J., 185, 202, 204
Rosenberg, M. J., 34
Ross, Lee, 2–24, 26–42
Roth, A. E., 11, 90, 91
Rothstein, R. L., 178n
Rubenfeld, D. L., 185, 203
Rubin, J. Z., 28, 300n
Rubinstein, Ariel, 5, 120–30
rule-making, negotiated, 288–89
Rush-Bagot Treaty (1817), 315n
Russia, Republic of, 301, 312, 313, 315, 319

Safra, Zvika, 121n, 122, 123, 124, 125
Salter, M. S., 284, 288
SALT II, 313, 318, 325
Salzburg Environmental Initiative, 151n, 297n
Samuelson, W. F., 54, 102, 103, 115
sanctions, endogenous vs. exogenous, 111
Sand, Peter H., 154n
Sandler, T., 215
Satterthwaite, Mark, 110
Saunders, M., 7
Schelling, T. C., 215, 224, 231, 237, 252
Schelling coordination problem, 72, 75
Schlaifer, R., 135
Schneider, S. H., 152n
Schmittberger, R., 11, 90
Schoeninger, D., 104
Schroth, H., 93
Schwarze, B., 11, 90
Science, 152n
Sebenius, James K., 6, 8, 150–82, 189, 221n
Selekman, B. M., 275

self-fulfilling warnings, 256n
selfish shifts, 99
Sen, A., 69
Senate, U.S., 240, 245, 247, 314, 315, 321
Sentis, K., 57, 65, 91, 92, 232
Setear, J., 190
Seymour, Whitney North, 184, 186
"shadow of the law," 112, 114, 119, 276
Shaklee, H., 68
Sherman, S. J., 67
side payments, 20, 170
Siegel, S., 16
Silverman, A. E., 203
Simkin, W. E., 287
Simmel, G., 96
Simmons, R. T., 67, 81
Simpson's paradox, 65–66
Sinden, J. A., 55
Siskind, E., 299n
Sivacek, J. M., 67
Skolnikoff, Eugene B., 152n
slavery, 238
Slovic, P., 60
small-scale (expanding) agreements, 179–81
Snyder, G. H., 214
Sobel, J., 249
social and psychological perspectives, 25–106
  benefit of optional play in anonymous one-shot prisoner's dilemma games, 62–85
  cognitive perspective, 44–60
  reactive devaluation in negotiation and conflict resolution, 26–42
  role of fairness considerations and relationships in a judgmental perspective of negotiation, 86–106
social order, as automaton, 129
social relationships, fairness and, 96–106
social utility functions, 91–92
soft vs. hard law, 173, 294
Solow, R. M., 89
Sondak, H., 97
Sonnenschein, Hugo, 121n, 128
South Africa, divestment of holdings in, 30–33
sovereignty, 308–9
Soviet Union, 85n, 230–31
  breakup of, 176, 312
  Law of the Sea Conferences and, 161, 163
  in nuclear arms negotiations, 29–30, 41, 312–13, 318–19, 321, 323, 328–29
  see also Russia, Republic of
stable coalitions, three configurations of, 224–25
Stanford Center on Conflict and Negotiation, 3n, 5
Stanford Child Custody Study, 3n
Stanford University, divestment controversy at, 30–33
Stanley, R. H., 165